Still Waiting for Tomorrow

Still Waiting for Tomorrow: The Law and Politics of Unresolved Refugee Crises

Edited by

Susan M. Akram and Tom Syring

CAMBRIDGE SCHOLARS

PUBLISHING

Still Waiting for Tomorrow:
The Law and Politics of Unresolved Refugee Crises,
Edited by Susan M. Akram and Tom Syring

This book first published 2014

Cambridge Scholars Publishing

12 Back Chapman Street, Newcastle upon Tyne, NE6 2XX, UK

British Library Cataloguing in Publication Data
A catalogue record for this book is available from the British Library

ISBN (10): 1-4438-5664-9, ISBN (13): 978-1-4438-5664-5

TABLE OF CONTENTS

FOREWORD

GUY S. GOODWIN-GILL*

The scholarly and thoughtful contributions to this volume cover a broad range of problems, and together should ensure that one question of principle in particular remains firmly on the international agenda. The issue can be simply stated: it is that of *responsibility*, the legal, political, and moral responsibility of States and other actors and stakeholders to find solutions to the displacements of people that are consistent with international law and concordant with justice.

Since the League of Nations first engaged with refugee issues in the 1920s, much has been achieved in developing a protective shield of rights for individuals in flight from risk of harm, and in bringing States together in pursuit of solutions; unfortunately, manifest deficiencies remain. At the time of writing, the Syrian refugee crisis had reached catastrophic proportions, presenting a scenario in which multiple armed militias, factionalism, and sectarianism all hinted strongly at a bleak, unresolved future. How long will the principal refugee receiving countries–Turkey, Lebanon, Jordan, Iraq–be left to cope with an exodus that could well top three million? What price must they pay, not in terms simply of dollars for assistance, but also in regard to their own development, security and community relations? This collection invites the reader to consider comparable problems for which resolution is still wanting, and to think ahead, about other potential causes of displacement, about how risks can be managed and preparedness enhanced.

History is there, but whether we can learn from historical examples is another matter. Clearly, history does not repeat itself in any simplistic sense, in the refugee context or otherwise, for causes, people, places, are not the same, and opportunities are infinitely variable. On the one hand, history does offer certain lessons, obvious though many of them are. It tells us of the human cost whenever solutions are left pending, of the transmissibility of despair through generations, and of its not infrequent translation into active militancy. It tells us of the political costs, borne especially by 'front-line' receiving States, but also in international relations more generally, as the displaced repeatedly raise their call for peace and justice.

On the other hand, solutions cannot be cut and pasted onto different scenarios. If history fails to offer prescriptive answers, in confirming the practical necessity and value of solutions for both individuals and communities, it nonetheless reveals the sorts of principles which must underwrite solutions if they are ultimately to be durable. Above all, it reminds us that political convenience cannot be substituted for protection and security, considered across the broadest spectrum of human endeavour; that the freedom to choose is critical, whether in the grand sense of self-determination and nationhood, or in the matter of individual life choices; that compensation, restitution or reparation can make the difference between success and failure; and that a special effort will always be required for those, such as the handicapped or the isolated, who might otherwise be left behind.

Fifty-five years ago or so, the plight of 'non-settled refugees,' primarily those who had been displaced by the Second World War or events immediately thereafter, was also a matter of concern. In 1957, the General Assembly requested the High Commissioner to intensify efforts to achieve permanent solutions for the maximum number of refugees remaining in camps, but without losing sight of the needs of others.[1] In the Third Committee the following year, the High Commissioner spoke of the 'Camp Clearance Programme' and of its aim 'to abolish camps as places of permanent residence for refugees.' His critique was that camps led to a feeling of isolation from the world, commonly left refugees unable to contribute economically and socially to life around them, resulted in a sense of hopelessness at the prospect of a camp life in perpetuity, and did great psychological damage.[2] The High Commissioner also brought up the idea for a 'World Refugee Year,' which was quickly endorsed by the General Assembly. The two aims for the Year were:

> '(a) To focus interest in the refugee problem and to encourage additional financial contributions from Governments, voluntary agencies and the general public for its solution,
> '(b) To encourage additional opportunities for permanent refugee solutions, through voluntary repatriation, resettlement or integration, on a purely humanitarian basis and in accordance with the freely expressed wishes of the refugees themselves.'[3]

Given its emphasis on 'a purely humanitarian effort'[4] and fund raising, World Refugee Year certainly had a positive impact. Over $70 million was contributed, and the High Commissioner could announce the completion of the camp clearance programme in Europe.[5] The General Assembly, in turn, noted that the Year had been a 'remarkable success' in many parts of the world, 'not only financially but also in promoting solutions of problems relating to large numbers of refugees, particularly those who are handicapped. . . '[6]

Looking back, however, it is important to locate this initiative not only in the prevailing political context, but also with due recognition for the nature of the issues then facing the international community of States (or at least those States whose interests led them to engage with the refugee question). First, the strong emphasis on the year as a 'purely humanitarian effort' meant that there was little or no engagement with the deep politics of unresolved refugee situations.[7] Second, as the numbers were already down, the emphasis in the Camp Clearance programme was very much on *individually* targeted measures for resettlement, integration or voluntary repatriation,[8] rather than on political solutions for refugee communities at large. Nevertheless, as the High Commissioner hoped, that programme will at least have demonstrated that, 'it is no solution to keep refugees in camps. . .'

As the contributions to this volume show, attaining durable solutions for refugee problems can be negatively affected by events and measures at both the national and the international level. A State's criteria for admission or resettlement may be so tightly drawn as to deny a solution to hundreds, even thousands, of refugees whose experience of suffering and flight may have exposed them to contact with armed groups, irrespective of any personal culpability as understood in the exclusion provisions of the 1951 Convention. 'National security,' though it has international implications, is a category which demands the closest scrutiny by domestic courts if it is to retain legitimacy in a democratic society.

Uncertainty is another problem. Prediction is not an exercise much favoured by High Commissioners for Refugees, but the climate change debate has certainly encouraged thinking about how to manage future risks and about preparedness for uncertainty. Not everything can be anticipated– the Palestinian dispersal was thought to be just a temporary phenomenon when States sat down to finalize the 1951 Convention–but the history of international refugee law and organization is also a lesson in the potentialities of co-operation, and in how working together is central to solutions.

As this collection shows, however, unresolved refugee situations reveal the gaps between principle and practice, the limits of laws and rules, and the temptation for various actors to exploit those gaps. They are clearly indicative of very real deficiencies in what is otherwise quite a sturdy international refugee regime, oriented in principle towards protection and the search for durable solutions, and possessed of institutional mechanisms which ideally should be the catalyst for effective action.

In 2009, after failing to reach consensus at its regular October meeting, the UNHCR Executive Committee did finally adopt a 'Conclusion' on protracted refugee situations.[9] It recognised that the *status quo*, the unresolved refugee situation, was not an acceptable solution, and then set out to identify the goals for the international community, declaring with all due emphasis that voluntary repatriation is to be preferred. It coupled this with recognition of the necessity to ensure, in appropriate circumstances, that restitution of property is guaranteed where refugees return to their countries of origin or, in the absence of restitution, that sufficient provision be made for compensation. It emphasised international solidarity and burden-sharing and that, notwithstanding the priority of return, there was also room for encouraging self-reliance amongst refugees and for promoting resettlement. Significantly, and in contrast to many 'historical' approaches to refugee issues, the Executive Committee identified countries of origin as important players in the search for solutions.

This combination of calls and proposals offers matters for co-operation with matters in which States might individually take initiatives, for example, by adjusting their own resettlement criteria towards the needs of those in protracted refugee situations, and therefore perhaps away from the self-interest which is otherwise almost always a major driver. However, while the Executive Committee stressed that solutions must be pursued with full respect for the rights of those affected, the 2009 Conclusion has its shortcomings, being less than forthright on those human rights which must play a central role in the politics of solution, and saying little about practicalities, such as how to make international co-operation work in specific situations. Thus, the Executive Committee emphasised, as it had done in its 2005 Conclusion,[10] that local integration is a matter of sovereign decision.[11] 'Sovereignty' is obviously a factor in the international refugee regime, but this traditional framing of the issue ignores those human rights considerations which may well push in the opposite direction, and fails also to give sufficient attention to special protection concerns and to the rights which international law requires to be protected, for example, in the case of unaccompanied children, of women at risk, and of those with disabilities.

The lessons of history are not there to be repeated, but they can provide moral and political guidance; they should also be the spurs to action, urging us ahead while equally keeping our focus on what is possible and viable. The seemingly intractable has been solved in the past, where the basic challenge–that of galvanising political will in matters apparently devoid of national self-interest–was no different from today.

It might be nice to think that World Refugee Year's simple agenda could be replicated today, but across the whole spectrum: to focus interest on the refugee problem, and to encourage additional opportunities for permanent refugee solutions, on a purely humanitarian basis and in accordance with the freely expressed wishes of the refugees themselves. The numbers needing solutions in 1959/1960, however, were considerably smaller than now, and the international environment quite different. The unresolved refugee situations described or touched on in this collection show that 'equitable burden-sharing' is clearly *not* the norm; on the contrary, the capacity of the international community to fulfil its political and legal responsibilities is fragmented, not so much by fundamental disagreement on relevant international legal principles, but on a lack of will and imagination in making solutions a reality in the face of pressing need.

The 2009 UNHCR Executive Committee conclusion, recognizing the importance of political will in reaching solutions, calls for 'comprehensive, multilateral and multi-sectoral collaboration and action', which would deal with root causes, avoidance of the necessity for flight, and full respect for the rights of those affected.[12] At one level, particularly given the dimension of international peace and security, solutions fall well within the remit of the Security Council and the General Assembly, and are the proper concern of UN organisations in addition to UNHCR, of regional organisations, and of individual States. But innovation is also needed, to promote co-ordination of effort among UN institutions and in ever pushing for action, both regionally and internationally. Just as the UN Secretary-General appointed a Special Representative for World Refugee Year, so today a Special Representative of the Secretary-General for Refugee Solutions at large might be considered. Political complexity, stalemate and overlapping organisational interests demand a mandate wider than the 'purely humanitarian' premise that governs UNHCR's efforts. An institutionally cross-cutting role could effectively exploit new opportunities for partnership, ensure that solutions are consistent with international law and relevant General Assembly resolutions, and take due account of such broader political processes as may be under way.[13]

Prolonged refugee situations are commonly the product of neglect–not benign neglect, but the surely conscious decision of many States to disregard and ignore those refugees whose intrinsic needs are integrally linked to hard political issues like self-determination, peace-making, peace-building, transitional justice, and development; or on whose behalf hard decisions must be taken, such as non-recognition, boycotts, or sanctions. In many respects, the issues *were* easier in the past. The camp clearance programme authorised by the General Assembly in the 1950s was premised on a given politics which framed the task in terms of the individual, rather than the community, and which, as High Commissioner Lindt remarked on many occasions, allowed due regard to individual choice. Many of today's unresolved situations, by contrast, engage the community in context, even if too little is done to ensure representative expression and due accounting of the community voice.

Now is the time for bold measures and for innovative steps to strengthen the international refugee regime and to bridge the responsibility gap between protection and durable solutions.

Notes

[*] Senior Research Fellow, All Souls College, Oxford; Professor of International Refugee Law, University of Oxford.

[1] G.A. Res. 1166 (XII), U.N. Doc. A/RES/1166 (XII), (Nov. 26, 1957).

[2] Statement of the UN High Commissioner, Auguste Lindt, to the U.N.G.A. Third Committee, Nov. 3, 1958. The High Commissioner also mentioned the 'Far East Programme', which was directed to refugees of European origin in the Far East, who had no possibility of integrating locally, and for whom emigration was seen as the main solution.

[3] G.A. Res. 1285 (XIII), U.N. Doc. A/RES/1285 (XIII), Dec. 5, 1958. The General Assembly urged States to co-operate in promoting the Year, 'as a practical means of securing increased assistance', and requested the Secretary-General to take such steps to this end as he considered necessary.' Dag Hammarskjöld appointed Claude de Kémoularia as his Special Representative and the Year ran from June 1959 to July 1969.

[4] Statement of the UN High Commissioner, Auguste Lindt, to the Economic and Social Council, July 20, 1959.

[5] *See* G.A. Res. 1388 (XIV), U.N. Doc. A/RES/1388 (XIV), (Nov. 20, 1959); G.A. Res. 1390 (XIV), U.N. Doc. A/RES/1390 (XIV), (Nov. 20, 1959).

[6] G.A. Res. 1502 (XV), U.N. Doc. A/RES/1502 (XV), (Dec. 5, 1960); Yearbook of the United Nations, Part 1, Sec. 2, Ch. VIII, 356-61 (1960), *available at* http://unyearbook.un.org/unyearbook.html?name=1960index.html.

[7] For example, while WRY generated additional funds for the UN Relief and Works Agency for Palestine Refugees in the Near East, it does not appear to have led to any relevant political initiatives; *see generally*, United Nations Yearbook, 1960, *supra* note 7, at 357.

[8] Statement of the UN High Commissioner, Auguste Lindt, to the Economic and Social Council, July 25, 1960.

[9] *See* UNHCR Executive Committee, *Report of the 60th Session*, §13, U.N. Doc. A/AC.96/1078, (Oct. 9, 2009); UNHCR Executive Committee, *Report of the*

Extraordinary Meeting of 8 December 2009 of the 61st Session, §5, U.N. Doc. A/AC.96/1080, (Dec. 29, 2009); UNHRC, Executive Committee, *Report of the 61st Session*, Annex II, U.N. Doc. A/AC.96/1095, (Oct. 12, 2010).

[10] UNHCR, Executive Committee, *Report of the 56th Session,* ¶22, U.N. Doc. A/AC.96/1021, (Oct. 7, 2005).

[11] UNHCR, *Report of the Extraordinary Meeting of 8 December 2009 of the 61st Session*, *supra* note 9, at §5(h).

[12] UNHCR, *Report of the Extraordinary Meeting of 8 December 2009 of the 61st Session*, *supra* note 9, at §5(a), (b).

[13] UNHCR, *Report of the Extraordinary Meeting of 8 December 2009 of the 61st Session*, *supra* note 9, at §5 (c), (n).

CHAPTER ONE

AN ESSAY ON THE CAUSES AND FACTORS OF THE UNRESOLVED PALESTINIAN REFUGEE PROBLEM: A VIEW FROM AN UNRWA COMMISSIONER GENERAL

KAREN KONING ABUZAYD*

I. Introduction

Long before the 1948 Arab-Israeli war when 750,000 people fled or were forced out of Mandate Palestine, the stage was set for Palestinians to become—and to remain—refugees. From the late 19th century the Zionist movement had conceived a plan for a Jewish return to the Holy Land. The movement foresaw the creation of a Jewish state, which by definition could not accommodate –or tolerate–Arab Palestinians living on the territory designated for the Jewish 'home' at that time. The ability of the Zionists to influence the 'big' powers in the first half of the 20th century was consolidated by the horrors of the Holocaust and the consequent attempt of those powers to make up for the events of World War II. Since the 1940s there have been few voices raised on behalf of Palestinians, particularly with regard to their right to an independent state or the right of those who remain refugees since 1948 to return home—the preferred solution for all refugees around the world.

This essay will review events from the early part of the 20th century until today, focusing on the origins of the Palestine refugee condition and the meager attempts by the 'international community' to protect Palestinian refugee rights.

II. Root Causes

On July 24, 1922, the League of Nations granted Britain a mandate to administer the territory covering what today is known as the occupied Palestinian territory (West Bank and the Gaza Strip), Jordan and Israel. The Mandate divided British authority between Transjordan, under Hashemite and indirect British rule and Palestine, under direct British rule. The latter was known as the British Mandate for Palestine, which made provision for 'a home for the Jewish people.' Over the following two decades, fluctuating cooperation and conflict among the British, Arabs and Zionists over immigration to Mandate Palestine culminated after World War II in Zionist and American pressure to create a Jewish State in Palestine.

In 1947, the British declared their intention to leave Palestine, returning their mandate to the United Nations and requesting the United Nations General Assembly ("UNGA") to make recommendations concerning the future of Palestine. The UNGA set up a UN Special Committee on Palestine ("UNSCOP") to ". . .investigate the cause of the conflict. . .and. . .prepare a report to the General Assembly and. . .submit such proposals as it may consider appropriate for the solution of the problem of Palestine."[1] The 11 nation members of UNSCOP, having considered a number of proposals, including that of a bi-national state, were apparently convinced that the enmity between Arab Palestinians and Jews would prevent their living together in one state. They, therefore, recommended partition into two states.

On November 29th 1947, the UN voted for partition in UNGA Resolution 181, awarding 61% of Mandate Palestine to a Jewish State. The British Mandate expired on May 14th 1948, the establishment of the State of Israel was declared and the Arab-Israeli war broke out on May 15th 1948. These events comprise the onset of what continues to be seen by Palestinians as 'al-Nakba' or 'the Catastrophe.' At the end of the war in March 1949, the new State of Israel kept the majority of the territory granted to it by Resolution 181 and took control over another 60% of what had been allocated to Arab Palestine, an irrefutable 'catastrophe' for Palestinians.[2]

The consequence of partition and the inevitable war which followed was the forced exile of 726,000 Palestinians from their homes in Mandate Palestine.[3] The majority of those fleeing made their way to neighboring territories or countries. They found refuge in what came to be known as the Palestinian Territory (West Bank and Gaza), the Hashemite Kingdom of Transjordan (since 1949, the Hashemite Kingdom of Jordan), the Syrian

Arab Republic, the Republic of Lebanon, the Arab Republic of Egypt and the Kingdom of Iraq (since 1958, the Republic of Iraq).[4]

III. Agencies established by the UN for Palestine refugees: UNCCP, UNRWA and UNHCR

A.The United Nations Conciliation Commission for Palestine (UNCCP)

On 11 December 1948, the UN General Assembly passed Resolution 194, creating the UN Conciliation Commission for Palestine ("UNCCP"). The UNCCP was expected to 'conclude' the 1948 war and work toward a 'final settlement' of all outstanding issues between the parties to the war. The issues of particular relevance to the Palestine refugees were dealt with in Section III, Article 11 of the Resolution as follows:[5]

(i) *'Right of return.'*

> Resolves that the refugees wishing to return to their homes and live at peace with their neighbors should be permitted to do so at the earliest practicable date, and that compensation should be paid for the property of those choosing not to return and for loss or damage to property which, under principles of international law or in equity, should be made good by the Governments or authorities responsible.

(ii) *'Repatriation, resettlement and economic and social rehabilitation.'*

> Instructs the CC to facilitate the repatriation, resettlement and economic and social rehabilitation of the refugees and the payment of compensation, and to maintain close relations with the Director of the United Nations Relief for Palestine Refugees and, through him, with the appropriate organs and agencies of the United Nations.

The Commission continues to present annual reports to the United Nations, passively keeping alive these issues most relevant to Palestine refugees: the 'right of return' and 'restitution,' issues which are repeatedly ignored rather than addressed in the off and on negotiations that have passed for a peace process since 1949.[6]

B. The United Nations Relief and Works Agency for Palestine Refugees (UNRWA)

In response to the recognized urgency of the needs of hundreds of thousands of refugees who fled from Palestine, the United Nations established the United Nations Relief and Works Agency for Palestine Refugees in the Near East ("UNRWA") by UNGA Resolution 302 (IV) on 8th December 1949 as a subsidiary organ of the UNGA, to provide relief and works services to the refugees.[7]

Today, some five million Palestine refugees (including the descendants of the 1948 refugees, according to the family unity principle applying to all refugees around the world) are registered with UNRWA in the West Bank and Gaza, Jordan, Syria and Lebanon.[8]

The UN operational definition of a Palestine refugee is 'any person whose normal place of residence was Palestine during the period between 1 June 1946 and 15 May 1948, and who lost both home and livelihood as a result of the 1948 Arab/Israeli conflict.'[9]

Palestine refugees are the sole group of refugees for whom there is an agency devoted exclusively to them. When the Office of the United Nations High Commission for Refugees was created in 1950 to protect and assist other refugees, the Palestine refugees were specifically excluded on the basis that they were already served by another UN agency.[10]

Today, UNRWA provides basic public services (primary education, primary healthcare, relief and social services, vocational training and microfinance programs). It is designed to promote self-reliance among Palestine refugees in a defined geographical environment.[11] UNRWA's 2013 General Fund budget (which covers the core services provided to the refugees) is $675 million, serving a population of 5.3 million refugees in the five separate, mainly urban, 'fields.'[12] This is a conservative expenditure when matched against comparable locations, services and numbers of beneficiaries. Its functions are carried out largely by 30,000 Palestine refugee staff, the majority of them professionals—teachers, medical workers, engineers and administrators.[13] UNRWA's success since 1949 can be measured by the fact that only one third of the refugees live in camps (which are usually peripheral parts of existing towns) and only 6% of the refugees are in need of social services.[14]

C. The United Nations High Commissioner for Refugees (UNHCR)

The Office of the United Nations High Commissioner for Refugees ("UNHCR") received its mandate in General Assembly Resolution 428 (V) in December, 1950 to 'provide, on a non-political and humanitarian basis, international protection to refugees and to seek permanent solutions for them.'[15] It functions on the basis of the 1951 Convention Relating to the Status of Refugees. 'Persons of concern' have, over the years, been added to its mandate, including some groups who are internally displaced and individuals who are stateless. Palestine refugees, in countries outside where UNRWA functions, are entitled to request UNHCR services and protection.[16]

III. International Legal Principles: Refugee Rights and State/UN Obligations

The 'right of return' and 'compensation' as promised in Resolution 194, and renewed annually at the UNGA, continue to resonate in the minds and hearts of Palestinians, who insist that the Resolution reinforces their legal and political rights to their original homes and the land they will be able to reclaim in their own independent state. These rights are a cornerstone for Palestinian resistance and essential to their persistence in identifying themselves as Palestine refugees who are still struggling for their right to statehood and Palestinian citizenship no matter where they are or what other status they have acquired.[17]

The 'right to return' and 'compensation' are core issues for Israeli-Palestinian 'final status' negotiations.[18] The UN view is that a just and durable solution to the issue of Palestine refugees must be found in accordance with international law and existing UN resolutions, including Resolution 194.[19] The parties are obliged to negotiate an outcome consistent with the principles of international law as affirmed by UN resolutions.[20]

IV. The Protracted Conflict over Claims

In considering how to address Palestine refugee 'claims,' it is necessary to underscore that Palestinian rights as refugees are not outside the framework of legal rights afforded other refugees. It is important to refer to the 'durable solutions' defined in the 1951 Convention Relating to the Status of Refugees, which governs UNHCR's activities and provides the framework for solutions for all refugees.[21] The Convention ensures a refugee's right to seek and enjoy asylum in another state, and eventually a 'durable solution' option, that is, voluntary repatriation, local integration or resettlement in a third country. Repatriation, or return to one's original home, is the solution usually preferred by the refugees and by both the country of origin and the country of asylum. It is the only 'right' that is absolute of the available durable solutions, as the right to return home is guaranteed under treaty and customary law and is a core obligation of all states of origin to accept the return of the inhabitants of their territory.[22] Each of the three durable solutions must be offered and agreed to by the refugees, by the countries of origin, and the asylum or resettlement states. Unlike the obligation on the state of origin to accept back the inhabitants of their territory, a country of asylum or resettlement is not legally obliged to accept an asylee or refugee permanently on its territory.

However, multi-state agreements to resolve major refugee crises involving return, host country absorption and third-country resettlement are often brokered by external parties—a UN agency, non-government parties engaged in conflict resolution or governments friendly to, or with an interest in, the refugees or the country of origin and/or asylum. In best case scenarios the 'brokers' have negotiation expertise, and use their skills impartially on behalf of all the parties involved. Moreover, these agreements usually begin with the premise that the right to return is a necessary prerequisite to a shared obligation amongst other states to accept a proportion of the refugee population unable or unwilling to return to the country of origin (conditions largely absent in discussions about Palestine refugees).[23]

The particular difficulty with realizing the preferred solution—repatriation—for Palestine refugees is obvious, given the 'threat' the State of Israel perceives would be posed to its defining characteristic, that of being a Jewish homeland. The fear that granting the 'right of return' would result in an influx of any number of Palestine refugees, sufficient to change the demographic majority of Jewish citizens, has been turned into a claim that the right of return requires the 'destruction' of the Israeli state. More discouraging for those who might attempt to realize a durable solution for refugees in a Palestinian state, these developments are rooted in religion and an unassailable belief by Israelis that they have a right to the 'biblical' land, while the Palestinians make their claim on the basis of being Palestinian, belonging to the land of Palestine (as in Resolution 194) and whose ancestors had lived on and tilled this same land for centuries before the declaration of the Israeli state.

Complicating the possibility of reaching agreement over what is regarded as negotiable on both sides is the pronounced inequality of the two parties to the conflict. Israel is home to what is described as the sixth most powerful army in the world and, more important, it has the unassailable political support of the United States of America,[24] from which it reportedly receives officially upwards of three billion dollars in aid a year.[25] Israelis, as well, are in the legally and morally reprehensible position of being the Occupying Power in the Palestinian territory of West Bank and Gaza since 1967. Palestine, on the other hand, for the past two decades has had a governing Authority (the Palestinian National Authority or Palestinian Authority in UN terminology) possessing little leverage to defend its past or even current geographical boundaries. Moreover, it has no substantive ability to function independently, either politically or economically, given the control exercised over essential aspects of state functions (land, sea and air border movements, airways control, customs collection, to name a few) by Israel, the Occupying Power.[26]

Given the origins and definition of Palestine refugees and the positions taken by powerful external actors on, inter alia, relevant UN resolutions, it is not surprising that decades-long negotiations to end Palestine refugee status, which began as part of Palestinian/Israeli peace talks and are inextricably linked with the creation of the Palestinian state, continue until today. Milestones along the way include the 1991 Madrid Conference, which was the catalyst for the 1993 (non-public) talks in Norway between Israel and the Palestinian Arabs that launched what became known as the Oslo peace process.[27] This led to the 1993 Declaration of Principles on Interim Self-Government Arrangements—known as the Oslo Accords[28]—and later to the 2000 Camp David meeting.[29] While no agreement was reached at Camp David, a trilateral (Israel, Palestine and America) statement was made conveying that efforts would continue and would be based on UN Resolutions 242[30] and 338,[31] promulgated at the end of the 1967 and 1973 wars, respectively, proclaiming that both sides were committed to eschewing violence.

To understand, in part, what has taken place on the ground over the past 20 years requires examining the Oslo Accords more closely, and more specifically, the Oslo II Agreement of 1995, which further complicated the possibility of reaching a Palestinian/Israeli peace agreement that would permit an independent, viable State of Palestine to exist and bring an end to Palestine refugee status. The Oslo Accords are based on a vision of a 'two state solution,' or a state of Israel and a state of Palestine living side by side in peace and security. Negotiators agreed to an odd (while not unique) step-by-step arrangement, decidedly disadvantageous to the

Palestinians. The Palestinian Authority would gradually demonstrate its ability to function as a reliable 'partner' (i.e., proving the ability to guarantee Israel's security), and would then be rewarded with gradually more independence and control over some of the lands left from the already reduced original Mandate Palestine.[32] However, precisely the opposite has occurred, as Palestinian West Bank and Jerusalem land continues to be taken over by Israeli settlers.[33]

A succinct summary of the most egregious content of the Oslo II Agreement (illustrated by a map) appears in the following paragraph from the Israeli Coalition Against House Demolitions ("ICAHD").

> Under the Oslo II Agreement of 1995, the West Bank was divided into three Areas: A, under full Palestinian Authority control; B, under Palestinian civil control but joint Israeli-Palestinian security control; and C, under full Israeli control. Although Area A was intended to expand until it included all of the West Bank except Israel's settlements, its military facilities and East Jerusalem—whose status would then be negotiated—in fact the division become a permanent feature. Area A comprises 18% of the West Bank, B another 22%, leaving Area C, a full 60%, including most of Palestinian farmland and water, under exclusive Israeli control. These areas, comprising 64 islands, shape the contours of the 'cantons' [former Israel Prime Minister Ariel] Sharon proposed as the basis of the future Palestinian state…In this scheme Israel will expand from its present 78% to 85-90%, with the Palestinian state confined to just 10-15% of the country.[34]

The Palestinians, under pressure from Western governments, agreed to function on, at most, 22% of British Mandate Palestine, all of which had once been their homeland.[35] Besides ignoring the right of return and the pre-1967 borders, this step-by-step arrangement has allowed the Israelis to control all of the West Bank and three of the Gaza borders. Furthermore, at first slowly and by now seemingly in a rush, the Israeli government has been creating 'facts on the West Bank and Jerusalem ground' by building settlements, roads, security areas, checkpoints, fences and walls. Peace negotiations have done nothing to slow down the massive and constant settlement construction. Consider the latest round of 'peace talks' brokered by U.S. Secretary of State Kerry, convened in August 2013 under a mediator with strong connections to Israel,[36] and which began with a token release of 100 long serving prisoners from Israeli jails at the same time an announcement was made approving the building of 2,000 new housing units in the occupied West Bank.[37]

Today more than 400,000 settlers populate the West Bank and 200,000 more have moved into what was deemed to be Palestinian East Jerusalem.[38]

There is no longer sufficiently contiguous territory in the West Bank that can be considered, or even function as, a viable state (quite aside from the separated and separately governed Gaza Strip, which is yet another obstacle to overcome).

Israeli laws and rules are cumulatively devised to make life increasingly complicated and oppressive for those who live in Jerusalem and the West Bank. Israeli policies make life miserable for any Palestinian who lives in the West Bank and has work, medical, education, international travel, family or other reasons to travel to Jerusalem and vice-versa.[39] Some argue these laws are intended to encourage (in some cases, clearly forcing) Palestinians to emigrate, a thinly disguised attempt at 'ethnic cleansing.'[40] There has also been a significant increase in settler violence perpetrated on Palestinian individuals and their property, as well as a continuing stream of displacements and removal of Palestinian structures. [41] Bedouin communities are particularly at risk of forcible displacement in the West Bank as Israel's proposed 'Prawer Plan' gains support in the Knesset and condemnation from, among other parties, the European Parliament.[42]

V. The Need for a Paradigm Shift

Is there a solution that will allow Palestinians and Israelis to live side by side, with dignity and security for both peoples? Israel, despite its military strength and international political influence, will continue to feel threatened by neighbors who have been and are being mistreated, discriminated against and denied their rights. The Palestinian territory today is a conglomerate of pockets, with its borders (and revenues) controlled by an occupying power. These factors do not advance the future citizenship of Palestinians in a state of their own, even one with the tentative and truncated Oslo boundaries. So what avenues might be explored which suit Palestinians, especially those steeped in resistance until their 'right' of return is granted—as promised by UNGA Resolution 194? What may be seen as positive elements to give the refugees hope that they and their children will not remain endlessly in a stateless, refugee limbo?

The elements are few, and, unfortunately, weak, particularly when set alongside the major obstacles already described, plus the length of exile and a deteriorating 'status quo,' which in itself obviates the possibility of reaching an agreement or (it is worth repeating) a viable state and an acceptable 'home' for refugees.

For their part, Palestinian officials, as they had begun to insist at the 1995 Taba negotiations, are adamant that their goal is to follow a path consistent with the principles of the UN Charter and international law in seeking resolution of all outstanding issues with Israel (borders, security, Jerusalem, refugees, settlements, water, land swaps). [43] Subsequent, although inconclusive—or ignored—proposals have been undertaken by the 'international community' (the 2002/3 Quartet's Road Map, for example) and neighboring states (the 2002 Arab Initiative).[44]

Today, following their newly acquired non-State observer status at the UN, Palestinian officials speak openly about what actions they will take if the current efforts fail.[45] They have prepared legal papers and documents to accede to UN Treaties and Agencies, including the International Criminal Court, and they propose to advance these applications and submit cases for judgment to the latter, including on alleged war crimes.[46] Among options under consideration are cases challenging violations of International Humanitarian Law by Israel, including under Article 49 of the Fourth Geneva Convention. Cases would build upon the International Court of Justice's Advisory Opinion of 9 July 2004 on the *Legal Consequences of the Construction of a Wall in the Occupied Palestinian Territory*, which found that Israeli settlements in the occupied Palestinian territories, including East Jerusalem, have been established in breach of international law. Specifically, Article 49, Paragraph 6 of the Convention provides that 'the Occupying Power shall not deport or transfer parts of its civilian population into the territory it occupies.'[47]

It follows that if current political efforts to achieve progress in the peace process flounder, then Palestinians may choose the path of international law to seek justice and redress their grievances. Such action could have consequences in terms of threats to funding for the Palestinian Authority from Western donors and all that would entail for a people and a government highly dependent on external aid to survive and function. Still, it could lead to international legal mechanisms once again, or for the first time, becoming the center of the dispute, a development which would benefit Palestinians, since international law and decades of UN resolutions favor the creation of an independent State of Palestine.

Meanwhile, proposals for a one state solution are gaining ground in the political and humanitarian literature, [48] and are discussed seriously at academic and other international events. [49] Briefly, in the 'one- state scenario,' Palestinians and Israelis will live equally and peacefully under one democratic government. Will the governments and the majority among the populations on either side agree?

For Israelis, this would constitute a demographic threat to the future of the Jewish state, a state they believe they have fought for and earned in the aftermath of World War II and the Holocaust, and a position for which there is firm support or at least sympathy among many Western governments. Palestinians would have to agree, at best, to accept a second-class citizenship, as already prevails in many ways for Palestinians who live in Israel and have Israeli citizenship.[50] For two peoples who have been unable to live peacefully in adjacent territories in 65 years, agreeing on how to live together amicably in one state seems to many somewhat of a fantasy.[51]

Beyond the historical, political, geographic and religious 'big picture,' there are human rights and refugee issues to be considered in the quest to afford Palestinians the rights which are guaranteed to them, as to all human beings, under the Universal Declaration of Human Rights (not one of the 30 UDHR rights is currently enjoyed by Palestine refugees).

One factor, often cited as an 'advantage' for Palestine refugees, is the uniqueness of having had an agency, UNRWA, created specifically for them. Yet Section II, Article 11 of Resolution 194 has been used to proscribe the role of UNRWA, interpreting it to confine the Agency's role to 'assistance.' UNRWA's achievements are often criticized both by those opposed to its work as well as by its supporters who contend that its mandate does not extend to international protection—at least not for seeking durable solutions. Its formal mandate, adopted in 1949, unlike UNHCR's mandate, does not specifically assign to it the 'protection' function, so when it addresses Palestinian rights issues, it is challenged by those who claim that UNRWA's intervention is 'political' or 'inappropriate.'[52]

Still, there is strong political support for UNRWA's work on protection as illustrated by the annual Resolutions adopted by the UN General Assembly on UNRWA operations. Resolution 66/74 of 12 January 2012, for example, states in operational Paragraph 3 that the UNGA "expresses special commendation to the Agency for the essential role it has played for over sixty years since its establishment in providing vital services for the well-being, human development and protection of the Palestine refugees and the amelioration of their plight." [53] These resolutions receive overwhelming support annually at the General Assembly.[54]

Additionally, because it offers wide-ranging services that would normally be provided by a state or local government, it faces accusations of 'perpetuating' the refugee problem and of creating refugee dependency. These allegations come not only from those who wish to deny Palestine refugees the right to decent living conditions, but also from those who seek to pre-empt a solution to the refugee issue in the context of the Middle East Peace negotiations. The false argument is advanced that handing the refugees over to UNHCR would be more appropriate, implying that this would also solve the right of return issue. This argument ignores the fact that refugees' right of return to their original homes is the preferred durable solution for other refugees served by UNHCR.

A similar interpretation is given to the presence of the Palestinian Authority (since November 2012 the occupied State of Palestine). Because the Palestinians have had a government and associated institutions to serve and represent them, including in international fora (if only as an observer), at least the refugees in West Bank and Gaza are expected to be satisfied as 'citizens' with their own 'state' institutions. This view does not take into account the fact of occupation, whereby the territory, the economy and the people—that is, the movement of both people and goods in and out of West Bank and Gaza--are under the heavy-handed administration and control of the Israeli Defense Forces (IDF) 'Civil' Administration.[55]

Since Oslo, the question of the future of the refugees has been dealt with by negotiators from, or associated with the Authority, which at every encounter left this most difficult issue to last as they tackled what they deemed to be more pressing issues or ones more amenable to discussion, such as security. Refugees (and Palestinians generally) have hesitated to criticize their own authorities, believing that their officials already face too many insurmountable difficulties with their Israeli counterparts, and wishing, in any case, to save their expressions of disagreement for the root cause of their problems, the occupation and the occupying power. However, it is a rare refugee (outside those among the Palestinian official establishment) who believes that she is well represented, particularly in peace negotiations regarding refugee rights, by those who have so far not seriously raised the right most important to them, that is, the right of return.

Although external parties often regard the possibility of refugees being able to return to their original homes or lands in any significant numbers as unrealistic, every refugee believes she has the right to return. The 'right' itself is not something a refugee (anywhere) will give up. This 'right' itself must be acknowledged in any negotiation, and compensation must be offered for material and psychological losses, as UNGA Resolution 194 asserts.[56]

Palestinians, like many refugees, are well known for their steadfastness and their resilience. They have been able to adapt over the years to the unrelenting discrimination and hardships they experience under occupation, and in some instances from governments and people in asylum countries.[57] While these attributes have been crucial to their survival as a strong and determined people over six and a half decades, they have also contributed to a superficial acceptance of their condition, reflected by the intermittent uprisings aside from the first and second *intifadas* in the West Bank and

Gaza. Otherwise, there has been a dearth of meaningful or consistent resistance to their oppression under occupation. Instead, there has been a dependence upon mainly externally generated and influenced international negotiations that have, for the most part, postponed discussion of the refugee issue and ignored provisions of international human rights and refugee law that would lead to justice for Palestinians, and, more specifically, for Palestine refugees.[58]

This adaptability, along with having to manage the hardships of their daily lives (particularly in the occupied Palestinian territories and Lebanon) has also contributed to the refugees' leaving decisions and actions to the Authority over the past 20 years. The Authority's elders appear to have been satisfied with a tentative (and misleading) international recognition, which has brought little meaningful improvement in the lives of their constituents. These leaders have grown increasingly out of touch with the Palestinian polity.

The widespread belief in the right of Palestinians to aspire to a state of their own, and the number of individuals and organizations that take an active interest in, and pursue actions on behalf of the Palestinian cause should give pause to elected (and other) governments around the world who do not show the same enthusiasm as their populations to defend and promote justice for Palestinians.

One must ask why such a popular—and just—cause, which receives consistent media coverage, does not garner more political support from world leaders or their legislatures.

VI. Conclusions

Where is international law in discussions regarding this struggle? Occupation is illegal.[59] Settlements,[60] settler violence and acquisition or seizure of territory,[61] destruction of property[62] and the wall, are all illegal.[63] UN Resolutions abound in defense and affirmation of an independent State of Palestine and the rights of Palestinian refugees.[64]

How might the widespread support and positive factors be parlayed into action? Are there too many negatives, too many contradictions and too much Israeli power and influence to find a way to ensure justice to the Palestinians? Do Israelis and the Israeli Government understand that there will be no peace in the region without justice for Palestinians?

The coming period will be decisive as it becomes clearer whether the Palestinian leadership or the Palestinian people will choose to follow a path to seek redress for their longstanding and just grievances. One factor is certain. Support for the Palestinian cause is increasing among the international community, as witnessed by recent votes at the United Nations and the growing international support for the Boycott, Divestment and Sanctions movement.[65]

A recent potentially far-reaching development, should it serve as an example to be followed, has been the EU Commission Notice of 15 July 2012 regarding 'the eligibility of Israeli entries and their activities in the territories occupied by Israel since 3 June 1967 for grants, prizes and financial instruments funded by the EU from 2014 onwards.'[66] The Notice states that the EU does not recognize the sovereignty over any of the 'territories,' which are defined as those comprising the Golan Heights, the Gaza Strip and the West Bank, including East Jerusalem. The related guidelines do not cover EU support to Palestinian entities in these same territories. Significantly, the 'aim' is stated as 'to ensure the respect of EU positions and commitments in conformity with international law . . .'[67]

At the United Nations, Palestinian statehood is no longer disputed. The outstanding issue is full membership, which requires the (unlikely to be secured) approval of the Security Council.

There are signs the political tide is turning, although translating this into an agreed (two state/one state?) solution is not yet within reach. If no progress is made on the political track, Palestinians may begin to exercise their right to pursue solutions for enforcement of their rights, anchored in international law, a path that might finally accord them justice, and both the Israelis and the Palestinians peace.

Notes

[*] Karen Koning AbuZayd, Commissioner-General of UNRWA (ret'd). This essay is based on a presentation at the Boston University School of Law Conference: Still Waiting for Tomorrow: The Law and Politics of Unresolved Refugee Crises, April 2, 2012. With thanks for comments and additions offered by Richard Wright, Director of the UNRWA Office at the United Nations, New York.

[1] U.N. Special Comm. on Palestine [UNSCOP], Report to the General Assembly, GAOR, 2d Sess., Supp. No. 11, U.N. Doc. A/364, (Sept. 3, 1947).

[2] Permanent Observer Mission of the State of Palestine to the United Nations, *1949 Armistice Agreement*, PERMANENT MISSIONS TO THE UNITED NATIONS, http://www.un.int/wcm/content/site/palestine/cache/offonce/pid/11600 (last visited Sept. 6, 2013).

[3] U.N. Conciliation Commission for Palestine, *Final Report of the United Nations Economic Survey Mission for the Middle East*, U.N. Doc. A/AC.25/6 (Dec. 28, 1949). In a June 2008 document, the Palestinian National Authority's Palestine Central Bureau of Statistics broke this figure down as follows: 280,000 in Gaza, 190,000 in the West Bank and 256,000 in Arab Countries. Press Release, The

Demographic Characteristics of the Palestinian Refugees, Palestinian National Authority, Palestinian Central Bureau of Statistics (June 2008).

[4] In the early years, the governments in Egypt and Iraq developed their own programs to support Palestine refugees. When leadership changes took place in these two countries and the Palestine refugees became less welcome, as in Egypt after Nasser and Iraq after Saddam Hussein, support for them was transferred to the Office of the United Nations High Commissioner for Refugees (see Section II, C).

[5] G.A. Res. 194 (III), ¶ 11, U.N. Doc. A/194 (Dec. 11, 1948).

[6] *See, e.g.,* United Nations Conciliation Commission for Palestine, *Nineteenth Progress Report*, U.N. Doc. A/4921 (Oct. 13, 1961) ("The right of Arab refugees to return to their homes in Jewish-controlled territory at the earliest possible date should be affirmed by the United Nations and their repatriation, resettlement and economic and social rehabilitation..."); United Nations Conciliation Commission for Palestine, Twenty-Fourth Progress Report, U.N. Doc. A/6451 (Sept. 30, 1966) (recalling the statement from the seventeenth progress report, "the work of identification and valuation is technical in nature and constitutes a prerequisite for any settlement with regard to the rights of individuals to their immovable property.")

[7] UNRWA's mandate has been renewed every three years by the UNGA. Its responsibilities were extended to cover persons displaced by the 1967 hostilities in the region. The current mandate runs until 30 June 2014. United Nations Relief and Works Agency for Palestine Refugees in the Near East, *Who We Are*, UNRWA.ORG, *available at* http://www.unrwa.org/who-we-are? (last visited Sept. 23, 2013).

[8] Another estimated five million Palestinians meeting the above definition reside in the wider Diaspora. United Nations Relief and Works Agency for Palestine Refugees in the Near East, *Statistics*, UNRWA.ORG, *available at* http://www.unrwa.org/etemplate.php?id=253 (last visited Sept. 6, 2013).

[9] Since some of those who fled were of nationalities other than Palestinian, the United Nations used the designation of 'Palestine refugees' rather than 'Palestinian refugees'. United Nations Relief and Works Agency for Palestine Refugees in the Near East, *Palestine Refugees*, UNRWA.ORG, *available at* http://www.unrwa.org/etemplate.php?id=86 (last visited Sept. 6, 2013).

[10] Article 1D in the July 1951 Convention relating to the Status of Refugees, July 28, 1951, 189 U.N.T.S. 150, which governs the application of the Convention towards Palestinian refugees states that "this Convention shall not apply to persons who are at present receiving from organs or agencies of the United Nations other than the United Nations High Commissioner for Refugees protection or assistance. When such protection or assistance has ceased for any reason, without the position of such persons being definitively settled in accordance with the relevant resolutions adopted by the General Assembly of the United Nations, these persons shall ipso facto be entitled to the benefits of the Convention." *See* LEX TAKKENBERG, THE STATUS OF PALESTINIAN REFUGEES IN INTERNATIONAL LAW (1998).

[11] Additional emergency programs (in 2012 amounting to around $500 million) are implemented by UNRWA during times of conflict, as in the first and second intifadas in the late 1980s and early 1990s and in the early 2000s, respectively. These interventions are not treated in this essay as they deserve separate analysis, along with the 2008-9 and 2012 attacks on Gaza and the Fatah/Hamas confrontation, which led to separate governance in the two parts of the territory. The Syria crisis has also necessitated a significant emergency program for Palestine refugees in Syria and for those who fled from Syria to neighboring countries ($290 million is the budget for these groups in the 2013 appeal). United Nations Relief and Works Agency for Palestine Refugees in the Near East, Syria Regional Crisis Response, July-Dec., 2013, UNRWA.ORG, http://www.unrwa.org/sites/default/files/201306071557.pdf.

[12] United Nations Relief and Works Agency for Palestine Refugees in the Near East, *UNRWA General Fund Programme Budget 2012-2013*, UNRWA.ORG, http://www.unrwa.org/userfiles/file/financial_updates/2011/Blue%20Book%202012-2013.pdf; United Nations Meeting in Support of Israeli-Palestinian Peace, Beijing, June 18-19, 2013, Presented by Richard Wright, Director of United Nations Relief and Works Agency for Palestine Refugees in the Near East, *available at* http://domino.un.org/pdfs/P1%20Richard%20Wright%20E.pdf.

[13] United Nations Relief and Works Agency for Palestine Refugees in the Near East, *Overview of UNRWA*, UNRWA.ORG, http://www.unrwa.org/etemplate.php?id=85, (last visited Sept. 6, 2013). *See* Lance Bartholomeusz, *The Mandate of UNRWA at Sixty,* 28:2-3 REF. SURVEY Q'LY 452 (2009) (explaining that UNRWA's Programme Budget relates to activities of all agency programmes such as education, health, relief and social services, microfinance, microenterprise, infrastructure and camp improvement).

[14] This percentage does not include the 827,000 refugees who receive food assistance as a consequence of the Gaza blockade. United Nations Relief and Works Agency for Palestine Refugees in the Near East, *Palestine Refugees*, UNRWA.ORG, http://www.unrwa.org/etemplate.php?id=86 (last visited Sept. 6, 2013).

[15] UN HIGH COMM'N FOR REFUGEES, SELF-STUDY MODULE 1: AN INTRODUCTION TO INTERNATIONAL PROTECTION. PROTECTING PERSONS OF CONCERN TO UNHCR 7 (Aug. 1, 2005), *available at* http://www.refworld.org/docid/4214cb4f2.html.

[16] *Supra* note 10. The UNHCR has issued several interpretations of the meaning and scope of Article 1D. For the most recent update on UNHCR's interpretation of its obligations towards Palestinian refugees, *see* U.N. High Commissioner for Refugees, *UNHCR Observations in the case C-364/11 El Kott and Others regarding the interpretation of Article 1D of the 1951 Convention and Article 12(1)(a) of the Qualification Directive*, REFWORLD.ORG (Oct. 27, 2011), http://www.refworld.org/docid/4eaa95d92.html (last visited Sept.19, 2013)

[17] *See* PLO Statement on the Intifada, *available at* http://www.jewishvirtuallibrary.org/jsource/History/PLOstatement88.html ("foremost among these rights are their right to repatriation, to self-determination, and to establish a free and independent state with Jerusalem as its capital"); *The*

PLO and the Right of Return, Interview with the PLO Department of Refugee Affairs, BADIL RESOURCE CENTER (Winter 2001), *available at* http://www.badil.org/en/al-majdal/item/741-the-plo-and-the-right-of-return-interview-with-the-plo-department-for-refugee-affairs; *Palestinian Parties and Organization to Abbas: Right of Return Non-Negotiable*, THE ELECTRONIC INTIFADA (September 25, 2008), http://electronicintifada.net/content/palestinian-parties-and-organizations-abbas-right-return-non-negotiable/858 ("The right of return is an individual right held by every Palestinian refugee and internally displaced person. The right is…an inalienable and indivisible right" and "The right of Palestinian refugees…to return is a collective right that is not limited to one group or another, and it is an integral part of the Palestinian right of self-determination.")

[18] Other 'core'—and some would say equally intractable—issues to be negotiated include security, Jerusalem, borders and water. Hussain Agha & Robert Malley, *Peace Process is Skewed,* MIFTAH.ORG (Sept. 8, 2010), *available at* http://www.miftah.org/Display.cfm?DocId=22555&CategoryId=5 (arguing that "what Israelis want from an agreement is something they have learned either to live without (Palestinian recognition) or to provide for themselves (security)"). Hussein Agha & Robert Malley, *Israel & Palestine: Can They Start Over?*, THE N.Y. REVIEW OF BOOKS (Dec. 3, 2009), *available at* http://www.nybooks.com/articles/archives/2009/dec/03/israel-palestine-can-they-start-over/?pagination=false (describing a persistent inability to reach a two-state settlement). Omar J. Dajani, *Stalled Between Seasons: The International Legal Status of Palestine During the Interim Period*, 26. DENV. J. INT'L L. &POL'Y 27 (1998).

[19] G.A. Res. 194, U.N. Doc A/RES/194 (Dec. 11, 1948).

[20] *See* S.C. Res. 242, U.N. Doc. S/RES/242 (Nov. 18, 1948); S.C. Res. 338, U.N. Doc. S/RES/338 (Oct. 22, 1973); S.C. Res. 368, U.N. Doc. S/RES/368 (Apr. 17, 1975); S.C. Res. 1398, U.N. Doc. A/RES/1398 (Mar. 15, 2002). *See also* Permanent Observer Mission of the State of Palestine to the United Nations, *General Assembly Resolutions*, PERMANENT MISSIONS TO THE UNITED NATIONS, *available at* http://www.un.int/wcm/content/site/palestine/pid/11865 (last visited Sept. 7, 2013) for the annual compilation of resolutions concerning 'The Question of Palestine' by the Permanent Observer of Palestine to the United Nations, which includes texts and votes.

[21] Convention relating to the Status of Refugees, July 28, 1951, 189 U.N.T.S. 150, *available at* http://www.unhcr.org/pages/49da0e466.html.

See U.N. General Assembly, *Statute of the Office of the United Nations High Commissioner for Refugees,* Dec. 14, 1950, A/RES/428(V) Ch.1 § 1, http://www.refworld.org/docid/3ae6b3628.html (last visited Sept. 23, 2013) (UNHCR's main mandate is to provide international protection to refugees falling within the scope of the statute and seeking permanent solutions for the problems of refugees).

[22] G.A. Res. 194 (III), ¶ 11, U.N. Doc. A/194 (Dec. 11, 1948). G.A. Res. 3236 (XXIX), ¶ 2, U.N. Doc A/3236 (Nov. 22, 1974) (reaffirming "the inalienable right of the Palestinians to return to their homes and property from which they have

been displaced and uprooted."); Universal Declaration of Human Rights, G.A. Res. 217 (III), ¶ 13, U.N. Doc. A/RES/217 (Dec. 10, 1948) (stating that everyone has the right to leave any country, including his own, and to return to his country).

[23] *See* Susan M. Akram and Terry Rempel, *Temporary Protection as an Instrument for Implementing the Right of Return for Palestinian Refugees*, 22 B.U. INT'L. L.J.1, 106 (Spring 2004) (reviewing the Comprehensive Plans of Action (CPA's) that, since the early 1970s have been the framework for successfully implementing shared-state obligations towards mass refugee flows, and arguing that the same framework should be applied to resolve the Palestinian refugee problem). *See also* Alexander Betts, *Comprehensive Plans of Action: Insights from CIREFCA and the Indochinese CPA*, UNHCR (Jan. 2006) (arguing that the CIREFCA and the Indochinese CPA were both successful examples of international cooperation of the refugee regime)

[24] America's uncritical role in backing Israel's actions, even those, such as occupation and settlements, that are clearly illegal under international law, is to a large extent based on the influence Jewish Americans have in important financial, economic, political and media structures in the U.S. along with the electoral influence of the American Israeli Political Affairs Committee (AIPAC) bolstered by American Christian Evangelicals. *See* RASHID KHALIDI, BROKERS OF DECEIT: HOW THE US HAS UNDERMINED PEACE IN THE MIDDLE EAST (2013); JOHN J. MEARSHEIMER AND STEPHEN M. WALT, THE ISRAEL LOBBY AND U.S. FOREIGN POLICY (2008). *See also* NASEER ARURI, DISHONEST BROKER: THE ROLE OF THE UNITED STATES IN PALESTINE AND ISRAEL (2003).

[25] *See* JEREMY SHARP, CONG. RESEARCH SERV., RL33222, U.S. FOREIGN AID TO ISRAEL (2002). *See also* Josh Ruebner, SHATTERED HOPES: OBAMA'S FAILURE TO BROKER ISRAELI-PALESTINIAN PEACE (Verso et al. eds., 2013) (showing that Obama has agreed to fund Israel 3.1 million in military aid and that Israel is granted loan forgiveness). *See also* 22 U.S.C.A. § 32 (the U.S. Forcign Assistance Act).

[26] Palestinian leverage may have somewhat increased as a result of the UNGA Resolution of November 29, 2012, granting Palestine the status of an observer 'non Member State'. The vote was 138 in favor, 41 abstaining and only nine against (among those were Israel, the United States and Canada), demonstrating a marked shift in support for the Palestinians, notably from Europe. A majority of European Union (EU) Member States voted in favor, and only one (the Czech Republic) voted against. Non-member observer status gives the State of Palestine access to UN Treaties and Instruments previously unavailable to them. *See* G.A. Res. 67/19, U.N. Doc. A/RES/67/19 (Nov. 29, 2012).

[27] *See The Madrid Conference*, 21:2 J. PALESTINE STUD. 117 (Winter 1992); Badea Abu Al-naja, *Madrid Dialogue Shows Unity: Ban,* WWW.MIFTAH.ORG (last accessed Sept. 23, 2013).

[28] *See The Oslo Accords*, MIDDLE EAST INFORMATION AND RESEARCH PROJECT (January 2001), *available at* http://www.merip.org/palestine-israel_primer/oslo-accords-pal-isr-
prime.html?ip_login_no_cache=af3979e1a59c4e2491dbb83e4532c174; Avi Shlaim,

The Oslo Accord, 23 J. PALESTINE STUD. 3 (1994) (discusses the process leading up to the Oslo accord and its aftermath); Scott Lasensky, *Paying For Peace: The Oslo Process and the Limits of Foreign Aid,* 58 MIDDLE EAST J. 2 (2004); A.G. Naidu, *Camp David Accords: A Study in American Foreign Policy,* 53 THE INDIAN J. OF POL. SCIENCE 3 (1992); *Ehud Barak on Camp David: "I Did Not Give Away a Thing,"* 33 J. PALESTINE STUD. 1 (2003); William A. Donohue, *Message Framing Surrounding the Oslo I Accords,* 53 J. CONFLICT RESOL. 1 (2009) (highlights the intersection between public rhetoric and private talks in the context of the Oslo I peacemaking).

[29] Hussein Agha and Robert Malley, *Camp; David: The Tragedy of Errors*, THE N.Y. REVIEW OF BOOKS (July 12, 2001), *available at* http://nybooks.com/articles/14380.

[30] S.C. Res. 242, U.N. Doc. S/RES/242 (Nov. 22, 1967). In the context of the establishment of a just and lasting peace in the Middle East, United Nations General Assembly Resolution 242 of 22 November 1967 calls for the withdrawal of Israel's armed forces from 'territories' occupied in the 1967 conflict. Forty-six years later, the Resolution remains unimplemented and the occupation persists.

[31] S.C. Res. 338, U.N. Doc. S/RES/388 (Oct. 22, 1973). United Nations General Assembly Resolution 338 of 22 October 1973 calls for a cease fire and the implementation of Resolution 242 in all its parts. Forty years have gone by ignoring this Resolution.

[32] *See* Declaration of Principles on Interim Self-Government Arrangements [Oslo I], Sept. 13, 1993, Isr.-P.L.O., 3232 I.L.M. 1525; Interim Agreement on the West Bank and the Gaza Strip, With Selected Annexes [Olso II], Sept. 28, 1995, Isr.-P.L.O., 36 I.L.M. 551. *See also* John Quigley, *Oslo Accords: More than Israel Deserves*, 12 AM. U. J. INT'L L. & POL'Y 285, 297 (1997) (arguing that even if Israel were to accede to all of Palestinian's demands presented at the Oslo agreements, Israel would still be in a better position than that to which it is entitled under international law).

[33] *See* Robert Serry, United Nations Special Coordinator for the Middle East Peace Process, Statement on Israeli Settlement Approvals (Feb. 22, 2012); Robert Serry, United Nations Special Coordinator for the Middle East Peace Process, Statement following the Announcement of Further Settlement Construction in the West Bank (June 7, 2012); Robert Serry, United Nations Special Coordinator for the Middle East Peace Process, Statement on the Announcement by Israel to Develop New Housing Units in East Jerusalem (Aug. 11, 2013). *See also* United Nations Office of the High Commissioner for Human Rights, Report of the independent international fact-finding mission to investigate the implications of the Israeli settlements on the civil, political, economic, social and cultural rights of the Palestinian people throughout the Occupied Palestinian Territory, including East Jerusalem, U.N. Doc. A/HRC/22/63 (Mar. 18, 2013) [hereinafter OHCHR Israeli Settlement Report].

[34] *Map: Defining the Palestinian Bantustan*, THE ISRAELI COMMITTEE AGAINST HOUSE DEMOLITIONS, *available at* http://www.icahd.org/node/442 (last visited Sept. 8, 2013).

[35] G.A. Res. 181(II), U.N. Doc. A/RES/181(II) (Nov. 29, 1947). President Mahmoud Abbas, Address before the United Nations General Assembly upon submitting a bid for United Nations Recognition of a Palestinian state (Sept. 23, 2011), *available at* http://www.haaretz.com/news/diplomacy-defense/full-transcript-of-abbas-speech-at-un-general-assembly-1.386385 ("we agreed to establish the State of Palestine on only 22% of the territory of historical Palestine - on all the Palestinian Territory occupied by Israel in 1967"). This compares with the original partition of 61% of territory for Israel and 39% for Palestine, which was never implemented. The land now potentially available to a future State of Palestine is half of what was already unfairly divided upon the dissolution of British Mandate Palestine. *Supra* note 2.

[36] John Hudson, *Israel, Palestine Backers Grudgingly Accept Indyk as Peace Talk Mediator*, FOREIGN POLICY [THE CABLE], July 22, 2013 (claiming that some Palestinians have "raised questions about Indyk's supposed neutrality, given his work as a deputy research director at the pro-Israel Public Affairs Committee in the '80s and later the Washington Institute for Near East Policy, which employs former AIPAC officials.")

[37] *Palestinians Warn Peace Talks at Risk Over Settlements*, FRANCE 24 (Aug. 13, 2013), *available at* http://www.france24.com/en/20130813-palestinians-warn-peace-talks-risk-over-settlements. On the release of political prisoners, *see* Guy Taylor, *Amid Mideast revolt, a chance for Israeli-Palestinian peace*, THE WASH. TIMES, July 29, 2013, *available at* http://www.washingtontimes.com/news/2013/jul/29/kerry-taps-indyk-envoy-israeli-palestinian-talks. On the building of new housing units, *see* Isabel Kershner, *Timing of Israeli Housing Plans May Be Part of a Political Calculation*, N.Y. TIMES, Aug. 12, 2013, *available at* http://www.nytimes.com/2013/08/13/world/middleeast/israel-names-palestinian-prisoners-to-be-released.html

[38] OHCHR Israeli Settlement Report, *supra* note 33.

[39] *See e.g. Israel: High Court Rulings Undermine Human Rights*, HUMAN RIGHTS WATCH (Jan. 30, 2012), *available at* http://www.hrw.org/news/2012/01/30/israel-high-court-rulings-undermine-human-rights (on The Citizenship and Entry into Israel Law). *See also* United Nations Office for the Coordination of Humanitarian Affairs, *East Jerusalem: Key Humanitarian Concerns* (March 2011), *available at* http://www.ochaopt.org/documents/ocha_opt_jerusalem_report_2011_03_23_web_english.pdf.

[40] *UN Expert Highlights Worsening Human Rights Situation in East Jerusalem*, UN NEWS CENTRE (Mar. 21, 2011), *available at* http://www.un.org/apps/news/story.asp?NewsID=37840#.Ujnx1byJT3E (statement by Richard Falk, the Special Rapporteur on the occupied Palestinian Territories: "the continued pattern of settlement expansion in East Jerusalem combined with forcible eviction of long residing Palestinians are creating an intolerable situation that can only be described…as a form of ethnic cleansing"). *See* ILAN PAPPE, THE ETHNIC CLEANSING OF PALESTINE (2007). *See also* newspaper coverage, including in Haaretz, Gideon Levy, *Ethnic cleansing of Palestinians, or democratic Israel at work*, HAARETZ, May 12, 2011, *available at* http://www.haaretz.com/print-edition/

opinion/ethnic-cleansing-of-palestinians-or-democratic-israel-at-work-1.361196; Robert Ross, *'Price Tag' Attacks and the ethnic cleansing of Palestinians*, MONDOWEISS,(July 2, 2013), *available at* http://mondoweiss.net/2013/07/attacks-cleansing-palestine.html.

[41] *See Israeli Settler Violence in the West Bank*, UNITED NATIONS OFFICE FOR THE COORDINATION OF HUMANITARIAN AFFAIRS (NOV. 2011), *available at* http://www.ochaopt.org/documents/ocha_opt_settler_violence_FactSheet_October_2011_english.pdf. *See also* Linah Alsaafin, *Israeli Settlers Escalate Violence Against Palestinians*, AL-MONITOR PALESTINE PULSE, June 3, 2013, *available at* http://www.al-monitor.com/pulse/originals/2013/06/israeli-settlers-violence-palestinians.html.

[42] *See Demolition and Eviction of Bedouin Citizens of Israel in the Naqab (Negev) – The Prawer Plan*, ADALAH: THE LEGAL CENTER FOR ARAB MINORITY RIGHTS IN ISRAEL, http://adalah.org/eng/?mod=articles&ID=1589#What-is-the-Prawer-Plan (last visited Sept. 8, 2013) for listings on 'The Prawer Plan,'.

[43] *The Taba Negotiations (January 2001)*, 31:3 J. PALESTINE STUD. 79 (Spring 2002); Miguel Moratinos, *European Union's Account of the Taba Talks* (Feb. 14, 2002), *available at* http://www.bitterlemons.org/docs/moratinos.html

[44] *A Performance-Based Roadmap to a Permanent Two-State Solution to the Israeli-Palestinian Conflict*, BCC (last updated Apr. 30, 2003), http://news.bbc.co.uk/2/hi/middle_east/2989783.stm. *Arab Peace Plan of 2002*, BBC (last updated Mar. 22, 2005), http://news.bbc.co.uk/2/hi/middle_east/1844214.stm.

[45] *See Abbas Warns of ICC Action if Israel Implements Settlement Plans*, THE PALESTINE CHRONICLE, Dec. 12, 2012, *available at* http://www.palestinechronicle.com/abbas-warns-of-icc-action-if-israel-implements-settlement-plans, though all such proposals are on hold to allow the recently convened 'Peace Talks,' in late-July 2013, a nine month chance to produce results. *See* Michael R. Gordon and Isabel Kershner, *Israel and Palestinians Set to Resume Peace Talks, U.S. Announces*, N.Y. TIMES, July 28, 2013, *available at* http://www.nytimes.com/2013/07/29/world/middleeast/israel-agrees-to-prisoner-release-clearing-way-for-talks.html.

[46] *See* John Quigley, *The Palestine Declaration to the International Criminal Court: The Statehood Issue*, *in* IS THERE A COURT FOR GAZA? A TEST BENCH FOR INTERNATIONAL JUSTICE (Chantal Meloni and Gianni Tognoni, eds., 2012); Press Release, Committee on the Inalienable Rights of the Palestinian People, Success in Resuming Peace Talks Vital, Top Negotiator Stresses at Meeting of Palestinian Rights Committee, U.N. Press Release GA/PAL 1269 (May 20, 2013) (Saeb Erakat, the chief Palestinian negotiator, stated that Palestine had prepared letters of accession to various agencies and conventions).

[47] *See* Legal Consequences of the Construction of a Wall in the Occupied Palestinian Territory, Advisory Opinion, 2004 I.C.J. 59-60 (July 9) ["The court is of the opinion that the construction of the wall and its associated regime impede the liberty of movement of the inhabitants of the Occupied Palestinian Territory (with the exception of Israeli citizens and those assimilated thereto) as guaranteed

under Article 12, paragraph 1, of the International Covenant on Civil and Political Rights."] *See also* Richard Falk, *Support for Wall Mocks International Law*, MIDDLE EAST RESEARCH AND INFORMATION PROJECT (July 20, 2004), *available at* http://www.merip.org/newspaper_opeds/oped072004 ("The International Court of Justice has rarely reached this degree of unanimity in big cases," noting the 14-1 vote of the illegality of the wall.)

[48] *See, e.g.,* EDWARD SAID, THE END OF THE PEACE PROCESS: OSLO AND AFTER(2000); VIRGINIA TILLEY, THE ONE-STATE SOLUTION: A BREAKTHROUGH FOR PEACE IN THE ISRAEL-PALESTINE DEADLOCK (2005); HANI FARIS, THE FAILURE OF THE TWO-STATE SOLUTION: THE PROSPECTS OF ONE STATE IN THE ISRAEL-PALESTINE CONFLICT (2013). *See also*, Ilene Prusher, *Influential Palestinians Say It's Time for a One-State Solution*, TIME, May 24, 2013.

[49] Conference, London One State Group and the SOAS Palestine Society, Challenging the Boundaries: a Single State in Israel/Palestine (Nov.17-18, 2007); Conference, Harvard University, The One State Conference: Israel/Palestine and the One-State Solution, (March 3-4 2012).Conference, Boston University, Right of Return (Apr. 6-7, 2013), http://rightofreturn.net/.

[50] *See Index of Currently Pending Discriminatory Bills in the 19th Israeli Knesset, available at* http://adalah.org/Public/files/Discriminatory-Laws-Database/Discriminatory-Bills-19th-Knesset-24-06-2013.pdf (last visited Oct. 6, 2013) (highlights the latest discriminatory laws against Palestinians in Israel); International Crisis Group (ICG), *Back to Basics: Israel's Arab Minority and the Israeli -Palestinian Conflict, available at* http://www.refworld.org/docid/4f61a4c72.html (last visited Oct. 6, 2013) (offers possible solutions for the integration of Palestinians in Israel and responses to systematic inequality); *The Palestinian Minority in The Israeli Legal System, available at* http://adalah.org/eng/Articles/1348/Array (last visited Oct., 6 2013) (details Israeli government discrimination, land appropriation, and discriminatory laws against Palestinians in Israel); *Discrimination Against Palestinian Citizens of Israel*, INSTITUTE FOR MIDDLE EAST UNDERSTANDING (September 28, 2011), *available at* http://imeu.net/news/article0021536.shtml.

[51] *See* Andrea Dessi, *Why a One-State Solution Won't Work: Interview with Aaron David Miller*, RESET DOC (Nov. 16, 2012), *available at* http://www.resetdoc.org/story/00000022123.

[52] Arlene Kushner, *UNRWA's Anti-Israel Bias*, 18 THE MIDDLE EAST Q. 84, 84 (2011) ("The propensity for senior UNRWA staff to make inappropriate, incendiary, and highly politicized statements–in stark contrast to the organization's mandate–has long been documented…"). *Cf.* Michael Kagan, *Is There Really a Protection Gap? UNRWA's Role vis-à-vis Palestinian Refugees*, 28 REF. SURVEY Q'LY 2-3 (2010) (stating that there is a protection gap of individual rights of Palestinian refugees, which the UNHCR and UNRWA have not addressed). *See also* Brenda Goddard, *UNHCR and the International Protection of Palestinian Refugees,* 28 REF. SURVEY Q'LY 2-3 (2010) (describing the difficulties of UNHCR and UNRWA adequately addressing the protection needs of Palestinian refugees).

[53] G.A. Res. 66/74, ¶ 3, U.N. Doc. A/RES/66/74 (Jan. 12, 2012).

[54] U.N. General Assembly, *Report of the Commissioner-General of the United Nations Relief and Works Agency for Palestine Refugees in the Near East*, U.N. Doc. A/54/13 (July 1, 1998), *available at* http://www.refworld.org/docid/3ae6aef30.html; United Nations Relief and Works Agency for Palestine Refugees in the Near East, U.N. General Assembly, *Report of the Independent International Fact-Finding Mission*, U.N. Doc. A/64/490 (Oct. 29, 2009), *available at* http://www.refworld.org/docid/4af15e652.html; U.N. General Assembly, *Assistance to the Palestinian People: Report of the Secretary General,* U.N. Doc A/68/76 (May 8, 2013), *available at* http://www.refworld.org/docid/51f8e77c4.html.

[55] Human Rights Watch, *Separate and Unequal, Israel's Discriminatory Treatment of Palestinians in the Occupied Palestinian Territories, available at* http://www.refworld.org/docid/4d1049e12.html (last visited Oct. 6, 2013) (describes cases showing institutionalized discrimination in the Occupied Palestinian Territories).

[56] *See, e.g.,* Memorandum Concerning Public Opinion about the Nusseibeh-Ayalon Position, Endorsed by eighty Palestinian community organizations, public institutions and political groups in Palestine (Oct. 2002), *available at* http://www.badil.org/en/al-majdal/item/1040-refugee-voices ("We reaffirm that the right of return is an individual and collective right. The right of return is non-negotiable. Governments or other second parties cannot waive or extinguish the right of return.")

[57] The treatment of Palestine refugees from Syria seeking refuge in neighboring countries since mid-2012 is the most recent example of discrimination.

[58] *See, e.g.,* Avi Shlaim, *It's Now Clear: the Oslo Peace Accords Were Wrecked by Netanyahu's Bad Faith*, THE GUARDIAN (Sept. 12, 2013), *available at* http://www.theguardian.com/commentisfree/2013/sep/12/oslo-israel-reneged-colonial-palestine (arguing that the Oslo Accords "did not address any of the key issues in this dispute: Jerusalem; the right of return of 1948 refugees; the status of Jewish settlements built on occupied Palestinian land; or the borders of the Palestinian entity.")

[59] *See* S.C. Res. 242, U.N. Doc. S/RES/242 (Nov. 22, 1967) ("*emphasizing* the inadmissibility of the acquisition of territory by war"). Hague Convention (IV) – Respecting the Laws and Customs of War on Land arts. 42-56, Oct. 18, 1907, 36 Stat. 2227, T.S. 539; Geneva Convention Relative to the Protection of Civilian Persons in Time of War arts. 27-34, 47-78, Aug. 12, 1949, 3 U.S.T. 3516, T.I.A.S. 3365.

[60] *See* U.N Human Rights Council, *Rep. of the Independent International Fact-Finding Mission to Investigate the Implications of the Israeli Settlements on the Civil, Political, Economic, Social and Cultural Rights of the Palestinian People throughout the Occupied Palestinian Territory, Including East Jerusalem*, 22nd Sess., U.N. Doc. A/HRC/22 (Mar. 22, 2013) (noting that Israeli settlements in occupied territories violate international law).

[61] *See* John Quigley, Book Review, 25 SUFFOLK TRANSNAT'L L. REV. 73, 78 (2001-2002)(reviewing THE OSLO ACCORDS: INTERNATIONAL LAW AND THE ISRAELI-

PALESTINIAN PEACE AGREEMENTS) (an "occupant who establishes settlement in the territory thereby gains no right to annex that territory").

[62] *See* S.C. Res. 471, U.N. Doc. S/RES/471 (June 5, 1980); S.C. Res. 904,S/RES/904 (Mar. 18, 1994).Convention IV Relative to the Protection of Civilian Persons in Time of War, Aug. 12, 1949, art. 53, 6 U.S.T. 3516, 75 U.N.T.S. 278 (stating that destruction of property by occupying power is prohibited unless when "rendered absolutely necessary by military operations.")

[63] *Supra* note 45. *See also* Ben White, *Five Years After ICJ Ruling, Israel Expands its Illegal Wall Onto More Palestinian Land*, WASH. REP. ON MIDDLE E. AFF., July 2009, at 18, *available at* http://www.wrmea.org/wrmea-archives/220-washington-report-archives-2006-2010/july-2009/3008-five-years-after-icj-ruling-israel-expands-its-illegal-wall-onto-more-palestinian-land.html.

[64] *See, e.g.,* S.C. Res.242, U.N. Doc. S/RES/242 (Nov. 22, 1967); S.C. Res.338, U.N. Doc. S/RES/338 (Oct. 22, 1973); S.C. Res. 369, U.N. Doc. S/RES/369 (May 28, 1975); S.C. Res. 378, U.N. Doc. S/RES/378 (Oct. 23, 1975); S.C. Res1397, U.N. Doc. S/RES/1397 (Mar. 12, 2002).

[65] *See* Ethan Bronner and Christine Hauser, *U.N. Assembly, in Blow to U.S., Elevates Status of Palestine*, N.Y. TIMES, Nov. 29, 2012, *available at* http://www.nytimes.com/2012/11/30/world/middleeast/Palestinian-Authority-United-Nations-Israel.html (explaining that over 130 states voted for Palestine's nonmember observer status at the United Nations). *See also* Nora Barrows-Friedman, *BSD Roundup: the BDS Movement, 7 Years On, 'Stronger, More Effective and More Diverse than Ever,'"* ELECTRONIC INTIFADA (July 11, 2012), *available at* http://electronicintifada.net/blogs/nora/bds-roundup-bds-movement-7-years-stronger-more-effective-and-more-diverse-ever; Palestinian BDS National Committee, *Palestinian BDS National Committee Stands in Solidarity with French Campaigners Facing State Repression*, BDS MOVEMENT (June 26, 2013), *available at* http://www.bdsmovement.net/2013/palestinian-bds-national-committee-stands-in-solidarity-with-french-campaigners-facing-state-repression-11107 ("The BDS movement is gaining fast growing support in the mainstream, persuading cultural figures to boycott Israel. . ."); Adam Horowitz and Philip Weiss, *The Boycott Divestment Sanctions Movement: BDS has become key battleground in the struggle over the future of Israel/Palestine*, THE NATION, June 28, 2010, *available at* http://www.thenation.com/article/boycott-divestment-sanctions-movement# (explaining that the divestment debate has spread to major public universities).

[66] Guidelines on the eligibility of Israeli entities and their activities in the territories occupied by Israel since June 1967 for grants, prizes and financial instruments funded by the EU from 2014 onwards, 2013 O.J.C 205/05.

[67] *Id.* at Section A. GENERAL ISSUES.

CHAPTER TWO

STATE OF EXILE: THE SAHARAWI REPUBLIC AND ITS REFUGEES

J.J.P. SMITH*

> "And remember when you were few and were reckoned weak in the land … He provided a safe place for you, strengthened you with His Help, and provided you with good things so that you might be grateful."[1]

> "[I]t is for the people to determine the destiny of the territory and not the territory the destiny of the people."[2]

Introduction–The dualities of a people in exile

The harsh, barren plain of the *hammada* that extends for hundreds of kilometers around Tindouf, Algeria is an improbable setting for the refugee camps of the Sahrawi people who have remained there for nearly four decades. A more inhospitable place of exile and a politically self-sustaining and internally governed refugee society is difficult to imagine. The 160,000 Sahrawi at Tindouf, together with some 120,000 others in that part of Western Sahara occupied by Morocco, are the last people in Africa yet to realize the "sacred trust" of the right to self-determination in a world at least formally free from European colonization.[3] It is a paradox that the insularity of the Sahrawi people in refugee exile has preserved their social, cultural, and national identity, while at the same time fostering their dependence on outside aid and the goodwill of the organized international community. This insularity has maintained their uniqueness and self-concept as a people, and generated support for their right to self-determination and liberation from a status as Africa's last colony.

The visual landscape of the Sahrawi refugee camps illustrates the dual aspects of Sahrawi refugee society.[4] The camps are at once permanent and impermanent, settled and transitory. They are widely spaced and named after the five principal cities in metropolitan Western Sahara–Auswerd,

Boujdour, Dakhla, El-Aauin and Smara, with the seat of the Sahrawi government a sixth at Rabouni camp. The Sahrawi people's history as a semi-nomadic desert society is reflected in the frequent presence of a traditional tent, the *khaima*, among mud walled houses built thick to withstand the searing temperatures of summer in the region.[5] Here, the Sahrawi people have settled into exile as they await a return to their native Western Sahara, and have fashioned a deliberately temporary place in Algeria, their host state. The setting of the camps is the starkest reminder of the dual aspects of the Sahrawi people: citizens of a self-declared state and refugees; members of a national liberation movement and a widely recognized nation-state; a people divided by military occupation with families divided by distance and, increasingly, time. The population is separated by the berm that partitions Western Sahara--built by Morocco at great cost from 1980 through 1987--the longest and most heavily land-mined fortification in the world.[6] The incongruities are manifest: the Sahrawi people subsist on no more than $50 million of annual aid while the value of natural resources taken from their territory is ten times greater; they have secured the promise of the organized international community to self-determination and independence, yet are denied exercise of those rights through the intransigence of the same community. As a matter of international law and fact, the Sahrawi at Tindouf are refugees. However, their self-governance and collective decision to continue in exile pending the exercise of their right to choose their political-national future is unique. The case of the Sahrawi people is important when considering protracted refugee situations, as it remains the classic example of conflicts that endure because of the inability of the international community to resolve such situations in their early stages. Western Sahara also yields relevant lessons to unfolding refugee crises today, such as the ongoing flight of Syria's refugees into neighboring states after 2011, and other mass refugee situations.

This chapter surveys the historical origins of the Sahrawi people as refugees, the construct of the Sahrawi refugee state and the involvement of that state with the international community. An assessment is offered about the situation of the Sahrawi people through the lens of international refugee law together with an analysis of the effects of a prolonged state-in-exile on the realization of self-determination. The chapter concludes with some observations relevant to protracted refugee situations in general.

I. The origins of a flight into exile and creation of the Sahrawi state

The exodus of the Sahrawi people from the then-territory of Spanish Sahara began in late 1975 with little forewarning. Following Spain's decision earlier in the decade to give up the colony (which it had held since the Congress of Berlin in 1884) and allow the Sahrawi people self-determination, the territory was invaded in October 1975 by Mauritania from the south and Morocco from the north.[7] Further to its announced withdrawal, Spain had in 1974 completed a census of the Sahrawi people pending its proposed referendum on the status of the territory. Later the same year, the United Nations General Assembly ("UNGA") requested the International Court of Justice to provide an advisory opinion about territorial claims to the colony.[8] The report of the UN's visiting mission to Western Sahara in May 1975, issued that October within a day of the ICJ's opinion, was unequivocal in its conclusion that the Sahrawi people wanted their independence. After all, a total population of 73,497 Sahrawi at the time was a manageable number to make the gauging sentiment uncomplicated.[9] For its part, the ICJ was clear about the historical legal record and the validity of claims to the territory by neighboring states. The ICJ found that at the time of Spanish acquisition, the territory was already long-inhabited by the Sahrawi people.[10] The Court also determined that neither Mauritania nor Morocco had tangible territorial claims over the territory, and certainly not sufficient claims to displace those of the Sahrawi people.[11] The Court went on to conclude that the Sahrawi people's right of self-determination originating in the UNGA's 1960 decolonization resolutions was undiminished.[12]

Spain's quickly fading control, and inability to counter the threat of annexation by neighboring Mauritania and Morocco, led to the Sahrawi fleeing their homeland. The colonial power's resolve to achieve an orderly decolonization of Spanish Sahara faltered, complicated by the death of Francisco Franco. In the face of the vacuum of power left by Spain, the organized international community was unable to prevent the annexation of Western Sahara by neighboring (and themselves formerly colonized) states.[13]

As events stood at the time, there might have been little impetus for a mass Sahrawi exodus in late 1975. The *Madrid Accords*, concluded that 14th of November between Spain, Mauritania and Morocco, created the framework for a seemingly acceptable transfer of responsibility for a self-determination referendum to the two occupying states.[14] Setting aside the expressed wishes of the great majority of the Sahrawi people and their representative assembly, the *Djemaa*, as well as the conclusions of the UN Visiting Mission and the ICJ, a semblance of normalcy continued that might have allowed for maintaining order in the territory. Even Morocco's so-called Green March, which began that 6th of November and threatened entry of up to 350,000 civilians across the border into Western Sahara, did not significantly penetrate the territory. And in the early days after Spain's transfer of control, there was little unrest and no immediate catalyst to displace most Sahrawi from the territory's urban areas.[15]

The semblance of normalcy changed dramatically with the subsequent armed invasion that caused the Sahrawi to flee in large numbers into the desert. The Sahrawi national liberation movement, the Polisario Front, adopted a war footing to repel Mauritanian and Moroccan armed units that entered Western Sahara in late October. Morocco in particular advanced with increasing violence, causing a spiral of fear in the civilian population. The Sahrawi people had not settled in Spanish colonial towns until after the Second World War, and so had been urbanized for only a generation. In 1975, even as now, the Sahrawi population turned to the desert for shelter. They fled the major towns of El-Aauin, Dakhla, Auserd, and Smara to temporarily seek refuge in the desert areas of Guelta Zemmur, Oum Dreyga, and Mahbas. Here they were attacked by Moroccan forces, including by the use of napalm and white phosphorus on the civilian population, most seriously at Oum Dreyga.[16] Recognizing the strength of the forces allied against them, the Sahrawi *Djemaa* reconvened on 28th of November 1975 and voted its own dissolution, declaring that it would not allow itself to be a "puppet institution" of the parties to the *Madrid Accords*.[17]

As is often the case during times of conflict, no accurate figures are available for the number of Sahrawi who were displaced across the desert to Tindouf. However, the 1974 census, details from the United Nations ("UN") voter registration process from 1991 until 2001, the numbers of people settling at Tindouf, as well as estimates of population growth in the camps in the generation since, suffice to make a reasonable approximation of the refugee population. Around three-quarters of the then-population of 80,000 Sahrawi fled Spanish Sahara. Not all came immediately to Tindouf, as a substantial number of armed men in the Sahrawi People's Liberation Army remained inside the territory. The civilian population that gathered at Tindouf may have suffered a mortality rate as high as five per cent from the violent attacks and the hardship of travel across the desert, including winter weather and a lack of food. However, estimates of an initial population of about 12,000 in each of the first four residential camps seem reasonable based on the known data.[18] What is noteworthy when comparable cases of refugee migration are considered is the considerable distance to Tindouf–inside the safe haven of Algeria across a narrow border strip–as well as the social cohesion of Sahrawi as they came together from widely separated locations in Western Sahara.[19] Equally remarkable was the absence of wider migration into diaspora communities. Algeria alone supported the Sahrawi exiles in what were initially conceived as temporary camps until 1977, when it became obvious there would be no quick or easy return for them to Western Sahara.[20] Indeed, over the next 14 years, active hostilities continued across much of inland Western Sahara, effectively barring the return of Sahrawi to their homeland.

In the first months of 1976 the political and exilic circumstances of the Sahrawi people became evident. On the 26th of February Spain informed the UN it would formally relinquish the colony two days later.[21] In response, the Provisional Sahrawi National Council declared the independence of the Saharawi Republic at Bir Lehlou, the nominal capital of the Sahrawi Arab Democratic Republic (the "SADR") in the eastern part of the territory.[22] Formal recognition of the SADR by African states followed. That April, Mauritania and Morocco agreed by treaty to partition the territory, with Mauritania establishing the province of Tiris el-Gharbia in the south (the former Río de Oro administrative area of Spanish Sahara) with Dakhla as its principal city.[23]

After the Sahrawi refugee population came under nominal protection around Tindouf, and in the face of the inability of the organized international community to challenge Mauritania and Morocco's hold on the territory, the Saharawi People's Liberation Army launched a wide-ranging guerilla campaign. Although isolated from the international community and under a tenuous existence, the Sahrawi were able to prosecute one of the twentieth century's more successful desert warfare campaigns. This feat has received little acknowledgement since the 1991 ceasefire. Soldiers of the Polisario Front's armed wing and the Sahrawi People's Liberation Army moved in small, fast-moving units through the desert to attack the occupiers as far afield as Nouakchott and El-Aauin, even seizing Spanish fishing vessels off the Atlantic coast of the territory.[24]

The sustained assaults across its long border with Western Sahara progressively weakened Mauritania financially and politically. In August 1979, Mauritania concluded a peace treaty with the Polisario Front, admitting it had engaged in an "unjust war."[25] When Mauritania left its part of Western Sahara, Morocco moved to occupy the entire coast of the territory. As with the armed conflict itself, such an enlarged presence ensured the Sahrawi refugees would not return home soon, and increased the enmity against the now sole occupying state. By 1979, continuing food aid from the World Food Programme made life in the camps more tolerable, and the start of an international solidarity movement based in Spain offered moral support for Sahrawi self-determination. While the hardship of life on the *hammada* led to an increase in infant and maternal mortality in the early years, birth rates began to increase in the 1980s after physical and food security was assured, and sustained population growth resulted.[26] The exceptional geographic isolation of the Sahrawi refugees at Tindouf and the continuing indifference of the international community to their insistence on self-determination were important causes for the exilic identity of the Sahrawi people. Their sense of strong cultural identity led to the creation of a functioning nation-state concerned with the maintenance of life in the camps and the political project of an independent Western Sahara.[27]

II. The Sahrawi state and national liberation movement in perspective

The character of the Sahrawi state reflects the circumstances in which its citizens now find themselves: a people divided by geography and unable to achieve the principal right of self-determination of non-self-governing peoples under modern international law. Governments of the developed world–the Global North–consider the Sahrawi as self-governing refugees, a perception at variance with the status previously accorded to African national liberation movements such as the South West Africa People's Organization ("SWAPO"). The Global North has displayed little motivation to engage the Sahrawi entity, deferring to the UN on the issue of self-determination, while at the same time refusing to recognize Moroccan sovereignty over the occupied part of Western Sahara.[28] Even the European Union, with its long-running fishing arrangements with Morocco on the Atlantic coast of Western Sahara, remained uninterested in considering Sahrawi views until the European Parliament voted in 2011 to reject extension of the 2007 EU-Morocco *Fisheries Partnership Agreement*.[29] In contrast, in the Global South there is wide recognition of the Sahrawi Republic, notably among African and Latin American states, including the SADR's membership in the African Union.[30] South Africa's statement on the opening of diplomatic relations with the Sahrawi Republic in 2004 is typical of the sentiment underlying recognition:

> For us not to recognise SADR in this situation is to become an accessory to the denial of the people of Western Sahara of their right to self-determination. This would constitute a grave and unacceptable betrayal of

> our own struggle … and our commitment to respect the Charter of the United Nations and the constitutive act of the African Union.[31]

Other developments legitimized the project of a Sahrawi state-in-exile. Among them were Algeria's formal recognition of the SADR on the 6th of March 1976, its acceptance of complete Sahrawi autonomy in the Tindouf camps, and material support, including allowing Sahrawi SPLA forces free passage to and from Western Sahara.[32] In the early years, the Sahrawi established a civil government, drafted (and periodically electorally amended) a constitution, created ministries to deliver services, developed legislative and treaty-making capacities, and fostered a democratic polity.[33] In part because of Algeria's cession of autonomy to the Sahrawi government at Tindouf–more accurately at Rabouni–and the SADR's control over the inland part of Western Sahara, a nominal statehood was realized early on.[34] While most of the elements of such statehood are evident, and uniquely established in the case of Western Sahara, there is a significant difference among other states in their approach to recognition of the Sahrawi Republic. Acceptance and bilateral relationships among African states has been widespread and lasting. The Latin American states have been largely consistent in their recognition. But the rest of the international community of states has not recognized the SADR.

The formal elements for Sahrawi statehood are evident, including a defined territory, an identifiable population, a competent government exercising a general jurisdictional capacity, and the conduct of international relations. The Sahrawi Republic functions at least as well as many others in Africa. Territory is the easiest element of the state to define, in part because of demonstrably certain, demarcated land frontiers accepted as Sahrawi by two of three neighboring states (Algeria and Mauritania), coupled with a universal rejection among the organized international community of Morocco's claim to Western Sahara. Moreover, a portion of Western Sahara continues to be governed by the SADR, with international acceptance through the UN's 1990 and 1991 ceasefire arrangements (of course, the international community has demurred in the partitioning of Western Sahara, there being almost no concern over Morocco's berm). The matter of a discrete or identifiable population in Western Sahara is also unique. The Sahrawi people were readily identified in Spain's 1974 referendum census, and were somewhat unusually in the post-colonial era in Africa, a singular ethnic-linguistic group. As refugees, the Sahrawi population remains homogeneous. They are divided because of the occupation of their territory, but have not been absorbed into the populations of host states or scattered to a diaspora. The other two formal requirements of statehood have also been maintained over the decades: a competent and functioning government in the refugee camps and in the "liberated zone" east of the berm, and diplomatic relations and international engagement with other states.[35] It is unfortunate that an organized international community reluctant to extend recognition to the Sahrawi Republic has overlooked the popular legitimacy of the state among its citizens, and the state's established democratic operation.

The unique features of the Sahrawi nation have become both strengths and weaknesses in its claim to self-determination. As a national liberation movement, the Polisario Front pursues a democratically legitimated mandate of self-determination (and, for 15 years until 1991, an armed campaign to that end) within the historic paradigm of African colonial liberation. As a state, the SADR acts to defend and provide necessities to its people while conducting relationships with other states, most notably Algeria, which claims an interest in the Sahrawi people. It also exercises sovereignty over the liberated zone east of the berm. Sahrawi statehood can hardly be considered embryonic, nor is it in stasis awaiting more formal definition upon independence. Emergence into full (or "fully restored") independence now appears more possible than a stalled, externally controlled self-determination process in the classic manner of national liberation movements during the 1960s and 1970s.[36]

Three particular aspects of the governance of the Sahrawi people underscore the important attributes of statehood. The first is that the 'state' institutions are democratically accountable to the Sahrawi population in the camps.[37] Governing organizations include an assembly that meets in congress for general legislative work and to confirm government appointments, a number of ministries similar to those in African and European governments, and quasi-non-governmental (or civil society) organizations such as the Sahrawi Red Crescent and the General Union of Sahrawi Workers, UGTSARIO.[38]

The second aspect of the Sahrawi state is its representation of all Sahrawi including those inside the occupied part of the territory. That representation has become an important part of the role of the government; a national identity construct fostered by the Polisario Front as the original liberation movement of the Sahrawi people. Even symbolically, none of the functions of the Sahrawi Republic have been ceded to the UN (for example through the ostensible self-determination related work of the United Nations Mission for the Referendum in Western Sahara, "MINURSO") or Algeria—other than immigration control over third country nationals who travel to the camps. The SADR government continues to provide services and to ensure the security of the Sahrawi in the camps in as ordinary a way as possible under the circumstances. In addition to providing basic services (education, healthcare, food distribution), the SADR government regulates what modest economy does exist and conducts external and defense affairs with surprising depth and sophistication given the limited monetary resources. The policy orientation of the Sahrawi government is to represent all Sahrawi, including those living west of the berm in the Moroccan held part of the territory, and to prepare for the restoration of independence, that is, the aftermath of self-determination.[39]

A third feature of the Sahrawi state is its capacity to engage in international relations. The 1979 peace treaty with Mauritania, together with AU membership and accession to regional treaties such as the *African Charter on Human and Peoples' Rights*, demonstrates this.[40] The SADR conducts wide-ranging diplomacy with African states and maintains unaccredited delegates to the UN at New York and Geneva, as well as the EU at Brussels. Even in states that have not granted recognition, such as Australia, Spain and The Netherlands, the SADR has representation, although with varying degrees of engagement. While there is considerable Sahrawi diplomatic representation in the international arena--demonstrably greater than Namibia and East Timor –in the absence of trade and consular affairs, the engagement is focused on political affairs.

Regardless of the strength of the Sahrawi state on the international stage, its domestic acceptance amongst the Sahrawi people is scarcely at issue. In the collective Sahrawi aspiration for self-determination, the state has considerable support as the formal, administrative and rule-making organization of the national liberation project.[41] SADR Constitutional norms reflect this, with a constitution popularly determined and revised by the electoral process over the years. The electoral process reflects broad support for the creation of the state and its governing institutions in a manner that anticipates independence as the only outcome of self-determination. It is important to note the close connection among the three main aspects of the "political communitarian project:" the Polisario Front, the standard bearer of political and existential aspiration; the collective and highly autonomous self-governing Sahrawi state in exile; and the state itself. The last is, of course, the tangible realization of determinacy, necessary to secure the place of the Sahrawi people in the international community.[42]

One notable phenomenon of the Sahrawi state in the era after the international administration of Timor-Leste and Kosovo is the absence of any UN or other tutelary-preparatory development of the state for (full) independence. Such mandates are now prescribed by the Security Council and no longer, as for Namibia, by the UNGA. The prospect of initial measures to provide for a transition to statehood or including capacity-building in exile is apparently too risky for the Security Council to contemplate in the post-1991 status quo, concerned as it is with the appearance of evenhandedness.[43] It is still possible for the African Union to play a useful role, but that has not been recently pursued. In any case, the institutions of the Sahrawi state are sufficiently developed that little societal consideration has been given to what will be required to transform the role of the state to one of "complete" governance.

III. States in the region: Their roles and influence

The Sahrawi Republic's relationship and legal position with Algeria is unique in the history of national liberation movements and refugee situations. The relationship respects the dual aspect of the Sahrawi people in exile in the context of their project for a permanent state while temporarily under forced displacement. The Sahrawi people and government have realized tangible advantages in the dual status accorded to them in the Tindouf camps. The most obvious is an exclusive internal governance or autonomy in the more or less informal cession of territory to them. Algerian support to the Sahrawi as refugees has been constant, including the provision of fuel, food and money, as well as water and electricity to the camps, and the use of Tindouf as an air and road transport hub.[44] Algeria also provides tertiary medical care and education in its metropolis, as well as travel documents (including passports) for Sahrawi who are unable or choose not to obtain a Spanish passport.[45] In the context of treaty and customary legal obligations, Algeria continues to accommodate the Sahrawi as refugees, notably through *non-refoulement* and freedom of movement, within the setting of their chosen residence in isolated refugee camps.[46]

It is this approach, one balanced between tangible political and material support for the Sahrawi national liberation project and the protection of the refugees as a collective, which has assured the unique viability and continuity of the camps. Algeria's position has been quietly criticized by the Arab League and more volubly by Morocco.[47] The formalist view, expressed in a 2008 report by Human Rights Watch, is that "notwithstanding Algeria's delegation of authority to the Polisario, the Algerian government remains ultimately responsible … for the human rights of all persons in its territory, including in the refugee camps around Tindouf."[48] There is presently no suggestion that Algeria will end its support for, or its *de facto* cession of territory, the SADR government. While that support has been understood by the several UN envoys responsible for talks between the Polisario Front and Morocco after 2004, it has not been challenged. This is a result of the resolve of the Sahrawi people to remain in the camps until self-determination as well as the inability to conceive how they might return to Western Sahara in the meantime.

In contrast, the African Union as an organization remains passive, even ambivalent, on the question of Western Sahara and involvement with the Sahrawi as refugees. While the AU maintains diplomatic ties with both Morocco and the SADR, it does not have influence over the occupation of Western Sahara or Sahrawi self-determination.[49] That is unfortunate, particularly in light of the early 1980s work of the Organization of African Unity to bring the two parties together. The Organization's efforts culminated in a 1983 resolution urging the parties to negotiate.[50] That, in turn, led to the UN Secretary-General's engagement of the question of Western Sahara, resulting in the 1988 peace proposal which secured the parties' agreement to ceasefire and referendum arrangements in 1990 and 1991.[51] The AU has since relinquished its role in the conflict, with UN envoys in the past decade consulting only the states directly concerned–Algeria, Mauritania, Morocco and the Polisario Front. While there may be opportunity for the AU to renew its advocacy for Sahrawi self-determination or to use its good offices in assisting the parties with negotiations, it now defers to the UN. Since the Tindouf camps are self-contained and there are few Sahrawi making refugee claims in African states or migrating without SADR, Spanish, Algerian or Mauritanian passports, the AU has not been overly concerned with the phenomenon of Sahrawi refugees. Without a "refugee problem," there is no particular impetus for the AU to become active under the circumstances.

Since it quit Western Sahara in February 1976, Spain's position has been one of official indifference to the circumstances of the Sahrawi refugees at Tindouf and to Morocco's occupation. While Spain may formally accept the Sahrawi people's right of self-determination, it does so with little effective diplomacy, continuing the official denial of responsibility for decolonization. Arguably, the 1975 *Madrid Accords* committed Spain to staying involved with the decolonization of the Sahrawi people, in partnership with Mauritania and Morocco. However, even from the outset, the *Accords* could not be implemented as a practical matter, whether or not Spain had grounds in international law to relinquish the administration of a non-self-governing people to other states. Under Law 45/1975, the *Cortes* abrogated Spain's responsibility to administer Western Sahara until the territory achieved self-determination. However, the statute authorized the Spanish government "to perform the acts and take such measures as may be necessary to carry out the decolonization of the Saharan dependent territory," suggesting a continuing domestic obligation.[52]

Several factors account for Spain's position in the early years of the occupation. These include fishing interests on the Saharan coast; Moroccan and Spanish commercial investments; the presence of each country's citizens in the other; Spain's efforts toward democracy; improving its international standing; and the long-running conflict with Morocco over the Ceuta and Melilla *presidios*.[53] Spain's hands-off approach contrasts starkly with that of Portugal towards East Timor. Portugal had maintained an active role in the UN vis-à-vis East Timor, as the colonial state with continuing responsibility for the territory–including through its agreement with Indonesia in May 1999 for a referendum in the territory.[54] In October 1980 Spain confirmed for the first time after the *Madrid Accords* its acceptance of the Sahrawi right of self-determination, a position it formally maintains today.[55] In the UN, Spain continues to assert that the principle of territorial integrity applies to its ongoing claim over Gibraltar, but not Western Sahara.[56]

Successive governments in Madrid have tolerated the Polisario Front's informal presence in mainland Spain, including low-level diplomatic connections and a liberal policy for the issuance of Spanish passports to Sahrawi. Spanish civil society is more outspoken in its support of the Sahrawi people themselves. The Spanish are the largest source of donor contributions and delegations to the camps, and host thousands of Sahrawi children every summer in family visits.[57] However, their ardent support has not translated into a change of Madrid's foreign policy. Spain maintains a neutral position of deference to the UN for resolution of the "question" of Western Sahara.[58]

IV. The Sahrawi under occupation

Another major aspect of the "question" of Western Sahara apart from the territory's partition is the separation of its people from each other. Almost half the population of the Sahrawi state-in-exile is inside the Moroccan-held part of Western Sahara. The Sahrawi statehood project is also driven by the cultural, political and international humanitarian circumstances of the population under occupation. The conditions of the Sahrawi under occupation are not lost on the Sahrawi in the Tindouf camps–though the effect of this solidarity is little understood. There is evidence that the occupation of part of the Sahrawi population tends to reinforce a homogeneous exilic identity. Personal accounts testify to the tangible human connection across the divided territory, and to the fact that human rights abuses occurring in the occupation reinforce a common Sahrawi moral and political aspiration for independence.[59] The Sahrawi are a people grounded in personal relationships: strong community relationships and a deep relationship to the land. Although these relationships have been re-ordered by colonization, urbanization, the upheaval of invasion and migration, and by the social dimensions of life in exile, they remain strong. The fact of the Sahrawi remaining in the territory after 1975 has reinforced the sense of communal identity and dislocation of those living in Tindouf.

In the aftermath of invasion, the Sahrawi who remained in the territory progressively urbanized. Under the constraints of heavy security, the civilian population has been increasingly denied the ability to live outside towns. The occupation has eliminated semi-nomadic life, compelling what remained of the Sahrawi population to enter into an urban, formal economy.[60] In recent years, the remaining Sahrawi have been more successful at publicizing the human and civil rights abuses they face under occupation. The protest camp at Gdeim Izek outside El-Aaiun, which was established in October 2010, showed the willingness of the Sahrawi in the occupied territory to challenge their circumstances. Over the following month the camp grew to some 15,000 protesters, concerned as much with social and financial disparities (including a lack of opportunity in the formal work economy) as with the absence of progress toward self-determination. On the 8th of November 2010, the same day negotiations between the Polisario Front and Morocco had been scheduled to resume in the United States, the occupying authorities forcibly dismantled Gdeim Izek.

The ongoing movement of Moroccan nationals as settlers into Sahrawi territory, subsidized financially and with state-provided housing, has resulted in the remaining Sahrawi population being outnumbered two to one. These figures do not include the 60,000 Moroccan FAR soldiers stationed on the berm, or the police and military presence of 20,000 more in the territory's cities.[61] The evidence of the Sahrawi people's conditions under occupation is mainly provided from those individuals who travel outside the occupied territory and increasingly from social media accounts of those who remain. It should be recalled that Sahrawi have limited opportunities to leave the territory. Passports are controlled by Morocco, which also maintains a heavy occupation presence within a fortified frontier. Moreover, the cost and immigration requirements of moving to third countries–other than Mauritania where some have family and kinship ties–are prohibited. While some Sahrawi work and study in Morocco, their numbers are not large.[62] Support for the Polisario Front remains high among the remaining Sahrawi, as well as the desire to fulfill the national self-determination project. These sentiments are matched by growing disdain for the UN over its inability to deliver on the promises of the 1990-91 referendum agreement.[63]

The occupation has facilitated the taking of natural resources from Western Sahara and forced the Sahrawi into second tier economic status. In recent years, particularly in Europe, the attention over resources has been on the fishery. In the Atlantic Ocean around Dakhla, the Canary Current Large Marine Ecosystem is Africa's richest fishery. From 1975 until 2011, Spanish and then other European vessels had worked the fishery under treaties with Morocco. In December 2011 the EU Parliament voted to reject extension of the most recent agreement, for which the European Commission had paid an annual rent of €36.1 million to Morocco. The Parliament's vote was based on three grounds which ensured wide acceptance for an unprecedented rejection of an EU Commission-negotiated treaty. The grounds included the apparent infringement of the Sahrawi people's right to their natural resources; the cost (and economic inefficiency) of the agreement; and the apparent lack of sustainability or inability to enforce regulations on fish stocks.[64]

A few months later Morocco took over the fishery with a few nationally flagged vessels and others chartered overseas, ending for a few years Europe's most substantial point of engagement with Western Sahara. In 2013, the two concluded negotiations for a new arrangement that would allow for resumption of EU fishing in 2014. The territory's other principal resource is phosphate rock. Phosphate is exported by the Moroccan state-owned *Office Chérifien des Phosphates* SA to fertilizer manufacturers such as Incitec Pivot in Australia and Potash Corporation in Canada. The value of the phosphate export trade–about $450 million in 2012, $330 million in 2013–is greater than the fishery, but not as well known internationally. The ongoing development of natural resources in the territory, at best a middling factor in Morocco's decision to invade, indirectly delays self-determination. It should be recalled that the cost to Morocco of continuing the occupation of Western Sahara is high compared to its national revenue, and is more than three times the value of resource revenues even in recent years of high market prices for fish and phosphate.[65] However, the extraction of natural resources does serve as a pretext for Morocco's economic development of the territory, including settlement of its nationals. The result is an increasingly informed and outspoken Sahrawi population, whose resentment and willingness to protest inside the occupied territory tends to reinforce the moral-political acceptability of the Sahrawi national project on both sides of the berm.

V. Indeterminacy: The UN and the organized international community

Refugees, as defined for purposes of identity and engagement of legal obligations by states, almost invariably become so due to circumstances of conflict or loss of social order, which themselves present problems for the organized international community, including the UN.[66] Syria's as yet non-international conflict, which began early in the 2011 Arab Spring, illustrates this, as does the long running conflict in eastern Congo. The case of Sahrawi refugees has the additional complicating elements of decolonization and denial of self-determination. Decolonization is the international community's structural approach to the "question" of Western Sahara, one which obscures the ongoing occupation and conflict that continues to cause dislocation of the population. In the current construct, the international community has concentrated on decolonization as an *a priori* requirement to resolve the Sahrawi refugee condition. What has arguably prevented the return of Sahrawi refugees at Tindouf (or integration into Algeria as a host state, or scattering into the diaspora) is the dual insistence upon, and failure of the UN to implement, meaningful self-determination. This is reinforced by the deference most states afford to the UN's singular role in the task. It is a responsibility in which the UN has dismally failed.

The UN's involvement with Western Sahara can be traced to the UNGA's self-determination and decolonization resolutions 1514 and 1541.[67] The two resolutions conferred on the organization the task of realizing what is described in the UN Charter as the "sacred trust" of promoting the well-being of the peoples of non-self-governing territories, including their self-determination. The particular right of self-determination in the colonial context (in contrast to the norms of self-determination for peoples seeking greater autonomy of secession in existing states, for example in South Sudan) was affirmed by the International Court of Justice in its 2010 Kosovo Advisory Opinion:

> During the second half of the twentieth century, the international law of self-determination developed in such a way as to create a right to independence for the peoples of non-self-governing territories and peoples subject to alien subjugation, domination and exploitation. A great many new States have come into existence as a result of the exercise of this right.[68]

The UN's engagement with Western Sahara is three-fold. The UN Charter is the politically accepted mandate to ensure decolonization of the territory. This manifests itself in several ways in the various UN bodies, particularly in a Security Council responsible for the maintenance of MINURSO and a UNGA charged with assessing progress toward self-determination. The UN has also involved the Secretary-General and successive Personal Envoys, which have been concerned with leading the negotiations between the parties.[69] Second, the UN supports refugees by the United Nations High Commissioner for Refugees' ("UNHCR") work in the Tindouf camps. In contrast with other refugee situations this presence is small, and not one immediately concerned with repatriation, integration into the host state, or much of the Sahrawi people's human security conditions. Until recently, the UN administered a limited "confidence building" program of family exchange visits on both sides of the berm.[70] The third aspect of the UN's engagement with Western Sahara remains unrealized. This is the enforcement of the law to end occupation, action from which the Security Council has resolutely abstained.

As for the UNGA, the conclusion of the International Court of Justice in the Western Sahara *Advisory Opinion* instructed: "The right of self-determination leaves the UNGA a measure of discretion with respect to the forms and procedures by which that right is to be realized."[71] However, with the exception of its admission of Palestine as a non-member observer state in November 2012, the UNGA has appeared unwilling to take an active role in furthering self-determination demands, revealing the changed dynamics of the UN system that apply to the few remaining decolonization cases. The underlying political-legal normative approach to Western Sahara or, more accurately, the status of the Sahrawi people as a holdover case of decolonization, is the single greatest factor in the occupation/refugee dynamic since 1975.

Whatever the general prescriptions of the UN Charter and the *jus cogens* norms which emerged from the UN's decolonization resolutions and state practice, the example of East Timor demonstrates the inability to impose compliance on a displaced (or departed) colonial state and an occupying successor state. Notwithstanding the involvement of UN Secretaries-General, the Security Council and the UNGA, together with the efforts of several UN envoys, the organization has been unable to act outside of a decolonization paradigm.[72] The Sahrawi people undoubtedly have the most fundamental of rights in the modern era, that is, the right to elect their political-legal status in the organized international community. However, the Sahrawi people are without the means to achieve the right for themselves in a formal legal context.[73]

History suggests that the UN will not itself arrive at any institutional change in the paradigmatic treatment of Western Sahara as a case of decolonization. Self-determination can be achieved in various ways, of course, and the majority of cases in Africa in the latter half of the twentieth century achieved autonomy through indigenous effort, with the acquiescence and occasional support of the parent colonial power and only limited UN involvement. Moreover, the Sahrawi people have already credibly determined their political-legal status in the creation and maintenance of the SADR and inside occupied Western Sahara by a persistent refusal to be a subordinate population. The UN's role in achieving legitimate Sahrawi self-determination may no longer be needed if superseded by events and the passage of time. It may be impractical to realize the promise of self-determination made by the UN in the face of continuing occupation. It is perhaps also unethical for the UN to hold out to the Sahrawi people a role to guarantee self-determination given the inability of the organization to realize the right.[74] However, what would replace a UN organized self-determination exercise remains uncertain.

VI. The long wait for a Sahrawi tomorrow

The span of time Sahrawi refugees have remained in exile is the result of many factors. A critical assessment yields empirical lessons for other long-running refugee situations and cases to come. Such factors also underscore structural weaknesses in the formal international order when attempting to resolve the causes of forced displacement of peoples over time in exile. This includes the limits of international law and the enforceability of the UN Charter in cases of territorial annexation. Western Sahara occupies the infamous place of being the last significant case of UN decolonization in Africa and the continent's longest running dispute.

There have been many delays in resolving the Sahrawi refugee situation. They stem from the unrealized decolonization program for the territory and its people. That phenomenon, discussed above, is the unfortunate confluence of a singular UN paradigm to resolve the status of the Sahrawi people, reinforced by the well-established deferral or acquiescence by the community of states to the UN in such a role. A second important factor is that the problem (or circumstances) of the Sahrawi at Tindouf is not acute in the comparative sense. Indeed, apart from the UNHCR and a Security Council annually renewing MINURSO's mandate, the conditions in the camps and the prospects for the health and security of the Sahrawi refugees receive little comment in the organized international community. A remarkable, self-perpetuating social order has been sustained in the camps that has diminished any sense of urgency.

A related consideration is the geographic remoteness of the camps. Sahrawi society is self-sustaining and does not present an immediate problem in the refugee sense because of the geography involved, which is uniquely beyond the view of states and an international public collective (the same dynamic has arguably been at work in eastern Congo, and was evident in the case of East Timor until 1991). The Sahrawi as refugees have also not been perceived as a regional security problem because of the remoteness of their territory and Sahrawi migration into third states in pronounced numbers has thus far been avoided. Even the secessionary split in nearby Mali in 2012 did not prompt the African Union to comment on negotiations between the Polisario Front and Morocco. The international and regional impetus to resolve the refugee situation has been absent for years in Western Sahara. Algeria's inability as host state to the Sahrawi refugees to influence the status quo is also part of this equation.

The case of the Sahrawi as refugees remains subordinate to the normative treatment of the "question" of Western Sahara, namely the prospect of self-determination. That approach by the organized international community, including by those states which formally recognize and conduct relations with the SADR, and the UN (particularly the Security Council) has been one with a goal of "just, lasting and mutually acceptable" resolution of the question of self-determination. This approach falls short of *implementing* self-determination, and undermines the immediacy of the refugee problem.

A substantial factor in the Sahrawi continuing their refugee existence is the decision to await an acceptable exercise of self-determination. This is not to suggest that the people of the Tindouf camps should elcct to return to the occupied part of Western Sahara, whatever the assurance for safe conduct and security on return. Rather, it is the strongly reinforced self-perception that the Sahrawi are not refugees, but rather are in exile, maintaining their society-state for the accepted eventuality of returning. This is born of a confidence in the rightness of that aspiration and the unyielding rejection of Morocco's claim. Much of the exilic discourse in Sahrawi society is concerned with the nation-project. As the Sahrawi artist-poet Mohamed Suleiman Labat laments:

My Homeland!
Lives inside of me though I do not live in it
It settled in my heart though I was born far away from it. [75]

Two aspects of the conflict in Western Sahara have little direct relevance to the Sahrawi as refugees: the settlement of Moroccan nationals in the occupied part of the territory and the taking of natural resources.

This stands in obvious contrast to other refugee cases, in terms of contributing to their origins and longevity. The Sahrawi were not first displaced by such activities nor do they continue to be. The factor of a Sahrawi population that remains divided is more difficult to assess. There remains a consensus for self-determination across both parts of the population. To the extent such a consensus holds across a divided, if single-minded community, it has been mutually reinforcing.

Refugee cases turn on questions of characterization and classification, including the identity and status of individual migrants. The resolution of refugee cases has historically succeeded when the return of refugees to their place of origin has been secured. For a return to be acceptable there must be a semblance of social order and a governing capacity by the state concerned. When it comes to Western Sahara such underlying conditions remain absent. What has made the case of Sahrawi refugees prolonged has been the parallel dynamics of a manifestly illegal occupation, one imposed by armed force and suppression of the rights of the remaining original population, coupled with the Sahrawi insistence on realizing the right of self-determination and a continuing rejection of any accommodation of the occupation. For the underlying circumstances to change and there to be a resolution for the Sahrawi who live in refugee exile, these dynamics must be addressed.

Notes

* Jeffrey Smith is a Canadian lawyer who has served as counsel to the Frente POLISARIO for the past four years. He was previously counsel to the United Nations and the government of East Timor (Timor-Leste) in that country for its maritime jurisdiction and oilfield development.

[1] QUR'AN 8:26 [Translation by the author].

[2] Judge Hardy C. Dillard, Western Sahara, Advisory Opinion, 1975 I.C.J. Reports 12, at 122 (separate opinion).

[3] The legacy of European colonization continues until today. Examples of European colonization in the formal sense include Tahiti, while the settlement and creation of the State of Israel after the Second World War is often described as a colonial project. Western Sahara may represent an extreme example of the legacy of colonialism in Africa, but the dissolution of state entities such as Eritrea-Ethiopia and Sudan-South Sudan also reflects the remnants of colonialism in the region.

[4] "Sahrawi" is used here as the name of the original people of the territory of Western Sahara, until 1975 the colony of Spanish Sahara. "Saharan" is applied in a geographic context while "Sahrawi" is used in the formal name of the Sahrawi Arab Democratic Republic. "Polisario Front" is the English language acronym of

the Sahrawi national liberation movement, the Popular Front for the Liberation of Saguiet el-Hamra and Río de Oro: وادي و الحمراء ساقية لتحرير الشعبية الجبهة الذهب

The Sahrawi population numbers about 350,000; some 160,000 in the Tindouf camps (including several thousand in the "liberated zone" in the east of the territory) and 120,000 in occupied Western Sahara, the remainder a diaspora found primarily in Mauritania and Spain. The most recent census of Sahrawi, known as the provisional voter list, was completed by the UN in late 1999, finding a total of 86,386 Sahrawi adults in the territory proper, the Tindouf camps and in other places eligible to vote in a self-determination referendum. *See* U.N. Secretary-General, *Report of the Secretary-General on the Situation Concerning Western Sahara*, U.N. Doc. S/2000/131 (Feb. 17, 2000).

[5] The *khaima* represents the ground or centre of Sahrawi society, home and meeting place, public and intimate all at once. For an insightful portrayal of residential housing in the Saharawi refugee camps, and the historical development of the camps themselves, *see* FRANZISKA BINER, LIVING (2011).

[6] The berm and its implications for the occupation of Western Sahara have been little considered by the UN or in academic literature. There is no doubt that the berm has secured Morocco's occupation. It also contributes to the resolve of the Sahrawi people in the Tindouf refugee camps to await the restoration of the entire territory. The berm's environmental impact is just becoming understood, including its disruption of surface water distribution and that it is a barrier to wildlife and grazing stocks.

[7] TONY HODGES, HISTORICAL DICTIONARY OF WESTERN SAHARA xxix (1982); *see also* U.N., *Milestones in the Western Sahara Conflict* (undated), *available at* http://minurso.unmissions.org/LinkClick.aspx?fileticket=b67SKR4JLik%3D&.

[8] Spain informed the U.N. on August 20, 1974 that it would conduct the referendum in the first half of 1975. This followed Portugal's earlier announcement of the rapid withdrawal from its colonies and Francisco Franco's promise in September 1973 to the Sahrawi *Djemaa* that "the population of [the Sahara] will freely determine its future." Letter of Spanish President Francisco Franco to the Djemaa (Sept. 21, 1973), *in* TONY HODGES, WESTERN SAHARA: THE ROOTS OF A DESERT WAR 167 (1984) [hereafter THE ROOTS OF A DESERT WAR].

[9] *Milestones in the Western Sahara Conflict*, *supra* note 7. The application of the results of the 1974 census would be a central issue in the efforts to conduct a self-determination referendum. It should be noted that some authors mistakenly refer to the figure of 73,497 persons as being the total adult voters.

[10] Western Sahara, Advisory opinion, *supra* note 2, at 31 ¶ 81.

[11] *Id.* at 68 ¶ 162.

[12] *Id.* ¶ 162. *See* G.A. Res. 1514 (XV), *Declaration of the Granting of Independence to Colonial Countries and Peoples*, U.N. Doc. A/L.323 (Dec. 14, 1960); *see also* G.A. Res. 1541 (XV), *Principles Which Should Guide Members in Determining Whether or not an Obligation Exists to Transmit the Information called for under Article 73e of the Charter*, U.N. Doc. A/4651 (Dec. 14, 1960). Principle VI of Resolution 1541 provides that "[a] Non-Self-Governing Territory

can be said to have reached a full measure of self-government by: (a) Emergence as a sovereign independent State; (b) Free association with an independent State; or (c) Integration with an independent State." And consider paragraph 6 of UNGA Resolution 742 (Nov. 27, 1953): "[T]he manner in which Territories . . . can become fully self-governing is primarily through the attainment of independence . . . ." G.A. Res. 742 (VIII), *Factors which should be Taken Into Account in Deciding whether a Territory is or is not a Territory Whose People not yet Attained a Full Measure of Self-Government*, U.N. Doc. A/2556 (Nov. 27, 1953).

[13] Western Sahara was not the only former European colonial state to face the paralysis of the international community in transforming a decolonized people into an independent state. East Timor was invaded a month after the Western Sahara invasion, on 7 December 1975. Both declared independence in part to secure recognition by other states when invasion and annexation were imminent. The cases of Namibia and Palestine are similar, although it should be recalled that the United Nations General Assembly, charged with administering decolonization, uniquely created the UN Council for Namibia to ostensibly govern the territory until independence from South Africa in 1990. For a comparative study of Western Sahara and Palestine see Rana B. Khoury, *Western Sahara and Palestine: A Comparative Study of Colonialisms, Occupations, and Nationalisms*, NEW MIDDLE EASTERN STUD. 1 (2011), *available at* http://www.brismes.ac.uk/nmes/archives/321.

[14] The *Madrid Accords* provided for shared sovereignty over Western Sahara (as the territory was then becoming known). All three states were ostensibly responsible to administer the territory and to ensure the Sahrawi people had the opportunity of a self-determination referendum. The *Accords*, known formally as the "Declaration of Principles on Western Sahara, Mauritania-Spain-Morocco" (Nov. 14, 1975) are found at 14 I.L.M. 1512. The *Accords* were contrary to international law, as Spain did not have the competency to transfer colonial administration to other states. They were accompanied by three annexes (protocols), not publicly disclosed until 2009, which provided for Spain's continuing involvement in the territory's natural resources, including the fishery (for the first five years to be without payment) and an ongoing 35% ownership of the Bu Craa phosphate mine and operation, relinquished by Spain in 2003. The annexes of the *Accord*s are available at http://www.gees.org/documentos/Documen-654.pdf. *See also* Cable from the US Embassy in Madrid, Possible US Investment in Spanish Sahara (Sept. 23, 1974), *available at* https://www.wikileaks.org/plusd/cables/1974MADRID05945_b.htmlalso ("Bu-Craa site will be up to 10 million ton annual [sic] production by end of 1975; a rate known reserves can maintain for 150 years. Production at this level will make Spain third or fourth largest producer in world just ahead or behind Morocco.").

[15] For a definitive contemporaneous history of the Green March and the events of late 1975, see THE ROOTS OF A DESERT WAR, *supra* note 8, at 197-239; *see also* JOHN MERCER, SPANISH SAHARA (1976). For a current history of the events of late 1975 see STEPHEN ZUNES & JACOB MUNDY, WESTERN SAHARA: WAR, NATIONALISM,

AND CONFLICT IRRESOLUTION 3 ff (2010).

[16] *See* THE ROOTS OF A DESERT WAR, *supra* note 8. *See also* PABLO SAN MARTIN, WESTERN SAHARA: THE REFUGEE NATION 108 ff (2010).

[17] *See Text of the Historic Document of El Guelta* (*The Guelta Zemmur Proclamation*), U.N. Doc. S/11902 (Dec. 10, 1975).

[18] *See* THE ROOTS OF A DESERT WAR, *supra* note 8, at 109 ("The number of refugees increased very quickly, from 9,000 in late 1975 up to approximately 70,000 in July 1976 and more than 100,000 at the end of that year, according to some estimates. Other estimates, more consistent with the population of the territory according to the [1974] census, put the figure at around 40,000.") [endnote omitted]. Dakhla camp is remote from the others, established at an oasis with a supply of water. After a few years Smara camp was moved several kilometers to its present location.

[19] Tindouf was an inevitable location for the Sahrawi to gather. It had previously been a place of refuge for 25,000–30,000 Sahrawi from Saguiet el-Hamra in 1957-58 displaced by the Franco-Spanish *Operation Ecouvillon* against the remnants of the Moroccan Liberation Army, and from 1970 through 1972 to Tan Tan and Tindouf after anti-Spanish demonstrations. *See* VIRGINIA THOMPSON & RICHARD ADLOFF, THE WESTERN SAHARANS: BACKGROUND TO CONFLICT 175 ff, 254 ff (1980).

[20] The use of the Tindouf area was negotiated in advance, and the majority of Sahrawi arrived around May 1976. They did not receive coordinated aid from the international community until a year later. *See* THE ROOTS OF A DESERT WAR, *supra* note 8, at 233. Importantly, it is the Sahrawi Red Crescent that administers the delivery of aid in the Tindouf camps, interposed between the Sahrawi population and international relief organizations. Interview with Yahya Bouhabeini, President of the Sahrawi Red Crescent, in Algiers (Dec. 16, 2012). *See also* SAN MARTIN, *supra* note 16, at 195 n.11.

[21] The situation had become untenable for Spain, with the few remaining officials and soldiers unable to cope with the invasion of the territory. Spain informed the UN that it considered "itself henceforth exempt from any responsibility of an international nature in connection with the administration of the said Territory, in view of the cessation of its participation in the temporary administration established for the Territory. [T]he decolonization of the Western Sahara will be reached when the opinion of the Saharawi population [is] validly expressed". Letter from the Representative of Spain to the Secretary-General (Feb. 26, 1976), U.N. Doc. A/31/56-S/11997.

[22] *See* Proclamation de la République Arabe Sahraouie Démocratique (Feb. 27, 1976), *available at* www.arso.org/03-1f.htm.

[23] Convention Concerning the State Frontier Line Established Between the Islamic Republic of Mauritania and the Kingdom of Morocco, Mauritania-Morocco, Apr. 14, 1976, 1977 U.N.T.S. 117 (entered into force Nov. 10, 1976).

[24] Spanish fishing vessels were seized in part as a political impetus for Spain to clarify its position on Sahrawi self-determination. *See* THE ROOTS OF A DESERT WAR, *supra* note 8, at 239.

[25] Mauritano-Sahraoui Agreement, Aug. 10, 1979, U.N. Doc. A/34/427 (annex) (also known also as the Peace Treaty signed in Algiers on August 5, 1979 between the Polisario Front and the Islamic Republic of Mauritania).

[26] Interview with Khadija Hamdi, SADR Culture Minister, in Camp 27 February (Oct. 18, 2010). The SADR maintains accurate archival records of births and deaths from the period that reflect this trend in population growth.

[27] *See* ELENA FIDDIAN-QASMIYEH, PROTRACTED SAHARAWI DISPLACEMENT: CHALLENGES AND OPPORTUNITIES BEYOND ENCAMPMENT (2011); SAN MARTIN, *supra* note 16; RANDA FARAH, *Sovereignty on Borrowed Territory: Sahrawi Identity in Algeria*, 11 GEO. J. INT'L AFF. 59 (2010-11); WAR AND REFUGEES: THE WESTERN SAHARA CONFLICT (Richard Lawless & Laila Monahan eds., 1987); TOBY SHELLEY, ENDGAME IN THE WESTERN SAHARA: WHAT FUTURE FOR AFRICA'S LAST COLONY? (2004).

[28] The governments of Norway and the United States have noted that their free trade agreements with Morocco do not extend to Western Sahara. However, the European Union acknowledged its 2007 *Fisheries Partnership Agreement*—the extension of which was rejected by the EU Parliament in December 2011—had contemplated exploitation of the territory's natural resources. *See* Letter of the EU Parliament Jurisconsult to Mr. Josep Borrelle Fontelles, Chair of the Committee of Development of the EU Parliament (July 13, 2009), *available at* http://www.wsrw.org/a159x1346. "More than two years after the entry into force of the FPA (28 February 2007) a first assessment of the implementation of the FPA can now be done . . . ." *Id.* at 2.

[29] *See* Jeffrey J. Smith, *Fishing for Self-determination: European Fisheries and Western Sahara—The Case of Ocean Resources in Africa's Last Colony*, 27 OCEAN Y.B. 267 (2013).

[30] In 1984 the SADR was formally admitted to the Organization of African Unity, now the African Union, which resulted in Morocco quitting the organization. The OAS first extended the invitation to join in 1982, and it was taken up in the December 1984 OAS Summit Conference. *See* AFRICA, Apr. 1982 at 36. *See also* Anthony G. Pazzanita, *Legal Aspects of Membership in the Organization of African Unity: The Case of Western Sahara*, 17 CASE WES. RES. J. INT'L L. 123 (1985); O.A.S., *Resolution on Western Sahara*, O.A.S. Doc. AHG/Res. 104-120 (XIX) (June 6-12, 1983).

[31] Letter from South African President Thabo Mbeki to King Mohamed VI (Aug. 1, 2004), *available at* http://arso.org/MBK.htm.

[32] *See generally* THE ROOTS OF A DESERT WAR, *supra* note 8. Additionally, the archival materials on display in the Sahrawi National Museum of Resistance outside Camp Rabouni are instructive. Algeria's support to the Sahrawi refugees is considerable but delivered at arm's length and without reciprocal obligation. For example, tertiary medical care is made available in Algerian hospitals and university education is broadly accessible by Sahrawi refugees.

[33] The Polisario Front has been democratic since its founding in 1973. On the composition and functioning of the SADR government, see ZUNES & MUNDY, *supra* note 15, at 126 ff. There is widespread Sahrawi involvement in local

government within the camps, and participation in the political life of the nation. The SADR's standing government, the 52-member Sahrawi National Council, is elected by the popularly determined General Popular Congress which convenes every four years. The Congress also chooses the government executive—the National Secretariat—including the Secretary-General of the Polisario Front who by office is President of the SADR. Four of 18 ministers in the Sahrawi National Secretariat are women. The SADR arguably remains the most democratic state in North Africa. *See* CONSTITUTION DE LA RASD (Sept. 4, 1999) (adopted by the 10th National Congress) [SADR Constitution], *available at* www.arso.org/03-const.99.htm.

[34] The extension of recognition to an emergent state by other states is an important political dimension in the legal status and acceptance of the state by the organized international community. The cases of Kosovo (in a secessionary construct) and Palestine (in a self-determination context) illustrate how vital widespread state recognition is to the realization of statehood. Thus, Algeria's recognition of the Sahrawi Republic and its conduct of a bilateral relationship on a government-to-government basis are important factors for Sahrawi statehood. *See generally* JAMES CRAWFORD, THE CREATION OF STATES (2006).

[35] The SADR routinely concludes bilateral and, in Africa, multilateral treaties with other states. While it is not able to accede to international treaties, it issues declarations stating an intention to be bound by them. For example, in 1975 Sahrawi authorities delivered a letter to the Swiss Federal Council confirming compliance with the 1949 Geneva Conventions. *See* INT'L COMM. OF THE RED CROSS, 1975 ANNUAL REPORT 8 (1976).

[36] The law, originating in General Assembly Resolutions 1514 and 1541, *supra* note 12, prescribes three options for the Sahrawi people: independence, autonomy-association with the colonizing state, and integration (or annexation) into the colonial administering state. Of them, integration with the parent colonial state—Spain—is out of the question. The proper (if formal) application of the law suggests that integration with Morocco (accepting that the necessary consent of the Sahrawi people while under occupation could be given) could only result after the realization of independence. On the other hand, international law and UN policy also provide for non-self-governing peoples a move to direct independence, as the majority of decolonization cases in Africa (and elsewhere) have demonstrated, including much of sub-Saharan Africa (*e.g.* Botswana and the former Portuguese colonies) and Western Sahara's three neighbouring states.

[37] The camps illustrate the cohesiveness of Sahrawi society in exile, their names demonstrating the aspiration to return as much as the desire to maintain a normal society. The camps are, strictly speaking, *wilaya* in the political-governance sense, each with a governor appointed from members of the Sahrawi National Council by the SADR prime minister. *See also* BINER, *supra* note 5, at 54 ff.

[38] The Sahrawi General Popular Congress numbers about 2,000 persons who are popularly elected every four years to convene on significant matters and appoint the National Council. Interviews with Kamal Fadel and Mohamed Burhi, SADR

delegates to Australia and Canada, respectively, in Camp Bojador (Dec. 15-16, 2012). *See also* SAHARA PRESS SERVICE, www.spsrasd.info.

[39] The policy underpinnings that inform the work of the SADR government are rooted in the state's constitution and evident in programs intended to be permanent, before and after the restoration of full independence and return of the Sahrawi to Western Sahara, for example in health care programs and the system of primary and secondary education. *Id.*; *see also* SADR Constitution, *supra*.

[40] African (Banjul) Charter on Human and Peoples' Rights, June 27, 1981, O.A.U. Doc. CAB/LEG/67/3 rev. 5, 21 I.L.M. 58 (1982). (entered into force Oct. 21, 1986). The SADR acceded to the Charter on May 2, 1986.

[41] Popular support for government and the national liberation project is evident in several ways, including election participation rates in the camps, individual and civic organization work toward self-determination and Sahrawi political independence, and a consensus among those in the camps that return to Western Sahara will only be acceptable under a Sahrawi government. *See generally* SAN MARTIN *supra* note 16; *see also* Vivian Solana, *'A Woman is Stronger than Our State': Performing Sovereignty on the Margins of the State*, 11 EXPLORATIONS IN ANTHROPOLOGY 57 (2011).

[42] THE ROOTS OF A DESERT WAR, *supra* note 8, at 120. It remains to be assessed to what extent the Sahrawi aspiration to realize a nation-state has been reinforced in a younger generation that is itself acquiring a political voice in the camps and in the occupied part of Western Sahara.

[43] The maintenance of the status quo by the Security Council can be seen in its reluctance to consider the addition of a human rights monitoring mandate for MINURSO, notwithstanding that the securing of human rights is implicitly part of the UN's role to assure the proper conditions for the conduct of a self-determination referendum. *See* U.N. Secretary-General, *Report of the Secretary-General Concerning the Situation in Western Sahara*, ¶ 72, U.N. Doc. S/20112/197 (Apr. 5, 2012) ("Frente Polisario continued to appeal for the protection of the human rights of Western Saharans and for an independent monitoring mechanism in the Territory during the [2011-12] period.").

[44] Algeria also supplies electricity for a nominal charge to the capital at Rabouni and Camp Boujdour (Bojador) (formerly Camp 27 February). Solar power is used extensively in the other camps for domestic purposes, including televisions and refrigerators. Petrol and cooking gas is supplied by road from northern Algeria, the former sold at market prices including to the SADR for government use, the latter supplied free by the Algerian Red Crescent.

[45]The SADR issues national passports to diplomats and citizens travelling to recognizing states.

[46] Algeria is a state signatory to the 1951 United Nations Convention Relating to the Status of Refugees, July 28, 1951, 189 U.N.T.S. 150, and its 1967 Protocol, Protocol Relating to the Status of Refugees, Jan. 31, 1967, 606 U.N.T.S. 267, as well as the 1969 O.A.U. Convention Governing the Specific Aspects of Refugee Problems in Africa, Sept. 10, 1969, 1001 U.N.T.S. 45. The UN High Commissioner for Refugees has noted Algeria's treaty (and customary international law)

responsibility to the Sahrawi people, referring to it as the "host state". *See* UNHCR, *Submission by the United Nations High Commissioner for Refugees for the Office of the High Commissioner for Human Rights' Compilation Report—Universal Periodic Review: ALGERIA* (2011), *available at* http://lib.ohchr.org/HRBodies/UPR/Documents/session13/DZ/UNHCR_UPR_DZA_S13_2012_UNCHR_E.pdf.

[47] On the involvement of the Arab League in the question of Western Sahara, *see* Stephen Zunes, *Algeria, the Maghreb Union, and the Western Sahara Stalemate*, 17 ARAB STUD. Q. 23 (1995) ("King Hassan [had] major influence in the Arab League and the Islamic Conference."). The ethical and religious precepts of Algerian support to the Sahrawi people have not been explored critically in western scholarship. The accepted view is that Algeria's foreign policy informs its approach. *See generally* ARAFAT MADI SHOUKRI, REFUGEE STATUS IN ISLAM: CONCEPTS OF PROTECTION IN ISLAMIC TRADITION AND INTERNATIONAL LAW (2011).

[48] Human Rights Watch, *Human Rights in Western Sahara and in the Tindouf Refugee Camps: The Report of Human Rights Watch (Excerpts)* (Dec. 19, 2008) ("Algeria's [*sic*] has effectively abdicated responsibility for human rights violations committed by the Polisario on Algerian territory. This is impermissible: the international community must hold the government of Algeria, along with the Polisario, accountable for any Polisario violations committed in Algeria."); WESTERN SAHARA: WHICH LEGAL REMEDIES FOR PEOPLES UNDER FOREIGN DOMINATION? 20-28 (Vincent Chapaux ed., 2010).

[49] The AU maintains a delegation office in El-Aauin. The AU does not participate in the "Group of Friends of Western Sahara." For a review of the OAU's early involvement in Western Sahara see Gino J. Naldi, *The Organization of African Unity and the Saharan Arab Democratic Republic*, 26 J. AFR. L. 152 (1982).

[50] O.A.U. Res. 104, *supra* note 30. King Hassan II of Morocco had stated a commitment at the 1983 OAU Summit to hold a self-determination referendum for the people of Western Sahara. Article 2 of the 1984 resolution urged "the Kingdom of Morocco and the POLISARIO Front, to undertake direct negotiations with a view to bringing about a ceasefire to create the necessary condition for a peaceful and fair referendum for self-determination of the people of Western Sahara, a referendum without any administrative or military constraints, under the auspices of the OAU and the UN …" *Id.*

[51] *Id.*; *see also* Gino Naldi, *Western Sahara: Suspended Statehood or Frustrated Self-Determination?*, 13 AFR. Y.B. INT'L L. 11 (2005). Then Secretary-General Javier Perez de Cuellar proposed the ceasefire and referendum terms in two reports to the Security Council, U.N. Docs. S/21360 (June 18, 1990) and S/22464 (Apr. 19, 1991). The first contained the agreed text of the 1988 settlement proposals and the Secretary-General's proposed implementation plan, adopted by the Security Council through Resolution 658 on 27 June 1990. The 1991 report provided for an Identification Commission to register voters within 11 weeks, and for a reduction of the Moroccan army in the territory to 65,000 personnel. This was to be achieved within a 35-week period to conduct the referendum and administer its results.

[52] Sobre Descolonización del Sahara, Ley 40/1975 (Nov. 19, 1975), *available at* http://www.boe.es/buscar/doc.php?id=BOE-A-1975-23743 ("The Government is authorized to perform such acts and adopt measures as may be necessary for the decolonization of the non-autonomous territory of the Sahara, safeguarding Spanish interests.") [Translation by the author].

[53] On fisheries, *see* Smith, *supra* note 29. On Spain's position after 1975 *see* THE ROOTS OF A DESERT WAR, *supra* note 8, at 352.

[54] Agreement between the Republic of Indonesia and the Portuguese Republic on the Question of Timor, Indon-Port., May 5, 1999, *available at* http://easttimorlawjournal.org/UN/indonesiaportugalquestionofeasttimor.html. Spain participates in the Security Council's Group of Friends, with France, Russia, the United Kingdom and the United States. The government of Spain also provides development aid to the Sahrawi in the camps through its international development agency, contributing €10 million in 2011. Interviews with Kamal Fadel and Mohamed Burhi, *supra* note 38.

[55] *See* LE MONDE, (Dec. 19, 1980) and the proceedings of the UN General Assembly Special Political and Decolonization Committee *available at* http://www.un.org/en/ga/fourth/archives.shtml.

[56] *See e.g.* Press Release, UNGA, Fourth Committee, Concluding Consideration of Decolonization, Approves Nine Draft Resolutions, U.N. Press Release GA/SPD/509 (Oct. 15, 2012).

[57] The holidays are known as "Vacations in Peace" (*Vacaciones en Paz*). They are arranged widely across Europe, including Italy and Austria. *See* SAN MARTIN, *supra* note 16, at 158.

[58] Spain's formal, continuing obligation for the decolonization of the Sahara and to the Sahrawi as refugees is obvious, although there has been no suggestion it could be engaged as a matter of the Responsibility to Protect doctrine. *See* Carlos Ruiz Miguel, *Spain's Legal Obligations as Administering Power of Western Sahara*, 311 GRUPO DE ESTUDIOS ESTRATÉGICOS GEES 1 (Dec. 19, 2008), *available at* http://www.isn.ethz.ch/isn/Digital-Library/Publications/Detail /?id=96664&lng=en.

[59] Interview with Khadija Hamdi, *supra* note 26.

[60] Author's observations in visits to the Tindouf camps over the years and from various interviews, including Interview with Khadija Hamdi, *supra* note 26 and Interviews with Kamal Fadel and Mohamed Burhi, *supra* note 38. Little study has been done of the social, economic, and political circumstances of the Sahrawi under occupation. Morocco does not publish statistical information or development figures for the territory in general, and not at all for the Sahrawi, notwithstanding the requirement found in G.A. Res. 1541 (XV), *supra* note 12. Occasional third party reports about social and economic conditions in the occupied territory address human rights, for example that by the Robert F. Kennedy Centre for Justice & Human Rights, *Robert F. Kennedy International Delegation Visit to Morocco Occupied Western Sahara and the Refugee Camps in Algeria* (Sep. 3, 2012), *available at* http://rfkcenter.org/rfk-center-observes-grave-human-rights-violations-in-western-sahara-3.

[61] There is little discussion and no acknowledgment of international humanitarian law applying in the occupied part of Western Sahara, notwithstanding the rejection of the organized international community of Morocco's claim to the territory, and the UN General Assembly's declaration of an occupation as such. A widely accepted view is that Morocco has simply succeeded to Spain's colonial obligations and is therefore not an occupying power.

[62] About 5,000 Sahrawi work and are students in Morocco. Interview with Emhamed Khadad and Kamal Fadel, Polisario Front ministers and delegates, at Geneva (Nov. 8, 2011).

[63] *See for example*, Letter of 31 Sahrawi Civil Society Organizations to the EU Commissioner for Trade (June 26, 2012), *available at* http://www.wsrw.org/files/dated/2012-06-26/2012.06.26_saharawi_ngos_dcfta.pdf.

[64] *See* Smith, *supra* note 29. Russia has maintained fisheries treaties with Morocco over the past decade, renewing for an extended term a three-year agreement which had been originally scheduled to end in January 2013. *Id.* at 276.

[65] Author's estimate. The value of fisheries and phosphate resources exploited in the territory can be calculated with considerable accuracy. The economics of the occupation have not been critically assessed. Morocco's state finances are not transparent enough to determine accurate figures, and military spending is not sufficiently detailed in wider state budgets. The annual direct military cost to occupy Western Sahara is at least $1.5 billion not including capital costs to construct the berm and procure arms to garrison the territory. Direct and indirect subsidies to settlers and industry development in the territory would appear to add at least another $1 billion to such annual cost. *See* Jeffrey J. Smith, *The Taking of the Sahara: The Role of Natural Resources in the Continuing Occupation of Western Sahara, in* L'AUTRE CÔTÉ DU MUR 162 (Denis Vericel ed., 2014).

[66] The latter term refers to events or conditions that are sufficiently serious or pronounced as to trigger involuntary migration, analogous to the accepted modern categorization of refugees as persons with a "well-founded fear of persecution."

[67] G.A. Res. 1514 (XV) and G.A. Res. 1541 (XV), *supra* note 12.

[68] Accordance with International Law of the Unilateral Declaration of Independence in Respect of Kosovo, Advisory Opinion, 2010 I.C.J. 403 ¶ 79 (July 22, 2010). *See* Richard Falk, *The Kosovo Advisory Opinion: Conflict Resolution and Precedent*, 105 AM. J. INT'L L. 50 (2011).

[69] *See Milestones in the Western Sahara Conflict, supra* note 7. The former United States diplomat Christopher Ross is the most recently appointed UN personal envoy for Western Sahara. In November 2012, following consultations in the region, he announced the postponement of direct negotiations between the Polisario Front and Morocco, saying the parties were too opposed for useful discussion. *See Accepting Status Quo on Western Sahara 'Serious Miscalculation,' Warns UN Envoy*, UN NEWS CENTRE (Nov. 28, 2012), *available at* http://www.un.org/apps/news/story.asp?NewsID=43629&Cr=western+sahara&Cr1=#.UL9_xBxipYU.

[70] 41,000 Sahrawi have registered for family exchange visits. The UNHCR plays a leading role in soliciting international aid, totaling $37 million in non-food aid budgeted for 2013. Interview with Yahya Bouhabeini, President of the Saharawi Red Crescent, in Algiers (15 Dec. 2012). *See also Western Sahara Territory*, UNHCR, *available at* http://www.unhcr.org/pages/49e4861f6.html.
[71] Western Sahara, Advisory Opinion, *supra* note 2, at 122 ¶ 71; *See also* G.A. Res. A/Res/66/86, *Question of Western Sahara*, U.N. Doc. A/Res/66/434 (Dec. 9, 2011) (reaffirming "the responsibility of the United Nations towards the people of Western Sahara.").
[72] For a useful contemporary discussion of the UN's role and responsibility in the "question" of Western Sahara, *see* Hans Morten Haugen, *The UN and Western Sahara—Reviving the UN Charter*, 25 ANUARIO ESPANOL DE DERECHO INTERNACIONAL 355 (2009).
[73] Consider the reasoning of the ICJ in the Timor Gap Treaty case, East Timor (Port. v. Austl.), 1995 I.C.J. Reports 90 ¶ 31 (June 30, 1995):

> For the two Parties, the Territory of East Timor remains a non-self-governing territory, and its people has the right to self-determination. Moreover, the General Assembly, which reserves to itself the right to determine the territories which have to be regarded as non-self-governing for the purposes of the application of Chapter XI of the Charter, has treated East Timor as such a territory. The competent subsidiary organs of the General Assembly have continued to treat East Timor as such to this day. Furthermore, the Security Council … has expressly called for respect for 'the territorial integrity of East Timor as well as the inalienable right of its people to self-determination in accordance with General Assembly resolution 1514 (XV)'.

[74] *See* ZUNES & MUNDY, *supra* note 15, at 260 ("Yet with regard to Western Sahara, the Security Council has largely turned a blind eye to Morocco's blatant contravention of the UN Charter, especially the laws governing the use of force in international relations (*jus ad bellum*) and laws governing war itself (*jus in bello*), including international humanitarian law.").
[75] Mohamed Suleiman Labat, *Southern Exposure*, 454 NEW INTERNATIONALIST 50 (2012).

CHAPTER THREE

TIBETAN DIASPORA IN THE SHADOW OF THE SELF-IMMOLATION CRISIS: CONSEQUENCES OF COLONIALISM

ROBERT D. SLOANE*

Self-immolation is a reclamation of sovereignty over one's own self within a state of siege. Biological life is taken in an assertion of political life. It is this possibility that is terrifying to the state in its quest to stabilize territorial sovereignty.
—Emily T. Yeh[1]

I.

From February 27, 2009, to date (at the time of this writing, July 17, 2013), in at least 120 confirmed cases,[2] Tibetans living in areas incorporated into the People's Republic of China ("PRC")[3] have set themselves on fire.[4] The media has referred to these tragic acts as self-immolation. Their pace has increased exponentially in recent years and months. In November 2012 alone, twenty-eight Tibetans self-immolated.[5] Contrary to common belief, self-immolation does not literally mean suicide by fire, which is more precisely denoted by the word *auto-cremation*. Rather, *self-immolation* literally means "offering of oneself as a sacrifice," particularly in the service of an ideal or deeply held belief.[6] It originates in "the Latin 'molare,' meaning to make a sacrifice of grain."[7] For Tibet, its etymological origin may be significant. It indicates perhaps the quintessential reason, so far as it may reliably be ascertained despite PRC censorship and other barriers to primary research,[8] that many Tibetans have recently decided to set themselves on fire. It is an act of profound dissent and protest, among other sentiments.[9]

Self-immolation is a comparatively recent phenomenon among both Tibetans within Tibet and, to a lesser extent, those residing in exile.[10] But for many years (since roughly 1959), and to date, Tibetans have expressed their rejection of Chinese rule in a less drastic way, namely, by fleeing occupied Tibet. At great personal risk, Tibetans of all ages—from young school children to the elderly—flee Tibet each year and seek refuge in India, Nepal, and (rarely) elsewhere, even though they thereby generally condemn themselves to statelessness, poverty, and permanent separation from family and friends, among other tragic consequences. For most of the past two and a half decades, between 2,500 and 3,500 Tibetans have fled Tibet annually. The exodus of Tibetans persists to this day despite the natural perils of a journey over the Himalayas and the political, especially security, perils of apprehension by Chinese police, military forces, and border patrols, which can lead to torture, detention, and, in extreme cases, extrajudicial killing. With a native Tibetan population of just 6 million, and in view of the risks involved, these numbers speak volumes. After a new wave of protests swept across Tibet in 2008, China intensified its chokehold over the region. It also—diplomatically, economically, and otherwise—coerced Nepal and India to adopt harsh policies that further discourage Tibetans from seeking greater freedoms in these states. The upshot, according to recent estimates, is that the number of Tibetans who manage to flee China annually has declined dramatically.

After more than fifty years, however, an estimated 150,000 Tibetans live in exile. In colloquial terms, their situation is one of the most enduring among the world's unresolved refugee crises—*colloquial* because few Tibetans in exile enjoy any, still less refugee, status under national or international law, including aid or protection from the United Nations High Commissioner for Refugees. Most reside in scattered settlements, some quite remote, in India and Nepal (approximately 125,000 and 25,000, respectively). Smaller communities exist in the United States, Canada, Switzerland, and a few other states. Neither India nor Nepal is a party to the 1951 Refugee Convention or its 1967 Protocol.[11] In part as a consequence, neither state recognizes refugees as such under its law or affords them comparable legal status. It would therefore be more accurate to characterize the roughly 150,000 Tibetans in exile as stateless.[12]

The reason for the Tibetan crisis of statelessness is not complicated: for the reasons detailed below, their true state of nationality has been under belligerent occupation for more than sixty years, since the People's Liberation Army ("PLA") invaded Tibet in 1950. One year later, China purported formally to annex and incorporate it into the PRC. Stateless Tibetans, in short, lack a state to which to return. Until internal political changes in China proper make negotiations over, at a minimum, a genuine autonomous arrangement for the Tibetan people plausible, there can be no resolution to the Tibetan refugee, or statelessness, crisis.

The tragic, and tragically neglected,[13] wave of self-immolations in Tibet in the past few years and the longstanding Tibetan refugee crisis share a common origin in China's colonization of Tibet. Since Tibet's occupation, China has treated the Tibetan people exactly as colonizer treats colonized.[14] Hence both the refugee crisis and the more recent self-immolation crisis represent sociopolitical and psychological consequences arising from the same colonial dynamic. By saying this, I mean to cast doubt on the predominant view, even among largely sympathetic scholars, activists, and politicians in (mostly Western) liberal democracies: namely, that Tibet is just another minority region within China and that the human rights violations suffered by its people, however serious, originate in China's generally inequitable treatment of its national minorities.[15] The truth is that, legally, Tibet is a country, a nation-state, under longstanding belligerent occupation,[16] and Tibetans qualify as a people, in every legal sense of the word, entitled under international law to exercise their right to self-determination—including the right to choose independence, associated statehood, or integration with another state.[17] The same right has been afforded to most every other formerly colonized people in the postwar era.[18]

Self-immolation is not just one more manifestation of political dissent in response to the denial of this right to self-determination; increasingly, it is the *only* available form of dissent possible in the police state in which Tibetans live. For an increasing number of Tibetans, it seems, self-immolation is preferable to a life of colonial exploitation or a worthwhile sacrifice to express their dissent from and protest of more than half a century of foreign occupation, human rights violations, and international neglect. Without appreciating the colonial status and colonization of Tibet and its people, respectively, the phenomenon of self-immolation can be, as it has often been, misunderstood—ascribed, for example, to socioeconomic factors.[19] The Tibetan refugee crisis, similarly, cannot be appreciated accurately apart from its colonial context. That crisis will persist, and Tibetans in exile will remain stateless, until the world recognizes the colonial status of their state and its belligerent occupation. In short, the same context that has led thousands of Tibetans to seek greater freedom outside their historic territory year after year has now led more than 120 Tibetans to set themselves on fire. The self-immolation crisis, which is likely to persist, is therefore of a conceptual piece with the diaspora of Tibetans in exile—and unlikely to end until Tibet's people enjoy their inalienable right to self-determination.

II.

The Trusteeship Council, one of the six original organs established by the UN Charter, suspended its work in 1994 after the tiny territory of Palau became an associated state (with the United States).[20] The Council deemed decolonization, the postwar process that dismantled Europe's colonial empires, thereby quadrupling the number of states in the world in less than half a century, complete. The Council still exists, but has suspended its operations indefinitely, because it believes colonies do not. In legal fact, Tibet, a colony the size of Western Europe, or roughly one-quarter the size of the United States, exists to this day. It is inhabited by about six million Tibetans but also, because of PRC tax breaks and similar economic incentives offered to Han settlers, by a greater number of Han who have migrated from China proper. Slowly but inexorably, these Han settlers (now estimated to constitute about 7.5 million, roughly 1.5 million more than the number of Tibetans) are overwhelming Tibet's indigenous population, as they did in Inner Mongolia decades ago, where Mongols now make up less than 20% of the population. Because of Han migration, Tibetans have likewise become a minority in Tibet, strangers in their own land.

As a contemporary colony, Tibet manifests the same morally repugnant characteristics as its predecessors and essentially the same dynamics that characterized the prewar colonies of European empires in Africa, Latin America, Asia, and elsewhere. These include brutal and discriminatory treatment of the colonized by the colonizer, theft and exploitation of the colony's natural resources, and appropriation of its territory for the benefit of the colonizer. As a de jure and de facto colony, Tibetans should enjoy the rare legal entitlement to what the Canadian Supreme Court has referred to as *external* self-determination, including a right to secede from the PRC if they so choose in a free and fair referendum.[21]

In 1945 (notably before Tibet's invasion), Article 2(4) of the UN Charter, to which China is an original party, established the prohibition on "the threat or use of force against the territorial integrity or political independence of any state" as what many deem the foundational axiom of the law governing relations between states in the postwar era. For one thing, after the defeat of the Nazis, Europe could no longer avoid the centrifugal sociopolitical dynamics breaking apart its erstwhile colonial empires. States also recognized, finally, the injustice of both aggression and colonization, predominant features of the world public order since the conventional origin of the classical law of nations after the Peace of Westphalia. And although the First World War's Allies largely reconfigured rather than dismantled colonialism at the Versailles conference, the moral bankruptcy of the practice became increasingly evident in the interwar period. The old norm of political legitimacy, statehood, and sovereignty based on the crude measure of effective control, which finds its classic expression in the *Tinoco* arbitration,[22] gave way to a theoretical entitlement to statehood based on the (at first, largely idealistic) Wilsonian principle of the self-determination of peoples.[23]

The self-determination of peoples, since its intellectual inception in the Wilsonian era, has begged the question what makes one group, but not another, a *people* for purposes of the principle. Scholars and politicians alike have long recognized that not all self-identified peoples can, as a practical matter, enjoy a legal entitlement to statehood or independence. Consequently, as a rule, self-determination must be respected *internally*.[24] I do not propose in this regard to break new ground or, indeed, analyze this issue in any depth within the limits of this chapter. It suffices to observe that Tibetans qualify as a people under *any* of the criteria enunciated in the mainstream international legal discourse since as early as the *Aaland Islands* precedent of the League of Nations[25] and, more recently, the influential decision of the Canadian Supreme Court in *Reference re Secession of Québec*.[26]

In the first place, unlike most of the states established as a consequence of decolonization after World War II, Tibetans share more than a common history of colonization or simple residence within (often arbitrary) lines that were later codified in conformity with the questionable post-colonial norm of *uti possidetis*.[27] As I have emphasized in past work, one persistent problem afflicting the debate over Tibet's historical status and its relationship to China is that "the distinctly modern Western conception of the nation-state, with precise borders and a single centralized government, is probably inapposite to pre-twentieth century China and Tibet alike."[28] But that is true for well over two-thirds of the nearly 200 states in existence as of 2013. Few, if any, of those states (and *China* is among them) have had their legitimacy or right to exist *as* a state questioned on that basis. Furthermore, Tibet, unlike a clear majority of the others, enjoys a genuine *national* history stretching back millennia, that is, a history of existence as a distinct polity (even before the Common Era) inhabited by a distinct people sharing a host of characteristics and common governance.

From its origins in antiquity until the 1200s of the Common Era, it is, to the best of my knowledge and research, undisputed among historians that the nation of Tibet existed and enjoyed complete political independence. Indeed, even "Chinese court historians recognized that by the eighth century, Tibet had become the most powerful nation in Asia," having "actually conquered several Chinese provinces."[29] In the ninth century, China and Tibet famously concluded a treaty, which provides in relevant part:

> Both Tibet and China shall keep the country and frontiers of which they are now in possession. The whole region to the east of that [demarcation] being the country of Great Tibet, from either side of that frontier there shall be no warfare, no hostile invasions, and no seizure of territory.[30]

China's historical claim to "own" Tibet, ironically, relies not on historical relations between China and Tibet inter se but on the political relationships between Tibet and two *foreign* (non-Chinese) dynasties that ruled China for centuries, namely, the Yuan (Mongol) (1271-1368) and the Qing (Manchu) (1644-1911) dynasties. During these periods, Tibet enjoyed more de facto political independence than China. Both the Mongols and the Manchus ruled China directly. In contrast, Tibet continued at all times to exercise most modern sovereign competences within the geopolitical and spiritual framework of the unique *cho-yun* (priest-patron) relationship that developed between Tibetan Buddhist leaders and first, the Mongol, and later, the Manchu emperors who conquered and governed China. In the interim, that is, during the reign of China's native Ming dynasty (1368-1644), the nation of Tibet enjoyed a cultural and political renaissance known as its "Second Kingdom." At that time, it exercised even greater political autonomy, largely free "of both Mongol and Chinese control."[31]

China finally overthrew the Manchus, which had long been weakened by European colonialism, among other forces, in 1911. Shortly thereafter, Tibet expelled the two Manchu *ambans* (diplomatic representatives)—the sole vestige of Manchu influence in Tibet—from Lhasa.[32] Their role had at any rate been largely symbolic for decades, if not centuries, not a meaningful indicia of Qing sovereignty or control. On February 13, 1913, the Thirteenth Dalai Lama, recognizing that modernity compelled urgent changes (political, social, military, and economic) and appreciating, in particular, the need for Tibet to emerge from its isolation and clarify its national status, formally proclaimed Tibet's independence as a sovereign state on the model of the European nation-state. Without detracting from its symbolic force, it bears emphasizing that this proclamation did not create, but rather described or confirmed, Tibet's status as an independent polity under, inter alia, the formal criteria elaborated by the European law of nations that had come to dominate the world in the twentieth century. Historians, legal scholars, and international fact-finding studies have uniformly concluded that even if Tibet's pre-twentieth century status were genuinely debatable, it would nonetheless remain undisputed that between the collapse of the Manchu Qing Dynasty in 1911 and the PLA's invasion of Tibet in 1950, Tibet enjoyed de jure and de facto independence, "the conditions of statehood as generally accepted under international law,"[33] that is, under the Montevideo or similar criteria.[34]

That leaves, as China's sole claim to sovereignty over Tibet, arguments based on its invasion and belligerent occupation of Tibet in and since 1950. Contemporary international law, of course, invalidates the annexation of territory by aggression, rendering it null and without legal force or effect. In 1950, Tibet qualified as an independent state. The PLA's aggression did not change that status. But almost before the ink dried on the UN Charter, China, despite having only recently expelled European and Japanese colonial powers from its own territory, ironically launched its own colonial adventure. In violation of Article 2(4) of the Charter, which prohibits the acquisition of territory by force against the "political independence of any state," the PLA marched into Tibet after winning the Chinese civil war. Tibet had relied for centuries on its difficult terrain and unusual geographic isolation for protection against foreign domination. But twentieth-century technology and geopolitical change weakened, if not vitiated altogether, these defenses. And although Tibet theoretically retained, under the nascent law of Article 51 of the UN Charter, an "inherent right"[35] to self-defense, with a small army of poorly armed and technologically ill-equipped soldiers, it had no serious chance of defending itself against the battle-hardened and technologically superior (not to mention far more numerous) forces of the PLA.

Of course, China vehemently denies that Tibet has ever enjoyed independence; in its view, Tibet has always been part of China. But this is a manifest fiction. Every comprehensive scholarly study concludes to the contrary.[36] Regardless, that is, even assuming the point were genuinely debatable rather than dogmatic (a product of longstanding, widespread, and effective propaganda by the PRC, both within China and abroad), a chief purpose of the UN Charter's core norm in Article 2(4) is precisely to insist that debates of this sort henceforth be resolved *peacefully*, that is, by one of the pacific methods of dispute settlement set forth in Article 33, paragraph 1, of the Charter. Otherwise Article 2(4) would have changed little from the prewar baseline. After all, seldom, if ever, did states in the centuries before the Charter's conclusion *not* justify their territorial wars and adventures, at least in part, by historical, cultural, religious, social, or legal claims, generally asserting that the invaded polity, for one or another such reasons, belonged to the invader. Saddam Hussein, for example, unsurprisingly did the same when he invaded Kuwait in 1990.

Together with Article 2(4), the principle of the self-determination of peoples theoretically established the consent of peoples, as expressed, if necessary, in free and fair referenda, as the postwar basis for sovereign legitimacy. But as China recognizes, any concession to the idea of a referendum on self-determination would lead to the immediate rejection of Chinese rule by the Tibetan people. So to this day, while China insists that the vast majority of Tibetans want to remain part of China, it refuses to consider letting Tibetans vote in a plebiscite that would establish the truth one way or the other. The reason is hardly recondite.

In retrospect, two historical contingencies facilitated Tibet's rapid and, in international relations, largely unnoticed absorption by China. First, it is a sad irony that "the isolation Tibet's government ha[d] self-consciously cultivated to *shield* Tibet from foreign domination proved the principal reason that Tibet found itself unable to achieve political recognition as a modern nation-state—and thus powerless to resist foreign domination by communist China."[37] Second, the Korean War broke out at the same time as China's invasion of Tibet. On June 25, 1950, North Korea crossed the 38th parallel, inaugurating the first of the hot wars that punctuated the Cold War, which would dominate international relations and global consciousness for the next forty years. Tibet is a casualty of that period. Its people, as one author aptly put it, remain orphans of the Cold War.[38]

Tibet's government sent a cable to the United Nations on October 25, 1950, pleading for international assistance to resist the PLA's aggression. Perhaps a few years later in postwar history, that cable would have led to action, prompting some kind of collective self-defense or military resistance. At a later time it may have prompted an international force under UN auspices, a U.S.-led military intervention of the sort that repulsed North Korea's invasion of South Korea, or a unilateral resistance by the United States such as its reaction to North Vietnam's aggression against South Vietnam years later.[39] As the Fourteenth Dalai Lama communicated to the nascent United Nations:

> The attention of the world is riveted on Korea, where aggression is being resisted by an international force. Similar happenings in remote Tibet are passing without notice . . . . We can assure you, Mr. Secretary-General, that Tibet will not go down without a fight, though there is little hope that a nation dedicated to peace will be able to resist the brutal effort of men trained to war, but we understand that the United Nations has decided to stop aggression whenever it takes place. The armed invasion of Tibet for the incorporation of Tibet in Communist China through sheer physical force is a clear case of aggression . . . . The problem is simple. The Chinese claim Tibet as a part of China. Tibetans feel that racially, culturally, and

> geographically they are far apart from the Chinese. If the Chinese find the reactions of the Tibetans to their unnatural claim not acceptable, there are other civilized methods by which they could ascertain the views of the people of Tibet; or, should the issue be surely juridical, they are open to seek redress in an international court of law . . . .[40]

More than half a century later, even young Tibetans who have never known an independent state of Tibet, and can hardly speak of it without fear, continue to feel—indeed, to *know*—as the cable puts it, "that racially, culturally, and geographically they are far apart from the Chinese." This is so despite the best efforts of the PRC, which have involved intense propaganda, economic incentives to Tibetans and ordinary Han, who have been encouraged to resettle in Tibet, and chronic human rights violations along with brutal repression of the remotest hint of Tibetan nationalism.

The unique characteristics of the Tibetan people constitute a second, independent criterion on the basis of which Tibetans must be deemed a people under contemporary international law. China has insisted for years that Tibetans constitute one of its fifty-five "minority nationalities," of which the Han allegedly constitute one, despite accounting for more than 90% of China's 1.3 billion residents. To those familiar with Chinese and Tibetan history, culture, sociology, or politics, the idea that Tibetans are a Chinese minority is preposterous. It will suffice to canvass a few of the most glaring distinctions between the Tibetan and Chinese peoples.

First, Tibetans speak their own language, which dates back millennia. It is not a dialect of Mandarin or Cantonese. It does not even bear an etymological relationship to the Chinese language group—unlike, for example, Japanese, which uses Chinese characters. Tibetan has its own alphabet and grammatical structure. In terms of etymology, linguists characterize it as part of the Tibeto-Burmese language group. The Tibetan language also does not contain a word for China that includes Tibet: In Tibetan, *Bod* refers to Tibet, while *Gyanag* means China. Only in the post-occupation period have Tibetans come to use the term *Zhonngguo* for the PRC (that is, for China including Tibet).

Second, the vast majority of Tibetans adhere to an intricate, unique, and highly distinctive religious tradition. The form of Buddhism that evolved over centuries in Tibet differs doctrinally and culturally from both Indian variants and the predominant Chinese sect, that is, *Chán* (Zen in Japanese). At any rate, only a minority of Han practice Buddhism, a tradition that entered China from India in the fifth century of the Common Era. Confucian, Taoist, and other spiritual or cultural traditions have for most of Chinese history been much more widespread and dominant within Chinese civilization than Buddhism. They remain so today. Tibetan

Buddhism, in contrast, originated in the unique fusion of Indian Mahayana Buddhism and the indigenous Tibetan religion or spiritual tradition of Bonpo, which, like the Tibetan language, dates back millennia, culminating in the Vajrayana tradition that came to prevail in Tibet and Mongolia.

Third, Tibetans differ racially from Han. "Han Chinese" is a tautology; there are no *non*-Han Chinese in a racial, cultural, or ethnic sense. The characterization of some Chinese citizens as "Han Chinese" originated in the postwar era. It is part of the fiction created and perpetuated by the PRC to justify Chinese colonization of areas, including Tibet and East Turkestan, which China calls Xinjiang. China characterizes these regions as part of a greater China, the "Motherland," not coincidentally, a project similar to (but more successful than) the effort of Slobodan Milosević and his allies to establish a "greater Serbia." China's policies towards Tibet reflect colonial motives, such as natural resource exploitation and the need for territory to accommodate China's huge Han population—as well as, I think, misplaced national pride. For Tibet is no more part of a Chinese "Motherland" than France could rightfully be said to be part of a hypothetically reconstituted Roman Empire. Even today, not only do most Tibetans not regard themselves as Chinese, most *Han* do not regard Tibetans as Chinese. China's elite has long considered China the literal and figurative center of civilization, the "Middle Kingdom." Tibetans historically had been one of the foreign peoples that China characterized as barbarians beyond its civilization's borders. The idea that Tibet is part of a Chinese "Motherland" is a twentieth-century invention.

Turning from history, culture, and sociology to law, yet another reason that has been proffered for Tibet's supposed status as part of China is treaty relations. Preliminarily, it is worth noting that Tibet's entry into numerous treaties with states including Nepal, India, Mongolia, the United Kingdom, and *China* in the first half of the twentieth century casts serious doubt on the assertion that China has always controlled Tibet's foreign affairs.[41] But the gravamen of this aspect of China's claim today is that regardless of Tibet's status historically, it became an inalienable part of China after the 17-Point Agreement of 1951.[42] That treaty states in strikingly irredentist language that "the Tibetan people shall return to the big family of the motherland—the People's Republic of China."[43] Because, with few exceptions, only states can be parties to treaties,[44] the very fact that China felt the need to ground its future relationship with the Tibetan people and their government on such a legal basis ironically implies, contrary to China's position, that Tibet had indeed been a state before the 17-Point Agreement. Why, after all, had Tibet left "the big family of the motherland"? Why did it need to "return"? Surely the answer cannot be, as China suggests, European colonialism. Only a literal handful of foreigners resided in Tibet before the Chinese invasion, and unlike China, no European state ever colonized Tibet. China nonetheless ascribes any Tibetan desire for independence or autonomy to foreign instigation, typically meaning Western states that allegedly want to "split" China. Again, the true wishes of Tibet's people could be readily ascertained by a plebiscite. China unsurprisingly refuses to consider this simple expedient.

An irredeemable defect at any rate invalidates the 17-Point Agreement: the PRC imposed it on Tibet by violence, including coercion of both Tibet (by the threat of an invasion of Lhasa and other areas) and its government's personal representatives (by the threat of violence against them if they refused to sign). Shortly after Tibet's belligerent occupation in 1950, the Dalai Lama, facing few real choices, sent official Tibetan delegates to Beijing to "negotiate." But "under duress that included both [threats of] personal violence and large-scale military retaliation against Tibet, [and] acting without the authority or approval of the Tibet government, [they] signed the so-called 17-Point Agreement."[45] The treaty is therefore "null and void *ab initio*"[46] under the law of treaties. Even if it were valid initially, the PRC abrogated the 17-Point Agreement almost immediately after its signature and continuing to date. China materially breached the treaty by, among other violations, coercively modifying Tibet's existing local government and imposing severe restrictions on the Tibetan people's freedom to practice their religion.[47]

Yet another reason that the Tibetan people qualify legally as a *people* and merit self-determination is China's history of persistent human rights violations in Tibet. These violations include not only violence against the person and restrictions on freedom of conscience and expression, but also complete refusal to allow Tibetans to exercise any form of internal self-determination—including, even though China deems Tibetans a minority, the de minimis minority nationality rights enumerated in Article 27 of the International Covenant on Civil and Political Rights ("ICCPR"). China denies to the Tibetan people the rights, among others, to freedoms of religion, speech, education, political participation, and economic or cultural autonomy. Nomads have recently been forcibly resettled and traditional, often historic, structures and homes in Lhasa demolished to make room for new Chinese construction. Serious civil and political rights violations include systematic torture, summary execution, and arbitrary detention, practices that have long been part of China's response to any manifestation of Tibetan nationalism or dissent from Chinese rule.[48] China's human rights violations continue to have grave consequences for the Tibetan people, most recently illustrated by its brutal crackdown on widespread political demonstrations in 2008, and even more recently, by its callous response to the tragic wave of self-immolations in Tibet.

For these reasons, as the Canadian Supreme Court suggested, Tibet's people may well have an additional claim to external self-determination based on China's persistent refusal to let them exercise internal self-determination (sufficient autonomy, political, cultural, and otherwise, within the larger nation-state), in combination with the PRC's severe and persistent human rights abuses[49]—a criterion intimated as early as the *Aaland Islands* precedent of the post-World War I era.[50] The PRC has shown consistently that it will not allow Tibetans even the minimal rights afforded to "ethnic, religious or linguistic *minorities*" (let alone those afforded to *peoples*) by international law, including the minority rights guaranteed by Article 27 of the ICCPR, "the right, in community with the other members of their group, to enjoy their own culture, to profess and practise their own religion, or to use their own language."[51]

In sum, Tibetans qualify as a *people* who should be entitled under international law to external self-determination under any definition of the latter term that does not reduce this central legal concept of the postwar era to a largely empty slogan. Yet for decades, the Fourteenth Dalai Lama, (until recently) Tibet's political and spiritual leader, has not insisted on self-determination. He has not asked for the referendum on Tibet's status to which his people remain legally entitled. His priority has been to secure meaningful cultural autonomy, an arrangement that would sacrifice political self-determination for the sake of preserving the Tibetan people's rich cultural, religious, ethnic, linguistic, and other heritage.[52] Because this modest request, too, has been met with obstinate refusal and a steady and inexorable process of Sinicization, it should not be surprising that Tibet's people today see few options except self-imposed exile, which perpetuates a crisis of statelessness, and more recently, self-immolation, a new response to what has rightly been described, colloquially even if not legally, as the cultural genocide of the Tibetan people.

III.

Predictably, China's position on the self-immolations, consistent with its approach to any manifestation of dissent in Tibet, is to blame the Dalai Lama. This position is both implausible and ironic in the face of, among other developments, the Dalai Lama's relinquishment of any claim to political authority and, for well over two decades before, his public and repeated affirmation that he seeks only greater cultural and religious autonomy for Tibetans. China's position on the self-immolations is as preposterous as it is tragic: that a nearly 80-year-old monk has managed to penetrate one of the most strictly controlled political societies in existence today in order to orchestrate a geographically widespread campaign of self-immolations from abroad in cooperation with Tibetan refugees and their foreign supporters. A representative article in the *China Daily* quotes Wang Chengxian, the deputy Communist Party Secretary of the Aba Tibetan and Qiang autonomous prefectures: "For the exiled 14th Dalai Lama and his [associates] in India, instigating self-immolation is just a means of realizing their political goal of splitting Tibet from China."[53] Similarly, Chinese Foreign Ministry spokesman Hong Lei said that "the Dalai Lama and his associates have been instigating Tibetan independence and creating 'disturbances' and that [he] and his associates 'single-handedly' planned" one of the self-immolations.[54] China has also characterized Tibetans who self-immolate as terrorists and enacted a new "public security offense" that subjects those who attempt it to criminal prosecution.[55]

The PRC's rhetoric, however divorced from reality and colored by its colonial agenda, betrays the true cause of the self-immolation crisis. Despite more than half a century of PRC effort—ranging from financial and social incentives, to censorship, to abduction of a six-year-old boy,[56] to "patriotic reeducation" sessions mandated for Tibet's monasteries and nunneries, to chronic human rights violations against the person, including torture, arbitrary detention, extrajudicial executions, and other forms of political violence—the PRC cannot convince some six million Tibetans that they are a minority nationality of the Chinese people. Tibetans know that they are not Chinese. They know that Tibet is not part of China.[57] They maintain a cultural, historical, religious, ethnic, linguistic, and perhaps above all, *national* identity that differs from that of the 1.2 billion plus Han who populate China proper.

Tibet is a sovereign state under illegal foreign occupation. It is the world's largest colony.[58] Only brute military force and the political and economic power of modern China today, combined with an intense propaganda campaign within China and abroad, obscure Tibet's colonization. Until that status changes, until China allows the Tibetan people to exercise their right *as* a people to self-determination, no effort "to control Tibetan discontent by means of carrot and stick" will be availing.[59] Hence the self-immolation crisis *within* Tibet casts considerable light on the unresolved refugee crisis *without*—where some 150,000 Tibetans reside in exile, largely as stateless persons.[60] Neither self-immolations nor the Tibetan diaspora will cease until Tibet's people receive the same right that every other formerly colonized people should receive in the postwar era: self-determination. As the world's largest remaining colony, Tibet's right to external self-determination, including, if its people so choose, independence as a sovereign state, should be legally undisputed.[61]

Notes

---

* Professor of Law and R. Gordon Butler Scholar in International Law, Boston University School of Law; and Chair, Board of Directors, Tibet Justice Center. I acknowledge with gratitude the suggestions of Michael J. Glennon, Fiona R. McConnell, and Nima R.T. Binara, and the research assistance of Beaudre Barnes and Julie Krosnicki.

1 Int'l Campaign for Tibet [ICT], *Storm in the Grasslands: Self-Immolations in Tibet and Chinese Policy*, 16 (2012), *available at* http://www.savetibet.org/wp-content/uploads/2013/06/storminthegrassland-FINAL-HR.pdf (quoting Emily T. Yeh, *On "Terrorism" and the Politics of Naming*, J. SOC'Y CULTURAL ANTHROPOLOGY (2012), *available at* http://www.culanth.org/files/HotSpot-Yeh.pdf) [hereinafter *Storm in the Grasslands*].

2 ICT, *Self-Immolations in Tibet: Fact Sheet* (last updated Feb. 27, 2013), *available at* http://www.savetibet.org/resource-center/maps-data-fact-sheets/self-immolation-fact-sheet [hereinafter *Self-Immolation Fact Sheet*].

3 By Tibet, I mean more than the Tibet Autonomous Region (TAR). The PRC established the TAR in 1965 and misleadingly suggests that it is coterminous with Tibet. By Tibet, apart from the TAR, I mean to refer to traditionally Tibetan areas of the PRC, namely, parts of the contemporary PRC provinces of Qinghai, Gansu, Sichuan, and Yunnan. The TAR corresponds roughly to the Tibetan province of Ü-Tsang. The PRC broke up the former Tibetan provinces of Amdo and Kham and incorporated them into, respectively, Qinghai and Gansu (Amdo), and Gansu, Sichuan, and Yunnan (Kham).

4 In addition, six Tibetans residing in exile have self-immolated. *See Self-Immolation Fact Sheet*, *supra* note 2. For a comprehensive symposium on the issue, see *Tibet is Burning — Self-Immolation or Political Protest?*, 25 REVUE D'ETUDES TIBÉTAINES (Katia Buffetrille & Françoise Robin eds., Dec. 2012)(Fr.), http://himalaya.socanth.cam.ac.uk/collections/journals/ret/pdf/ret_25.pdf.

5 *Self-Immolations Hit 90 Mark*, RADIO FREE ASIA (Nov. 30, 2012), *available at* http://www.rfa.org/english/news/tibet/burning-11302012155443.html.

6 *See* THE NEW OXFORD AMERICAN DICTIONARY 1538 (Erin McKean ed., 2d ed. 2005); *see also* CONCISE OXFORD ENGLISH DICTIONARY (Catherine Soanes & Angus Stevenson eds., 11th rev. ed. 2009).

7 *Storm in the Grasslands*, *supra* note 1.

8 Since the international community first took notice of the crisis of self-immolations in Tibet, the PRC has imposed a media blackout throughout Tibet and

deployed the full resources of the state's propaganda machinery in an effort to blame the self-immolations on the Dalai Lama and the Tibetan government-in-exile. *See, e.g.*, Cui Jia, *Monks Vent Anger at Self-Immolation*, CHINA DAILY, Dec. 3, 2012. China also responded to the self-immolations in Tibetan areas by imposing curfews, banning kerosene and other incendiary materials, further abridging human rights, and intensifying its "patriotic reeducation" campaigns in monasteries and elsewhere.

[9] *Tibet's Future: The Limits of Despair*, ECONOMIST, Mar. 9, 2013.

[10] *See generally* Carole McGranahan & Ralph Litzinger, *Self-Immolation as Protest in Tibet,* FIELDSIGHTS – HOT SPOTS, CULTURAL ANTHROPOLOGY ONLINE (Apr. 9, 2012), *available at* http://www.culanth.org/fieldsights/93-self-immolation-as-protest-in-tibet.

[11] Convention Relating to the Status of Refugees, July 28, 1951, 189 U.N.T.S. 150; Protocol Relating to the Status of Refugees, Jan. 31, 1967, 606 U.N.T.S. 267. *See* Tibet Justice Center [TJC], *Tibet's Stateless Nationals: Tibetan Refugees in Nepal* 44 (2002) [hereinafter *Tibet's Stateless Nationals: Nepal*]; TJC, *Tibet's Stateless Nationals II: Tibetan Refugees in India* 41 (2011) [hereinafter *Tibet's Stateless Nationals: India*]. Both reports can be found at http://www.tibetjustice.org/reports/.

[12] The Convention Relating to Stateless Persons, Sept. 28, 1954, 360 U.N.T.S. 117, defines a stateless person as "a person who is not considered as a national by any State under the operation of its law." *Id.*, art. 1. The vast majority of Tibetans residing in exile in India and Nepal qualify as stateless, so defined, and the remainder should be characterized as de facto stateless: in practice, they lack the nationality, or any of the generally associated rights and privileges, of any state. *See Tibet's Stateless Nationals: India, supra* note 11, at 51-58; *Tibet's Stateless Nationals: Nepal*, *supra* note 11, at 46-48.

[13] Self-immolation, in general, is a phenomenon so rare and shocking to the collective political conscience that a single act grips the world's attention, as did the self-immolation of Thich Quang Duc in Vietnam in 1963, *see, e.g.*, Robert F. Worth, *How a Single Match Can Ignite a Revolution*, N.Y. TIMES, Jan. 21, 2011, or, more recently, Tarek al-Tayeb Mohamed Bouazizi in Tunisia in 2011, *see, e.g.*, *Tunisia's Troubles: Sour Young Men*, ECONOMIST, Jan. 6, 2011. It is remarkable and sad that some 120 self-immolations in a span of just over three years have led to little more than a few articles in the press and pusillanimous expressions of concern from UN officials and institutions. *See, e.g.*, Edward Wong and Jim Yardley, *100th Self-Immolation Reported Inside Tibet*, N.Y. TIMES, Feb. 14, 2013; *Self-Immolation in Tibet: The Burning Issue*, ECONOMIST, Dec. 9, 2012; *Tibet's Growing Tragedy: Self-Immolation Protests Reach 105*, FORBES, Feb. 25, 2013.

[14] For the seminal account of these dynamics, *see generally* ALBERT MEMMI, THE COLONIZER AND THE COLONIZED (1965).

[15] *See, e.g.*, U.S. DEP'T OF STATE, BUREAU OF DEMOCRACY, HUMAN RIGHTS, AND LABOR, COUNTRY REPORTS ON HUMAN RIGHTS PRACTICES FOR 2011: CHINA

(INCLUDES TIBET, HONG KONG, AND MACAU) (2012) (comparing Tibet to "other predominantly minority areas" of the PRC) [hereinafter U.S. DEP'T OF STATE REPORTS ON HUMAN RIGHTS PRACTICES FOR 2011].

[16] *See infra* text accompanying notes 40-50.

[17] *See infra* text accompanying notes 39-40.

[18] For an overview of the meaning and history of self-determination, *see generally* Gary Lawson & Robert D. Sloane, *The Constitutionality of Decolonization by Associated Statehood: Puerto Rico's Legal Status Reconsidered*, 50 B.C. L. REV. 1123, 1132-36 (2009). For the application of these issues to Tibet, *see generally* Robert D. Sloane, *The Changing Face of Recognition in International Law: A Case Study of Tibet*, 16 EMORY INT'L L. REV. 107, 129-55 n.85 (2002) [hereinafter Sloane, *Recognition*]. *See also, e.g.*, TJC & Unrepresented Nations and Peoples Org. [UNPO], *The Case Concerning Tibet: Tibet's Sovereignty and the Tibetan People's Right to Self-Determination* (1998) (by Andrew G. Dulaney & Dennis M. Cusack, TJC, & Michael C. van Walt van Praag, UNPO) (update added by TJC, Feb. 13, 2013), *available at* http://www.tibetjustice.org/reports/sovereignty/the_case_concerning_tibet-updated2013.pdf [hereinafter *Tibet's Sovereignty and the Tibetan People's Right to Self-Determination*]; UNPO et al., *China's Tibet: The World's Largest Remaining Colony: Report of a Fact-Finding Mission and Analyses of Colonialism and Chinese Rule in Tibet* (1997) [hereinafter UNPO Report, *China's Tibet: The World's Largest Remaining Colony*].

[19] *See, e.g.*, Barry Sautman, *Tibet's Suicidal Politics*, EAST ASIA FORUM, (Mar. 21, 2012), *available at* http://www.eastasiaforum.org/2012/03/21/tibet-s-suicidal-politics/. Sautman's editorial is reflective of a trend in global opinion. For a response, *see* Robert D. Sloane, *Tibet, Cynical Sinicism, and the Tragedy of Self-Immolations*, EAST ASIA FORUM, (May 9, 2012), *available at* http://www.eastasiaforum.org/2012/05/09/tibet-cynical-sinicism-and-the-tragedy-of-self-immolations/.

[20] For a description of the evolution and status of associated statehood in international law, see Lawson & Sloane, *supra* note 18, at 1137-40.

[21] *See* Reference re Secession of Quebec, [1998] S.C.R. 217, ¶¶ 126-39 (Can.). For a brief overview of the import of this case, which expresses the consensus view on contemporary self-determination; *see generally* Lawson & Sloane, *supra* note 18, at 1132-40.

[22] Tinoco Concessions (Gr. Brit. v. Costa Rica), 1 R.I.A.A. 369 (1923).

[23] It is no accident that the twin pillars of the postwar international human rights treaties, the International Covenant on Civil and Political Rights, *adopted by the General Assembly* Dec. 16, 1966, art. 1, 999 U.N.T.S. 171 (entered into force Mar. 23, 1976) [hereinafter ICCPR], and the International Covenant on Economic, Social, and Cultural Rights, *adopted by the General Assembly* Dec. 16, 1966, art. 1, 993 U.N.T.S. 3 (entered into force Jan. 3, 1973) [hereinafter ICESCR], each begin by affirming that "all *peoples* have the right of self-determination" and that

"by virtue of that right they freely determine their political status and freely pursue their economic, social and cultural development." ICCPR art. 1, ¶1 (emphasis added); ICESCR art. 1, ¶ 1 (same). Equally, the UN Charter proclaims as one of its paramount purposes the "develop[ment] of friendly relations among nations based on . . . [the] *self-determination of peoples*." U.N. Charter art. 1, ¶ 2 (emphasis added).

[24] *See* Reference re Secession of Quebec, *supra* note 21, at ¶ 126.

[25] *The Aaland Islands Question: Report Submitted to the Council of the League of Nations by the Comm. of Rapporteurs*, League of Nations Doc. B7.21/68/106 (1921) [hereinafter *The Aaland Islands Question*]; *Report of the Int'l Comm. of Jurists Entrusted by the Council of the League of Nations with the Task of Giving an Advisory Opinion upon the Legal Aspects of the Aaland Islands Question*, League of Nations Doc. 69.20/4/238 (1920).

[26] *See* Reference re Secession of Quebec, *supra* note 21, at ¶¶ 132-34.

[27] For a general critique, *see* Steven R. Ratner, *Drawing a Better Line:* Uti Possidetis *and the Borders of New States*, 90 AM. J. INT'L L. 590 (1996).

[28] Sloane, *Recognition*, *supra* note 18, at 131 n.85.

[29] *Tibet's Sovereignty and the Tibetan People's Right to Self-Determination, supra* note 18.

[30] Sino-Tibetan Treaty, China-Tibet, 821/823 A.D., *reprinted in* MICHAEL C. VAN WALT VAN PRAAG, STATUS OF TIBET: HISTORY, RIGHTS AND PROSPECTS IN INTERNATIONAL LAW app. 2 (1987). This is only one of multiple treaties entered into by the Tibetan nation. *See* Sloane, *Recognition*, *supra* note 18, at 148 n.147. In 2007, scholars discovered the original text of an additional treaty entered into between Tibet and Mongolia in 1913. *See* Phurbu Thinley, *Tibet-Mongolia Treaty of 1913, a Proof of Tibet's Independence: Interview with Elliot Sperling*, PHAYUL.COM (Nov. 12, 2008), *available at* http://www.phayul.com/news/article.aspx?id=23205&t=1.

[31] *Tibet's Sovereignty and the Tibetan People's Right to Self-Determination, supra* note 18, at 7.

[32] *Id.* at 40

[33] *See* Sloane, *Recognition*, *supra* note 18, at 146-47 & n.144-45 (quoting, inter alia, a report by the International Commission of Jurists, and collecting authorities); *see generally* VAN WALT VAN PRAAG, *supra* note 30 (supplying a comprehensive study of the legal issues and, insofar as they may be relevant to the law, the historical background, and concluding that Tibet is a sovereign state under illegal foreign occupation).

[34] Convention on the Rights and Duties of States, Dec. 26, 1933, 49 Stat. 3097, 165 L.N.T.S. 19.

[35] U.N. Charter art. 51.

[36] *See, e.g.*, LEE FEIGON, DEMYSTIFYING TIBET (1998); CHARLES BELL, TIBET PAST AND PRESENT (1992); REBECCA REDWOOD FRENCH, THE GOLDEN YOKE: THE LEGAL COSMOLOGY OF BUDDHIST TIBET (1999); MELVYN GOLDSTEIN, A HISTORY

OF MODERN TIBET, 1913-1951 (1989); WARREN SMITH, TIBETAN NATION (1996); Dawa Norbu, *Selfdetermination in the Post-Soviet Era: A Case Study of Tibet*, 34 J. INT'L L. STUD. 237 (1997); Conference of International Lawyers on Issues Relating to Self-Determination and Independence for Tibet, Jan. 6-10, 1993, *Tibet: The Position in International Law* (1994); Legal Inquiry Committee on Tibet, *International Commission of Jurists, Tibet & The Chinese People's Republic*, ¶¶ 5-6 (1960).

[37] Sloane, *Recognition*, *supra* note 18, at 136; *see generally id.* at 136-40.

[38] JOHN KENNETH KNAUS, ORPHANS OF THE COLD WAR: AMERICA AND THE TIBETAN STRUGGLE FOR SURVIVAL (1999).

[39] To be clear, I do not mean to express any view here on the propriety or legality—still less the advisability—of the Vietnam War, either internationally or domestically (from the perspective of U.S. law). I mean only to suggest, descriptively, that historical contingency rather than principle accounts for the distinct treatment of the reactions to China's invasion of Tibet, on the one hand, and Iraq's invasion of Kuwait or Indonesia's invasion of East Timor, on the other. *See*, in this regard, Sloane, *Recognition*, *supra* note 18, at 130-31, 145, 178-83.

[40] Cablegram from the Kashag and the National Assembly of Tibet to the U.N., U.N. Doc. A/1549 (Nov. 11, 1950), *reprinted in* VAN WALT VAN PRAAG, *supra* note 18, at 334 [hereinafter Cablegram from the Kashag and the National Assembly of Tibet to the U.N.].

[41] *See* Sloane, *Recognition*, *supra* note 18, at 147 n.148 (citing multiple treaties entered into by Tibet). For a complete list, see TJC, *Treaties and Conventions Relating to Tibet*, *available at* http://www.tibetjustice.org/materials/ (last visited Apr. 14, 2013).

[42] *See* Agreement of the Central People's Government and the Local Government of Tibet on Measures for the Peaceful Liberation of Tibet, China-Tibet, ¶ 1, May 23, 1951 [hereinafter 17-Point Agreement], *reprinted in* VAN WALT VAN PRAAG, *supra* note 30, at 337.

[43] 17-Point Agreement, *supra* note 42, at art. 1.

[44] Vienna Convention on the Law of Treaties art. 1, May 23, 1969, 1155 U.N.T.S. 331, *reprinted in* 8 I.L.M. 679.

[45] Sloane, *Recognition*, *supra* note 18, at 152.

[46] VAN WALT VAN PRAAG, *supra* note 30, at 165.

[47] *See* 17-Point Agreement, *supra* note 42, arts. 4, 6, 7; Sloane, *Recognition*, *supra* note 18, at 154.

[48] Recent reports and other documentation include, for example, U.S. DEP'T OF STATE REPORTS ON HUMAN RIGHTS PRACTICES FOR 2011, *supra* note 15; Amnesty Int'l [AI], *People's Republic of China: Tibet Autonomous Region: Access Denied*, AI Index ASA 17/085/2008 (June 18, 2008); Human Rights Watch [HRW], *"I Saw It with My Own Eyes": Abuses by Chinese Security Forces in Tibet, 2008-2010* (July 21, 2010).

[49] *See* Reference re Secession of Quebec, *supra* note 21, at ¶ 134.

[50] *The Aaland Islands Question*, *supra* note 25, at 27-28.
[51] ICCPR, *supra* note 23, art. 27.
[52] Dalai Lama, Address to the U.S. Congressional Human Right's Caucus: Five Point Peace Plan (Sept. 21, 1987) (transcript *available at* http://www.dalailama.com/messages/tibet/five-point-peace-plan).
[53] *Monks Vent Anger at Self-Immolation*, *supra* note 8; *see also Dalai Lama Behind Tibet Protest Self-Immolation, Says China*, TELEGRAPH (Mar. 27, 2012), http://www.telegraph.co.uk/news/worldnews/asia/tibet/9168885/Dalai-Lama-behind-Tibet-protest-self-immolation-says-China.html.
[54] *Dalai Lama Behind Tibet Protest Self-Immolation, Says China*, *supra* note 53.
[55] *See* Edward Wong, *From the Tibetan Monastery at the Heart of Self-Immolations, an Explanation*, N.Y. TIMES, June 3, 2012, at A6.
[56] *See, e.g.*, *Tibet's Missing Spiritual Guide*, BBC NEWS (last updated May 16, 2005), *available at* http://news.bbc.co.uk/2/hi/asia-pacific/4551425.stm; Interfaith International, *Written Statement on Panchen Lamas Case*, UNPO (Feb. 13, 2006), *available at* http://www.unpo.org/article/3948.
[57] *See* Cablegram from the Kashag and the National Assembly of Tibet to the U.N., *supra* note 40. Today, of course, China refuses to allow independent research of any sort to ascertain what Tibetans in Tibet believe about their national identity or political situation, among many other issues, and to that extent it is impossible to verify this assertion with certainty. But the objective evidence, not least, recently, the statements of Tibetans who have self-immolated, *see generally Storm in the Grasslands, supra* note 1, strongly supports the statement in the text. The author has also personally interviewed hundreds of Tibetans who have fled Chinese-occupied Tibet. Without exception, and in a variety of contexts, they have expressed the same sentiment with remarkable force and passion.
[58] *See* UNPO Report, *China's Tibet: The World's Largest Remaining Colony*, *supra* note 18.
[59] *Tibet's Future: The Limits of Despair*, *supra* note 9.
[60] *See supra* text accompanying notes 10 to 11.
[61] Reference re Secession of Quebec, *supra* note 21, at ¶ 132.

CHAPTER FOUR

SELF- DETERMINATION, STATEHOOD, AND THE REFUGEE QUESTION UNDER INTERNATIONAL LAW IN NAMIBIA, PALESTINE, WESTERN SAHARA, AND TIBET

SUSAN M. AKRAM*

Introduction to the Legal Framework on Namibia, Palestine, Western Sahara and Tibet

This chapter addresses the significance of the legal framework established by the United Nations ("UN") for resolution of the core issues underlying the conflicts in South West Africa/Namibia, Palestine, Western Sahara ("W. Sahara"), and Tibet. The chapter will examine what elements were present in the UN framework for self-determination in South West Africa/Namibia that contributed to Namibia's ultimate independence and the solution of its refugee problem that are present or absent in the cases of Palestine, W. Sahara, and Tibet.[1] The chapter will conclude with examining which of these elements appears necessary to resolving the ongoing refugee problem in each of these cases, suggesting the utility of various strategies to build on the Namibia precedent.

Namibia and Palestine are closely analogous cases from the perspective of the legal principles applicable to them in the UN. The two territories have parallel histories in terms of how their campaigns towards self-determination and independence began, and in the way their status was addressed at the League of Nations and the UN. The decolonization effort for W. Sahara took a somewhat different course through the UN, and the UN has not viewed Tibet as an occupied or colonized territory. However, comparing the histories of these territories through the lens of the UN, and comparing that to broader international law principles, is helpful to understand the different ways in which law provides a framework for resolving the core self-determination problems at the heart of these conflicts. What are the key elements in the UN approach towards Namibia that allowed it to secure independence in fulfillment of self-determination? Are those elements present or absent in the UN's approach to the cases of Palestine, W. Sahara and Tibet? Which of those elements appears necessary to resolving the refugee issues in these cases? Can what Namibia achieved be achieved by any of these other territories or peoples in the near future?

The UN's Framework for Decolonization and Self-Determination

Self-determination as a legal concept, and then as a right of "peoples" to be implemented by the community of states and the UN, evolved between the two world wars.[2] At the end of WWI, the great powers incorporated various kinds of supervisory relationships with former colonial or Ottoman territories into the League of Nations Covenant and the Treaty of Lausanne (ending the Ottoman Empire).[3] This plan created three classes of territories, claimed to be at different stages of development, and placed them under the Mandate, or supervision, of one or other of the great powers.[4] The Mandates system was a compromise between the notion of self-determination and the interests of the colonial powers.[5] The League of Nations Covenant placed Palestine among the Class A mandates, or those closest to readiness for independence, along with Iraq, Lebanon, Syria, and Transjordan.[6] Britain was given Mandatory power over Palestine.[7] South West Africa/Namibia was among the Class C mandate countries and considered farthest from independence under the League of Nations Covenant, Article 22—in fact, independence was not contemplated at all by the League for the Class C territories.[8] Namibia was placed under South Africa's Mandate.[9] On April 18, 1946, the League dissolved, leaving all the Mandate countries continuing under the terms of Covenant Article 22 as trusteeships under the new United Nations Organization, with the exception of Syria, Lebanon, and Transjordan, which had by then become independent.[10]

With the dissolution of the League of Nations and the establishment of the United Nations, self-determination as a concrete aim of the international community of states became a cornerstone of the UN Charter. Article 1 of the Charter included among the Purposes of the United Nations, "To develop friendly relations among nations based on respect for the principle of equal rights and self-determination of peoples, and to take other appropriate measures to strengthen universal peace."[11] The General

Assembly's ("UNGA") two Resolutions, 1514 (XV) and 1541 (XV), passed one day apart in 1960, marked a watershed in the long march towards ending colonialism and recognizing self-determination as a legal right of certain "peoples." UNGA Resolution 1514, the Declaration on the Granting of Independence to Colonial Countries and Peoples, stated, "all peoples have the right to self-determination which entails freely determining political status." It declared that:

> 5. Immediate steps shall be taken, in Trust and Non-Self-Governing Territories or all other territories which have not yet attained independence, to transfer all powers to the peoples of those territories, without any conditions or reservations, in accordance with their freely expressed will and desire, without any distinction as to race, creed or colour, in order to enable them to enjoy complete independence and freedom.
> 6. Any attempt aimed at the partial or total disruption of the national unity and the territorial integrity of a country is incompatible with the purposes and principles of the Charter of the United Nations.[12]

Resolution 1514 set out a list of Principles for member states to follow in order to determine when states had an obligation to transmit information to the UN concerning the status of territories to be decolonized under Chapter XI of the Charter. Principle VI of the Resolution lists three ways in which decolonization could take place and self-determination of the territory in question could be realized: full independence; free association with an independent state; or integration with an independent state. The Resolution describes what is required for any of these options to meet the criteria for fulfillment of self-governance. Free association would have to be based on "free and voluntary choice by the peoples of the territory . . . through informed and democratic processes." Integration should be "on the basis of complete equality between the peoples of the Self-Governing Territory and those of the independent country. . . " as well as on "equal status and rights of citizenship and equal guarantees of fundamental rights and freedoms without distinction or discrimination."[13] The definition of self-determination in Resolution 1514 was incorporated in 1966 as Article 1 in the two UN human rights covenants, the International Covenant on Civil and Political Rights ("ICCPR") and the International Covenant on Economic, Social and Cultural Rights ("ICESCR"). However, the Charter, the Declaration, the Covenants, nor any other international law instrument define the "peoples" who hold the right. The meaning of "self-determination" and "peoples" are highly disputed and appear to fluctuate widely with UN practice.[14]

What "peoples" are nationals of a territory and entitled to rights in and to that territory, and when a territory becomes a state, are also highly contested, as the cases of Namibia, Palestine, W. Sahara and Tibet painfully illustrate. [15] The determination of who the 'nationals' are of a territory that has undergone a change in status depends on the reasons for the territorial change. If the territorial status has changed as a result of occupation, international law is quite clear that such occupation cannot deprive the habitual residents of that territory of their nationality rights in it, nor can the occupier's settlers acquire nationality in that territory –the transplantation of settlers into occupied territory is manifestly illegal.[16] On the other hand, if the change in territorial status is due to state succession in the absence of occupation, the rules governing nationality rights for habitual residents and nationals of the prior territory are more complex. Simply put, the thrust of the rules on successor states is that habitual residents of the territory are presumptively granted the nationality of the successor state; they cannot be 'arbitrarily' deprived of the new nationality of the successor state; they must have the voluntary choice of national status if they are entitled to more than one nationality; and the successor state cannot deprive habitual residents of nationality under any circumstances if to do so would render them stateless.[17]

Of course, the trigger question in the situations examined here is whether the territories are occupied as a matter of international law. In the Namibia case, the consensus view by 1945, when the UN Charter came into force, was that classic 'colonization' was occupation, and illegal under the Charter, whether through the Mandate system or otherwise. The colonization determination has not been so clear for the other territories under consideration, making the decision of who their 'nationals' are, a far more contested matter. Bound up with the right of "peoples" to self-determination in the context of decolonization are the complicating factors from the perspective of the UN of territorial aggression, prolonged occupation, and settler implantation. These factors were present in Namibia, but did not prevent ultimate independence. They remain major barriers to the realization of self-determination in the three other cases under consideration, and despite *jus cogens* and peremptory norms prohibiting them, the UN has been incapable of enforcing the prohibitions in favor of realizing self-determination for the peoples in question.

When a territory becomes a 'state' is yet another difficult question demanding a formula to help resolve which peoples have rights to that particular territory. There are two views of exactly when a territory or people are a "state" as a matter of international law, and the global community of states has not acted consistently on the issue.[18] The most commonly accepted standard for the elements of statehood is the

Montevideo Convention on the Rights and Duties of States (1933).[19] This Convention defines the criteria of a state as a permanent population with a defined territory, government, and the capacity to enter into relations with other states.[20] Since Montevideo, it is also claimed that an additional element is required for statehood: independence.[21] One position is that statehood is a function of the declaration and recognition by other states; the other is that statehood is a function of recognition plus other factors, which may or may not include independence.[22] Historically, there are many examples of states that have been recognized without having territorial independence, including our primary illustration, Namibia.[23]

A struggle over territory and the rights of peoples to it, inevitably involves armed conflict, and the right to resort to force of arms is intrinsically connected with the self-determination question. The use of armed force *against* a people recognized as having the right to self-determination is absolutely prohibited under the UN Charter, as a peremptory or *jus cogens* norm of international law. The prohibition against preventing dependent peoples from realizing self-determination "reached peremptory status in the course of the massive decolonization process."[24] The UN Charter is explicit on the prohibition of the use of force in Article 2(4), and authorizes the Security Council ("UNSC") to intervene militarily or otherwise to prevent "breaches of the peace and acts of aggression" under Chapter VII. In 1975, the UNGA defined what constituted "acts of aggression" in UNGA Res 3314, including:

> The invasion or attack by the armed forces of a State of the territory of another State, or any military occupation, however temporary, resulting from such invasion or attack, or any annexation by the use of force of the territory of another State or part thereof.[25]

The Rome Statute of the International Criminal Court (ICC), adopted in July 1998, although listing the "crime of aggression," did not initially incorporate a definition. In June 2010, the definition of the "crime of aggression" was incorporated into Article 8 of the Statute, reading, in relevant part:

> 1. For the purpose of this Statute, "crime of aggression" means the planning, preparation, initiation or execution, by a person in a position effectively to exercise control over or to direct the political or military action of a State, of an act of aggression which, by its character, gravity and scale, constitutes a manifest violation of the Charter of the United Nations.

> 2. For the purpose of paragraph 1, "act of aggression" means the use of armed force by a State against the sovereignty, territorial integrity or political independence of another State, or in any other manner inconsistent with the Charter of the United Nations. Any of the following acts, regardless of a declaration of war, shall, in accordance with United Nations General Assembly resolution 3314 (XXIX) of 14 December 1974, qualify as an act of aggression:
>
> (a) The invasion or attack by the armed forces of a State of the territory of another State, or any military occupation, however temporary, resulting from such invasion or attack, or any annexation by the use of force of the territory of another State or part thereof. . . [26]

Military occupation, whether short or long term, constitutes a crime of aggression under contemporary international law under the Rome Statute, and can be prosecuted in the ICC. The feasibility of prosecution in the cases under consideration is another matter, but the illegality of the acts involved in the occupations in these cases precedes the codification of 'aggression' in the Rome Statute. The laws and legal proscriptions on occupation long pre-date the UN Charter, going back to the 1907 Hague Convention Respecting the Laws and Customs of War on Land and Its Annex: Regulations Concerning the Laws and Customs of War on Land.[27] Neither the Hague Regulations nor the Fourth Geneva Convention prohibit occupation *per se* but even they place limitations on acts an occupier can take in the territory occupied. Among those limitations are the proscription against changing the laws in place in the territory, imposing its own laws, and exploiting the resources or property of the occupied area for its own economic benefit.[28] Two corollary prohibitions under the law of occupation are now war crimes under the Rome Statute of the International Criminal Court: [29] the prohibition against the transfer of an occupier's population into occupied territory and the deportation of the indigenous people outside of the occupied area.[30] Moreover, the Geneva Conventions of 1949 expanded the definition of "occupation" and "protected persons" to periods of occupation that are not militarily opposed.[31]

The thrust of these rules is clear: an occupier does not acquire sovereignty over the territory it occupies, regardless of the length of occupation. Whether occupation is legal or illegal in general (depending on the binding nature of the governing treaties), in the cases of Namibia, W. Sahara, and Palestine, the actions of the occupiers have been viewed as illegal or in contravention of the right to self-determination of the peoples involved as a matter of customary law, underscored by specific pronouncements as such from the International Court of Justice ("ICJ.").[32] Although there is a strong basis to conclude that Tibet is illegally occupied under general international law, in the consensus of academics, civil society and within certain governments, such consensus is for the most part lacking from the UN political organs and in the public positions of most UN member states.[33]

Finally, as part of its decolonization framework, the UN has very explicitly authorized the use of force for liberation movements seeking to implement the right of self-determination. The right of resistance against colonialism or denial of self-determination has been spelled out in a series of UN resolutions since at least 1970. UNGA Resolution 2621 (XXV) of October 12, 1970, articulates the right to act against and resist subjugation, domination, and exploitation. In two important paragraphs, the Resolution states that the UNGA: "declares the further continuation of colonialism in all its forms and manifestations a crime" constituting a violation of the UN Charter, and "reaffirms the inherent right of colonial peoples to struggle by all necessary means at their disposal against colonial powers."[34] The Resolution incorporated very specific language that member states had an obligation to support the struggle of African territories against apartheid, through sanctions and other means against South Africa. The principle of the right to resistance through armed struggle is confirmed by Art. 1(4) of Protocol 1 of the Fourth Geneva Convention (1977), which defines the fight for self-determination as an international armed conflict and a "war of liberation."[35] Art. 1 recognizes the right of resistance in wars of national liberation, including the use of military force.[36] The UN has explicitly endorsed this right for Namibia, W. Sahara, and Palestine.[37]

What made Namibia's bid for independence successful in the face of enormous odds, while W. Sahara, Tibet, and Palestine have been unable to achieve self-determination or independence with similar (though not identical) forces against them? Has the UN's intervention differed in any meaningful way in these cases? Is territorial independence a *sine qua non* to resolving these protracted refugee problems, or are there other options consistent with the UN's approach toward these issues? Must Palestine, W. Sahara, and Tibet also succeed in obtaining independence like Namibia in order to resolve their refugee crises, or does the UN's framework in these cases suggest other strategies towards resolution? How does the Namibian case help identify strategies for Palestine, Tibet, and W. Sahara to resolve their protracted refugee situations?

These questions require unpacking the key factors that contributed to achieving independence and the return of refugees in Namibia, beginning with the UN's view of self-determination and its perspectives on each of the refugee crises.

The UN's Approach to Self-Determination and Refugees: Namibia, Palestine, W. Sahara and Tibet

Namibia

South Africa sought to fully incorporate Namibia as South African territory during the Mandate period. However, the UN refused South Africa's bid of territorial incorporation and the UNGA voted to put Namibia under trusteeship under Ch. XII of the UN Charter.[38] South Africa objected, beginning a lengthy battle in the UN Almost immediately, the UNGA filed the first of three requests for Advisory Opinions from the ICJ on various questions relating to the status of Namibia.[39] The UNSC later filed another request for an Advisory Opinion with the ICJ,[40] and Liberia and Ethiopia filed a contentious case challenging South Africa's apartheid policies and failure to comply with UN requirements towards South West Africa.[41]

In the first of the UNGA's requested advisory opinions, the International Status of South West Africa, the ICJ found that South Africa retained its obligations as Mandatory, that the UNGA was legally bound to perform supervisory functions formerly performed by the League, that South Africa had to submit to UNGA supervision and file annual reports, but that it did not have to put Namibia under UN Trusteeship.[42] However, the ICJ also found that South Africa could not unilaterally modify the status of Namibia because that required UN consent. South Africa rejected the Opinion. The UNGA submitted two subsequent advisory opinions relating to South West Africa/Namibia: Voting Procedures on Questions Relating to Reports and Petitions Concerning the Territory of South West Africa, and Admissibility of Hearings of Petitioners by the Committee on South West Africa. [43]

In a series of resolutions following the first Advisory Opinion in 1950, the UNGA established multiple UN Committees to address the South West Africa issue: The Committee on South West Africa (1953); the Good Offices Committee (1957); and two Special, or *Ad Hoc*, Committees on South West Africa (1970).[44] The UNGA as early as 1957 requested the Committee on South West Africa to determine what legal action was available to the UN to ensure that South Africa complied with its obligations. In response, the Committee submitted a special report discussing what legal actions were open to the UN to compel South Africa to comply.[45] It was on the recommendation of this report that Ethiopia and Liberia, former members of the League of Nations and now UN members, decided to file a contentious case in the ICJ—the case that was ultimately filed as the South West Africa Cases (*Ethiopia and Liberia vs. South Africa*). The Committees were tasked with furthering the goal of independence for Namibia; for example, the *Ad Hoc Committee for South West Africa* was required to recommend "means of administering South West Africa to enable the people of the territory to exercise self-determination and achieve independence."[46] Throughout this period, South Africa refused to put Namibia under trusteeship or to fulfill any mandate obligations.

In October 1966, the UN terminated South Africa's Mandate and placed Namibia under direct UN responsibility. In 1967, the UNGA established the Namibian Council to administer the territory until independence.[47] The UNSC then sought an Advisory Opinion asking what states' obligations were given South Africa's continuing intransigence.[48] In its Advisory Opinion to the UNSC, the ICJ affirmed the legal framework set up by the UNGA, and held that the ultimate objective of the Mandates was self-determination and independence of the administered states.[49] The ICJ further found that South Africa's Mandate was properly terminated, its continued presence in Namibia was illegal, and it was required to withdraw from the territory. The Court also found that member states were obliged not to recognize or support South African presence in Namibia, including the obligation not to enter into treaties and economic and other dealings with South Africa.

The UNSC accepted the Opinion, declared South African occupation an internationally wrongful act, threatened Ch. VII action, and requested a review of treaties involving South African relations in Namibia.[50] The UNGA dissolved the Special Committee and transferred the question of South West Africa to the Special Committee on the Situation with regard to the Implementation of the Declaration on the Granting of Independence to Colonial Countries and Peoples (Special Committee of Twenty-Four). Following the first report of this Committee, the UNGA passed Resolution 1899, which required all states to refrain from supplying arms, equipment, petroleum and other goods to South Africa, and to "refrain from any action which might hamper implementation of the present resolution and prior UNGA resolutions on South West Africa."[51] These led to the initiation of the sanctions regime against South Africa.

Meanwhile, refugees had been fleeing Namibia to neighboring states since 1960, and in increasingly large numbers through the 1970s and 1980s, primarily to Zambia and Tanzania. With the establishment of the South West Africa People's Organization ("SWAPO") and its military arm, the People's Liberation Army of Namibia ("PLAN") in 1960, the reception and maintenance of the refugees was organized and coordinated directly by these entities representing the Namibian government-in exile.[52] In 1976 the UNSC passed Resolution 385, a legal framework for the transfer of power, free elections, and territorial integrity of Namibia. The Secretary General drafted a settlement that was later adopted by the UNSC as Resolution 435. In Resolution 435, the UNSC adopted the Secretary General's view that the return of the refugees should not be contingent on independence, but that refugee return was a prerequisite to a fair pre-independence electoral process.[53]

According to the Proposal for a Settlement of the Namibian Situation, addressed to the President of the UNSC, the UN "will ensure that Namibians remaining outside of Namibia are given a free and voluntary choice whether to return. Provision will be made to attest to the voluntary nature of decisions made by Namibians who elect not to return to Namibia."[54] The United Nations High Commissioner for Refugees (UNHCR) was tasked to oversee a repatriation process that was to take place within six weeks of UN authorization, to ensure that all repatriations were voluntary, and to assist in resettlement of those not choosing to return.[55]

SWAPO committed to the UN framework on behalf of the Namibian people's liberation movement. Actual implementation of the Resolution was delayed for a decade, however, due to the ongoing conflict between SWAPO and its Cuban and Angolan supporters on the one hand and South Africa on the other, and the refusal of South Africa to give full amnesty to the returning refugees. Still, the repatriation of over 40,000 refugees took place prior to the elections of November 1989, ensuring an easy victory of SWAPO to form the first independent Namibian government.[56] The small number of refugees compared to the number of Sahrawi, Palestinian, and Tibetan refugees must be understood in the context of the small population of Namibia at the time of barely 1.6 million people. UNHCR maintained a short presence after independence, with almost no involvement in reintegration of returnees, which was entirely taken over by the SWAPO government.

Ultimately, South Africa entered into an agreement with Cuba and Angola about withdrawal of all troops, and recognized the right of self-determination, independence, and equality for South West Africa. Most states refused to recognize South Africa's claims to Namibia after Resolution 435, even though independence did not come about until 1990, after the 1988 tripartite agreement with Cuba and South Africa.[57] In other words, most of the world community of states dealt with the Namibian Council as the lawful administrative authority over Namibia at least a full decade before actual independence. During this time, within the UN's framework, Namibia was able to consolidate resources on its territory, set the sanctions regime against South Africa in place, and continue its armed resistance until final withdrawal of foreign forces and the agreement for independence from South Africa.[58] In the Namibia case, then, independence was not a prerequisite to achieving the main goals of self-determination—the end of apartheid, non-recognition of South African claims to its territory, its right to armed resistance to achieve the withdrawal of South Africa, and return of refugees in advance of elections or territorial independence.

Although South Africa did not recognize Namibian independence and did not withdraw from its territory until 1988-1990, the world community, following the actions taken at the UN and at the ICJ, created a defined legal framework for Namibia's status, declared its independence, imposed sanctions on South Africa, and created the mechanisms to implement independence over a period of 20 years before independence was actually achieved. And this was so, even though the UNSC never actually voted to take Chapter VII enforcement action to force South African withdrawal from South West Africa. Much of these developments occurred through a robust legal strategy involving submissions to the ICJ from the start, and the aggressive work, led by the Afro-Asian bloc and the Non-Aligned states along with the Committee of Twenty-Four in the UNGA to assert, advocate for, and litigate to preserve Namibian rights and resources within and outside the UN itself.

The UN's approach towards the Namibian, Palestinian, Sahrawi, and Tibetan claims to self-determination has meant something different in each of these cases. In W. Sahara, the UN's position evolved from a framework for self-determination and independence to a commitment today to a negotiated referendum that could include an independent state or some other form of autonomy within the Moroccan state. On W. Sahara, the ICJ has articulated an obligation for the international community *erga omnes* not to recognize Morocco as the colonial power, but the UN appears to have backed away from that commitment in favor of a negotiated framework with Morocco over terms of a referendum.

In the case of Palestine, the UN has interpreted self-determination as meaning full independence, but has changed its position on the question of *from* which country Palestinians are entitled to self-determination. Prior to 1947, Palestine as a Class A mandate territory was to exercise this right in all of historic Palestine as a former colony of the Ottoman Empire; the self-determination framework adopted by the UN in the late 1960's positions this right vis-à-vis Israel as the occupying power in only the West Bank and Gaza. Thus, the UN has insisted on an 'independent state' in noncontiguous territory with borders roughly on the 1967 Armistice Lines of the West Bank and Gaza for Palestine, in an area which is no more than 22% of mandate Palestine. [59]

In both the Palestinian and W. Sahara cases, although their claims towards territorial independence have ripened within the UN and the view of the international community, the UNSC has been unwilling or unable to engage Chapter VII action to secure the legal rights it claims to have guaranteed. The UN's approach towards Tibet has focused on curbing Chinese human rights violations against the Tibetan people and perhaps, at maximum, an endorsement of some type of Tibetan political representation within China.

Palestine

Palestinians were recognized as a distinct nationality under international law by 1924, by virtue of their inclusion as such in the Treaty of Lausanne of August 6 of that year. In 1925, Britain, holding the Mandate over Palestine, passed legislation conforming to the international status that recognized Palestine citizenship, and issued thousands of Palestinian passports pursuant to its citizenship legislation.[60] British (and other) courts recognized Palestinian nationality in decisions throughout the Mandate period, and Israeli courts did so as late as 1950. [61] In fact, in enacting its 'Citizenship (Nationality) Law,' Israel expressly repealed Palestinian citizenship—an act that UN bodies have challenged as illegal under international law because of its discriminatory basis, which is discussed below.

The territory of Palestine was administered as a Class A mandate through the League of Nations, and was the only one of the Class A territories *not* to achieve independence by the time the League terminated in 1946.[62] In 1946, the Arab states objected to continuing Palestine's UN trusteeship status. Similar to South Africa's Mandate over Namibia, the UN accepted Britain's commitment to its Mandate obligations rather than put Palestine under direct UN trusteeship. It is important to note the inconsistencies in Great Britain's role as mandatory power: Great Britain had, on the one hand, committed to bringing Palestine to independence, while simultaneously committing to a national home for the Jewish people in Palestine through the Balfour Declaration.[63] The UNGA's *Ad Hoc Committee* to study proposals on the future government of Palestine rejected the Arab and other states' initial proposals to seek an ICJ Advisory Opinion and instead recommended Partition.[64]

The UNGA then passed Resolution 181 in November 1947, recommending partition of Palestine into two states.[65] By the end of 1947, there were 1,230,000 Palestinians, comprising 2/3 of the population of Palestine, and 610,000 Jews, comprising 1/3 of the population. The Jewish community owned no more than 7% of the land of Palestine. The Partition Resolution, however, allocated 55% of Mandate Palestine to the 'Jewish State' and 44% of Palestine to the 'Arab State.'[66] Resolution 181 was a compromise between satisfying the demands of the Zionist movement and the commitment to the independence of the Palestinian 'peoples' in the League Covenant under its Article 22, and later by the United Nations.

The Resolution referred to the Arab and Jewish communities living in Palestine as the 'two Palestinian Peoples' and required that each of the new states enact a constitution specifically guaranteeing equal rights for all citizens of the territory, the protection of religious and political rights of minorities, and the free choice of citizenship in either of the new states. The territories were to remain under UN supervision until they enacted constitutions meeting these requirements.[67] It is important to note that, in contrast to the recognition of Palestinian nationality, the UN did not, through Resolution 181 or any subsequent Resolution, recognize 'Jewish nationality.' The national groups to be granted citizenship in the new states under 181 were Palestinian nationals recognized as such under the 1925 Mandate legislation and their descendants, as well as all those, Jews and Arabs, who were habitual residents of Palestine at the time of the Partition Resolution. The Resolution did not recognize the claims of the Zionist movement to 'Jewish nationality' on an extraterritorial basis (that is, to Jews around the world who were not territorially connected to Palestine). As the King-Crane Report had stated: "For a national home for the Jewish people is not equivalent to making Palestine into a Jewish State; nor can the erection of such a Jewish State be accomplished without the gravest trespass upon the civil and religious rights of existing non-Jewish communities in Palestine."[68]

When the inevitable armed conflict ensued in response to Resolution 181, the Zionist militias gained control of 77% of historic Palestine beyond the borders of territory designated under Resolution 181 and Israel declared its state in the enlarged territory on May 1948. Israel failed to comply with the prerequisites of the Resolution in proclaiming its state.[69] Unlike Namibia, however, the UN did not affirm the territorial integrity of Palestine, or move to enforce the terms of Resolution 181. Surprisingly, after Resolution 181 passed, the UNSC first asked members to study partition of Israel/Palestine, but then backed away from it, requesting the UNGA to reconsider alternatives, including a possible trusteeship for

Palestine.[70] However, also unlike Namibia, which was eventually placed under UN trusteeship, UN trusteeship over Palestine never materialized. The UN instead admitted Israel as a member in 1949, pending compliance with UNGA Resolution 194. This key Resolution, passed on December 11, 1948, incorporated the individual rights of refugee return, restitution and compensation.[71] As with Resolution 181, Israel failed to comply with the critical provisions of Resolution 194 concerning the obligation to accept return of the refugees after its admission to the UN.

Soon after 181 passed, the UNGA and the UNSC began to act in very different and inconsistent ways towards Palestine. The UNGA developed a significant body of Resolutions affirming both individual rights—refugee return, property restitution, and compensation—and collective rights of self-determination, statehood, and independence. After 1967, these Resolutions framed the collective rights only with respect to the part of Palestine not recognized as sovereign Israeli territory, that is, the territories occupied by Israel since 1967. The UNGA, however, has insisted on the framework of both individual and collective rights for peace negotiations.[72] In contrast, the UNSC's framework has almost exclusively focused on Resolutions 242 and 338 as the basis of a negotiated solution.[73] These two resolutions create the "land for peace" formula that suggest that the only legal framework necessary to resolve the conflict is Israeli withdrawal from the 1967-Israeli Occupied Palestinian Territory (OPT), including the option of some exchange of territory, for a permanent peace.[74]

Without outside pressure to push back against the consistent US veto supporting Israel's positions at the UNSC, the UNSC has remained consistent in reaffirming only Resolutions 242 and 338 as the basis for a negotiated peace, and has refused to accept the framework for individual refugee rights.[75] In other words, the UNSC's framework focuses solely on satisfaction of the collective right to self-determination within some part of the 1967 territories, without incorporating resolution of the individual rights of Palestinian refugees. In turn, the negotiation framework from Oslo onwards has referenced only Resolutions 242 and 338 and none of the UNGA individual rights resolutions.[76] The negotiations framework to date has proceeded on the premise that 'Palestine' is or will be a state in the OPT. Even the most recent framework established in April 2002 by the 'Quartet'—comprising the Russian Federation, the United States, the European Union, and the UN—assumes that a Palestinian state could be established prior to the conclusion of final status negotiations with Israel.[77] The Quartet's framework is that, based on negotiated agreements, the Palestinian Authority (PA) can assert its claim to statehood with provisional borders and attributes of sovereignty even before full Israeli withdrawal. That was also the basis of the Oslo Accords.[78]

In 2013, 5.3 million Palestinian refugees were registered with the United Nations Relief and Works Agency ("UNRWA"), the specialized agency established to provide humanitarian assistance for Palestinian refugees under UNGA Resolution 302(IV) of December 8, 1949.[79] As Karen AbuZayd notes, the UNGA passed Resolution 194 (III) on December 11, 1948, hard on the heels of the massive exodus of between 700,000-800,000 refugees from Palestine.[80] Resolution 194 established the first agency with a protection mandate for the Palestinian refugees, the United Nations Conciliation Commission for Palestine ("UNCCP"). However, because of the UN's view that Palestinians were a separate and special refugee situation, Palestinian refugees have been defined differently by various UN agencies and in treaties affecting their rights.

The "refugees" whose "rights, property and interests" the UNCCP was designed to protect were defined on a group or category basis: all persons displaced from their homes in Palestine due to the 1947-1949 conflict.[81] This definition encompasses over 8 million Palestinians today. The UNCCP was unable to fulfill its mandate of ensuring the return, property restitution and compensation for losses of the refugees as required by Resolution 194's para. 11 on the one hand, and mediate a final resolution to the conflict between the warring parties, as required by Resolution 194's para. 6, on the other.

Nevertheless, the existence of the UNCCP with an explicit international protection mandate towards the refugees, and the establishment of UNRWA to provide international humanitarian assistance towards the refugees, led the UN delegates drafting the statute of the UNHCR, the 1951 Refugee Convention/1967 Protocol and the 1954 Convention on Stateless Persons to preclude the application of those instruments to Palestinian refugees. The dual UN agency framework of UNCCP and UNRWA for achieving the prescribed solution explains the Palestinian "exclusion clauses" of Article 1D in the Refugee Convention, paragraph 7 (c) in the UNHCR Statute, and Article 1(2) of the Convention on Stateless Persons. The UN intended the para. 11 formula to apply to all Palestinians encompassed in the group definition of Resolution 194, not just the subset of Palestinian refugees registered with UNRWA—that is, all Palestinians displaced from Palestine as a result of the 1947-49 conflict, the over 8 million persons mentioned above who fit this definition today.[82]

The ambiguities created by the differing mandates of UN agencies and differing definitions of "Palestinian refugee" have led to widely divergent interpretations of who *are* Palestinian refugees, to what benefits they are entitled, and who is covered by the various legal obligations the UN has mandated for them through Resolutions and UN institutions.[83] The exclusion clauses in the various instruments defining and affecting Palestinians as refugees have led to a "protection gap" for this population since the *de facto* demise of the UNCCP.

UNRWA provides assistance to the subset of Palestinian refugees registered with the Agency in the host countries in which most of them reside, yet UNRWA has no mandate to seek or implement durable solutions for them. UNHCR has no mandate over Palestinians in the UNRWA host states, but has interpreted the exclusion clause in its Statute, para. 7(c) as meaning that it does have a mandate towards Palestinian refugees outside the UNRWA areas. UNHCR has not, however, intervened to protect the rights and interests of Palestinians as spelled out in Resolution 194, particularly their right of return, and has not intervened to protect their rights as stateless persons. Despite the ambiguities, the UNGA has never wavered from the para. 11 formula in Resolution 194. In fact, this Resolution is of a unique character, as it has been affirmed through an overwhelming majority vote every year by the UNGA since its passage, representing the consensus of the community of states that the refugees must be allowed to return "to their homes," obtain restitution of their properties and compensation for losses, regardless of what territorial solution is ultimately negotiated.[84]

The political organs of the UN have been outpaced by the work of the human rights bodies, however, which have developed a significant body of soft law in the form of Concluding Observations and Human Rights Council resolutions.[85] Beginning in the late 1990s, the human rights treaty bodies began a sustained focus on the violation of individual rights of Palestinians, including refugees and displaced persons. All of the treaty bodies have rejected Israel's position that its obligations under the human rights treaties do not extend to the OPT, declaring that to be a violation of each of the treaties. The Committee on Economic, Social and Cultural Rights ("CESCR") has found systemic treaty violations with regard to Israel's treatment of Palestinians through the institutionalized discrimination against Palestinians emanating from the "excessive emphasis on the State as a 'Jewish State'", and through such laws as the Israeli Nationality Law and the Absentee Property laws.[86] The CESCR has affirmed that Israeli settlements, removal of Palestinians and expropriation of their properties, demolition of Palestinian homes, and denial of Palestinian family reunification and residency rights violate Israel's obligations under the treaty. For example, in its June 2003 Concluding Observations, the CESCR noted:

> 18. The Committee is particularly concerned about the status of 'Jewish nationality,' which is a ground for exclusive preferential treatment for persons of Jewish nationality under the Israeli Law of Return, granting them automatic citizenship and financial government benefits, thus resulting in practice in discriminatory treatment against non-Jews, in particular Palestinian refugees. The Committee is also concerned about the practice of restrictive family reunification with regard to Palestinians, which has been adopted for reasons of national security.[87]

The institutionalized discrimination against Palestinians on the basis of legislation preferencing Jews over non-Jews is at the heart of the denial of Palestinian refugee return and property restitution, and has been consistently declared a violation of the human rights treaties not only by the CESCR, but by the Committees Against Torture ("CAT"), Rights of the Child ("CRC"), Against Racial Discrimination ("CERD"), and Discrimination Against Women ("CEDAW").[88] The CERD has found Israel's institutionalized preferencing of its Jewish citizens in land, citizenship/nationality and other laws, both within Israel and in the OPT, to be illegal discrimination under the Convention. In particularly strong language in its 2012 Concluding Observations, the CERD found that the separate legal regime applicable to Palestinians in East Jerusalem and the OPT to be "racial segregation and apartheid" in violation of Article 3 of the Convention.[89]

The Human Rights Council's 33 resolutions on Israel since 2006 have condemned violations of human rights and humanitarian law concerning Palestinians, particularly with regard to the denial of their rights to self-determination. In March, 2007, for example, the Council resolved that:

> The construction of the wall by Israel, the occupying Power, in the Occupied Palestinian Territory, including East Jerusalem, along with measures previously taken, severely impedes the right of the Palestinian people to self-determination. . . . [The Council] [s]tresses the need for respect for and preservation of the territorial unity, contiguity and integrity of all of the Occupied Palestinian Territory, including East Jerusalem. . . [and] [u]rges all Member States and relevant bodies of the United Nations system to support and assist the Palestinian people in the early realization of their right to self-determination. . . .[90]

These resolutions and concluding observations have been important sources of lawmaking for Palestinians, both refugees and non-refugees, in addition to the ICJ Advisory Opinion on the Wall, discussed below. On November 22, 1974, the UNGA adopted Resolution 3237, which granted the Palestine Liberation Organization ("PLO") "Observer" status within the UN, [91] allowing it to participate in all the sessions and the work of the UN, effectively as a "quasi-state."[92] In 1975, the UNGA passed Resolution 3376, establishing the *Committee on the Exercise of the Inalienable Rights of the Palestinian People*, entrusted to work towards Palestinian independence and sovereignty, and to implement the individual rights spelled out in prior UNGA resolutions. The Committee was also tasked to work with civil society organizations to accomplish its goals. Subsequently, on 2 December 1977, the *Division for Palestinian Rights* was set up by UNGA Resolution 32/40B, to support and assist the Committee in its work, and to be a liaison with civil society organizations working on Palestinian issues. Over the years, a network of over a thousand such organizations has cooperated in various ways with the Committee to help pursue these goals. Moreover, the Palestinian cause has a solid bloc of support within the UN, support that has been underutilized by the Palestinian leadership in achieving its goals.

Today, Palestine, like Namibia, has statehood recognition by the overwhelming majority of states, as well as "non-member state" status in the UNGA Statehood recognition, however, has been granted based on the condition that Israeli sovereignty over the part of Palestine conquered in 1948 is respected, that is, Palestinian statehood and independence is to be exercised only in the 1967 OPT. The practical consequences of such recognition cannot be realized because Israel has refused to recognize Palestinian statehood and continues to occupy its territory. Finally, the UN's approach is conflicted: the world community has recognized Palestinian statehood through its overwhelming vote at the UNGA, but because of the US veto the UNSC has not recognized Palestine as a UN member state. [93] Thus, from the UN political organ's perspective, Palestinian statehood and independence, as well as a solution of the refugee problem, must be the outcome of a peace agreement with Israel, rather than insisting on a settlement in accordance with international law.

Western Sahara

W. Sahara, unlike Palestine and Namibia, was not a League of Nations Mandate, but a Spanish colony from 1885-1975. In the decolonization efforts following the adoption of the UN Charter, W. Sahara was declared first a non-self-governing territory, and then entitled to self-determination by the UN[94] Resolution 1514 became the foundation for the UNGA's position that W. Sahara was entitled to self-determination, and it passed several resolutions calling on Spain to bring about Sahrawi independence through a UN supervised referendum.[95] Spain took steps to grant more autonomy to W. Sahara, and established a local government for the territory in the face of competing claims by Morocco and Mauritania, which sought some form of union between W. Sahara and their countries.[96]

The Sahrawi took matters into their own hands, establishing the *Popular Front for the Liberation of Saguia el-Hamra and Rio de Oro,* the POLISARIO Front, in 1973, and negotiating an agreement with Spain to protect their interests and to demand a UN brokered referendum. [97] In 1974, the UNGA, prompted by Morocco and Mauritania, requested both an Advisory Opinion on the status of the territory, and that Spain postpone the referendum. In quick succession, a UN mission called for by the Committee of Twenty-Four found that the Sahrawi by an overwhelming majority sought independence, and, on request by the UNGA, the ICJ issued its W. Sahara Advisory Opinion.[98] The Opinion stated that the territory had not been *terra nullius*; the Sahrawi people were the indigenous inhabitants of the territory, they were entitled to self-determination in their territory, and neither Morocco nor Mauritania had any superseding claims to the territory.[99] The ICJ W. Sahara Advisory Opinion drew two important conclusions. First, the Court found that the legal basis for self-determination for the territory was in its relationship to Spain, the former colonial power, not Morocco, the occupying power. Second, the Opinion interpreted UNGA Resolution 1514, the Declaration on Colonial Countries, as "confirming that the application of the right of self-determination requires a free and genuine expression of the will of the peoples concerned."[100] The 'peoples concerned' were the Sahrawi people.

Spain gave up its claims under the Madrid Accords of 1975, and declared an interim administration that included Morocco and Mauritania.[101] Under the Agreement, Spain relinquished administration, but not sovereignty (which it did not possess) over W. Sahara to Morocco and Mauritania. According to the Agreement, Spain was to "set up an interim government in the territory with the participation of Morocco and Mauritania and the collaboration of the Yema'a. The responsibilities and powers as administrative authority will be transferred to this government."[102]

In defiance of the Advisory Opinion, Morocco organized its "Green March" in October of 1975, in which hundreds of thousands of its citizens invaded W. Sahara to claim it as Moroccan territory. Other than re-affirming the Sahrawis' right to self-determination, the UN did not intervene, and fighting broke out between Moroccan and Mauritanian forces on the one hand and the POLISARIO Front on the other, compelling thousands of Sahrawi to flee to Algeria. On February 27, 1976, the POLISARIO declared the independence of the Sahrawi Arab Democratic Republic ("SADR"), and Morocco and Mauritania reacted by partitioning the territory.[103] The Moroccan-Mauritanian treaty of partition gave Morocco about two-thirds of the territory of W. Sahara, and when Mauritania relinquished its claims in 1979, Morocco moved in to occupy what was left. Today, Morocco occupies eighty percent of W. Sahara; with the Sahrawi population divided between the Moroccan-occupied area and the Tindouf camps in Algeria, separated by the Moroccan-constructed berm.[104]

From 1976-1983, the UN relinquished responsibility over the W. Saharan question to the Organization of African Unity ("OAU") as a regional issue. In July, 1978, the OAU Assembly established an Ad Hoc Committee of Heads of State and Government to seek a solution of the W. Sahara problem on the basis of self-determination.[105] The Ad Hoc Committee presented a set of conclusions that called for the free exercise of the right to self-determination through a referendum to be administered by the UN and the OAU. The OAU Assembly endorsed the Committee's conclusions at the 16th Ordinary Session a year later.[106] The referendum proposal was accepted, in principle at least, by the King of Morocco, and the OAU Assembly proceeded to establish an Implementation Committee to carry out the referendum process.[107] The OAU established the framework for participation in a referendum on self-determination through the work of the Implementation Committee.[108] The framework included a proposal to establish an impartial interim administration with the mandate to set up and conduct the referendum; an arrangement for secret ballots to include options for independence or integration with Morocco; and a cease-fire to be monitored by a peace-keeping force. These proposals were all endorsed by the OAU Assembly.[109] Morocco refused any further cooperation in carrying out the proposals for a referendum, and the OAU decided to recognize the SADR as a member of that body in November, 1984.

Subsequent to recognition of the SADR by 26 of the OAU states, the SADR was admitted to the OAU Council of Ministers. Morocco resigned from the OAU in protest. The SADR went on to be a founding member of the African Union ("AU"), while Morocco remains the only African country that refuses to become an AU member. From 1986 onwards, in the face of stalemate at the OAU/AU, the issue returned to the UN.[110] UN Secretary-General Perez de Cuellar initiated a cease-fire and referendum proposal to the POLISARIO Front and Morocco in 1988. The Secretary-General, however, moved away from the OAU proposal of a referendum leading directly to independence. Rather than a framework to be instituted and enforced by the UN, the Secretary General's Settlement Plan called for a referendum to be accomplished through direct negotiations between the parties.[111] Under the Plan, the UN would supervise a ceasefire between Morocco and the POLISARIO Front, followed by a referendum giving the Sahrawi the option of independence or integration with Morocco.[112] The Plan required establishment of an Identification Commission to "implement the agreed position of the parties that all Western Saharans counted in the 1974 census undertaken by the Spanish authorities and aged 18 years or over will have the right to vote, whether currently present in the Territory or outside as refugees or for other reasons."[113]

In April 1991, the UNSC established the United Nations Mission for the Referendum in W. Sahara ("MINURSO"), a monitoring force for the ceasefire.[114] MINURSO was charged with a multi-pronged mission beyond the ceasefire monitoring that included the release and exchange of prisoners, implementing repatriations, identifying and registering qualified voters, and organizing a free and fair referendum. To date, the UN's efforts through MINURSO and the Secretary-General have resulted in a voting list of 84,251 names, with many appeals pending, but the Identification Commission set up through MINURSO suspended its work in 2003 with no further progress on the referendum. The POLISARIO Front, along with Algeria and Mauritania as observer countries, accepted the criteria for voter eligibility, but Morocco rejected them. Meanwhile, the Plan (including subsequent versions, the "Baker Plans" of 1997-2004), has stalemated on the eligibility question.

The ICJ W. Sahara Advisory Opinion and UNGA Resolution 1514 established the terms of the self-determination question for the territory and people of W. Sahara.[115] When Spain relinquished her claims, neither Morocco nor Mauritania obtained legal recognition for a claim of sovereignty over W. Sahara—not by the ICJ, nor through the 1975 Madrid Accords. The UNGA confirmed this in Resolution 3458 (XXX).[116] The ICJ has since proclaimed self-determination as a right *erga omnes*.[117] At least in the decolonization context of W. Sahara, the meaning of Resolution 1514 is that self-determination confers on the colonized people a right to free choice about the means to achieve independent statehood, a choice that is to be implemented by the international community as a non-negotiable matter. However, the UN's perspective on W. Sahara has shifted from the obligation to ensure statehood to committing to a referendum on self-determination that *may include* the freedom to choose independence. Falling short of the commitment the UN made towards Namibia, the UN has not been unconditionally committed to independence as the ultimate legally required goal for W. Sahara.[118]

Although the initial UN construct of decolonization of W. Sahara from Spain might have helped advance the independence process for the

Sahrawi at a time when the decolonization framework was a major focus of the UN bodies, the U. N. has all but forgotten Spain's *de jure* continuing colonial administration role or obligation today. The UN appears to have been unable to bridge its ambiguity between recognizing its obligation towards W. Sahara as a former colony entitled to decolonization under UNGA Resolution 1514 and 1541—a position enshrined in the ICJ Advisory Opinion and thus binding on the UN as a matter of law—and Morocco's territorial claims, however specious, that refer to the Sahrawi as a minority population of Morocco. The UNS.C. has not explicitly declared Morocco an illegal occupier of W. Sahara, although the UNG.A. has declared W. Sahara to be occupied in a series of Resolutions since the 1970's. [119] The UN Secretaries-General have also exhibited this ambiguity, with Perez de Cuellar from 1985-1991 advocating for the integration of W. Sahara into Morocco, rather than confirming the ICJ's position in the W. Sahara Advisory Opinion.[120] Meanwhile, many states and particularly large private corporations have *de facto* dealt with Morocco as if it had lawful title over the territory, including entering into economic agreements for the exploitation of W. Sahara mineral, oil and fisheries resources.[121]

As for attributes of statehood, Jeffrey Smith makes the case that most of the Montevideo criteria have been met: defined territory, defined population, and capacity to enter into relations with other states. He underscores the democratic nature of the SADR institutions and their accountability to the entire Sahrawi population in the divided and occupied territories. [122] The SADR's internal structures of democratic accountability are an impressive achievement for a besieged and occupied people, but they have not brought the Sahrawi closer to actual recognition by the community of states. Less than half of the UN member states have recognized the SADR, and the UN has not accepted it as a member of the organization.[123] Yet, neither the UN nor the world community has formally or legally recognized Moroccan title to any part of W. Sahara. At the same time, there appears to be no contest about whom are the "peoples" belonging to the territory of W. Sahara; there is no contest over nationality rights between the Sahrawi and the Moroccans from the perspective of the UN or international consensus.

In W. Sahara, too, the UN perspective is conflicted: the UNGA has made a clear commitment that W. Sahara comprises a defined people and territory with the right to choose the form of self-determination; yet the Secretaries-General and the UNSC have been unwilling (or unable) to take Chapter VII measures to enforce this legal framework. This is particularly problematic following a quarter century of failed efforts to arrange a self-determination referendum.

At the same time, the UN human rights mechanisms, particularly the treaty bodies, have not been silent on W. Sahara. The CESCR has issued Concluding Observations in 2000, 2006, and 2011, focusing on the denial of self-determination.[124] Likewise, the Human Rights Committee, CAT, CRC and CEDAW have issued Concluding Observations decrying violations of human rights as well as Morocco's persistent denial of the Sahrawi's right to self-determination.[125] In 1999, the HRC specifically commented on the referendum process:

> The Committee remains concerned about the very slow pace of the preparations toward a referendum in Western Sahara on the question of self-determination, and at the lack of information on the implementation of human rights in that region.[126]

In 2012, the Human Rights Council held its Universal Periodic Review of Morocco, and ten state delegates for the first time raised Morocco's violations of human rights and the denial of self-determination in W. Sahara.[127] This Review was a breakthrough in terms of challenging Morocco directly within the human rights machinery by UN member states. Unfortunately, the companion effort to introduce a human rights monitoring mechanism into the MINURSO mandate failed at the UNGA the same year.[128] However, the terms of reference for MINURSO—found in the 1990 and 1991 arrangements for the Mission—require securing the public order and establishing the necessary conditions among the civilian population for a referendum to take place. This aspect of the mandate necessarily encompasses a human rights observation and reporting, if not a protection, function.[129] Nevertheless, further progress on realizing Sahrawi self-determination has stalemated in tandem with the stalemate of the referendum itself.

Today, between 150,000 and 200,000 refugees from W. Sahara live in one of four of the remote desert camps of Tindouf, in Algeria.[130] Most live in tents, but many now have more permanent sand-brick homes. UNHCR provides many of the basic necessities for survival for the refugee communities, with other community needs met by the SADR and by Algeria itself. The widespread support for Sahrawi civil and political rights has helped establish a network of official and non-official relationships in neighboring countries that provide education and relatively easy access to work and study in Algeria, Spain and other states. The unique *Vacaciones en Paz*, established by the Asociacion Amigos de Pueblo Saharaui, a Spanish NGO, provides summer programmes with host families in Spain for 7,000 to 10,000 Sahrawi children each year.[131] These summer sojourns establish contacts through informal relationships that help build civil society knowledge and support for the Sahrawi cause. Meanwhile, UNHCR sponsors family visits across the divided territory, and intervenes to ensure family unity for separated Sahrawi families or spouses between the Tindouf camps and occupied W. Sahara, as well as Algeria, Morocco, and Mauritania proper.[132] These transnational networks and relationships are critical for relieving the isolation of the refugees, but are also opportunities for Sahrawi youth to access education, travel, and employment opportunities, ensuring their integration in a globalized society. The refugees, in this sense, are not 'forgotten' or left behind, while their rights to return and implementation of self-determination are on hold. As a practical or legal matter, the return of Sahrawi refugees is not a major factor in ending the conflict or finding an ultimate resolution of the occupation of W. Sahara.

Tibet

In distinct contrast to the cases of Namibia and W. Sahara, the UN has not viewed Tibet as a colonial project entitled to the international commitment towards decolonization embodied in UNGA Resolution 1514.[133] Arguably, of the four territories under examination, Tibet may have the strongest historical claim as an independent state with territorial integrity prior to the United Nations Charter. From 1911 until 1950, Tibet functioned as an independent state, with a centralized government, cabinet, currency, civil service and defined territory and population. In 1913, the 13th Dalai Lama formally proclaimed the restoration of Tibetan independence, and during this period, Tibet engaged in diplomatic relations and executed treaties with other states.[134] In October 1950, China invaded Tibet and coerced a surrender agreement, causing the exodus of the leadership under the Dalai Lama and thousands of refugees.[135] According to van Walt van Praag, "Few scholars seriously challenge the notion that Tibet possessed actual independence at least between 1911 and 1950."[136]

The UN has had minimal intervention in Tibet, providing an extremely weak legal framework on which to base Tibetan self-determination claims. The UNGA has passed only three resolutions on Tibet: 1353 (1959), calling for respect for human rights of the Tibetan people; 1723 (1961), demanding an end to violations of Tibetan human rights and freedoms including the right to self-determination; and 2079 (1965), decrying the continued violation of the fundamental freedoms of the Tibetan people. The UN has never recognized Tibet as an independent state, and the majority of states did not recognize it as such prior to China's invasion in

1950. Neither the UNGA nor the UNSC condemned China for its invasion as a violation of the UN Charter, and the UN appears to have accepted Chinese rule over the "Tibetan Autonomous Region, *de facto* if not *de jure*."[137] Nor has there been reaction from the main UN organs over the effective dismantling of the framework of the 17-Point Agreement by China—already defunct and widely discredited as the result of coercive action over non-representative members of the Tibetan community left behind after the exodus. The agreed-upon Tibetan "self-rule" has been replaced with the national minority policy and direct Chinese Communist Party rule.[138] At the same time, there has been no real contest over Tibetans as a distinct nationality. The Chinese Government itself refers to Tibetans as one of its 'national minority' groups receiving special status under China's Law on Regional National Autonomy.[139]

The UN's perspective on Tibetan self-determination has been confined to a single statement in one of the three UNGA resolutions that were passed between 1959 and 1965. In UNGA Resolution 1723, the UNGA called for a "cessation of practices which deprive the Tibetan people of their fundamental human rights and freedom including their rights to self-determination . . . ."[140] The UNGA Resolutions have called for respect for the "fundamental freedoms" of the Tibetan people, but even in the immediate aftermath of China's invasion of Tibet, the UN failed to condemn Chinese aggression or call for an end to China's occupation of Tibet.[141] That framework has not changed to date, and neither the UN nor the community of states has labeled China an occupying power in Tibet. Not surprisingly given China's seat as a permanent member of the UNSC, that body has never passed a resolution on Tibet.

The weak UN position contrasts sharply with Article 2 of the UN Charter, enshrining the right to self-determination; the expert and academic consensus embodied, for example, in the International Commission of Jurists report on its Fact-Finding Mission to Tibet; and the many governmental statements at an informal level reiterating Tibet's entitlement to self-determination.[142] It is safe to say that Tibet's status as an independent state until 1950, as a matter of the UN Charter and general international law, did not change as a result of China's occupation or the 17-Point Agreement. China's aggressive occupation of Tibet in 1950, a violation of the UN Charter, remains so today, and as a legal matter cannot alter the status of Tibetan territory it occupies. Likewise, the 17-Point Agreement, even if it were legal at the time of signing, has been breached by China both *de facto* and *de jure*, and has been repudiated by the Tibetan leadership, as well.[143] Regardless of the legitimacy of Tibet's historic and legal claim to self-determination under international law, the UN political bodies presently offer no framework to realize such a claim.

The UN treaty bodies have not addressed China's actions towards Tibet in terms of occupation or denial of self-determination, but have done so in terms of the rights of Tibetans as a minority group, and through the lens of ethnic, religious or racial discrimination. The CERD, CAT, CEDAW and CESCR have all issued Concluding Observations on China's treatment of Tibetans that are human rights-focused.[144] CESCR issued Concluding Observations on China for the first time in 2005. Its framing of the violations are typical of the treaty body reports:

> 38. The Committee notes with concern the reports regarding the discrimination of ethnic minorities in the State party, in particular in the field of employment, adequate standard of living, health, education and culture. In this regard, the Committee regrets the insufficient information provided by the State party regarding the enjoyment of economic, social and cultural rights enshrined in the Covenant by populations in the ethnic minority areas. The Committee notes with concern the reports from sources other than the State party relating to the right to the free exercise of religion as a right to take part in cultural life, and the use and teaching of minority languages, history and culture and the Xinjiang Uighur Autonomous Region (XUAR) and the Tibet Autonomous Region (TAR).[145]

China's second report is due for review in 2014, and non-governmental organizations have raised, in parallel reports on China, the occupation of Tibet and the violation of the right of self-determination as the root causes of the legal issues at stake.[146] Unfortunately, the CESCR did not include occupation or denial of self-determination in the "List of Issues" to which it has asked China to respond in its upcoming review.[147]

The Tibetan refugee problem is both an issue of internal displacement and exile, as Chinese policies have resulted in massive forcible internal relocation of Tibetans as well as institutionalized Tibetan exile settlements in India and Nepal. The Tibetan Relief Committee estimates that about 145,150 Tibetans live in India, Nepal and Bhutan, while smaller numbers live in Canada, Switzerland and the United States.[148] The majority of Tibetan exiles are in India, and the Government in Exile under the Dalai Lama has been operating in MacLeod Ganj in Dharamsala, India, since 1960 as 'honored guests' of the Indian state.

India is not a party to the 1951 Refugee Convention and has not incorporated domestic refugee legislation. India thus does not recognize Tibetans as having legal status as refugees. India's policies towards Tibetan exiles have been *ad hoc* and have changed over time in response to political relations between India and China. Indian Foreigners legislation governs the treatment of Tibetans in the same way as other non-Indians residing or visiting India.[149] The Registration Certificates which Tibetans must obtain in India, are valid for up to six months, must continually be renewed, and do not entitle Tibetans to residence or citizenship. Unless they can obtain third state citizenship, Tibetans in India, as in other neighboring states, are *de facto* stateless.[150]

Initially, the Dalai Lama, as the formal leader of Tibetans in exile, in his Five-Point Peace Plan, laid out the "Middle Way," expressly renouncing violence as a means to securing self-determination and other rights. The Tibetan leadership's commitment to the 'Middle Way'" has eroded as a matter of a shift in power to groups such as the Tibetan Youth Congress, which have expressly refuted non-violence. The shocking increase in self-immolations among the Tibetan communities, particularly monks, can also be understood only as a resort to violence in desperate calls for attention to systemic violations of human rights.[151] At the same time, the Tibetan leadership in exile has suspended its commitment to the 'Middle Way' in the face of China's lack of response to Tibetan demands for genuine autonomy to preserve their cultural, social, economic, and political life within the Tibetan region, and a completely defunct peace process.[152]

The UN's view of Tibetans within the Tibetan Autonomous Region ("TAR") as defined by China, and Tibetan refugees, is through a purely human rights framework. The first UNGA Resolution passed concerning Tibet in 1959, defined the problem to be resolved as the "violation of Fundamental Human Rights of the Tibetan People, suppression of their distinctive culture and religious life."[153] UNGA Resolution 1723 (1961), quoted above and Resolution 2079 (1965), echoed the emphasis on human rights violations, although Resolution 1723 also added that the denial of rights included "their right to self-determination."[154] From the UN's view, then, the return of Tibetan refugees is tied to China's human rights policies vis-à-vis Tibetans as a minority within China, while from the Tibetan perspective, it is a function of securing real political autonomy for the entire Tibetan region *from* China in recognition of Tibetan self-determination.

Implications of *Erga Omnes* Obligations for Solving the Self-Determination and Protracted Refugee Problems

Violations of *jus cogens* norms give rise to third state responsibility, particularly those of non-recognition and non-assistance in illegal acts.[155]

The International Law Commission's Draft Articles on State Responsibility list the acts that constitute serious breaches of fundamental legal obligations that would give rise to third state responsibility.[156] The prohibitions against wars of aggression, denial of self-determination, population transfers and settler implantation have been recognized as *jus cogens,* or at least peremptory, norms that trigger obligations by third states.[157] Such third state obligations—or obligations *erga omnes*—have been articulated by the ICJ in its Advisory Opinions vis-à-vis Namibia, W. Sahara, and Palestine.[158] The UNGA has also expanded on the *erga omnes* obligations of states in many resolutions specifically with regard to W. Sahara and Palestine.[159]

In its Advisory Opinion on Legal Consequences for States of the Continued Presence of South Africa in Namibia, the Court outlined the sanctions obligations as:

> [M]ember states are under obligation to abstain from entering into treaty relations with South Africa in all cases in which the Government of South Africa purports to act on behalf of or concerning Namibia. With respect to existing bilateral treaties, member States must abstain from invoking or applying those treaties or provisions of treaties concluded by South Africa on behalf of or concerning Namibia which involve active intergovernmental cooperation. . . Member States . . . are under obligation to abstain from sending diplomatic or special missions to South Africa including in their jurisdiction the Territory of Namibia, to abstain from sending consular agents to Namibia, and to withdraw any such agents already there . . . [the Resolutions] impose upon member States the obligation to abstain from entering into economic and other forms of relationship or dealings with South Africa on behalf of or concerning Namibia which may entrench its authority over the Territory . . . .[160]

By 1971, the legal framework for Namibia was agreed upon by the UNSC, UNGA and the ICJ, with the key components of independence, self-determination, equal rights, non-discrimination, end of apartheid, and the obligation of all states through a sanctions regime to bring those about. UNSC Resolution 283 reiterated the obligations of third states: to declare South African presence in Namibia illegal; to refrain from diplomatic and other relations with South Africa and withdraw diplomatic representation; to cease any investments or corporate relations with South Africa in Namibia; and to review and terminate any treaties with South Africa as applicable to Namibia. All states were required to report to the UN on the measures taken to comply with the Resolution.

The UNSC did not enforce the sanctions demanded by the UNGA or call for intervention, because of French, United States, and United

Kingdom vetoes. Yet because of the ICJ's endorsement of sanctions against South Africa, and the Court's insistence that all Member States were obligated to bring about Namibian independence, the sanctions regime was "legalized" to support individual states' actions in imposing sanctions on South Africa.[161]

In the W. Sahara Advisory Opinion, the ICJ was not specific about what obligations third states had with regard to the self-determination of W. Sahara. In a single paragraph, the Court cited language from UNGA Resolution 2625, the Declaration on Principles of International Law Concerning Friendly Relations and Co-Operation Among States in Accordance with the Charter of the United Nations:

> Every state has a duty to promote, through joint and separate action, realization of the principle of equal rights and self-determination of peoples in accordance with the provisions of the Charter, and to render assistance to the UN in carrying out the responsibilities entrusted to it by the Charter regarding the implementation of the principle, in order: . . . (b) To bring a speedy end to colonialism, having due regard to the freely expressed will of the peoples concerned.[162]

Following the Advisory Opinion, the UNGA tasked the Secretary-General to implement Sahrawi self-determination, and continued to support the Secretary-General and OAU efforts under the Settlement Plan.[163] However, no UN Resolution directly addressed third states' *erga omnes* obligations as a follow up to the ICJ reference. The UNSC took up the matter after the 1975 invasion, condemned the Green March, called for Moroccan withdrawal, and reaffirmed UNGA Resolutions 1514 and 3292 with regard to W. Sahara.[164] However, the UNSC failed to specifically condemn the attempt to acquire Sahrawi territory by force as violations of the Charter. Nor did it call on other states to refuse to recognize the illegal seizure of territory.

Thus, although the UNSC and UNGA initially agreed that W. Sahara was a former Spanish colony with defined territory and a people entitled to self-determination, they have not agreed on what to do about the relationship of Morocco to W. Sahara beyond recognizing that Morocco has no tenable territorial claim there.[165] This ambiguity has permitted Morocco and its allies to block any UNSC action against Morocco's use of force and transfer of population in W. Sahara, and to prevent the call for sanctions or obligations of third states against Morocco. The ICJ's W. Sahara opinion implies that there were obligations *erga omnes* on the community of states not to support any claim of right to W. Sahara by Morocco, but that has not been taken up by a sufficient number of state supporters of W. Sahara to counteract the powerful interests of Morocco and its allies at the UNSC

The ICJ's Advisory Opinion on the Legal Consequences of the Construction of a Wall in the OPT is both the most explicit instruction of *erga omnes* obligations concerning violations of *jus cogens* norms, as well as the most important pronouncement on the law concerning Israel-Palestine. Although it was confined to issues relating to the construction of Israel's wall inside the OPT, it addressed many of the critical contested questions relating to self-determination and the human rights of the Palestinian people. In a near-unanimous decision, the ICJ found that Israel's wall construction, as well as the "associated regime" of permits and access zones, were a violation of international law and that Israel should immediately cease construction, dismantle the portion already built, and terminate the permit regime.[166] The ICJ further found that Israel was required to provide restitution and reparations for all damages it had caused to Palestinian landowners in confiscating land and constructing the wall.

The ICJ then discussed both third state obligations and the responsibilities of the UN to bring about an end to the Israeli violations involved in the wall construction. As to the first, the ICJ found: "All states are under an obligation not to recognize the illegal situation resulting from the construction of the wall and not to render aid or assistance in maintaining the situation created by such construction."[167] It reminded States parties to the Fourth Geneva Convention of their obligations under that treaty "to ensure compliance by Israel with international humanitarian law." As to the UN's obligations, the ICJ stated: "The United Nations, and especially the UNGA and the UNSC, should consider what further action is required to bring an end to the illegal situation resulting from the construction of the wall and the associated regime, taking due account of the present Advisory Opinion."[168]

The ICJ found that the *erga omnes* obligations flowed from the prohibition against acquisition of territory by force by Israel. The Court was explicit that Israel's violation of the self-determination of the Palestinian people, the land expropriation and other human rights abuses against Palestinians involved in the property takings, and the wall construction within Palestinian territory constitute grave breaches of the Fourth Geneva Convention.[169] It found that the wall construction was designed to further Israeli settlements and settler implantation, and was prohibited by Art. 49(6) of the Fourth Geneva Convention.

These violations of *jus cogens* norms triggered the duty of non-recognition and non-assistance by third states as well as the UN in Israel's actions. The Advisory Opinion, in near-unanimity on every point, called on all the organs of the UN to take action to implement the Opinion.[170] The UNGA adopted the Advisory Opinion on 20 July 2004, and demanded that Israel comply with the obligations spelled out by the ICJ.[171] The UNGA also called on UN member states to comply with the *erga omnes* obligations set out by the Court, and for States Parties to the Fourth Geneva Convention to ensure Israel's compliance, as well. The UNGA tasked the Secretary-General with creating a Register of Damages for restitution and compensation to Palestinians victimized by the wall construction.[172]

The Wall Advisory Opinion was not the first pronouncement from the UN organs on *erga omnes* obligations vis-à-vis Israel's violations of Palestinian self-determination and Israeli occupation in Arab territories. Beginning in the 1980's, the UNSC issued a series of Resolutions finding obligations on third states relating to Israel's territorial aggression, occupation, and violation of Palestinian self-determination in East Jerusalem and the OPT, as well as in the Syrian Golan Heights. Very similar to resolutions on Namibia, the UNGA has called on all states to initiate boycotts and sanctions on Israel. In particularly strong language, UNGA Resolution Es-9/1 condemned Israeli 'aggression' into the Golan Heights, and called upon all UN Member States to suspend weapons supplies or military assistance; economic, financial and technological assistance and co-operation; and to sever diplomatic, trade and cultural relations to or from Israel.[173] These Resolutions were clearly the work of the PLO and its allies in the UN during the 1970's and '80's—an alliance which has all but disappeared with the collapse of the PLO as the representative body of the Palestinian people today.

Moreover, the UNGA's success in submitting the question of the wall construction to the ICJ was itself a watershed in the long-running impasse at the UNSC at producing any resolution critical of Israel. The question whether the UNGA had the authority to refer the question to the ICJ related to Art. 12(1) of the Charter and the scope of Resolution 377 (V), the 'Uniting for Peace' Resolution. Art. 12(1) of the Charter states that "While the UNSC is exercising in respect of any dispute or situation the functions assigned to it in the present Charter, the UNGA shall not make any recommendation with regard to that dispute or situation unless the UNSC so requests."

Resolution 377(V) had been passed in 1950 precisely to break the repeated political deadlock at the UNSC so that the UNGA could act on urgent issues, especially when conflict was imminent or ongoing. Resolution 377(V) provides that if the UNSC fails to act because one or more Permanent Member fails to agree in situations of a 'threat to peace, breach of the peace, or act of aggression…' the UNGA shall consider the matter in emergency special session.[174] UN Charter Art. 96 specifically grants the UNGA and the UNSC the right to request an advisory opinion from the ICJ 'on any legal question.'[175] Thus, the issue was not whether the UNGA had the authority to take a question for an advisory opinion to the ICJ, but whether it could do so if or when the UNSC was 'seized of the matter.'

The ICJ itself ruled on this question in the Wall Opinion, finding that as long as the UNSC was not debating the precise issue that was the subject of the Advisory Opinion request at the same time as the UNGA was considering it, then Resolution 377(V) authorized the UNGA to raise the question to the ICJ.[176] This ruling has significant reach for each of the cases here, as Palestine. W. Sahara and Tibet face opposition by powerful vote-holders in the UNSC who block more aggressive action, certainly Ch. VII action, to advance their rights through that body. The ICJ Wall Opinion ruling on the legality of the Uniting for Peace Resolution to bypass a stalemate at the UNSC is a major breakthrough for building the foundations for *erga omnes* obligations through ICJ Advisory Opinions brought directly by the UNGA The Wall Opinion was a milestone with regard to UN findings on *erga omnes* obligations vis-à-vis Israeli violations of *jus cogens* norms and war crimes against Palestine and the Palestinians. Since the Opinion, there has been a steady expansion of UN bodies, special procedures and fact-finding missions promoting third state and corporate responsibility for complicity with Israeli violations of peremptory norms.[177] The General Assembly and the Human Rights Council have adopted these reports and conclusions, forming a solid legal foundation for the institution of a sanctions regime.

Lessons Learned from Namibia

Law is a necessary, but of course insufficient element for resolving prolonged refugee crises with roots in denial of self-determination and ongoing occupation. Too frequently, law is disregarded as either irrelevant or minimally relevant to the resolution of long-running conflicts, in which armed struggle and raw political power are seen as the key determinants of outcome. This view, however, fails to take into account that customary international law is based on the actual practice of states. States and individual government actors respond to the pressure of civil society, and civil society is persuaded to act by a perception of injustice, persuasively articulated as a violation of legal norms. The case of Namibia is precedential for the contemporary conflict and refugee situations discussed here for its illustration of the critical role law can play in accomplishing self-determination and durable solutions for refugees. The resolution of the Namibia question took a path from legal normative framework set out by the UN, to civil society action—operating in tandem with an armed struggle under relatively unified leadership—to the utilization of international legal machinery to bring about self-determination and ultimate independence. Although each case is unique, the Namibia 'lesson' is an important one for the people of W. Sahara, Tibet and Palestine to accomplish their objectives.

In the Namibia case, the UNGA and UNSC ended up with an agreement on the underlying legal framework *against* UNSC member consensus. The UNSC came to agree with the UNGA reluctantly and late because of the actions of several of the permanent members blocking a vote. It ended up being forced to that position because the ICJ's four advisory opinions (one in answer to the UNSC itself) consistently articulated what the law required.[178] And because of the efforts of numerous Committees within the UN, particularly the aggressive Committee of Twenty-Four, the Namibian Council, the leadership of SWAPO, and the commitment of a grassroots anti-apartheid movement, states responded to the ICJ rulings to impose sanctions without UNSC Chapter VII action.

The creation of the Committee for South West Africa and the Council for Namibia that interceded in the governance of Namibia were distinguishing features of Namibia compared to Palestine and W. Sahara that may have helped move Namibia to independence. They were instrumental in using the weight of UN consensus to support the creation and implementation of the sanctions regime, making inroads in protecting Namibia's resources, and acting as the UN's authority within the territory in enforcing the framework for independence. The extent of their influence in the ultimate outcome is debatable, however, compared to the impact of the armed struggle waged by the ANC and PAC as well as the Namibian political and militant organizations, PLAN, SWAPO, SWANU and the South West Africa National United Front (SWANUF).[179] These entities were further supported by the global solidarity movement against apartheid.[180] It was the continuation of the armed struggle, the international community's imposition of a sanctions regime against South Africa, a (relatively) united leadership in the struggle, and sustained civil society pressure against apartheid that brought about Namibia's independence. What the Namibian case shows is that for 20 years before actual independence, Namibians and their supporters had a strong legal strategy, combined with the political and the armed struggle that resolved many of the key issues allowing the non-rejectionist states to make statehood meaningful by the time actual independence came about. It certainly advanced the Namibian case that apartheid was morally exhausted and universally rejected from at least 1988.

As noted earlier, Namibia's right to independence of the entire territory of South West Africa was acted upon as a matter of legal right almost immediately after the Mandate period ended, despite its Class C status.[181] Namibian refugees were guaranteed their rights to safe haven in neighboring countries, in settlements run directly by their government-in-exile, SWAPO, until they could return safely and voluntarily. SWAPO kept the rights of the refugees, and the connection of the refugees to the political polity, central to the resolution of their struggle. The UN's considerations in refugee return were guaranteeing voluntary choice and safety, and then carrying out orderly repatriation processes. Right to return, the choice of resettlement, and protection against *non-refoulement* were not in question for the refugee framework vis-à-vis Namibia. Furthermore, the place of return for the refugees was to their original homes in all of territorial Namibia. The refugees were able to return to Namibia even before a final agreement ended the conflict because the UN adopted an approach to self-determination that included protection of the territorial integrity of the country and statehood with full independence and sovereignty—underscored by an agreed-on framework from the ICJ, the UNGA and the UNSC

Unlike in Namibia, the UNGA and UNSC approaches have been in conflict with regard to both Palestine and W. Sahara, with the UNSC disregarding the legal framework articulated by the UNGA and reinforced by the ICJ in the Advisory Opinions in both cases.[182] While Palestine's efforts appear to have been defeated by the veto of permanent members of the UNSC, and W. Sahara's efforts marginally advanced in efforts to implement a referendum, the legal strategies were not defeated by permanent member vetoes at the UNSC in the Namibian case. In comparison to Namibia, however, the UNGA and the UNSC have neither jointly developed the actual foundation for recognition, nor the legal framework for Palestinian or Sahrawi independence. Moreover, in both the W. Sahara and the Palestinian cases, there has been very limited effort to follow up on the Advisory Opinions, particularly with regard to the *erga omnes* obligations that in the Namibia case were critical to the sanctions regime but have not been pursued with the community of states for sanctions against Israel or Morocco. Nor have there been efforts to obtain additional rulings from the ICJ to articulate what obligations states have to achieve realization of Palestinian or Sahrawi self-determination following the recognition of statehood by both the ICJ and the UNGA

For Palestinians, the UNSC has failed to explicitly affirm their inalienable rights—self-determination and statehood, right of refugee return, and Israeli withdrawal from the 1967 territories—that have been the focus of the UNGA's framework for resolution of the conflict.[183] The UNSC has also blocked UN sponsored conferences by vetoes or by refusing to consider UNGA recommendations.[184] The UNSC's approach has been framed by the "land for peace" political formula as a basis for negotiations, with almost no reference to legal rights. Moreover, in marked contrast to Namibia, the 2004 Advisory Opinion on the Wall represents the sole submission to the ICJ on behalf of Palestinian rights in over sixty years of conflict.[185] Similarly, although the UNSC has authorized MINURSO as a peacekeeping and monitoring body on the ground in W. Sahara, it has also failed to act on the body of UNGA resolutions concerning Sahrawi independence, and has seemingly backed away from an initial commitment to independence to commitment to a *process* for a referendum to be agreed on by the conflicting parties. As for Tibet, since the UNSC has never spoken and there has been no Advisory Opinion request put to the ICJ on the question, there is no UN framework to speak of on the self-determination question, and no established framework for articulating *erga omnes* obligations against China.

In the cases of both Palestine and Tibet, the UN has not protected the territorial integrity of either mandate Palestine or the entire Tibetan region, promoting self-determination, statehood, independence, and sovereignty in a small part of Palestine; and imprecise 'self-determination' along with civil, economic, social and cultural rights to Tibetans as an ethnic minority in a truncated part of Tibet. For the Palestinians, this framework leaves the area of Palestine/Israel where the majority of the refugees should exercise their rights outside the recognized Palestinian self-determination unit, and for Tibetans, it presents the same problem for the internally displaced and the Tibetan refugee exile community—a recognized right to remain or to resettle in only the truncated 'Tibetan Autonomous Region' that excludes the provinces of Tsinghai and Sikang, an integral part of the historical Tibetan homeland.[186] This effectively prevents the option of Namibia, where the solution for the refugees was implemented in the context of independence and territorial integrity.

Although the UNGA and the UNSC are divided over when and how statehood should be recognized in the case of Palestine, and although the UNGA—unlike the UNSC—has a longstanding record of affirming individual refugee rights in addition to Palestinian statehood, independence, and sovereignty, both the UNGA and UNSC agree that independence, sovereignty, and a solution for the refugees are to be achieved in peace negotiations with an Israeli regime that rejects all three. Israeli consensus even refuses to recognize the majority of Palestinians as refugees, and rejects out of hand their right to return to their original homes and lands and restitution of their properties within Israel, or even the vast swaths of Palestinian properties confiscated since 1967 in the West Bank. *De facto*, this is similar to the position the UN has taken for both W. Sahara and Tibet: emphasizing the denial of individual human rights, but leaving resolution of the self-determination and refugee issues to negotiations between the POLISARIO and Morocco in the former, and Tibetan leadership in exile and China in the latter. Both states, Morocco and China, reject any meaningful negotiation on the question. Forced relocation, settler implantation and land confiscation also mark Morocco's and China's actions towards the Sahrawi and Tibetan populations. Forced relocation is particularly acute for Tibetans, with 50-80% of Tibetan herders (of a population of approximately 2.25 million) to be removed from their lands as a result of China's 'Western Development Strategy.'

Just as critical for Namibia's successful independence bid as a unified UN strategy and recognition of territorial integrity were the factors of unified leadership and close collaboration with civil and UN actors. In contrast to SWAPO, the Namibian Council and civil actors have been working together to preserve rights and pursue joint strategies, the Palestinian leadership has been deeply divided, has acted less in concert with its civil society than against it, and has less and less legitimacy in the eyes of its people. The strategies it has pursued have been fractured and inconsistent, both within and outside the UN framework. In the mid-1960s, in response to the decolonization efforts within the UN of the African states, the PLO made a very deliberate change in its UN strategy. By 1969, the resolutions proposed and passed at the UN on Palestinian issues had changed their language from that of individual rights to calling for rights of the Palestinian people—collective rights.[187] This may have seemed like an appropriate strategy at the time, but by failing to merge individual rights with the collective, the PLO has been forced at the negotiating table to exchange one set of rights for another.

Moreover, the Palestinian leadership has agreed to severance of the majority of the Palestinian population—the refugees—from the political representation on the statehood question. Only Palestinians within the West Bank and Gaza are acknowledged to be represented by the PA, meaning that only approximately 30% of the Palestinian people were permitted to vote in the last elections in which Fatah prevailed in the West Bank and Hamas won in Gaza. In none of the other cases here has the leadership permitted severance of their population for purposes of representation of their interests and durable solutions. The Palestinian strategy has focused on ending occupation and on international humanitarian law protections rather than a combined strategy demanding fulfillment of both individual rights and the collective rights of self-determination and independence.

Prior to and following the request for the Advisory Opinion on the Wall issued in 2004, there has been little or no effort by the Palestinian delegation at the UN to build on it as part of a distinct legal strategy. [188] This is surprising, in light of the PLO's solid support within the UNGA, especially with the Group of Non-Aligned States. In contrast to the four Advisory Opinions and the contentious case litigated over decades for Namibia, the single Advisory Opinion in the Palestinians' favor on many of the most contentious issues of the conflict has lost its strategic value due to the failure of any follow-up in using it as an effective legal tool.[189]

Additionally, the PLO and PA have failed to work within the European Union, utilize regional and other mechanisms, or facilitate the filing of lawsuits in domestic courts.[190] The Palestinian leadership appears to have failed to incorporate legal strategies in its negotiations frameworks, as well. For example, it has failed to insist that Resolution 194, in addition to Resolutions 242 and 338, must be incorporated in all negotiations. It has also failed to insist on inclusion of the West Bank, Gaza Strip, and East Jerusalem as a single territorial entity in all negotiation proposals.

In all three cases, there has been a systematic omission of law in favor of a political solution from the UN In the Palestinian case, this is obvious from the UNSC's failure to reaffirm the UNGA's individual rights resolutions and the 'Quartet's' framework that a Palestinian state can be reached prior to Israeli withdrawal. In the Sahrawi case, the UN's move from implementing independence directly as a decolonization obligation to negotiating the terms of a referendum with the occupying state, Morocco, illustrates the same paradigm. The Palestinian, Sahrawi and Tibetan leadership have also taken an almost entirely political, rather than a law-based approach to the UN. The PA, for example, has failed to, or refused, collaboration with the civil society groups working with the Palestine Committee and the Division to expand and build on the roles of these UN institutions. On the contrary, the PA has frequently been at odds with these organizations and with civil society activists engaged with the UN, preventing the kind of deep collaboration necessary to put a multi-pronged, solid legal strategy in place. At the negotiations level, too, there has been a critical lack of a robust legal approach. No legal department advised the PLO-PA until after the Oslo Accords, when the Adam Smith Institute established the first legal affairs department for the PLO. Since then, it appears that the PA has not incorporated much of the legal affairs unit's work at the international level. One can safely conclude that the leadership in all these cases has failed to see the importance that legal strategies have alongside political, negotiation, media, civil society collaborations, and the armed struggle, in achieving their goals.[191]

Strategies for Civil Actors

A large proportion of the people of W. Sahara, Tibet, and Palestine remain both internally displaced and refugees, with no indication that their displacement will end in the near future. Yet resolving the refugee problem is not an equally critical factor in finding an overall resolution to each of these prolonged conflicts. A few comparisons help to illustrate how the Namibian example can show ways forward for the other three cases to accomplish their most critical objectives that will lead to resolution of the refugee questions, as well.

The greatest imperative for the Palestinians for the foreseeable future is a united leadership; the Hamas/Fatah division has been devastating for their cause. In the absence of uniting Hamas and Fatah, the global Palestinian community will need to reconstitute the PLO and make it fully representative of the widely-scattered Palestinians, particularly the refugees. The Palestinians have, in the last few years, succeeded in changing the popular perception of their cause in their favor and, as discussed above, have overwhelming support within the UN—as illustrated by the massive majority vote for state recognition in the UNGA in December 2012. Advocacy for Palestinian rights has been robust in the UN machinery since at least the mid-1980's. The sustained effort within the UN human rights mechanisms that has brought about the far-reaching reports and Concluding Observations described above has all been the result of the work of civil society non-governmental organizations. Many of the Concluding Observations and reports from the treaty bodies and the Special Rapporteurs were cited as support for the findings of the ICJ in the Advisory Opinion on the Wall.[192]

In contrast to the PLO/PA, civil society, particularly international solidarity groups, have been very pro-active, not only in developing the soft law within the UN, but also in pressuring states and corporations to cease cooperating with Israel's occupation activities. The Boycott, Divestment and Sanctions ("BDS") campaign instituted in 2005 and coordinated by the Palestinian BDS National Committee has started gaining significant traction, with the announcement by the European Union prohibiting loans to Israeli ministries, public bodies and businesses operating in the OPT.[193] In order to move to implementation of the *erga omnes* obligations as articulated by the ICJ—not to recognize or cooperate with Israel's wall construction and related regime of separation —as well as to build on norms prohibiting apartheid, settler implantation, ethnic cleansing and aggression, much more will be required beyond what civil society alone can do. The PA knows how to use the Uniting for Peace resolution successfully in bringing a request for an Advisory Opinion to the ICJ, and they can do it again to follow-up on the Wall Opinion. The achievement of 'non-member state' recognition opens enormous opportunities for prosecutions through the ICC, individual complaint and other processes through the specialized UN agencies, and, most important, diplomatic advocacy for a sanctions regime against Israel.

The Palestinians do not need to obtain an independent state to resolve the refugee problem. The effort to secure legal equality for Palestinian citizens of Israel began many years ago, and is more likely to succeed in repealing the discriminatory laws that prevent Palestinian refugee return and property restitution than the effort for a viable Palestinian state. The Israeli settlement project has made the "two-state solution" impossible, despite the UNSC and international political commitment to it. Refugee return, in any case, can precede any territorial outcome in Israel/Palestine, as illustrated by Namibia and by many subsequent Comprehensive Plans of Action incorporating mass refugee repatriation around the world for decades. Refugee return and property restitution can take place in a single state, confederation of states, or any other territorial configuration. For the Palestinians, diplomatic isolation of Israel, particularly if the "S" of BDS develops, will be critical to breaking the impasse on recognizing the refugees' rights to return to their original homes and lands. In any event, massive changes in demographic realities will have significant consequences for Israel's efforts to maintain exclusive Jewish-privileged statehood; Palestinians are today the majority population between the Jordan River and the Mediterranean Sea, making a state of Israel/Palestine in the not-too-distant future almost inevitable.

As for the Sahrawi, as Jeffrey Smith points out, they do not see theirs as primarily a refugee problem. The majority of the refugees are living as a "community in exile" with a government based in Tindouf that represents the occupied areas declared as part of the SADR, as well as the refugee population.[194] Since the Sahrawi do not define themselves primarily as refugees, they do not rest their claims on the right of 'refugee return.' In fact, the right to return to that part of W. Sahara from which individuals have been displaced is uncontested as a matter of international consensus. There is also no issue that the displaced cannot be accommodated as a matter of demography, as there is sufficient territory for them to reside in their original homes and lands. Like the Namibian refugees, the Sahrawi are not widely dispersed or far from their homes of origin. For the Sahrawi, then, the question of the refugee—or "exile"—return is bound up in resolution of the self-determination and prolonged occupation questions. The Sahrawi, like the Namibians, have refused, at least formally, to give up the armed struggle, which has forced the international community to maintain the UN presence through MINURSO as a peacekeeping effort. On the other hand, the Saharawi have been scrupulous in observing the 1991 ceasefire terms, and they may have *de facto* relinquished the armed struggle. Meanwhile, UNHCR has intermittently carried out family visits and family reunification efforts for the divided communities, reestablishing after the 1991 ceasefire the connections for a refugee repatriation plan that could precede independence along the lines of the Namibian pre-independence refugee return.

The Sahrawi leadership has focused on building their internal governance, an effort that has garnered legitimacy internally and externally. However, it has not developed a legal strategy of any note—whether working to establish a UN Committee on W. Sahara or collaborating closely with the non-governmental organizations trying to enforce boycotts against or divestment from corporations exploiting W. Saharan resources. The Sahrawi leadership should move to build on the Advisory Opinion through advocacy around the *erga omnes* obligations articulated by the ICJ, or use its support in the UNGA to make requests for additional Advisory Opinions on the legality of exploiting Sahrawi resources, the construction of the berm, or the movement of settlers into Sahrawi territory. All could be framed as violations of *erga omnes* obligations, based on the *jus cogens* or peremptory norms discussed at the outset.

As opposed to the Palestinian leadership, the Sahrawi have shown widespread support for their leadership, and confidence in the representative nature of their internal election process. From the point of view of the majority of the Sahrawi, the SADR leadership is democratic and participatory, and plays an effective internal governance role. From the perspective of international relations and international strategies to advance Sahrawi rights, however, that confidence is less obvious. Within the UN, the SADR could use the Group of Non-Aligned states to help establish a body equivalent to the Namibian Council or the Committee on South West Africa to advance Sahrawi claims in the UN machinery. There is undoubtedly enough support in the UNGA for Sahrawi rights to establish such an entity. The Sahrawi do not have a persistent opponent in the permanent veto-wielding members of the UNSC as Tibet and Palestine do, but so far there has been little visible effort to obtain UNSC resolutions and action to enforce the referendum process.

However, in the absence of meaningful UNSC intervention, the Sahrawi could develop a more robust legal effort through the UNGA and follow up Advisory Opinion requests to the ICJ to obtain legal authority for non-recognition and sanctions against Morocco by UN member states. So far, it does not appear that the SADR leadership has instituted a 'Boycott, Divestment and Sanctions' campaign patterned on the Namibian sanctions effort or the current Palestinian civil society strategy. The fundamentals for non-recognition and sanctions are the elements articulated by the ICJ in the W. Sahara Advisory Opinion: the *erga omnes* obligation to bring about an end to colonialism and the denial of self-determination, including economic, social, and cultural development. Bound up in the right to self-determination is territorial integrity of the self-determination "unit," and rights over the natural resources attached to the territory.[195] Namibia benefited from a very explicit UNGA Resolution on the issue of rights to natural resources. In Resolution 33/182, the UNGA stated:

> [T]he natural resources of Namibia are the birthright of the Namibian people and that the exploitation of those resources by foreign economic interests under the protection of the repressive racist colonial administration . . . is illegal and contribute to the maintenance of the illegal occupation régime.[196]

The SADR could generate momentum in the UNGA to follow up on the elements from the first Advisory Opinion for a subsequent Opinion spelling out the precise obligations on third states that result from their participation in exploiting the resources of W. Sahara. Agreements between Morocco and other states that exploit resources belonging to the territory of W. Sahara fall under the *erga omnes* obligation of non-recognition—a position repeatedly raised by the SADR with foreign states and corporations exploiting W. Sahara oil and gas, fisheries and phosphates.[197] This effort has begun, but primarily through grassroots advocacy and Sahrawi solidarity work conducted primarily in Europe, led by Western Sahara Resource Watch.[198] Despite Jeffrey Smith's position that the refugee question is not tied to the issue of Saharan resource exploitation, the Namibian example reflects that a key element to bringing an end to illegal occupation is draining the occupier of the economic benefits of occupation. The costs to Morocco of continuing the occupation of W. Sahara appear to far exceed the benefits it is receiving in mineral and other resource extraction.[199] If a sanctions regime against Morocco seems difficult to contemplate, depriving Morocco of economic benefits may be easier to achieve through raising the stakes for partnership agreements over resource exploitation with third states or corporations.[200] Economic pressure and diplomatic isolation helped bring an end to South African occupation of Namibia; the same can bring Morocco to agreement on the terms and eligible voters to the referendum demanded by the SADR. In the absence of UNSC action, the Sahrawi leadership can still generate greater legal legitimacy for non-recognition and non-cooperation with Moroccan actions through pressure in the other organs of the UN. [201]

The effort in the UN to buttress Tibetan rights is nascent. The Tibetan leadership has yet to seriously engage within the UN machinery. This is particularly distressing considering that of all the cases at issue, the Tibetans' plight is the best-known among global civil society, and has garnered the greatest sympathy and public activism worldwide. There has not been an effort to develop legal competence within the Tibetan government-in-exile, and to engage with NGO's that are using legal strategies to advocate for Tibetans within the UN machinery. At the same time, the great strength of the Tibetan people is unified, venerated and credible leadership. These two factors alone suggest that identifying and acting on legal strategies within and outside the UN should not be a complicated process (as compared to the fractured Palestinian leadership, for example).

There is a long road ahead to developing a significant body of soft law to crystallize a framework through the UN that can support further diplomatic and political effort in light of the leadership's disavowal of an armed struggle, and in the absence of UNSC intervention. The return of refugees to Tibet is, like the Palestinians, not dependent on achieving independence. It is, however, dependent on insistence of human rights protections for Tibetans within the broader Tibetan region, not just the reduced territory of the TAR. It will require insistence on equality and non-discriminatory treatment of Tibetans in all spheres: employment, housing, benefits, and particularly, protection of religious, linguistic, and cultural rights. Obtaining UN intervention to protect and monitor the economic, social and cultural rights of Tibetans will be essential to refugee return prior to real efforts to regain autonomy and political rights as a first step to meaningful self-determination. Despite potential obstacles in the UNGA, Tibetan solidarity groups can utilize the Namibian example to develop a robust UN strategy in the human rights mechanisms and generate momentum in the UNGA for Advisory Opinion requests to the ICJ to support findings of obligations *erga omnes* against China for its human rights violations and denial of self-determination of the Tibetan people.

As discussed above, the Uniting for Peace resolution provides a method for the Sahrawi and the Tibetan leadership to obtain Advisory Opinions that clarify the underlying legal issues on which they need international consensus and commitment, and a framework for establishing *erga omnes* obligations to put pressure on their occupying states. China is far less vulnerable to boycott and divestment efforts than Morocco or Israel, and sanctions are not feasible with China's veto at the S.C. However, China is very sensitive to state and UN criticism, and consistently reacts negatively to criticism on Tibet. Thus, a sustained effort within all the UN human rights machinery to highlight Chinese abuses of Tibetan rights, and a unified call for meaningful political autonomy for the Tibetan people, is necessary and may generate concessions from the Chinese central government in halting the dispossession and development policies that are causing Tibetan human rights abuses, and perhaps incremental political concessions. The most recent policy changes illustrate China's sensitivity to sustained criticism on its 'minority populations' policies. From developing a body of 'soft law' on Tibetan rights in the UN mechanisms—as the Palestinians have done for the last few decades—the Tibetan leadership could also obtain support in the UNGA for an Advisory Opinion to follow up on the meaning and *erga omnes* obligations in implementing Resolution 1723. With legal principles articulated by the ICJ, or even the UN treaty bodies, that all states have obligations not to recognize China's actions in Tibet, or engage in economic cooperation in the Tibetan region, there may be slow progress towards greater autonomy for Tibet. This is not simple, but the Namibians have shown how it may be feasible.

The comparison of these three cases with Namibia illustrates the importance of a clear body of soft and hard law to support the recognition of self-determination by the UN in order to accomplish the demands of the Sahrawi, Palestinian, and Tibetan people. For each of the refugee cases involved, refugee rights can be achieved in the absence of full independence, but only if the key elements discussed above are present. In each case, success in achieving the end of these protracted refugee crises depends on the existence of a unified leadership with a sustained UN strategy. That leadership must, in turn, be capable of transforming the UN legal framework into diplomatic action with the community of states—legalized through *erga omnes* imprimatur—to establish a non-recognition, non-cooperation or sanctions regime against the occupying state. Without these critical elements, the Sahrawi, Tibetan, and Palestinian people will not get what they deem most important: the fulfillment of their individual rights to return, restitution of their properties, and collective rights of full recognition as a people connected with their own, undivided, territory.

Notes

* Clinical Professor, Boston University School of Law. The author thanks BUSL law students Eileen Morrison, Emelie Kogut and Chloe Brighton for their invaluable research assistance for this chapter. A short version of the research on Namibia and Palestine appears as a chapter in ABORTED STATE? THE U.N. INITIATIVE AND NEW PALESTINIAN JUNCTURES (Noura Erakat & Mouin Rabbani eds., 2013). The author also thanks Jeffrey Smith, Robert Sloane, John Dugard and Ingrid Jaradat Gassner for their reviews of, and insightful comments on, the W. Sahara, Tibet, Namibia and Palestine sections respectively; the author takes full responsibility for all her own errors.

[1] The author is indebted to the work done by others on the subject, in particular, *see* Stephanie Koury, *The European Community and Member States' Duty of Non-Recognition Under the EC-Morocco Association Agreement: State Responsibility and Customary International Law, in* INTERNATIONAL LAW AND THE QUESTION OF W. SAHARA (Karin Arts & Pinto Leite eds., 2007); Stephanie Koury, *Legal Strategies at the United Nations: A Comparative Look at Namibia, Western Sahara, and Palestine, in* INTERNATIONAL LAW AND THE ISRAELI-PALESTINIAN CONFLICT: A RIGHTS BASED APPROACH TO MIDDLE EAST PEACE (Susan Akram, Michael Dumper, Michael Lynk & Iain Scobbie eds., 2011); *see also* John Quigley, THE STATEHOOD OF PALESTINE: INTERNATIONAL LAW IN THE MIDDLE EAST CONFLICT (2010).

[2] *See* Atlantic Charter art. 3, 1941, U.K.–U.S., 55 Stat. 1603.

[3] Treaty of Peace with Turkey Signed at Lausanne: The Convention Respecting the Regime of the Straits and Other Instruments Signed at Lausanne, July 24, 1923, *available at* http://wwi.lib.byu.edu/index.php/Treaty_of_Lausanne.

[4] League of Nations Covenant art. 22, *available at* http://www.unhcr.org/refworld/docid/3dd8b9854.html.

[5] *See* Daniel Thurer & Thomas Burri, *Self-Determination,* MEPIL, 2013, para. 4, *available at* http://ilmc.univie.ac.at/uploads/media/self-determination_empil.pdf.

[6] The Council of the League of Nations: The Mandate for Palestine (1922), *available at* http://www.fordham.edu/halsall/mod/1922mandate.html.

[7] *Id.*

[8] League of Nations Covenant, *supra* note 4, at art. 22.

[9] *See* Nele Matz, *Civilization and the Mandate System Under the League of Nations as Origin of Trusteeship*, 9 MAX PLANCK YEARBOOK OF U.N. LAW 47, 76 (2005).

[10] *Documents on the League of Nations: Resolution for the Dissolution of the League of Nations, Adopted by the Assembly on April 18, 1946*, 1 INTERNATIONAL ORGANIZATION 246, 246-51 (1947).

---

[11] U.N. Charter art. 1, para. 2.
[12] G.A. Res. 1514 (XV), U.N. Doc. A/RES/1514 (XV) (Dec. 14, 1960), *available at* http://www.un.org/en/decolonization/declaration.shtml.
[13] *Id.*
[14] *See* Matthew Saul, *The Normative Status of Self-Determination in International Law: A Formula for Uncertainty in the Scope and Content of the Right,* 11 HUM. RTS. L. REV. 4 (2011) (describing how the concept of self-determination is one of the most unsettled terms in international law).
[15] United Nations High Commissioner for Refugees [UNHCR], *Statelessness in Southern Africa,* (2011), *available at* http://www.refworld.org/docid/50c1f9562.html.
[16] Refugees International, *Nationality Rights for All: A Progress Report and Global Survey on Statelessness, available at* http://www.refworld.org/docid/49be193f2.html.
[17] International Law Commission, *Articles on Nationality of Natural Persons in Relation to the Succession of States,* Supp. No. 10 (A/54/10) *available at* http://www.refworld.org/docid/4512b6dd4.html; PAUL WEIS, NATIONALITY AND STATELESSNESS IN INTERNATIONAL LAW (1979).
[18] William Thomas Worster, *Law, Politics, and the Conception of the State in State Recognition Theory*, 27 B.U. INT'L L.J. 115, 118-19 (2009).
[19] Montevideo Convention on the Rights and Duties of States, Dec. 26, 1933, 165 L.N.T.S. 19, *available at* http://www.cfr.org/sovereignty/montevideo-convention-rights-duties-states/p15897.
[20] *Id.* at art. 1.
[21] Quigley, *supra* note 1, at 207-08.
[22] *Id.* at 119.
[23] Other examples include the previous Soviet satellite states of Belorussia, now Belarus, and the Ukraine. Bosnia was also admitted as a UN member without having control over territory or independence. S.C. Res. 757, U.N. Doc. S/RES/757 (May 30, 1992), *available at* http://daccess-dds-ny.un.org/doc/RESOLUTION/GEN/NR0/011/16/IMG/NR001116.pdf?OpenElement. Monaco, though a mini-state (1.95 square kilometers and 5000 citizens), is widely recognized as such, though France controls its domestic and foreign policy through treaty (1918 and 1930). Treaty Establishing the Relations of France with the Principality of Monaco, Fr.-Monaco, July 17, 1918, 981 U.N.T.S. 363. The US Marshall Islands is a UN Member even though the US maintains full authority over defense and security. Compact of Free Association, U.S.-Marsh. Is., June 25, 1983, U.S. Pub. L. 99-239. *Cited in* Quigley *supra* note 1, at 222.
[24] Lauri Hannikainen, *The Case of Western Sahara From the Perspective of Jus Cogens, in* INTERNATIONAL LAW AND THE QUESTION OF WESTERN SAHARA 62 (Karin Arts & Pedro Pinto Leite eds., 2007).
[25] G.A. Res. 3314 (XXIX), U.N. Doc. A/RES/3314 (XXIX) (Dec. 14, 1974), *available at* http://daccess-dds-ny.un.org/doc/RESOLUTION/GEN/NR0/739/16/IMG/NR073916.pdf?OpenElement; *see* Roger Clark, *Western Sahara and the United Nations Norms on Self-Determination, in* INTERNATIONAL LAW AND THE

QUESTION OF WESTERN SAHARA 54-55 (Karin Arts & Pedro Pinto Leite eds., 2007).

[26] The Rome Statute of The International Criminal Court, July 17, 1998, 37 I.L.M. 999, *available at* http://www.refworld.org/docid/3ae6b3a84.html [hereinafter Rome Statute].

[27] International Conferences (The Hague), *Hague Convention (IV) Respecting the Laws and Customs of War on Land and Its Annex: Regulations Concerning the Laws and Customs of War on Land,* Oct. 18, 1907, *available at* http://www.refworld.org/docid/4374cae64.html [hereinafter Hague Regulations].

[28] *See id.* at arts. 52, 53.

[29] Rome Statute, *supra* note 26. Of course, prosecution of war crimes at the ICC depends on state membership. The issue currently pending at the ICC of whether Palestine can be treated as a state for purposes of acceding to the Rome Statute and to the International Criminal Court (ICC) was not resolved through recognition of statehood. Summary of the Submissions on Whether the Declaration Lodged by the Palestinian National Authority Meets Statutory Requirements, ICC, *available at* http://www.icc-cpi.int/menus/icc/structure%20of%20the%20court/office%20of%20the%20prosecutor/comm%20and%20ref/palestine/summary%20of%20submissions%20on%20whether%20the%20declaration%20lodged%20by%20the%20palestinian%20national%20authority%20meets (last visited Aug. 25, 2011) (providing all the materials submitted to the ICC on the issue that is still before the court and is yet to be decided).

[30] *See* Convention IV Relative to the Protection of Civilian Persons in Time of War, Aug. 12, 1949, art. 49(6), *available at* http://www.icrc.org/ihl/INTRO/380 [hereinafter Fourth Geneva Convention]; *see also* Rome Statute, *supra* note 26, at art. 7 (defining deportation or forcible transfer of population as a crime against humanity); Rome Statute, *supra* note 26, at art. 8 (defining unlawful deportation or transfer as a war crime).

[31] Art. 4(1) of the Fourth Geneva Convention states that "Persons protected by the Convention are those who, at a given moment and in any manner whatsoever, find themselves, in case of a conflict or occupation, in the hands of a party to the conflict or Occupying Power of which they are not nationals."

[32] *See, e.g.*, Legal Consequences for States of the Continued Presence of South Africa in Namibia (South West Africa) Notwithstanding UNSC Resolution 276, Advisory Opinion, 1971 I.C.J. 53, ¶ 118 (June 21) [hereinafter Namibia Advisory Opinion], *available at* http://www.icj-cij.org/docket/files/53/5595.pdf ("South Africa, being responsible for having created and maintained a situation which the Court has found to have been validly declared illegal . . . ." and "… the presence of South Africa in South West Africa is illegal"); Legal Consequences of the Construction of a Wall in the Occupied Palestinian Territory, Advisory Opinion, 2004 I.C.J. 131, ¶ 142 (July 9) [hereinafter Wall Advisory Opinion], *available at* http://www.icj-cij.org/docket/files/131/1671.pdf ("The Court accordingly finds that the construction of the wall, and its associated régime, are contrary to international law" and discusses what "further action is required to bring to an end the illegal situation resulting from the construction of the wall and the associated régime"); W

Sahara, Advisory Opinion, 1975 I.C.J. 61, ¶ 162 (Oct. 16) [hereinafter W. Sahara Advisory Opinion], *available at* http://www.icj-cij.org/docket/files/61/6195.pdf (finding insufficient legal ties between Morocco and W. Sahara to stifle W. Sahara's right to self-determination and "those legal ties that the court found to exist at the time of Spanish colonization between W. Sahara and Morocco…were not of such a character as to justify today the reintegration or retrocession of the territory without consulting the people").

[33] Robert Sloane, *The Changing Face of Recognition in International Law: A Case Study of Tibet*, 16 EMORY INT'L. L. REV. 107, 144 (2002) (highlighting El Salvador's efforts to get a draft resolution on the agenda at the UNGA in 1950 to condemn China's invasion of Tibet as a violation of UN Charter Art. 2(4), an effort that was defeated by the UK, the US, and India).

[34] G.A. Res. 2621 (XXV), U.N. Doc. A/RES/2621 (Oct. 12, 1970), at paras. 5 and 6.

[35] Protocol Additional to the Geneva Conventions of 12 Aug. 1949, and relating to the Protection of Victims of International Armed Conflicts (Protocol I), June 8, 1977, Art. 1(4).

[36] *See* Monique Chemillier-Gendreau, *Resistance, Right to, International Protection, in* MAX PLANCK ENCYCLOPEDIA OF PUBLIC INTERNATIONAL LAW [MPEPIL] ¶ 13-14, 2013.

[37] G. A. Res. 3246 (XXIX), U.N. Doc. A/RES/3246 (Nov. 29, 1974) ("3. Reaffirms the legitimacy of the peoples' struggle for liberation from colonial and foreign domination and alien subjugation by all available means, including armed struggle . . . 7. Strongly condemns all Governments which do not recognize the right to self-determination and independence of peoples under colonial and foreign domination and alien subjugation, notably the peoples of Africa and the Palestinian people…"). The UN has reaffirmed the right to resort to armed struggle for people under colonial and foreign domination in, among others, G.A. Res. 3236 (XXIX), U.N. Doc. A/RES/3236 (Nov. 22, 1974) ("1. Reaffirms the inalienable rights of the Palestinian people in Palestine, including a) The right to self-determination without external interference b) The right to national independence and sovereignty…2. Reaffirms also the inalienable right of the Palestinians to return to their homes and property from which they have been displaced and uprooted, and calls for their return."); G.A. Res, 33/24 (XXXII), U.N. Doc. A/RES/33/24 (Nov. 29, 1978); G.A. Res. 34/44 (XX), U.N. Doc. A/RES/34/44(Nov. 23, 1979); G.A. Res, 2672 (XXV), U.N. Doc. A/RES/2672 (Dec. 8, 1970); G.A. Res. 2535 (XXIV), U.N. Doc. A/RES/2535 (Dec. 10, 1969); G.A. Res, 41/101, A/RES/41/101 (Dec. 4, 1986) ("2. Reaffirms the legitimacy of the struggle of peoples for their independence, territorial integrity, national unity and liberation from colonial domination, apartheid and foreign occupation by all available means, including armed struggle…" especially in relation to Namibia and Palestine); G.A. Res, 35/35, A/RES/35/35 (Nov. 14, 1980) ("2. Reaffirms the legitimacy of the struggle of peoples for independence, territorial integrity, national unity and liberation from colonial and foreign domination and foreign occupation by all available means,

including armed struggle..." in relation to W. Sahara); G.A. Res, 36/9, A/RES/36/9 (Oct. 28, 1981) ("Takes note of... the decisions of its Implementation Committee to organize and conduct a general and free referendum on self-determination in W. Sahara.")

[38] Charter of the United Nations Ch. XII: International Trusteeship System, art. 77, *available at* http://www.un.org/en/documents/charter/chapter12.shtml (June 26, 1945); *see also* G.A. Res, 2145 (XXI) A/RES/2145 (Oct. 27, 1966) (rejecting and terminating the mandate of South Africa over Namibia placing the territory under the direct responsibility of the United Nations); G.A. Res, 2248 U.N. Doc. A/RES/2248 (May 19, 1967) (establishing the UN Council as the legal administering authority for Namibia until independence); G.A. Res, 45/21, U.N. Doc. A/RES/45/21 (Nov. 20, 1990) (reaffirming the inalienable right to self-determination and independence).

[39] International Status of South-West Africa, Advisory Opinion, 1950 I.C.J. 10 (July 11) [hereinafter International Status of South-West Africa Advisory Opinion], *available at* http://www.icj-cij.org/docket/files/10/1891.pdf. Voting Procedure on Questions Relating to Reports and Petitions Concerning the Territory of South-West Africa, Advisory Opinion, 1955 I.C.J. 67 (June 7) [hereinafter Voting Procedure Advisory Opinion], *available at* http://www.icj-cij.org/docket/files/24/2145.pdf (finding that the UNGA's practice of 2/3 majority vote on questions regarding Southwest Africa appropriate). Admissibility of Hearings of Petitioners by the Committee on Southwest Africa, Advisory Opinion, 1956 I.C.J. 36 (June 1) [hereinafter Admissibility of Hearings Advisory Opinion], *available at* http://www.icj-cij.org/docket/files/31/5503.pdf (granting petitioners oral hearings based on South Africa's refusal to file reports).

[40] Namibia Advisory Opinion, *supra* note 32.

[41] In 1962, Liberia and Ethiopia filed a contentious case in the I.C.J. against South Africa for failing to submit reports and to comply with the League Covenant requirements. The parties claimed that South Africa's apartheid policies violated the requirements of the mandate. South-West Africa Cases (Eth. v. S. Afr.; Liber. v. S. Afr.), Preliminary Objections, 1962 I.C.J. Rep. 319 (Dec. 21), *available at* http://www.icj-cij.org/docket/index.php?sum=286&code=lsa&p1=3&p2=3&case=47&k=f2&p3=5. The ICJ dismissed the case for lack of standing. South West Africa Cases, Second Phase (Eth. v. S. Afr.; Liber. v. S. Afr.), 1966 I.C.J. 46 (July 18), *available at* http://www.icj-cij.org/docket/files/47/4955.pdf.

[42] International Status of South-West Africa Advisory Opinion, *supra* note 39.

[43] Voting Procedure Advisory Opinion, *supra* note 32 (finding the UNGA's practice of 2/3 majority vote on questions regarding Southwest Africa appropriate); Admissibility of Hearings Advisory Opinion, *supra* note 32.

[44] G.A. Res. 749 (VIII) A, U.N. Doc. A/RES/749 (VIII) (Nov. 28, 1953); G.A. Res. 1143 (XII), U.N. Doc. A/RES/1143 (XII) (Oct. 25, 1957); S.C. Res. 276, U.N. Doc. S/RES/276 (Jan. 30, 1970) (first Ad Hoc Committee established on Jan 30, 1970 and the second on July 29, 1970).

[45] G.A. Res. 1060 (XI), U.N. Doc. A/RES/1060 (XI) (Feb. 26, 1957).

[46] Koury *supra* note 1, at 148; G.A. Res. 1702 (XVI), ¶ 2, 1083rd plen. mtg. (Dec. 19, 1961), *available at* http://daccess-dds-ny.un.org/doc/RESOLUTION/GEN/NR0 /167/55/IMG/NR016755.pdf?OpenElement.

[47] Stephanie Koury, *Legal Strategies at the United Nations: A Comparative Look at Namibia. Western Sahara, and Palestine*, INTERNATIONAL LAW AND THE ISRAELI-PALESTINIAN CONFLICT: A RIGHTS-BASED APPROACH TO MIDDLE EAST PEACE 148, 149 (Susan M. Akram et al. eds., 2011); *see* G.A. Res. 2248 (S-V), U.N. Doc. 2248 (S-V) (May 19, 1967).

[47] Namibia Advisory Opinion, *supra* note 32.

[48] Namibia Advisory Opinion, *supra* note 32.

[49] Namibia Advisory Opinion, *supra* note 32 (affirming the resolutions and mandates put forth by the UNGA and UNSC).

[50] S.C. Res. 385, U.N. Doc. S/RES/385 (Jan. 30, 1976) ("recalling the advisory opinion of the International Court of Justice of 21 June 1971 that South Africa is under obligation to withdraw its presence from the Territory").

[51] G.A. Res. 1899 (XVIII), U.N. Doc A/RES/1899 (XVIII) (Nov. 11, 1963).

[52] *See* Ngila R. L. Mwase, *The Repatriation, Rehabilitation and Resettlement of Namibian Refugees at Independence*, 25 COMMUNITY DEV. J., no. 2, 2008, at 113-14.

[53] *See* UNHCR, THE STATE OF THE WORLD'S REFUGEES 2000: FIFTY YEARS OF HUMANITARIAN ACTION 134 (2000) ("From the start, UNTAG considered that the return and peaceful reintegration of the Namibian refugees was a prerequisite for elections and for the successful transformation of Namibia into an independent, democratic country.").

[54] Proposal for a Settlement of the Namibian Situation, Letter dated Apr. 10, 1978 from the President of Security Council, U.N. Doc. S/12636 (Apr. 10,1978), *available at* http://www.ucdp.uu.se/gpdatabase/peace/SyA%2019780712.pdf.

[55] Mwase, *supra* note 52, at 115.

[56] THE STATE OF THE WORLD'S REFUGEES 2000: FIFTY YEARS OF HUMANITARIAN ACTION, *supra* note 53, at 134-36.

[57] Tripartite Agreement, Angl.-Cuba-S. Afr., Dec. 22, 1988, *available at* http://peacemaker.un.org/angola-tripartite-agreement88.

[58] UNITED NATIONS CONVENTION ON THE LAW OF THE SEA, 1982: A COMMENTARY (Myron Nordquist ed., 1989) (highlights the role of the UN Council in the accession of Namibia to the 1982 UN Law of the Sea Convention in 1982); Karin Arts, *The Legal Status and Functioning of the United Nations Council for Namibia,* 2 LEIDEN J. OF INT'L L. (1989) (describes the establishment, the structure, the functions and the powers of the Council with attention paid to questions concerning the legal status of the UNCN); S.C. Saxena, *Namibia and the United Nations, in* 36 INDIAN J. OF POL. SCI. 3, *available at* http://www.jstor.org/stable/41854677 (critically examines the role of the United Nations in Namibia's struggle for independence); *United Nations Council for Namibia: Decree on the Natural Resources of Namibia, in* 13 Intl. Legal Materials 6 (1974), *available at* http://www.jstor.org/stable/20691361 (a decree enacted by

the UN Council for Namibia declaring the "right of peoples and nations to permanent sovereignty over their natural wealth and resources").

[59] The UN's position has been affirmed through the recognition of the state of Palestine in the Territories occupied by Israel by 138 member states voting for its status as a "non-member observer state" in the UNGA.

[60] 'Mandate Palestine' or 'historic Palestine' as referred to here is the territory known as British mandate Palestine from June 1919-14 May 1948, described by the League of Nations. See the Mandate of Palestine Confirmed by the Council of the League of Nations in Moore [ed.] vol. III, 75-84. References to 'the OPT' or 'occupied Palestine' is to the territories occupied by Israel since 1967. The West Bank and Gaza or the OPT are the approximately 22% of what remains of historic Palestine that remain occupied by Israel since 1967. Only the OPT have been recognized by the UN as comprising the State of Palestine that was voted as a non-member state of the UN by the UNGA in December 2012.

[61] On Palestinian Nationality as a matter of international law, see MUTAZ M. QAFISHEH, THE INTERNATIONAL LAW FOUNDATIONS OF PALESTINIAN NATIONALITY (2008). For cases recognizing Palestinian nationality, see R. v. Ketter, 1 K.B. 787 (1940) (UK); A.B. v. M.B. 17 ILR 110 (1950) (Israel).

[62] *See* The Council of the League of Nations: The Mandate for Palestine, *supra* note 6.

[63] *See id.*; The Balfour Declaration, Nov. 2, 1917, *available at* http://www.mfa.gov.il/MFA/Peace%20Process/Guide%20to%20the%20Peace%20Process/The%20Balfour%20Declaration (last visited Aug. 22, 2011).

[64] UN Special Committee on Palestine, *Report to the General Assembly*, U.N. Doc. A/364 (Sept. 3, 1947), *available at* http://unispal.un.org/unispal.nsf/0/07175de9fa2de563852568d3006e10f3.

[65] G.A. Res 181 (II), U.N. Doc. A/RES/181(II) (Nov. 29, 1947), *available at* http://domino.un.org/unispal.nsf/0/7f0af2bd897689b785256c330061d253.

[66] Susan M. Akram and Michael Lynk, *Arab-Israeli Conflict*, 1 THE MAX PLANCK ENCYCLOPEDIA OF PUBLIC INTERNATIONAL LAW 502 (R. Wolfrum ed., 2012).

[67] G.A. Res 181 (II), U.N. Doc. A/RES/181(II) (Nov. 29, 1947), *available at* http://domino.un.org/unispal.nsf/0/7f0af2bd897689b785256c330061d253.

[68] Henry C. King and Charles R. Crane, *The American King-Crane Commission of Inquiry Report, in* DOCUMENTS ON THE ARAB-ISRAELI CONFLICT (M. Cherif Bassiouni ed., 2005).

[69] The Declaration of the Establishment of the State of Israel, May 14, 1948, *available at* http://www.mfa.gov.il/MFA/Peace+Process/Guide+to+the+Peace+Process/Declaration+of+Establishment+of+State+of+Israel.htm (last visited Aug. 15, 2011).

[70] U.N. SCOR, 3rd year, U.N. Doc. S/PV271 (Mar. 19, 1948), *available at* http://unitednationstrusteeshippalestine1948.blogspot.com ("a temporary trusteeship for Palestine should be established under the Trusteeship Council of the United Nations to maintain the peace and to afford the Jews and Arabs of Palestine, who must live together, further opportunity to reach an agreement regarding the future

government of that country"); Kermit Roosevelt, *The Partition of Palestine: A Lesson in Pressure Politics, in* 2 MIDDLE EAST J. 1 (1948), *available at* http://www.jstor.org/stable/4321940; Itzhak Galnoor, *The Zionist Debates on Partition, in* 14 ISRAEL STUD. 2 (2009), *available at* http://www.jstor.org/stable/30245854.

[71] G.A. Res. 194 (III), U.N. Doc. A/RES/194 (III) (Dec. 11, 1948), *available at* http://unispal.un.org/UNISPAL.NSF/0/C758572B78D1CD0085256BCF0077E51A.

[72] *See* G.A. Res. 302 (IV), U.N. Doc. A/RES/302 (IV) (Dec. 8, 1949) (establishing assistance for Palestinian refugees); G.A. Res. 394 (V), U.N. Doc. A/RES/394 (V) (Dec. 14, 1950) (providing a progress report on establishing repatriation, resettlement, and restitution for Palestinian refugees).

[73] S.C. Res. 242, U.N. Doc. S/RES/242 (Nov. 22, 1967), *available at* http://unispal.un.org/unispal.nsf/5ba47a5c6cef541b802563e000493b8c/7d35e1f72 9df491c85256ee700686136?OpenDocument (" . . . should include the application of both the following principles: (i) Withdrawal of Israeli armed forces from territories occupied in the recent conflict; (ii) Termination of all claims or states of belligerency and respect for and acknowledgment of the sovereignty, territorial integrity and political independence of every State in the area and their right to live in peace within secure and recognized boundaries free from threats or acts of force"); S.C. Res. 338, U.N. Doc S/RES/338 (Oct. 22, 1973), *available at* http://unispal.un.org/unispal.nsf/0/7FB7C26FCBE80A31852560C50065F878 ("The Security Council 1) calls upon all parties to the present fighting to cease all firing and terminate all military activity immediately . . . *in the positions they now occupy*; 2) calls upon the parties concerned to start immediately after the cease-fire the implementation of Security Council resolution 242 (1967) in all of its parts" (emphasis added)).

[74] The UNSC in the 1970s and 1980s condemned Israeli violations of human rights and international law; affirmed the *de jure* applicability of the Four Geneva Conventions; established committees to study Israeli settlements; appointed fact-finding missions; and requested the Secretary General to report on Israel's compliance. *See* S.C. Res. 279, U.N. Doc S/RES/279 (May 12, 1970); S.C. Res. 298, U.N. Doc S/RES/298 (Sep. 25, 1971); S.C. Res. 476, U.N. Doc S/RES/476 (Jun. 30, 1980); S.C. Res. 636, U.N. Doc S/RES/636 (July 6, 1989). Nevertheless, its approach has been focused on the illegality of Israel's expansion in the Occupied Territories and violations of humanitarian law, but not on the underlying violations of Palestinians' individual and collective inalienable rights as the UNGA has long insisted upon. *See* S.C. Res. 605, U.N. Doc S/RES/605 (Dec. 22, 1987). Even concerning international human rights violations, the UNSC has taken no enforcement action, and has vetoed a number of resolutions on such violations. *See* International Crisis Group (ICG), *Curb Your Enthusiasm: Israel and Palestine after the U.N.*, Middle East Report N°112, *available at* http://www.refworld.org/docid/4e6ef0102.html. In this last area, though, it was not different from Namibia, in that Namibia was not successful in obtaining UNSC enforcement action on resolutions in its favor.

[75] *See, e.g.*, S.C. Res 1243, ¶1, U.N. Doc. S/RES/1243 (May 27, 1999); S.C. Res. 1605, ¶1, U.N. Doc. S/RES/1605 (June 17, 2005). These are just a small number of UNSC Resolutions calling upon the parties to implement resolution 338 (1973).
[76] Taba Negotiations: The Moratinos Non-Paper, EU SPECIAL REPRESENTATIVE TO THE MIDDLE EAST PROCESS, Jan. 2011, *available at* http://www.mideastweb.org/moratinos.htm; The Wye River Memorandum, U.S. DEPT. OF STATE, Oct. 23, 1998, *available at* http://www.state.gov/www/regions/nea/981023_interim_agmt.html; Declaration of Principles on Interim Self-Government Agreements, ISRAEL MINISTRY OF FOREIGN AFFAIRS, Sept. 13, 1993, *available at* http://www.mfa.gov.il/MFA/Peace%20Process/Guide%20to%20the%20Peace%20 Process/Declaration%20of%20Principles; Camp David Accords, ISRAEL MINISTRY OF FOREIGN AFFAIRS, Sept. 17, 1978, *available at* http://www.mfa.gov.il/MFA/Peace+Process/Guide+to+the+Peace+Process/Camp+ David+Accords.htm.
[77] U.N. Secretary General, Letter dated Apr. 10, 2002 from the Secretary-General addressed to the President of the Security Council, U.N. Doc. S/2002/369 (Apr. 10, 2002) (establishing Russia, the US, the EU, and the UN as the Quartet, a group designed to address the escalating conflict in the Middle East).
[78] The Israeli-Palestinian Interim Agreement on the West Bank and the Gaza Strip (The Oslo Peace Accord), Washington, D.C., Sept. 28, 1995, *available at* http://foeme.org/www/?module=regional_data&record_id=4 (last visited Aug. 23, 2011).
[79] United Nations Relief and Works Agency for Palestine Refugees in the Near East, *In Figures: As of 1 Jan. 2013*, UNRWA.ORG (Jan. 2013), http://www.unrwa.org/sites/default/files/2013042435340.pdf.
[80] See Karen AbuZayd's chapter, *An Essay On the Causes and Factors of the Unresolved Palestinian Refugee Problem: A View from an UNRWA Commissioner General,* in this volume.
[81] G.A. Res 394 (V), U.N. Doc A/RES/394 (Dec. 14, 1950), *available at* http://unispal.un.org/unispal.nsf/d0911f77d9bb1f14852574050052b8d6/2e009c237 2d9e9f9852560eb006d0d8c?OpenDocument&Highlight=0,UNCCP ("Ensure that refugees, whether repatriated or resettled, will be treated without any discrimination either in law or in fact"). United Nations Conciliation Commission for Palestine (UNCCP), *The Question of Reintegration by Repatriation of Resettlement (Working Paper),* A/AC.25/W/82/Rev.1 (Oct. 2, 1961); United Nations Conciliation Commission for Palestine (UNCCP), *Definition of a "Refugee" under Paragraph 11 of the General Assembly Resolution of 11 December 1984*, A/AC.25/W/61, Apr. 9, 1951, *available at* http://unispal.un.org/UNISPAL.NSF/0/418E7BC6931616B485256CAF00647CC7 (stating that the categories of Palestinian refugees covered by the terms of Res. 194 include 1. 'persons of Arab origin who were Palestinian citizens and, after 29 November 1947, left territory at present under the control of the Israel authorities'; 2. 'stateless persons of Arab origin who after 29 November 1947 left that territory where they had been settled up to that date'; 3. 'persons of Arab origin who were

Palestinian citizens and left the said territory after 6 August 1924 and before 29 November 1947 '; and 4. 'persons of Arab origin who had opted for Palestinian citizenship, left that territory before 6 August 1924, and retained their citizenship up to 29 November 1947'). *See* Susan M. Akram, *Palestinian Refugees and Their Status: Rights, Politics and Implications for a Just Solution,* 31 J. OF PALESTINE STUD. 3 (2002) (stating that 'Palestine refugee' is a term used by UNRWA to refer to both Palestine refugees and their descendants and displaced persons and their descendants. According to the UNRWA, Palestine refugees refer to "any person whose normal place of residence was Palestine during the period 1 June 1946 to 15 May 1948 and who lost both home and means of livelihood as a result of the 1948 conflict." Displaced persons refer to those who are not Palestine refugees and fall within the UNGA Resolution 2252 (July 4, 1967) and subsequent UNGA Resolutions.). Michael Fischbach, *The United Nations and Palestinian Refugee Property Compensation*, *in* 31 J. OF PALESTINE STUD. 2 (2002), *available at* http://www.jstor.org/stable/10.1525/jps.2002.31.2.34 (explaining that the primary mandate of the UNCCP was conciliation between the parties as well as refugee repatriation and compensation).

[82] Susan M. Akram and Terry Rempel, *Temporary Protection as an Instrument for Implementing the Right of Return for Palestinian Refugees*, 22 B.U. INT'L. L.J. 1, 54-56 (Spring 2004).

[83] For a summary review of the various definitions of "Palestine refugee" and Palestinian refugees, see Susan M. Akram, *Myths and Realities of the Palestinian Refugee Problem*, *in* INTERNATIONAL LAW AND THE ISRAELI-PALESTINIAN CONFLICT: A RIGHTS-BASED APPROACH TO MIDDLE EAST PEACE 13-44, (Susan M. Akram et al. eds., 2011).

[84] See Karen AbuZayd's chapter, *An Essay On the Causes and Factors of the Unresolved Palestinian Refugee Problem: A View from an UNRWA Commissioner General*, in this volume; G.A. Res. 169, U.N. Doc. A/RES/169 (Dec. 15, 1980), at art. 66; S.C. Res. 237, U.N. Doc. S/RES/237 (June 14, 1967).

[85] U.N. Human Rights Council, *Report of the Human Rights Council on its 7th session,* A/HRC/7/78 (July 14, 2008), *available at* http://www.refworld.org/docid/49997ae80.html; U.N. Human Rights Committee, *Concluding Observations, Israel*, CCPR/C/79/Add.93 (Aug. 18, 1998), *available at* http://www.refworld.org/docid/3ae6b0284.html.

[86] Norwegian Refugee Council/Internal Displacement Monitoring Centre, *Israel: CESCR echoes NGO concerns over displacement, available at* http://www.refworld.org/docid/4ed8d3360.html (highlighting NGO concern with Israel's forced evictions and displacement of Palestinians and Bedouins in Israel and the occupied Palestinian Territory); Committee on Economic, Social and Cultural Rights, 19th Session (Dec. 4, 1998) (explains the substantive violations by Israel).

[87] U.N. Committee on Economic, Social and Cultural Rights [CESCR], *Concluding Observations, Israel*, E/C.12/1/Add.90 (June 26, 2003), *available at* http://www.refworld.org/docid/3f242abc7.html; BADIL RESOURCE CENTER & ASYLUM & HUMAN RIGHTS CLINIC, SUBMISSION TO THE COMMITTEE ON ECONOMIC,

CULTURAL AND SOCIAL RIGHTS REGARDING ISRAEL'S SERIOUS BREACH OF ITS OBLIGATIONS UNDER THE INTERNATIONAL COVENANT ON ECONOMIC, SOCIAL AND CULTURAL RIGHTS (ICESCR) (2010), *available at* http://www.badil.org/en/documents/category/40-other?download=846%3Abadil-sub-to-cecsr-regarding-israel-icescr-4thsession-nov2010.

[88] United Nations Committee on Economic, Social and Cultural Rights [CESCR], *Concluding Observations, Israel*, E/C.12/1/Add.27 (1998); CESCR, Concluding Observations, *Israel*, E/C.12/1/Add.69 (2001); CESCR, *Concluding Observations, Israel,* E/C.12/1/Add.69 (2001); CESCR, *Concluding Observations, Israel,* E/C.12/1/Add.90 (2003); CESCR, *Concluding Observations, Israel,* E/C.12/ISR/CO/3 (2012). Committee Against Torture [CAT], *Concluding Observations, Israel,* CAT/C/ISR/CO/4, (2009); CAT, *List of Issues prepared by the Committee prior to the submission of the fifth periodic report of Israel*, CAT/C/ISR/5, (2012). United Nations Human Rights Committee [HRC], *Concluding Observations, Israel,* CCPR/C/79/Add.93, (1998); HRC, *Concluding Observations, Israel,* CCPR/CO/79/ISR, (2003); HRC, *Concluding Observations, Israel,* CCPR/C/ISR/CO/3 (2010). Human Rights Council, *First Special Session*, A/HRC/S-1/3, (2006); Human Rights Council, *3rd Special Session: Israeli Military Incursions in Occupied Palestinian Territory*, A/HRC/S-3/2, (2006); Human Rights Council, *6th Special Session: Human Rights Violations Emanating from Israeli Military Incursions in the Occupied Palestinian Territory, including the Recent Ones in Occupied Gaza and West Bank of Nablus*, A/HRC/S-6/2 (2008); Human Rights Council, *9th Special Session: "The Grave Violation of Human Rights in the Occupied Palestinian Territory including the Recent Aggression in the Occupied Gaza Strip,"* A/HRC/S-9/2, (2009); Human Rights Council, *12th Special Session: "The Human Rights Situation in the Occupied Palestinian Territory and East Jerusalem,"* A/HRC/S-12/1, (2009). United Nations Committee on the Rights of the Child [CRC], *Concluding Observations, Israel,* CRC/C/15/Add.195, (2002); CRC, *Concluding Observations, Israel,* CRC/C/OPAC/ISR/CO/1, (2010); CRC, *Concluding Observations, Israel,* CRC/C/ISR/CO/2-4, (2013). United Nations Committee on the Elimination of Discrimination Against Women [CEDAW], *Concluding Comments, Israel,* CEDAW/C/ISR/CO/3, (2005); CEDAW *Concluding Observations, Israel,* CEDAW/C/ISR/CO/5, (2011).

[89] Committee on the Elimination of Racial Discrimination [CERD], Concluding Observations, Israel, CERD/C/ISR/CO/14-16 (2012), *available at* http://www2.ohchr.org/english/bodies/cerd/docs/CERD.C.ISR.CO.14-16.pdf.

[90] H.R.C. Res. 7/17, U.N. Doc. A/HRC/7/17 (March 27, 2008).

[91] G.A. Res. 3237 (XXIX), U.N. Doc. A/RES/3237 (Nov. 22, 1974).

[92] Quigley, *supra* note 1, makes the case that, with or without majority state recognition, Palestine satisfies all the conditions of the Montevideo Convention—a permanent population, defined territory, government, and the capacity to enter into relations with other states. He concludes that Palestine does not need territorial independence to be a state.

[93] One hundred and thirty-eight nations voted in favor of Palestinian statehood recognition. *See* Press Release, General Assembly, General Assembly Votes Overwhelmingly to Accord Palestine "Non-Member Observer State" Status in United Nations, U.N. Press Release G.A./11317 (Nov. 29, 2012), *available at* http://www.un.org/News/Press/docs/2012/ga11317.doc.htm.

[94] *See* G.A. Res 1874, U.N. Doc. A/RES/1874 (Jun. 23, 1963); G.A. Res. 2229, U.N. Doc. A/RES/2229 (Dec. 20, 1966).

[95] *See* G.A. Res. 1514, U.N. Doc. A/RES/1514 (Dec. 14, 1960); G.A. Res. 33/31, U.N. Doc. A/RES/33/31 (Dec. 13, 1978).

[96] As Jeffrey Smith and others have pointed out, Spain's relinquishment of its role in W. Sahara through the 1975 Madrid Accords has actually complicated the decolonization process. The lack of colonial consideration of the treatment of the territory has allowed Morocco to assume the role of primary party responsible for the territory of W. Sahara, not as an occupying state, but by a claim of sovereignty over the territory. *See* Thomas Marks, *Spanish Sahara: Background to Conflict*, 75 AFRICAN AFF. 298 (Jan. 1976), *available at* http://www.jstor.org/stable/721863; B.O. Okere, *The Western Sahara Case*, 28 INT'L AND COMP. L. 2 (Apr. 1979), *available at* http://www.jstor.org/stable/758602.

[97] The POLISARO Front is an acronym for the Popular Front for the Liberation of Saguia el-Hamra and Río de Oro, in Spanish, Frente Popular para la Liberación de Saguia el-Hamra y Río de Oro.

[98] W. Sahara Advisory Opinion, *supra* note 32, at ¶ 162.

[99] W. Sahara Advisory Opinion, *supra* note 32, at ¶ 162 (stating the materials and information show "the existence of rights, including some rights relating to the land, which constituted legal ties between the Mauritanian entity, as understood by the Court, and the territory of Western Sahara.").

[100] W. Sahara Advisory Opinion, note 32, at ¶ 55.

[101] The November 1975 Madrid Accords did not provide for local governance or the involvement of the Djemaa. *See* Declaration of Principles on Western Sahara by Spain, Morocco, and Mauritania (Nov. 1975) (stating "Morocco and Mauritania will participate in collaboration with the Djemaa and to which will be transferred all the responsibilities and powers referred to in the preceding paragraph.").

[102] *Id.*

[103] As of 2012, 85 states have given diplomatic recognition to the SADR, and it has been a member of the AU since 1984. Partition of the territory became official in April 1976, but it may have been both a reaction to recognition of the SADR and to the fact that territorial partition was already a reality on the ground. Terrence McNamee & Greg Mills & J Peter Pham, *Morocco and the African Union: Prospects for Re-Engagement and Progress on Western Sahara,* Discussion Paper 1/2013, *available at* http://www.thebrenthurstfoundation.org/Files/Brenthurst_Commisioned_Reports/Brenthurst-paper-201301-Morocco-and-the-AU.pdf (holding that the SADR has received diplomatic recognition by 85 states as of 2013, and 40 states have diplomatic relations with the SADR); see Jeffrey Smith's chapter, *State of Exile:*

The Saharawi Republic and Its Refugees, in this volume (highlighting the Mauritania and Morocco treaty regarding the territorial partition, and the international community's response to the partition. *See also* Benjamin MacQueen, AN INTRODUCTION TO MIDDLE EAST POLITICS (2013) (explaining that the POLISARIO declared the independence of the SADR on February 27, 1976).

[104] Construction began in 1981, and was completed in 1987, physically preventing the armed conflict from continuing across the divided territory. *See* United Nations Map No. 3691, Rev. 53 U.N. (Oct. 2006), *available at* http://www.un.org/Depts/Cartographic/map/dpko/minurso.pdf.

[105] Organization of African Unity [OAU], *Resolution of the Question of the Question of the Western Sahara*, AHG/Res. 92 (XV) (July 22, 1978).

[106] OAU, AHG/Res. 114 (XVI) (June 6-12, 1983), cited in Gino Naldi, *Western Sahara: Suspended Statehood or Frustrated Self-Determination?* 13 AFR. Y.B. INT'L L. 11 (2005).

[107] OAU Res. AHG/103 (XVIII) (June 24-27, 1981).

[108] OAU, *Resolution on the Question of Western Sahara*, AHG/Dec. 114 (XVI) (October 17, 1979); OAU, *Resolution on Western Sahara*, AHG/Dec. 103 (XVIII) (June, 24-27,1981). *See also* OAU, AHG/Res. 104 (XIX) (June 6-12, 1983) (OAU Peace Plan), *available at* http://www.africaunion.org/root/au/Documents/Decisions/hog/sHoGAssembly1983.pdf.

[109] OAU, AHG/Res. 104 (XIX) (June 6-12, 1983). *See also* Naldi, *supra* note 106, at 16-17.

[110] The re-engagement of the UN at this time was marked by the intervention of Secretary General Perez de Cuellar himself. *See* Yahia Zoubir & Anthony Pazzanita, *The United Nations' Failure in Resolving the Western Sahara Conflict,* 49 MIDDLE EAST J. 4 (Sept. 1995).

[111] *Cf.* S.C. Res. 1359, U.N. Doc. S/RES/1359 (June 29, 2001) with S.C. Res. 1754, U.N. Doc S/RES/1754 (April 30, 2007).

[112] *See* S.C. Res. 621/88, U.N. Doc. S/RES/621/88 (Sept. 20, 1988).

[113] U.N. Secretary-General, *The Situation Concerning Western Sahara*, ¶ 61, U.N. Doc S/21360.

[114] S.C. Res. 690, ¶ 4, U.N. Doc. S/RES/690 (April 29, 1991) (establishing MINURSO); *see, e.g.,* S.C. Res. 2099, ¶ 1, U.N. Doc. S/RES/2099 (April 25, 2013) (deciding to extend the mandate of MINURSO until April 2014).

[115] W. Sahara Advisory Opinion, *supra* note 32. *See also* Accordance with International Law of the Unilateral Declaration of Independence in Respect of Kosovo, Advisory Opinion, 2010 I.C.J. 403 (July 22), *available at* http://www.icj-cij.org/docket/files/141/15987.pdf.

[116] *See also* Res. 2625 (XXV) 1970 Declaration on Principles of International Law Concerning Friendly Relations and Cooperation among States in Accordance with the Charter of the United Nations.

[117] Case Concerning East Timor (Port. v. Austl.), 1995 I.C.J. Gen. List No. 84, (June 30), *available at* http://www.refworld.org/docid/40239bff4.html.

[118] The UN did oversee a referendum process for Namibia, but as a pre-requisite for the required outcome of realizing self-determination that incorporated the principle of majority vote for black Namibians, as the I.C.J. had established.
[119] *See* G.A. Res. 34/35, U.N. Doc. A/RES/34/35 (Nov. 21, 1979); G.A. Res. 34/37, U.N. Doc. A/RES/34/37 (Nov. 21, 1979) (stating that it "deeply deplores the aggravation of the situation resulting from the continued occupation of W. Sahara by Morocco and the extension of that occupation to the territory recently evacuated by Mauritania"); G.A. Res. 43/33, U.N. Doc. A/RES/43/33 (Nov. 22, 1988).
[120] *See* John Dugard, *Advisory Opinions and the Secretary General*, *in* INTERNATIONAL LAW AND THE QUEST FOR ITS IMPLEMENTATION 415 (Marcelo Kohen & Laurence Boisson de Chazournes eds., 2010).
[121] Spain had agreements with Morocco over W. Sahara fisheries until 1986, and after that the EU has entered into such agreements. Private corporations including Kerr McGee, Wessex Exploration, Sterling and Premier, have also contracted with Morocco regarding petroleum rights in Saharan territory, an issue on which Sahrawi rights activists are heavily engaged. *See* Helen Campbell, *Oil Companies Very Keen on Western Sahara*, WESTERN SAHARA RESEARCH WATCH (May 2005), *available at* http://www.wsrw.org/a193x1971.
[122] Smith notes the additional singular features of Saharawi autonomy such as self-rule, control and governance over the inland part of W. Sahara not occupied by Morocco. See also Jeffrey Smith's chapter, *State of Exile: The Saharawi Republic and its Refugees*, in this volume.
[123] Hannikainen, *supra* note 24, at 68.
[124] United Nations Committee on Economic, Social and Cultural Rights [CESCR], *Concluding Observations, Morocco*, E/C.12/1994/5 (May 30, 1994), *available at* http://www.refworld.org/docid/3ae6ae6514.html ("concerned that the right to self-determination has not been exercised . . . "); CESCR, *Concluding Observations, Morocco*, E/C.12/1/Add.55 (Dec. 1, 2000) ("With regard to the situation in the W. Sahara, the Committee regrets that there has not been a definite solution to the question of self-determination."); CESCR, *Concluding Observations, Morocco*, E/C.12/MAR/CO/3 (Sept. 4, 2006), *available at* http://www.refworld.org/docid/45c30ba60.html ("no clear solution has yet been found to the question of self-determination . . . straitened circumstances endured by people displaced by the conflict . . .").
[125] United Nations Committee Against Torture [CAT], *U.N. Committee against Torture: Conclusions and Recommendations, Morocco*, CAT/C/CR/31/2 (Feb. 5, 2004), *available at* http://www.refworld.org/docid/411745864.html; United Nations Committee on the Rights of the Child [CRC], *U.N. Committee on the Rights of the Child: Concluding Observations, Morocco*, CRC/C/15/RESP/ Add.211 (Part I) (Dec. 1, 2004), *available at* http://www.refworld.org/docid/42d284f34.html.
[126] United Nations Human Rights Committee [HRC], *Concluding Observations, Morocco*, CCPR/C/79/Add.113 (Nov. 1, 1999), *available at* http://www.refworld.org/docid/3ae6b01218.html; *see also* HRC, *Concluding*

Observations, Morocco, CCPR/CO/82/MAR (Dec. 1, 2004), *available at* http://www.refworld.org/docid/42ce96954.html; HRC, *Concluding Observations, Morocco,* CCPR/CO/C/79/Add.44, *available at* http://www.refworld.org/docid/3ae6b02724.html.

[127] United Nations Human Rights Council, *Report of the Working Group on the Universal Periodic Review: Morocco*, A/HRC/21/3 (July 6, 2012), *available at* http://www.refworld.org/docid/50c997852.html; Universal Periodic Review 13th Session, Joint Report Submitted by RFK Center for Justice and Human Rights & BU Asylum and Human Rights Program (Nov. 21, 2011), *available at* http://www.scribd.com/doc/95531621/Universal-Periodic-Review-13th-session-RFK-Center.

[128] Robert F. Kennedy Center for Justice and Human Rights, *Nowhere to Turn: The Consequences of the Failure to Monitor Human Rights Violations in Western Sahara and Tindouf Refugee* Camps (Apr. 2013), *available at* http://rfkcenter.org/images/attachments/article/1884/NowhereToTurnLoRes.pdf (stating that "in spite of all the evidence of human rights violations, the Security Council has extended MINURSO's mandate more than 20 times, but has not approved a human rights mandate for MINURSO."); UNSC Rep. of the Security Council, , *Report of the Secretary-General on the situation concerning Western Sahara*, S/2012/197 (Apr. 5, 2012), *available at* http://www.refworld.org/docid/4fbf7a8f2.html.

[129] *See* Jeffrey Smith's chapter, *State of Exile: The Saharawi Republic and Its Refugees,* in this volume (stating that "the maintenance of the status quo by the Security Council can be seen in its reluctance to consider the addition of a human rights monitoring mandate for MINURSO, notwithstanding that the securing of human rights is implicitly part of the UN's role to assure the proper conditions for the conduct of a self-determination referendum.").

[130] UN Secretary-General, *Report of the Secretary-General on the Situation Concerning Western Sahara*, U.N. Doc. S/2000/131 (Feb. 17, 2000).

[131] DETERRITORIALIZED YOUTH: SAHRAWI AND AFGHAN REFUGEES AT THE MARGINS OF THE MIDDLE EAST 6 (Dawn Chatty, ed.,,2010).

[132] Press Release, UNHRC, Agreement Reached on Increased Family Visits for Long-Separated Sahrawi Families (July 3, 2013), *available at* http://www.unhcr.org/51d430029.html.

[133] There may be consensus among states and civil society that Tibet is a colonized or an occupied nation, at least as an informal matter. *See* Sloane, *supra* note 33. National courts have issued decisions and judgments that recognize Tibet as an occupied state. *See, e.g., Spanish Court Acknowledges Tibet As An Occupied State Under International Law,* TIBET JUSTICE CENTER, *available at* http://www.tibetjustice.org/features/audencia-nacional-ruling/ (last visited Oct. 28, 2013). However, as academics and legal experts have conceded, formal state recognition of Tibet as such remains elusive, including from the UN. *See* Jayshree Bajoria, *The Question of Tibet*, COUNCIL OF FOREIGN RELATIONS (Dec. 5, 2008), *available at* http://www.cfr.org/china/question-tibet/p15965#p2; Barry Sautman, *Tibet's Putative Statehood and International Law*, 9 CHINESE J. INTL. L. 1 (2010);

Ellen Bork, *Tibet's Transition: Will Washington Take a Stand?,* WORLD AFF. J., Sept./Oct. 2012, *available at* http://www.worldaffairsjournal.org/article/tibet's-transition-will-washington-take-stand.

[134] See Robert Sloane's chapter, *Tibetan Diaspora in the Shadow of the Self-Immolation Crisis: Consequences of Colonialism,* in this volume; Sloane, *supra* note 33 (arguing that Tibet has been recognized on many levels as being occupied territory and long entitled to independence, as well as explaining historical reasons for Tibet's failure to achieve self-determination, including its political isolation to avoid being colonized by European powers). *See also* Robert Barnett, *Did Britain Just Sell Tibet?* N.Y. TIMES at A31 (Nov. 24, 2008) (detailing the British shift of position on Tibet).

[135] *See The Tibetans,* CONFLICT EARLY WARNING SYSTEMS, UNIVERSITY OF SOUTHERN CALIFORNIA, *available at* http://www.usc.edu/dept/LAS/ir/cews/database/Tibet/tibet.pdf.

[136] Michael C. Davis, *Tibet, in* MAX PLANCK ENCYCLOPEDIA OF PUBLIC INTERNATIONAL LAW [MPEPIL] ¶ 5, 2013; Michael van Walt van Praag, THE STATUS OF TIBET (Wisdom Publications, 1987); Michael van Walt van Praag, POPULATION TRANSFER AND THE SURVIVAL OF THE TIBETAN IDENTITY (New York US Tibet Committee, 1986).

[137] Minorities at Risk Project, *Assessment for Tibetans in China*, Dec. 31, 2003, *available at*, http://www.refworld.org/docid/469f3a69c.html (stating that "no country to date has challenged Beijing's claim that Tibet is a part of China.").

[138] Davis, *supra* note 136, at ¶ 11.

[139] Law of the People's Republic of China on Regional National Autonomy 1984 (the Autonomy Law), *available at* http://www.china.org.cn/english/government/207138.htm.

[140] G.A. Res. 1723 (XVI), U.N. Doc. A/RES/1723 (Dec. 20, 1961).

[141] *See* G.A. Res. 1353 (XIV), U.N. Doc. A/RES/1353 (Oct. 21, 1959); G.A. Res. 2079 (XX), U.N. Doc. A/RES/2079 (Dec. 18, 1965).

[142] INTERNATIONAL COMMISSION OF JURISTS, TIBET: HUMAN RIGHTS AND THE RULE OF LAW (1997), *available at* http://www.icj.org/tibet-tibet-human-rights-and-the-rule-of-law/ (finding that the Tibetans are a "people under alien subjugation," entitled to the right of self-determination.); Tenzin Bhagen-Tsang, *Tibet, The United Nations and Human Rights,* JAMES MADISON UNIVERSITY: STUDENT FOR A FREE TIBET, *available at* http://www.jmu.edu/orgs/tibet/tibetandun.html; *Countries Support Self-Determination for Tibet at 58th U.N. Commission on Human Rights*, INTERNATIONAL CAMPAIGN FOR TIBET, Mar. 28, 2002, *available at* http://www.savetibet.org/countries-support-self-determination-for-tibet-at-58th-un-commission-on-human-rights/ (stating that Germany, Guatemala, The Netherlands, and Switzerland were among the countries that raised self-determination for Tibet at the UN Commission of Human Rights in 2002).

[143] *See* Sloane, *supra* note 33, at 154.

[144] Committee on the Elimination of Racial Discrimination [CERD], *Concluding Observations, China*, CERD/C/CHN/CO/10-13 (2009); Committee Against Torture

[CAT], *Concluding Observations, China*, CAT/C/20/Add.5 (1996); Committee Against Torture [CAT], *Concluding Observations, China*, CAT/C/CHN/CO/4 (2008); Committee on the Elimination of Discrimination against Women [CEDAW], *Concluding Observations, China*, CEDAW/C/CHN/CO/6 (2006).

[145] United Nations Committee on Economic, Social and Cultural Rights [CESCR], *Concluding Observations, China*, E/C.12/1/Add.107 (2005), *available at* http://daccess-dds-ny.un.org/doc/UNDOC/GEN/G05/422/45/PDF/G0542245.pdf?OpenElement.

[146] Tibet Justice Center and Boston University Asylum & Human Rights Program, *Parallel Report Submitted to the Committee on Economic, Social and Cultural Rights (CESCR) for Consideration of the Report on China Concerning the Rights of the Tibetan People* (April 1, 2013), *available at* http://www.tibetjustice.org/reports/un/Tibet_Parallel_Report_CESCR_2014.pdf [hereinafter Parallel Report].

[147] United Nations Committee on Economic, Social and Cultural Rights [CESCR], *U.N. Committee on Economic, Social, and Cultural Rights: Addendum to the Initial Reports Submitted by States Parties, People's Republic of China*, E/1990/5/Add.59, *available at* http://www.refworld.org/docid/45377f760.html.

[148] Davis, *supra* note 136, at ¶ 9-10; *see also* Tibet Justice Center, *Tibet's Stateless Nationals II: Tibetan Refugees in India* (Sept. 2011).

[149] *See* Foreigners Act No. 31 (1946); Registration of Foreigners Act No. 16 (1939), codified in India Code (1993).

[150] *See* TIBET JUSTICE CENTER, TIBET'S STATELESS NATIONALS II: TIBETAN REFUGEES IN INDIA 45 (2011). *See also* Namgyal Dolkar v. Ministry of External Affairs, W.P. (C) 12179/2009 (High Court of Delhi) (India) (holding that Tibetans born in India between January 26, 1985 and July 1, 1987 are Indian citizens by operation of the Indian Citizenship Act, which affects 30,000 Tibetans born in India during those years while those born before and after remain in 'foreigner' and stateless status).

[151] Parallel Report, *supra* note 146, at ¶ 1, 21 (stating that 114 Tibetans have self-immolated against their treatment under Chinese rule. Nearly all self-immolators who had left behind a final statement had called for "basic rights and freedoms, including the rights to practice their own religions, learn their mother tongue, wear Tibetan clothes and be united.").

[152] *See* Sloane, *supra* note 33.

[153] G.A. Res. 1353 (XIV), U.N. Doc. A/RES/1353 (Oct. 21, 1959).

[154] G.A. Res. 1723 (XVI), U.N. Doc. A/RES/1723 (Dec. 20, 1961).

[155] Lea Brilmayer & Isaias Yemane Tesfalident, *Third State Obligations and the Enforcement of International Law,* 44:1 NYU J. OF INTL. L. AND P. 1 (2010), *available at* http://nyujilp.org/wp-content/uploads/2010/06/44.1-Brilmayer-Tesfalidet.pdf (third state obligations consist of "a global obligation, on the part of every State, to undertake heroic measures to pressure, prevent or punish every violation of international law.").

[156] International Law Commission, *Draft Articles on Responsibility of States for*

Internationally Wrongful Acts, at art. 1-3, Supplement No. 10 (A/56/10), *available at* http://www.refworld.org/docid/3ddb8f804.html. *See also* Commentary to article 19 of 1976 Report to the UNGA (" a serious breach of an international obligation of essential importance for the maintenance of international peace and security, such as that prohibiting aggression....safeguarding the right of self-determination of peoples, such as that prohibiting the establishment or maintenance by force of colonial domination.")

[157] Rafael Nieto-Navia, *International Peremptory Norms (Jus Cogens) and International Humanitarian Law,* COALITION FOR THE INTERNATIONAL CRIMINAL COURT (Mar. 2001), *available at* http://www.iccnow.org/documents/WritingColombiaEng.pdf.

[158] *See* Namibia, W. Sahara, and Palestine Advisory Opinions, *supra* note 32. *See also* Accordance with International Law of the Unilateral Declaration of Independence in Respect of Kosovo (Request for Advisory Opinion), 2010 I.C.J. Gen. List No. 141 (July 22), ¶ 79 and 82, *available at* http://www.refworld.org/docid/4c5151002.html (*erga omnes* obligations as articulated by the ICJ with respect to Kosovo). *See also* S.C. Res. 497, U.N.Doc. S/RES/497 (Dec. 17 1981) (declaring invalid Israel's annexation of the Golan Heights).

[159] *See* S.C. Res. 497, U.N. Doc. S/RES/497 (Dec. 17, 1981) (invalidating Israel's annexation of the Golan Heights); G.A. Res, 2546, U.N. Doc. A/RES/2546 (Dec. 11, 1969) ("Recalling the humanitarian resolutions regarding the violations of human rights and fundamental freedoms in the territories occupied by Israel"); G.A. Res. 34/37, U.N. Doc. A/RES/34/37 (Nov. 21, 1979) (reaffirming the inalienable right of the people of W. Sahara to self-determination and independence).

[160] Namibia Advisory Opinion, *supra* note 32, at paras. 122-124.

[161] *See* S.C. Res. 283, U.N. Doc. S/RES/283 (July 29, 1970).

[162] W. Sahara Advisory Opinion, *supra* note 32, ¶ citing G.A. Res. 2625 at ¶ 2.

[163] *See* G.A. Res. 3458 (XXX), U.N. Doc. 3458 (XXX) (Dec. 10, 1975); G.A. Res. 31/45, U.N. Doc. A/RES/31/45 (Dec. 1, 1976); G.A. Res. 33/31, U.N. Doc. A/RES/33/31 (Dec. 13, 1978).

[164] S.C. Res. 377, U.N. Doc. S/RES/377 (Oct. 22, 1975); S.C. Res. 379, U.N. Doc. S/RES/379 (Nov. 2, 1975); S.C. Res. 380, U.N. Doc. S/RES/380 (Nov. 2, 1975). *See* Koury, *supra* note 47, at 153-54.

[165] W. Sahara Advisory Opinion, *supra* note 32, at ¶ 162 (court held that neither Mauritania nor Morocco had any ties of sovereignty, that is, a tenable territorial claim to W. Sahara).

[166] Wall Advisory Opinion, *supra* note 32, at ¶ 121.

[167] Wall Advisory Opinion, *supra* note 32.

[168] *Id.* (The Court's rulings on the main points were almost unanimous. The Justices voted 14 to 1 that the construction of the wall was contrary to international law; 14 to 1 that Israel was under an obligation to immediately terminate its breaches of international law related to the wall construction; 14 to 1 that Israel was under an obligation to make reparation for all damages caused by the wall; 13

to 2 that all states are under an obligation not to recognize the illegal occupation; and 14 to 1 that the United Nations should consider what further action should be taken to resolve the illegal situation).

[169] *Id.*, at ¶ 75 ("The Security Council, after recalling on a number of occasions 'the principle that acquisition of territory by military conquest is inadmissible'"); at ¶ 88 ("The Court also notes that the principle of self-determination of peoples has been enshrined in the United Nations Charter and reaffirmed by the UNGA in Resolution 2625(XXV)…"); at ¶ 89-94 (on the application of the Fourth Geneva Convention to Palestine's occupation).

[170] *See* Dugard, *supra* note 119, at 405.

[171] G.A. Res. ES/10-15, U.N. Doc. A/RES/ES/10-15 (Aug. 2, 2004) (150 member states voted yes, 6 member states voted no, with 25 abstentions).

[172] *See* Koury, *supra* note 47, at 161-62 (member states to impose sanctions on any entities involved in the wall construction and to deny Israeli settlers' entry to their states as well as refuse settler products in their markets. The Movement also made specific requests to the UNSC and the Secretary-General to take steps to ensure compliance with the I.C.J. Opinion).

[173] G.A. Res. ES-9/1, U.N. Doc. A/RES/ES-9/1 (Feb. 5, 1982).

[174] G.A. Res. 377(V), U.N. Doc. A/RES/377(V) (Nov. 3, 1950).

[175] U.N. Charter art. 96, para. 1.

[176] Advisory Opinion on the Wall, ¶¶ 27 and 28.

[177] *See* Human Rights Committee, *Report of the Special Rapporteur on the situation of human rights in the Palestinian territories occupies since 1967, Richard Falk*, A/HRC/22/62 (Dec. 28, 2012); Human Rights Committee, *Report of the Special Rapporteur on the situation of human rights in the Palestinian territories occupies since 1967, Richard Falk*, A/HRC/20/32 (May 25, 2012); Human Rights Committee, *Human Rights Situation in Palestine and other Occupied Arab Territories*, A/HRC/23/NGP/66 (May 29, 2013), *available at* http://unispal.un.org/UNISPAL.NSF/0/5708AD7472C846CC85257B7F004D64F1 ; UNGA, *Report of the Special Rapporteur on the situation of human rights in the Palestinian territories occupied since 1967*, A/67/379 (Sept. 19, 2012); UN General Assembly, *Report of the United Nations Fact-Finding Mission on the Gaza Conflict*, A/HRC/12/48 (Sept. 25, 2009); H.R.C. Res. 19/17 [Israeli settlement in the Occupied Palestinian Territory, including East Jerusalem, and in the Occupied Syrian Golan], U.N. Doc. A/HRC/RES/19/17 (Mar. 22, 2012); United Nations Committee on the Elimination of Racial Discrimination [CERD], CERD/C/ISR/CO/14-16, ¶ 24-38, (Mar. 9, 2012), *available at* http://www2.ohchr.org/english/bodies/cerd/docs/CERD.C.ISR.CO.14-16.pdf.

[178] *See* Namibia Advisory Opinion (responding to question put forth by the UNSC), *supra* note 32; International Status of South West Africa Advisory Opinion, *supra* note 39. Voting Procedure Advisory Opinion and The Admissibility of Hearings Advisory Opinion, *supra* note 32.

[179] South West Africa Peoples' Organization (SWAPO), comprising primarily Ovambo people, was established to create a "free, democratic government in South West Africa…and to rid our continent of all forms of foreign domination."; South

West Africa National Union (SWANU) was established to "unite and rally the people of South West Africa into one national front…and to lead them in the struggle for national independence and self-determination"; the African National Congress was formed in 1912 to unite all Africans in the struggle for freedom; the Pan-Africanist Congress broke off from the ANC in 1959 to form a separate organization dedicated to the struggle of only black Africans and repudiating collaboration with whites. *See* The South West Africa/Namibia Dispute: Documents and Scholarly Writings on the Controversy between South Africa and the United Nations (John Dugard, Ed., 1973);

[180] For views on the effectiveness of these entities, *see id.*; *See also* Submissions to the United Nations General Assembly Special Political and Decolonization Committee (Fourth Committee), The Question of Western Sahara and the Natural Resources of the Territory (submitted by Jeffrey Smith), New York, Oct. 4-6, 2011 (recommending that UNGA Special Political and Decolonization Committee to consider how the creation of a Council of W. Sahara, similar to the Council for Namibia, could govern for and legislate in the case of occupied W. Sahara).

[181] *See* League of Nations Covenant, *supra* note 4.

[182] *See* UNSC, *Peaceful settlement of the question of Palestine*, Nov. 29 2004, A/59/574 S/2004/909*, *available at* http://www.refworld.org/docid/426df5754.html; Iain Scobbie, *Advisory Opinion on the Legal Consequences of the Construction of a Wall in the Occupied Palestine Territory for the Responsibility of the U.N. for Palestine*, 16 EUROPEAN J. OF INTL. L. 5 (2006), *available at* http://www.ejil.org/pdfs/16/5/331.pdf; Moshe Hirsch, *The Impact of the Advisory Opinion on Israel's Future: International Relations Perspective,* 1 J. OF INTL. L & INTL. REL. 2 (2011), *available at* http://www.jilir.org/docs/vol1no1-2/JILIR%201(1-2)%20Hirsch-Impact%20of%20Advisory%20Opinion%20on%20Israel's%20Future%20Policy.pdf.

[183] Koury, *supra* note 47, at 156.

[184] *Id.* at 156-57.

[185] Wall Advisory Opinion, *supra* note 32.

[186] *See* Michael C. van Walt van Praag, *Tibet and the right to Self-Determination,* 26 WAYNE L. REV. 279 (1979).

[187] *See, e.g.,* G.A. Res. 2649 (XXV), ¶5, U.N. Doc. A/RES/2649 (Nov. 30, 1970).

[188] Wall Advisory Opinion, *supra* note 32. Although not binding as an advisory opinion, it is a significant decision on major legal issues underlying the Israeli-Palestinian conflict. In coming to the conclusion that the Wall and its associated regime of permits and closures are illegal, the Court dismissed Israel's main arguments undermining the applicability of international humanitarian law and human rights law. The opinion narrowly defined the scope of the necessity defense; confirmed that both international humanitarian law and human rights law apply in the Occupied Palestinian Territories; dismissed the "missing reversioner" argument to find the Fourth Geneva Convention fully applicable; and placed clear obligations on all signatory states to take measures to enforce the four Geneva Conventions (under *erga omnes* obligations). Further, the ICJ recognized the

standing of the PLO to appear in the proceedings; established that Israel was bound by articles of state responsibility and other legal principles to restitute Palestinian property. Susan M. Akram and Michael Lynk, *The Wall and the Law: A Tale of Two Judgments*, 24:1 NETHERLANDS Q. OF HUMAN RIGHTS 61, (2006).

[189] Ali Abunimah, *Opinion: Recognizing Palestine?*, AL JAZEERA (April 13, 2011, 16:15), *available at* http://english.aljazeera.net/indepth/opinion/2011/04/2011413152522296883.html (criticizing the PA's failure to follow up with mobilization and legal strategies after the ICJ Opinion).

[190] The host of lawsuits that have been filed in domestic courts in many countries on behalf of Palestinian victims and against Israeli defendants or corporations working with Israel in its occupation activities have been the work of private lawyers and non-governmental organizations in the Palestinian solidarity communities. *See* Matar et al. v. Dichter, 563 F.3d 9 (2nd Cir. 2009); Belhas v. Ya'alon, 515 F.3d 1279 (D.C. Cir. 2008); Corrie et al. v. Caterpillar, Inc., 503 F.3d 974 (9th Cir. 2007); Doe v. State of Israel, 400 F.Supp.2d 86 (D.D.C. 2005); Abu-Zeineh v. Fed. Labs., Inc., 975 F.Supp. 774 (W.D. Pa. 1994).; R (Hassan) v. the Secretary of State for Trade and Industry [2007] EWHC 2630 (Admin) (U.K.). *See also* The Associated Press, *Dutch Lawyers Seek Arrest of Minister Ayalon for 'War Crimes,'* HAARETZ (Oct. 7, 2008), *available at* http://www.haaretz.com/news/dutch-lawyers-seek-arrest-of-minister-ayalon-for-war-crimes-1.255137; *Spanish Court Green-Lights Gaza Probe*, YNET NEWS (Feb. 27, 2009), *available at* http://www.ynetnews.com/articles/0,7340,L-3678624,00.html; *War Crimes Suit Filed Against Barak, Livni in Belgium*, YNET NEWS (June 23, 2010), *available at* http://www.ynetnews.com/articles/0,7340,L-3909745,00.html.

[191] *See* LAURA ZITTRAIN EISENBERG & NEIL CAPLAN, NEGOTIATING ARAB-ISRAELI PEACE: PATTERNS, PROBLEMS, POSSIBILITIES 211 (2010); Jeff Halper, *A Strategy Within a Non-Strategy: Sumud Resistance, Attrition, and Advocacy*, 35 J. PALESTINE STUD. 45 (2006). *See also* Koury, *supra* note 47.

[192] Wall Advisory Opinion, *supra* note 32, ¶¶ 109, 110, 112, 133; H.R.C., *Special Rapporteur on the situation of human rights in the Palestinian territories occupied since 1967, John Dugard,* U.N. Doc. A/HRC/4/17 (Jan. 29 2007); H.R.C., *Special Rapporteur on the situation of human rights in the Palestinian territories occupied since 1967, Richard Falk,* U.N. Doc. A/HRC/16/72 (Jan. 10, 2011).

[193] *See* Press Release, Boycott, Divestment and Sanctions (BDS), EU acknowledges obligation to not recognize Israeli colonisation and annexation of occupied Palestinian territory (July 18, 2013), *available at* http://www.bdsmovement.net/2013/eu-guidelines-press-release-11211#sthash.MBTeQfJH.dpuf ("European Investment Bank to stop loans to 'virtually all' major Israeli businesses and public bodies. New European Union guidelines will prevent Israeli ministries, public bodies and businesses that operate in occupied Palestinian territory from receiving loans worth hundreds of millions of Euros each year from the European Investment Bank, it emerged today. The EU will also stop awarding grant funding to Israeli ministries, public bodies or private

businesses for activities that take place in occupied Palestinian territory, even if they are headquartered inside Israel's pre-1967 borders."). The European Commission's recent directive is clearly meant to bind EU institutions in prohibiting loans to Israeli entities involved in or operating from the occupied territories of Palestine. *See* Guidelines on the eligibility of Israeli entities and their activities in the territories occupied by Israel since June 1967 for grants, prizes and financial instruments funded by the EU from 2014 onwards, OJ 2013/C 205/05 (July19, 2013), *available at* http://eur-lex.europa.eu/LexUriServ/LexUriServ.do?uri=OJ:C:2013:205:0009:0011:EN:PDF.
See also 2012 O.J. (L-298) 55, at art. 58(1)(c) (the European Investment Bank is a section 58(1)(c) institution and is therefore bound by the 2013 directive).

[194] Ronnie Hansen [Norwegian Refugee Council], *Generations in Exile from Africa's Last Colony,* 27 FORCED MIGRATION R. 76 (Jan. 2007), *available at* http://www.fmreview.org/FMRpdfs/FMR27/51.pdf.

[195] W. Sahara Advisory Opinion, *supra* note 32, at ¶ 55. *See also* Declaration of Permanent Sovereignty over Natural Resources, G.A. Res. 1803 (XVII) A/RES/1803 (Dec. 14, 1962). *See* Stephanie Koury, *The European Community and Member States' Duty of Non-Recognition Under the EC-Morocco Association Agreement: State Responsibility and Customary International Law, in* INTERNATIONAL LAW AND THE QUESTION OF WESTERN SAHARA 171-72 (Karin Arts & Pedro Pinto Leite eds., 2007).

[196] G.A. Res. 33/182, U.N. Doc. S/RES/33/182 (Dec. 21, 1978); *see also* Vincent Chapaux, *Question of the European Community-Morocco Fisheries Agreement, in* INTERNATIONAL LAW AND THE QUESTION OF WESTERN SAHARA, 231-2 (Karin Arts & Pedro Pinto Leite eds., 2007).

[197] *See* Koury, *supra* note 196, at 177. *See also* Carlos Wilson, *Foreign Companies Plundering Western Saharan Resources,* in INTERNATIONAL LAW AND THE QUESTION OF WESTERN SAHARA, 249-65 (Karin Arts & Pedro Pinto Leite eds., 2007).

[198] Wilson, *supra* note 198, at 250-51.

[199] Jeffrey Smith makes the point that the occupation costs Morocco a great deal more than the country's gain in resource extraction from the territory. He estimates military expenditure alone to cost no less than US $1.5 billion per year. Pedro Pinto Leite and Jeffrey Smith, *The Question of Western Sahara: from Impasse to Independence*, PAMBAZUKA NEWS (Feb. 27, 2013),
http://www.pambazuka.org/en/category/features/86407/print. *See* Interview with Jonas Gahr Støre, Norwegian Minister of Foreign Affairs, in Norwegian Parliament (Feb. 23, 2011), *available at* http://vest-sahara.no/a123x1646 (stating that "Morocco does not exercise internationally recognized sovereignty with regard to Western Sahara. As a point of departure, therefore, Morocco does not have the right to exploit the area's resources as if they were its own in light of the 1907 Hague Convention."); Toby Shelley, Address at the Oxford Middle East Studies Centre (Feb. 18, 2012), *available at* http://www.arso.org/TSh180205.htm (making an initial assessment of what Morocco has lost and gained by holding and settling W. Sahara).

[200] *See, e.g.*, Jeffrey Smith, *Fishing in Self-Determination: European Fisheries and Western Sahara – The Case of Ocean Resources in Africa's Last Colony*, *in* OCEAN YEARBOOK 27 (Aldo Chircop et al. eds. 2013).
[201] Smith argues that one major UN agency of particular interest to the Sahrawi is UNFAO, in which he urges their participation in fisheries surveys on the Saharan coastline.

CHAPTER FIVE

THE IRAQI REFUGEE CRISIS AND THE US RESPONSE

MICHELE R. PISTONE*

In the years following the US-led invasion of Iraq that began in March 2003, approximately four million Iraqis were displaced from their homes. Half of this population was internally displaced; that is, about two million Iraqis were forced to move from one Iraqi town to another.[1] Of the remaining two million refugees who fled over Iraq's borders, the vast majority remained in the Middle East. At the height of the crisis, Syria was host to approximately 1.2 million Iraqis and Jordan approximately 450,000 refugees.[2] Other Iraqis fled in large numbers to Lebanon, Turkey and Egypt.[3] Indeed, in absolute terms, the refugee movement out of Iraq was, and remains, one of the largest refugee movements since World War II.[4]

Representatives of a wide range of groups are among the refugees. Iraqis have been forced to flee their homes because of persecution or a fear of persecution on account of their religion, nationality, political opinion or imputed political opinion, or because of their associations with particular groups. The refugees thus include religious minorities–Assyrian-Christians,[5] Sabean, Madean, Yezedis, Ba'hai, and Jews, as well as people who lived in mixed religious neighborhoods or who were part of mixed religious families, including Shia's who are married to Sunnis. The refugees and displaced include men, women, children, and the elderly. They include intellectuals, academics and artists. They include students. They include interpreters and others who worked alongside US military soldiers. They are contractors who supplied goods and services to US troops in Iraq. They come from all over Iraq and from all walks of life. For the most part, the refugees were persecuted or their family members were persecuted, in the form of kidnapping, torture, rape, or murder, because of who they are or what they believe.

The United States government responded slowly–and initially, extremely ineffectively–to the Iraqi refugee crisis. Indeed, even though the

United States had a direct hand in creating the refugee crisis, it was five years before the Bush Administration created a minimally adequate infrastructure to process requests by refugees living abroad seeking refugee resettlement into the United States. Only after such an infrastructure was developed did the necessary work of processing and relocating refugees to the United States begin. To date–about ten years after the start of the war–the United States has accepted only 74,599[6] of the 4 million displaced Iraqis.[7] This number pales in comparison to earlier post-war refugee resettlements to the United States. For example, at the end of the Vietnam War in 1975, more than 130,000 refugees from Southeast Asia were resettled to the United States in one year alone; five years later, 168,000 refugees were resettled.[8]

This chapter begins with an overview of the origins of the crisis and its unusual characteristics in comparison to most other refugee movements. The second section discusses some of the most prevalent problems faced by the Iraqi refugees and IDPs. The third section of the chapter discusses options available to refugees who have sought protection from the US government. Finally, the chapter ends with recommendations for future action.

Origins of the Iraqi Refugee Crisis

A large-scale flight of Iraqi refugees did not occur at the onset of the war. Rather, the vast majority of the refugees did not start fleeing their homes until 2006, three years into the war. The immediate cause was the sectarian violence that erupted in the aftermath of the 22 February 2006 bombing of the Samarra mosque.[9] Heightened sectarian violence by insurgents persisted in earnest for almost two years and was directed at moderate Iraqis, particularly those who were perceived as supporting the US military efforts in Iraq. The refugees who could not find safety within Iraq fled mainly to other countries in the Middle East.

The Iraqi refugee population differs from many other refugee movements in several significant ways. First, a majority of Iraqi refugees are educated–indeed, even highly educated[10]–with moderate political leanings. As to the latter point, in fact, Samir Shankir Mahmud Sumaida'iye, Iraq's ambassador to the United States, characterized Iraqi refugees as constituting a "flight of moderation."[11] Many of the refugees were persecuted and fled because of their association with, or perceived support for, the US government and its military efforts in Iraq. As a result of the flight of this population of politically moderate, educated citizens,

Iraq is now finding that it is without many of the people who would be critical to help rebuild the country and its political system after the war.

In addition, unlike most refugee populations that settle in refugee camps close to their national border, Iraqi refugees settled in urban centers.[12] To some extent, at least, the urban concentration of Iraqi refugees was due to their educational attainment and middle-class status, which provided them sufficient resources to, for example, rent apartments for limited periods. As a result, Iraqi refugees blended into the native populations of their host countries. This explains why, despite a refugee population numbering in the millions, there were no images of thousands of refugees streaming across a border displayed on video or television screens, as frequently shown during other refugee crises. And, of course, there were no photos of Iraqi refugee camps either. Rather, the Iraqis are urban refugees, living in or on the outskirts of Damascus, Amman, Beirut, Cairo and other cities.

Problems Faced by Iraqi Refugees

With a refugee crisis of this magnitude it is easy to forget a central point: four million refugees mean four million tragedies. Individual tragedies unfold in many distinct ways, but the common core of the tragedy for the refugee experience is that it causes one to lose one's past, present and future. Being uprooted means the loss of one's place, work, home, and community. Refugees live in a disorienting fog of constant and unwanted change. Forces over which they have little power, and perhaps no understanding, assault and endanger them. Refugee life also can result in the loss of one's sense of autonomy and purpose, so much so that all initiative and ambition is lost. Futures may be lost as well. Changes in one's health can be permanent; losses of family can be overwhelming; a lifetime of savings and achievement can disappear; and the consequences of lost opportunity for continued-- or even any-- education can be permanent. All of this can happen suddenly, sometimes in a day, and the imprint can last for years, even decades. Some of the most pressing problems faced by Iraqi refugees and internally displaced are discussed below.

a. Trauma: The Psychological Costs

Forced migration creates extreme stress. Studies of different refugee populations have found mental and severe emotional problems to be common among members of refugee populations. The most prevalent psychiatric disorders among refugee populations are Post Traumatic Stress Disorder (PTSD) and depression.[13] Although many studies of refugee populations occur during or immediately after flight, recent longitudinal studies suggest problems associated with PTSD can become chronic despite intensive treatment.[14]

Studies have found that refugees who live through prolonged armed conflict may be particularly susceptible to trauma-related psychological damage. A survey by the United Nations Refugee Agency (UNHCR) of Iraqi refugees in Syria, for example, found that every person interviewed had experienced a traumatic event prior to flight.[15] Nearly one out of every five refugees registering with UNHCR between October 2007 and November 2008 claimed to be a direct victim of torture and/or violence in Iraq.[16] The survey also showed eighty-nine percent suffered from depression, while more than eighty percent suffered from anxiety and sixty-seven percent suffered from PTSD.[17] Iraqi refugees in Egypt expressed similar problems, with doctors noting an increase in stress related illnesses, such as heart disease.[18] While the percentage of those suffering from psychological ailments in Jordan and Lebanon is not quite as striking, an International Organization for Migration (IOM) study determined that over half of the Iraqi refugees surveyed in those places displayed distress factors indicating high levels of emotional and psychological anxiety.[19]

Moreover, a recent meta-analysis of research conducted on refugees shows pre-displacement factors may affect their mental health. For instance, refugees with higher levels of education and socioeconomic status before displacement (common traits among Iraqi refugees), had worse mental health after displacement compared to those ranking lower on these socioeconomic parameters.[20] Women, also, have worse mental health than men or children.[21]

Typical symptoms of trauma among refugees include recurrent nightmares or daytime images of trauma, severe emotional distress, irritability, short-term memory problems, hopelessness, and suicidal thoughts.[22] Occasionally these psychological stresses can even manifest themselves in physical pain and ailments.[23] PTSD may also increase immediately after finding a safe harbor, as new pressures emerge to learn a new culture and language, find work, create new social ties, and regain previous social status.[24]

b. Illness and Loss of Medical Services

Another immense problem for refugee populations concerns disease and its treatment. First, for several reasons, refugees are particularly likely to develop various medical conditions. Stress, prolonged and sometimes extreme physical hardship, and crowded or unsanitary conditions all play a part. So does the fact that refugee populations–even before their displacement–typically lack quality medical care or face deteriorating levels of care in the period before their flight. For example, Jordan, a country that was measles-free for nearly two decades, saw a recurrence of the disease among its refugee and native populations.[25] Similarly, the Iraqi health system had already started to decline by 2003 because of pre-war sanctions.[26] In the aftermath of the US invasion, conditions worsened further, with more than half of Iraq's doctors leaving the country, and one in seven killed or kidnapped.[27]

The availability of medical treatment typically does not improve after a refugee flees his or her homeland; health problems may even be exacerbated by the stress and turmoil of flight. The problems of Iraqi refugees in obtaining health care, for example, have been well documented. While working in Syria, for example, the International Medical Corps, an American non-governmental organization, estimated that eighty-five percent of Iraqi refugees there had little or no access to health care.[28] The fate of Iraqis seeking medical care in Jordan has been similarly bleak, with almost ninety-five percent of them asserting that they could not afford medical care, and seventy-four percent strongly asserting the point.[29] Jordan has a national system of health insurance for Jordanian citizens, but it is not open to foreigners, who must rely on private insurance.[30] Most private insurance in Jordan does not include costly surgical procedures or treatment.[31] Jordan also subsidizes basic medical care, but Iraqi refugees usually cannot cover even the small, required fees.[32] Refugees avoid the hospital until absolutely necessary and then are forced to pay cash up front.[33]

In Lebanon, Iraqi refugees must pay a doctor to certify that they are sick before being eligible for treatment paid by local non-governmental organizations.[34] Refugees often complain that they are considered ineligible for these services because they arrived in the country with financial resources.[35] For many Iraqis there, the savings they brought with them have dwindled to almost nothing, leaving them no way to pay for needed medical care and ineligible for help from local organizations.[36]

The difficulties faced by Iraqi refugees in obtaining medical treatment are by no means uncommon among refugee groups; indeed, other groups have fared far worse. Substantial delays or denials of medical care not only make more difficult the already stressful path of being a refugee, but also can lead to death or permanent disability. For certain diseases, delays and denials of health care can also create epidemics, as untreated disease can spread quickly among populations living in crowded conditions, as refugees often are.[37]

c. Inability to Obtain Gainful Employment

Refugees often cite the inability to access gainful employment as one of the principal obstacles they face after fleeing their homes. Once a family member can obtain a job, many of the other issues facing the family–such as the need for housing, food, water, health care and education–can begin to be addressed.

Among the Iraqi refugee and IDP population, the lack of employment opportunities presents particular complications. The governments of Jordan and Syria both prohibit Iraqi refugees from working while living there as "guests."[38] Even those Iraqis displaced within Iraq have found it difficult to find jobs. Research by the International Organization for Migration found that 75% of the members of the Iraqi IDP population cite employment as their principal need.[39] Some of this need stems from the overall lack of economic opportunity within Iraq. Others have found it hard to obtain a job in an area of the country in which they do not have family members or friends, or do not speak the native language, such as those IDPs who have settled in the Kurdish region in northern Iraq.

d. Loss of Secure, Stable and Affordable Housing

For refugees fleeing their homes, finding shelter is one of the most pressing, if not the most pressing, of problems. It begins immediately upon the uprooting of family from their home and persists until a final resolution of the refugee condition. For the Iraqi refugee population, finding housing has not been an easy task. As noted above, unlike other refugee flows, Iraqi refugees did not settle in refugee camps that could be created, paid for and managed by a refugee organization, as is common for many mass refugee movements. Rather, this group moved into urban centers, where adequate housing was scarce and costly. While many refugees did flee with cash, making it possible to pay rent for some time after their flight, the inability to work in their host countries meant that these finite cash reserves dwindled rapidly. The race to zero savings was hastened by the fact that many fled to the same few cities–Amman, Beirut,

Cairo, Damascus–causing an imbalance between housing demand and supply, which allowed landlords to increase rents.[40]

Not only is housing a problem for refugees in temporary host communities abroad, it is also a pressing issue for the looming population of internally displaced Iraqis and those considering return.[41] The capital of Baghdad presents particular problems. The majority of the IDP population "originates from Baghdad, where violence triggered most of the internal and external displacement."[42] Baghdad is also host to "an estimated forty percent of these IDPs."[43] Yet it has been difficult for those who were displaced from their homes to regain possession of them. Before the war began, it was not uncommon for Sunnis, Shias and Christians to all live peacefully in the same neighborhood of Baghdad. These communities that were once inhabited by families from a variety of religious faiths have since been "cleansed," particularly during the 2006-08 period of sectarian violence, and now are inhabited by members of a single group. After refugees fled their homes, the homes were either destroyed or were occupied by any number of groups, including squatters, armed groups, and others. In some cases, the homes were even sold fraudulently to unsuspecting buyers who now occupy them. Consequently, even those IDPs who want to return home find that they do not have a "home" to which they can safely return.[44] Many fear for their lives and personal safety if they return to their former neighborhoods and try to regain possession of their homes.[45] Indeed, according to a 2010 UNHCR survey, "sixty-one percent of returning refugees regretted returning to Iraq, with the majority citing insecurity and personal safety concerns."[46]

While the Iraqi government, as well as international relief organizations, has recognized the problems associated with a general lack of enforcement of real property rights, no system has yet been established to resolve these real property disputes.[47] In fact, only limited information is available about the scope of this problem. The data that has so far been compiled by the International Organization for Migration, the Iraqi government, and some international and national actors is far from complete. And there is reason to believe that even after such a dispute resolution system is established, the process will not be simple, and the anticipated results may be difficult to achieve. Indeed, many of the property disputes that arose before 2003, during the Ba'ath Party era, remain unresolved. For those claims, the Iraqi government established the Commission for Resolution of Real Property Disputes (CRRPD).[48] Yet, only 60,000 of the 170,000 claims that arose from Ba'ath Party era property violations have been resolved to date.[49] Even for those that have been resolved on paper, "rule of law remains weak in Iraq and the CRRPD may not be able to enforce its decisions."[50]

e. Loss of Educational Opportunities

One of the systemic problems for refugees is the loss of educational opportunities. During the period of flight, of course, formal education is impossible. Even afterward, however, substantial obstacles remain. Language barriers in one's new place of residence may make formal education inaccessible. So might prejudice and discrimination. Limited financial resources, stretched to the limit by the costs of flight, may be insufficient to pursue further education. The loss of supporting networks can force the abandonment of the dream of education because of the need to support oneself. Other priorities can emerge as well–family responsibilities, for example–and the window of opportunity for pursuing education may be lost for good.

The problem is acute even for younger students, some of whom may be forced to work to help their family survive.[51] In the case of Iraqi refugees, a 2007 study by UNICEF estimated that 220,000 displaced Iraqi children had their primary school education interrupted, adding to the 760,000 children out of school in 2006.[52] Among Iraqi school-aged refugee children, school attendance ranged from eleven percent in Syria to twenty-eight percent in Jordan.[53] The consequences of severely diminished educational opportunity can hardly be overestimated–they are unremittingly negative and reach far into the future.

f. Increases in Domestic Violence, Prostitution, and Sex Trafficking

With family structures coming under the disorienting pressure of refugee life and the loss of social support systems, refugee communities also experience a rise in domestic violence, prostitution, and sex trafficking. A study of the Iraqi refugee population in Jordan found that twenty-five percent of Iraqi women reported domestic abuse.[54] A 2012 article in *Health Care for Women International* found that thirty percent of Iraqi refugee women in Syria experienced domestic violence, with twenty percent experiencing abuse within a year of flight from home.[55]

As with all domestic violence cases, underreporting is a problem in calculating totals. This is especially true among Iraqi women because cultural norms encourage women to tolerate such behavior in silence.[56] Children are likewise affected by an increase in domestic violence.[57] In 2007, the Iraq Psychologists Association conducted a study that found that between March 2003 and 2007 ninety-one percent of refugee children questioned reported an increase in aggression at home, and thirty-eight percent displayed serious bruising from beatings.[58] A non-governmental organization in Jordan suggested domestic violence was a problem for Iraqi children outside Iraq as well.[59] An additional troubling fact is that non-governmental organizations that aid victims of domestic violence may themselves become targets of violence because they challenge traditional beliefs.[60] Threats of violence are ample disincentive for such organizations to refrain from publicizing the availability of their assistance.

The abrupt dislocation and disruption caused by refugee life also ensures that even as violence grows within the family, it flourishes outside the home. Thus, an increasing number of Iraqi women and girls have reported being the victims of rape or sexual or gender-based violence (SGBV) in Syria and Jordan.[61] Forced prostitution was also a problem for young Iraqi refugee girls in Syria.[62] "Voluntary" prostitution also occurs as women, particularly those who are heading households, "turn to prostitution to feed their families."[63] This practice has been referred to as "survival sex" because of its direct correlation with poverty.[64] Members of female-headed households are also particularly vulnerable to abuse and exploitation.

g. Unrest in Syria

The outbreak of violence in Syria and ongoing civil uprising has created serious problems for Iraqi refugees who were living in Syria at the start of the violence. Some crossed back into Iraq and joined the population of internally displaced persons within Iraq.[65] These newly arriving returnees are putting pressure on the already strained government, as joblessness remains high, housing options are limited and sectarian violence continues.[66]

For those who remain in Syria, conditions are deteriorating.[67] Reports from Syria are that thousands are displaced, seeking temporary housing in schools, which have had to shift their focus from education to housing as a result. There are also reports that, taking advantage of the chaos in Syria, Iraqis are crossing into Syria to hunt Iraqi refugees who had fled to Syria to find safety from persecution in Iraq.[68]

Moreover, in recent months, Syrian refugees have fled into Iraq to escape the violence in Syria.[69] The Iraqi government and the United Nations have responded by establishing refugee camps for Syrian refugees in Iraq, close to the Syrian and Iraqi border. Others, for example, Syrian Kurds, fled to the Kurdistan region of Iraq, where camps have also been established.[70]

The US Government's Response to the Iraqi Refugee Crisis

The Bush Administration's response to the Iraqi refugee crisis and its concomitant human costs was inadequate and slow. First, as explained in subsection a below, the Bush Administration was slow to create and implement an adequate legal process to protect Iraqi refugees by providing them with legal immigration status in the United States. But even a robust response on this issue, under any conceivably practical approach, would leave most refugees unaffected. As explained further in subsection b, the response was also inadequate because it did not do enough to address the plight of refugees living overseas.

a. Protecting Iraqi Refugees under US Immigration Law

By the end of the Bush Administration, about 13,000 refugees from the 2003 war were living in the United States.[71] The refugees came to the United States under a variety of legal processes, most of which required some affirmative action on the part of the US government.

The largest potential legal avenue of relief for most refugees is the overseas refugee resettlement program. Through that program, refugees living abroad can apply for protection and are resettled in the United States. In recent years the target number for this program has been around 50,000-70,000 refugees worldwide.[72] This number is set each year by the Administration, in consultation with members of Congress, and can be adjusted upward or downward in response to conditions around the world.

What is surprising is that the Bush Administration did not initiate a more robust overseas refugee resettlement program for the Iraqis. In 2007 about 1,600 Iraqis were resettled by this program–in 2008, the first year that a specific allocation was made for Iraq, the allocation increased to 12,000.[73] That allocation represented barely one-quarter of one percent of the then-estimated two million refugees from Iraq. By 2009 the allocation increased to 18,000 refugees, still minimal compared to the need.[74]

The overseas refugee resettlement program has long been criticized because it has been applied in a way that subordinates humanitarian concerns to larger foreign policy objectives. Indeed, Professor Steven Legomsky has commented that "[p]residents have generously admitted those refugees fleeing Communist countries while largely turning a deaf ear to almost all others."[75] For instance, over the years, most of the refugee numbers for Latin America and the Caribbean region went to Cuban refugees.[76] In contrast to the ideological comfort of admitting communist-country refugees, admitting large numbers of Iraqi refugees was apparently not so politically comforting. The Bush Administration wanted to portray an Iraq that was on the mend and would soon be independent and prosperous. A refugee resettlement program that brought hundreds of thousands of refugees to our shores would have undermined that policy objective.

After much prodding by non-governmental organizations and members of its own military, the Bush Administration did, however, create certain limited legal protections for people who assisted US military efforts in Iraq. In January 2008, a special immigrant visa for Iraqis who served the US military and have "experienced or are experiencing an ongoing serious threat" because of their work for the United States military was created.[77] This visa category initially was capped at 5,000 individuals for each fiscal year through 2012 with any remaining slots carrying over to Fiscal Year 2013.[78]

Humanitarian parole–a third alternate route–was also made available to Iraqi refugees. This category of protection is available to people with extraordinary situations that warrant humanitarian action by the US government, such as people with severe medical needs. The same statutory provision that authorizes humanitarian parole[79] also authorizes a fourth type of visa that was used by Iraqi refugees–"significant public benefit parole."[80] Significant public benefit parole is available to Iraqis who assisted the US war effort and whose service "put their lives in imminent, documented danger."[81] In all, this provision helped roughly several hundred Iraqis gain temporary entry into the United States.[82]

Because of the scope of the need and the paucity of legal options for reaching safety in the United States, many Iraqis had to risk traveling to the United States through circuitous routes and apply for asylum at its borders. Our treaty obligations not to return refugees to persecution arise once refugees arrive in the US or at its border. But arriving here is hard to do. There are countless formal and informal barriers along the way–among other things, costs, difficulties in procuring legal travel documents, corruption, and various physical dangers and threats. In dire fear and without other legal options, many Iraqis took costly, risky and dangerous paths to freedom in the United States. However, upon arriving in the United States, the claims of Iraqi asylum seekers have tended to have a high rate of success—at least based on the experiences of Iraqi refugees represented through the asylum clinic at Villanova Law School.

b. Protecting Refugees Overseas

As is typical of countries on the receiving end of massive refugee flight, neither Syria nor Jordan was prepared for the Iraqi influx. The receiving countries can hardly be blamed for their lack of preparedness–Iraqi refugees in Jordan and Syria at one time "represent[ed] almost [ten] percent of the populations in Syria and Jordan."[83] The impact on the existing infrastructure, from housing, to education, to health care, was real. For example, Jordan complained that it did not have enough potable water for their Iraqi guests.[84] And the educational infrastructures in both countries were strapped to incorporate the additional school-aged children into the public school system. This created animosity and ill feelings among the native as well as the refugee populations.

Such large influxes can have severe political consequences as well. For example, Nicholas Kristof noted the possibility of Jordan being destabilized by the pressures of a large refugee population, and warned that "[i]f Jordan were to collapse in part from such pressures, [it] would be a catastrophe."[85]

Despite the costs of the refugee flight to the region, the US was slow to provide necessary resources. Over the last eight years, US efforts to deal with the perceived threat from Iraq and Afghanistan have cost over one *trillion* dollars. Over the same period of time, the US contribution to UNHCR–the main organization dedicated to assisting refugees and the internally displaced–has amounted to less than four billion dollars, or approximately 500 million dollars a year. The funds expended on the wars in Iraq and Afghanistan, accordingly, represent the equivalent of our funding for UNHCR for two thousand (2,000!) years. "UNHCR's total annual budget for operations across the globe"–for food, security, shelter, etc.–also is "vastly exceed[ed]" by the amounts spent in the developed world on determining the status of the many fewer persons who, having crossed a developed country's border, ask for recognition as asylees.[86]

In another article I offered a plan that would provide immediate help to refugees in the aftermath of significant refugee movements.[87] The US government must recognize the costs of refugee movements on the region and act with appropriate speed and generosity to help the receiving countries cope with the arrival and stabilization of refugee populations.

Recommendations

Crises of the magnitude suffered by the Iraqi refugees and internally displaced require both short-term and long-term response capability. Policy makers must recognize the costs of refugee movements, and proceed to address them by–among many other things–amending some laws affecting potential refugees and re-conceptualizing and expanding the structures, programs, and entities capable of assisting them. As the recommendations below indicate, what is required most of all is a change in overall outlook. Such a change, I hope, would produce major proposals, beyond those presented here, whose enactment would signal to all that a new day has dawned in the treatment of refugees and the internally displaced. It is important for the United States to show those struggling to realize the principles of democracy and globalization in their homelands that the US recognizes the fragility of their lives and is making meaningful attempts to improve it. The burden is one that the United States must bear–as the Council on Foreign Relations Independent Task Force on US Immigration Policy suggested, the US commitment to providing a safe haven for refugees "is enshrined in international treaties and domestic US laws that set the standard for the rest of the world; [and] when American standards erode, refugees face greater risks everywhere."[88]

For a long time, the suffering of the refugees from the Iraqi conflict was regarded merely as collateral damage, and acknowledgement of the human cost discouraged as politically inconvenient and inimical to the achievement of larger goals.[89] The hope was that once the refugees decided to return to Iraq, the problem would simply go away. While in the longer term, voluntary repatriation is the best possible solution to a refugee crisis, large-scale repatriation to Iraq, especially during the Bush Administration, was a pipedream. Indeed, even years later, most parts of Iraq remain unsafe for voluntary repatriation. This is evident in the case of Iraqis returning home to escape the violence in Syria. They are returning to nothing–and are simply joining the already significant number of internally displaced without homes or jobs within Iraq. An initial short-term plan involving large-scale repatriation would never have been feasible. But for the longer term, it is appropriate to search for permanent solutions for the internally displaced.

The initial response by the US government was slow and inadequate, in part because there were practical limits to how many people could be processed through the then-existing administrative bureaucracy. US immigration laws and the concomitant refugee processing bureaucracy needs to be fortified to resolve the short and long-term problems that arose in the initial years of the Iraqi refugee flight so that when the inevitable next time occurs the US is better prepared to respond to a humanitarian crisis of this magnitude. Expedited resettlement for those refugees in need of immediate help should be a focus for the present.

In October of 2011, the Department of State's Bureau of Population, Refugees and Migration (PRM) noted that the United States sometimes took longer than eight to ten weeks to resettle refugees with life-threatening emergencies.[90] The delays were caused by security clearances, face-to-face interview requirements, and positive tuberculosis (TB) tests found to be negative after further testing.[91] Regional guidelines that focus on a particular country like Iraq, with targeted time frames, should be implemented to improve both consistency and efficiency when expediting resettlement.[92] Security clearance issues can be streamlined if US agencies continue to coordinate and work with security vetting agencies.[93] Security vetting agencies have shown the potential to quickly return interagency security checks–in some limited cases security checks were completed in five working days.[94]

Technology may help to streamline and expedite the interviewing process, in particular to shortcut the problems caused by requirements that US agencies have face-to-face interviews with refugees. Significant numbers of refugees could be processed for resettlement by having their interviews conducted by videoconferences, especially in cases where in-person interviews cannot be conducted for security reasons.[95] Immigration courts currently use videoconferencing for immigration court adjudications;[96] that technology could be expanded for use in the refugee resettlement adjudication process. Similarly, the use of technology has already shown to improve the resettlement process–the Department of Homeland Security recently adopted a more streamlined process that allows applicants to email petitions directly to processing offices, which has resulted in quicker responses and processing times.[97] The delays resulting from suspected TB cases can also be ameliorated if an alternative and quicker form of testing is implemented to prevent individuals who do not have TB from being unnecessarily retested.[98]

Moreover, immigration laws that were enacted to respond to the Iraqi crisis–for example, the special immigrant visas made available for interpreters–must be expanded to apply to interpreters and others who assist the US military in any operation without regard to geographic location. Going forward, US immigration laws need to be amended and the concomitant refugee processing bureaucracy needs to be expanded to respond to the immediate short-term needs of the refugee population, without the need for Congressional action each time a crisis arises. The better response is to create legal mechanisms that bring refugees to safety more quickly. Ideally, a yearly or bi-yearly renewable temporary protected status for refugees–modeled on the traditional TPS—should be instituted that could provide temporary protection efficiently to larger numbers of refugees. Such a program could begin on a trial basis immediately. Nevertheless, those programs already in place must be restructured because they are not functioning as Congress intended.[99] For instance, while the rate of processing of Iraqis has improved, around 20,000 interpreter visas remain unused.[100] The special immigrant visa program for Iraqis ends in September 2013.[101] According to the State Department, applications that have not been processed at that time will simply not be processed at all, leaving the visas that Congress expressly authorized to languish unused.[102]

A second program should have been expanded some time ago, that is, the issuance of large numbers of student visas to Iraqis in Syria and Jordan, so that the next generation of Iraq's leaders, teachers, doctors and lawyers could have been studying to prepare themselves to rebuild Iraq when the time came for rebuilding. One cannot presume that all who fled during the war have no intention to return in the future to a peaceful, post-war Iraq. Visas could also have been extended to larger numbers of Iraqi scientists, educators, and scholars on cultural exchanges so that they could have continued their work and avoided the stress and other costs of refugee flight.

Congress passed the first *Torture Victims Relief Act* more than a decade ago to combat the multiple disabling conditions and long-term consequences associated with incidents of torture.[103] The studies cited earlier show that Iraqi refugees have experienced high rates of torture, underscoring the great need for rehabilitation services.[104] It is necessary to implement efficient and effective screening programs that can help identify distress quickly, and begin the support or treatment necessary to combat the burden of long-term physical or psychological illness.[105] The *Torture Victims Relief Act*, which can provide urgently needed funds to torture programs both in the US and abroad, should be reauthorized.[106]

When refugees receive decisions denying them resettlement, they must have an efficient and useful mechanism available that provides them with review of the denial.[107] Under current procedure, refugees can request review of their denial, but the process is so complicated that most refugees have great difficulty understanding what evidence is required to overcome the denial. Denials, moreover, do not come with substantive explanations or information explaining what is necessary for a positive decision.[108] A refugee denied for security reasons will not receive a clear indication of the basis of the security concern, and therefore cannot provide a detailed or adequate response.[109] This process must be amended to provide sufficient information to enable those denied a meaningful opportunity of review.[110] If resettlement is denied for security reasons, there should be a clear indication of those reasons, and the denial should be accompanied by a clear explanation of the quality and nature of the information relied upon for the denial.[111]

The US government must put an administrative infrastructure in place at the inception of a war to respond to the inevitable refugee flow. Such short-term response capability must be institutionalized because the onset of a crisis often comes suddenly. Indeed, if we do not learn from our mistakes and do something to improve our preparation for the next crisis, unpreparedness will be perceived as policy, not misfortune. As noted earlier, at the end of the Vietnam War in 1975, we resettled more than 130,000 refugees from Southeast Asia in one year alone; five years later, we resettled 168,000.[112] So 12,000, even 20,000 a year from one country is plainly below what the United States is capable of doing. In this regard, the White House must assume a strong leadership role and communicate that refugee issues are to be given greater priority.[113] Because refugees interact with numerous agencies, the White House should institute an annual interagency cabinet level meeting to coordinate federal efforts on a variety of protection efforts, including refugee resettlement and asylum matters.[114] The advice given by the Council on Foreign Relations Independent Task Force on US Immigration Policy should be followed–which suggests that there should be "greater priority for refugee issues . . . within the White House."[115]

The US must devote much more substantial resources to establish a permanent and upgraded short-term response capability. Establishing such a capacity not only will alleviate much human suffering and give national leaders more flexibility in responding, it also will send an important message: that the US is fully capable of responding both to major security and humanitarian crises, and can do so in a timely manner.

The US should have acted towards the Iraqi refugee crisis urgently, and with all the means at its disposal. The US needed to support and protect Iraqi refugees so that they could have been in a position to help rebuild a peaceful, vital Iraq in the future. Instead, we have had to re-learn from this crisis that refugee movements are costly–costly in terms of human suffering, costly to the host countries, and costly to the project of rebuilding Iraq. Iraq lost many of its intellectuals, academics and doctors, its moderates and its middle class. The country even lost its religious diversity.[116] The refugees represent the human capital that would have rebuilt Iraq. Now as Iraq tries to recover post-conflict, its resources are strained to the limit; the country cannot tap into the human capital and potential that once set it apart from other countries in the Middle East. That loss is significant and will persist for years into the future. The US, like the other countries involved in the Iraqi conflict, must learn from the humanitarian crisis that ensued and ensure that the many mistakes will not be repeated when the next crisis comes along.

Notes

[*] Professor of Law, Villanova University School of Law; and Founding Director of the Clinic for Asylum, Refugee, and Emigrant Services (CARES), in which she and her students provide free legal representation to asylum seekers fleeing persecution in their home countries.

[1] The United Nations defines internally displaced persons as:

> persons or groups of persons who have been forced or obliged to flee or to leave their homes or places of habitual residence, in particular as a result of or in order to avoid the effects of armed conflict, situations of generalized violence, violations of human rights or natural or human-made disasters, and who have not crossed an internationally recognized State border.

Guiding Principles on Internal Displacement, transmitted by memo dated July 22, 1998 from the Director, Division of International Protection addressed to all Directors, Chiefs of Section, Chiefs of Unit, Heads of Desks, all UNHCR Field Offices, ¶ 2, U.N. Doc. E/CN.4/1998/53/Add.2 (Feb. 11, 1998), *available at* http://www.refworld.org/docid/3c3da07f7.html.

[2] Because of the nature of their flight, it is difficult to quantify the scope of the refugee flight in exact numbers. These are estimates based on numbers supplied by a number of sources, including the host countries and non-governmental organizations. UNHCR, *Iraq Situation*, *in* UNHCR GLOBAL REPORT 2009, at 169, 171 (2010), *available at* http://www.unhcr.org/4c08f25e9.html. In 2010 slightly more than three million Iraqis were displaced, with that number almost evenly divided between refugees and internally displaced persons. *Id.*

[3] *See* UNITED NATIONS HIGH COMM'R FOR REFUGEES, IRAQ SITUATION UPDATE–AUGUST 2008, at 2 (2008), *available at* http://www.unhcr.org/491956a02.html.

[4] On March 20, 2003 the United States instituted Operation Iraqi Liberation, a military attack on and invasion of Iraq. Later, "post-conflict" stages of the invasion were named Operation Iraqi Freedom. Since the invasion began, there has been a waxing and waning of sectarian violence in Iraq. With the increase in sectarian violence after the inception of Operation Iraqi Freedom, it created what one diplomat called, "the largest exodus in the history of the Middle East." Imad Moustapha, Ambassador of Syria to the U.S., Address at Villanova University School of Law's Second Annual Matthew J. Ryan Forum on Law and Public

Policy (Apr. 4, 2008). [This may, however, be exceeded by the refugee crisis from Syria—Ed. Note].

[5] As of September 2006, Muslims comprised ninety-seven percent of the Iraqi population; three percent consisted of Christians, with Chaldeans and Assyrians being the two largest Christian groups. U.S. DEP'T OF STATE, BUREAU OF DEMOCRACY, HUMAN RIGHTS, AND LABOR, *Iraq*, *in* INTERNATIONAL RELIGIOUS FREEDOM REPORT 2006, *available at www*.state.gov/g/drl/rls/irf/2006/71422.htm. Despite the fact that Christians made up such a small part of the total Iraqi population at the start of the war, they represented nearly 40 percent of the refugees who emigrated out of Iraq. Zaid Sabah & Rick Jervis, *Christians, Targeted and Suffering, Flee Iraq*, USA TODAY, Mar. 23, 2007, *available at* http://usatoday30.usatoday.com/news/world/iraq/2007-03-22-christians-iraq_N.htm.

[6] *See* U.S. DEP'T OF HOMELAND SEC., 2011 YEARBOOK OF IMMIGRATION STATISTICS 40 (2012), *available at* http://www.dhs.gov/sites/default/files/publications/immigration-statistics/yearbook/2011/ois_yb_2011.pdf; DANIEL C. MARTIN & JAMES E. YANKAY, OFFICE OF IMMIGRATION STATISTICS, U.S. DEP'T OF HOMELAND SECURITY, REFUGEES AND ASYLEES: 2012, at 3 (2013) *available at* http://www.dhs.gov/sites/default/files/publications/ois_rfa_fr_2012.pdf.

[7] *See More than 4 Million Iraqis have Fled Home as Situation Worsens*, UN NEWS CTR., June 5, 2007, *available at* http://www.un.org/apps/news/story.asp?Cr=Iraq&Cr1=&NewsID=22786#.UZ52BbWTgb0.

[8] *See* JOYCE C. VIALET, REFUGEE ACT REAUTHORIZATION: ADMISSIONS AND RESETTLEMENT ISSUES 5-6 (1983), *available at* http://www.hsdl.org/?view&did=14799. When the Refugee Act was enacted in 1980, 168,000 of the 231,000 allotment went to Southeast Asian refugees for two consecutive years. *See id.*; and *cf. also* Bill Frelick's chapter in this volume. East Asia continued to receive the lion's share of the resettlement allocations, with more than 40,000 refugees allocated for that region (Cambodia, Vietnam, and Laos) each year through 1998. *See* KAREN MUSALO ET AL., REFUGEE LAW AND POLICY: A COMPARATIVE AND INTERNATIONAL APPROACH 77-79 (2011). Over the 18-year period, the total number of resettled refugees from Southeast Asia was well over one million people. *See* MAX NIEDZWIECKI & TC DUONG, SOUTHEAST ASIA RESOURCE ACTION CTR., SOUTHEAST ASIAN AMERICAN STATISTICAL PROFILE 10 (2004), *available at* http://www.searac.org/sites/default/files/seastatprofilemay04.pdf.

[9] The violence erupted on February 22, 2006, when one of Shiite Islam's holiest shrines was bombed. Ellen Knickmeyer & K.I. Ibrahim, *Bombing Shatters Mosque In Iraq*, WASH. POST, Feb. 23, 2006, at A01. Although no one died in the bombing, it led to riots that killed more than 170 people. Robert F. Worth, *Muslim Clerics Call for an End to Iraqi Rioting*, N.Y. TIMES, Feb. 25, 2006, at A6. Violence erupted again on November 22, 2006, when a string of coordinated bombings killed 138 people in Sadr City, a Shiite section of Baghdad. Sudarsan Raghavan &

Nancy Trejos, *Assault on Iraqi Civilians is Deadliest Since 2003*, WASH. POST, Nov. 24, 2006, at A01. The aim of the United States' "surge" of troops in the fall of 2007, as well as a cease fire between the Iraqi Prime Minister and local militias, was to promote an environment of reconciliation. *Iraq: Violence On Downturn In Southern Al-Sadr City* (Radio Free Europe/Radio Liberty broadcast Apr. 28, 2008), *available at* http://www.refworld.org/cgi-bin/texis/vtx/rwmain?docid=481870cfa. The cease-fire ended in March 2008, and militias attacked American and Iraqi positions in March and April. *Id.*

[10] "[I]rrespective of sect or ethnicity, academics, medical doctors, and other highly educated professionals—all of whom have been targeted by armed groups in Iraq—predominate among the refugees." REINOUD LEENDERS, GETTING THE "LADDER OF OPTIONS" RIGHT—THE ILLUSIVE AND REAL SECURITY FALLOUT OF THE IRAQI REFUGEE CRISIS 5 (Middle East Institute & Fondation pour la Recherche Stratégique 2010), *available at* http://www.refugeecooperation.org/publications/iraq/pdf/01_leenders.pdf (noting that Iraqis having a university degree were found to constitute thirty-one percent of the refugee population in Syria and that in Jordan, close to half of the adult refugees had completed higher education at the bachelor level or higher).

[11] *Id.*

[12] *See* JEFF CRISP ET AL., SURVIVING IN THE CITY: A REVIEW OF UNHCR'S OPERATION FOR IRAQI REFUGEES IN URBAN AREAS OF JORDAN, LEBANON AND SYRIA 49-51 (2009), *available at* http://www.unhcr.org/4a69ad639.html; Géraldine Chatelard, *Iraqi Refugees: Making the Urban Refugee Approach Context-Specific*, HUMANITARIAN EXCHANGE MAGAZINE, July 2011, *available at* http://www.odihpn.org/humanitarian-exchange-magazine/issue-51/iraqi-refugees-making-the-urban-refugee-approach-context-specific.

[13] For a good discussion of the mental health issues commonly faced by refugees and other displaced persons, see RICHARD F. MOLLICA, HEALING INVISIBLE WOUNDS: PATHS TO HOPE AND RECOVERY IN A VIOLENT WORLD (2006).

[14] J. David Kinzie, *Immigrants and Refugees: The Psychiatric Perspective*, 43 TRANSCULTURAL PSYCHIATRY 577, 584 (2006); *see also* Grant N. Marshall et al., *Mental Health of Cambodian Refugees 2 Decades After Resettlement in the United States*, 294 J. AM. MED. ASS'N 571, 576-77 (2005) (finding high rates of PTSD and depression among Cambodians after two decades in America); Richard F. Mollica et al., *Longitudinal Study of Psychiatric Symptoms, Disability, Mortality, and Emigration among Bosnian Refugees*, 286 J. AM. MED. ASS'N 546, 551-52 (finding, in a follow-up survey, that forty-three percent of Bosnian refugees continued to have PTSD).

[15] UNHCR, SECOND IPSOS SURVEY ON IRAQI REFUGEES: FINAL RESULTS 12-13 (2008), *available at* http://www.unhcr.org/cgi-bin/texis/vtx/home/opendocPDF Viewer.html?docid=4795f96f2 [hereinafter SECOND IPSOS SURVEY ON IRAQI REFUGEES]. The report used the Harvard Trauma Survey (HTS) as the instrument to assess trauma. The HTS is tailored to fit different refugee populations and their own unique political, social, and historical experiences. *See* Marwa Shoeb, Harvey Weinstein & Richard Mollica, *The Harvard Trauma Questionnaire: Adapting a*

Cross-Cultural Instrument for Measuring Torture, Trauma and Posttraumatic Stress Disorder in Iraqi Refugees, 53 INT'L J. SOC. PSYCHIATRY 447, 449-51 (2007) (discussing trauma studies in the Middle East).

[16] SECOND IPSOS SURVEY ON IRAQI REFUGEES, *supra* note 15.

[17] *Id.*

[18] INTEGRATED REG'L INFO. NETWORKS (IRIN), EGYPT: HIGH RATES OF TRAUMA, SICKNESS AMONG IRAQI REFUGEES (2008), *available at* http://www.unhcr.org/cgi-bin/texis/vtx/refworld/rwmain?docid=47cbc62d1e.

[19] INT'L ORG. FOR MIGRATION (IOM), ASSESSMENT ON PSYCHOSOCIAL NEEDS OF IRAQIS DISPLACED IN JORDAN AND LEBANON 70 (Guglielmo Schininà, Elena Bartoloni & Rocco Nuri eds., 2008), *available at* http://www.iom.int/jahia/webdav/shared/shared/mainsite/published_docs/brochures_and_info_sheets/report_psy_assessment.pdf.

[20] Matthew Porter & Nick Haslam, *Predisplacement and Postdisplacement Factors Associated with Mental Health of Refugees and Internally Displaced Persons*, 294 J. AM. MED. ASS'N 602, 610 (2005).

[21] *Id.*

[22] DAVID R. JOHNSON, HELPING REFUGEE TRAUMA SURVIVORS IN THE PRIMARY CARE SETTING 5-6 (The Center for Victims of Torture 2005), *available at* http://www.cvt.org/sites/cvt.org/files/u11/Helping_Refugee_Trauma_Survivors_Primary_Care.pdf.

[23] *Id.* at 8-9.

[24] *Id.* at 8. *See* Marshall et al., *supra* note 14 (explaining continuing problems of Cambodian refugees two decades after arriving in America).

[25] *See* Khetam Malkawi, *35 New Measles Cases Detected; Immunisation Campaigns Intensified*, JORDAN TIMES, May 2, 2013, *available at* http://jordantimes.com/35-new-measles-cases-detected-immunisation-campaigns-intensified. Officials believe the prevalence of measles, particularly in Syrian refugees, is related to the interruption of national vaccination programs due to the ongoing Syrian conflict. *Id.*

[26] INT'L COMM. OF THE RED CROSS (ICRC), IRAQ: NO LET-UP IN THE HUMANITARIAN CRISIS 9 (2008), *available at* http://www.icrc.org/eng/assets/files/other/icrc-iraq-report-0308-eng.pdf.

[27] *Id.* at 9 (estimating that by 2008, out of 34,000 doctors, 20,000 had left Iraq, 2200 had been killed and 250 had been kidnapped).

[28] Press Release, Int'l Med. Corps, International Medical Corps Becomes First American NGO to Operate in Syria (Mar. 27, 2008), *available at* http://www.imcworldwide.org/content/article/detail/1703.

[29] SHANNON DOOCY ET AL., INT'L MED. CORPS, HEALTH NEEDS AND PERCEPTIONS OF PATIENTS IN JORDANIAN RED CRESCENT AND CARITAS CLINICS 15-16 (2008), *available at* http://www.internationalmedicalcorps.org/Document.Doc?id=80.

[30] *"The Silent Treatment": Fleeing Iraq, Surviving In Jordan*, HUMAN RIGHTS WATCH, Nov. 2006, at 62-63, *available at* http://www.hrw.org/sites/default/files/reports/jordan1106webwcover.pdf.

[31] *Id.* at 63.

[32] *Id.*
[33] *Id.* at 64.
[34] *Rot Here or Die There: Bleak Choices for Iraqi Refugees in Lebanon*, HUMAN RIGHTS WATCH, Nov. 2007, at 57, *available at* http://www.unhcr.org/cgi-bin/texis/vtx/refworld/rwmain?docid=47565c202.
[35] DANISH REFUGEE COUNCIL (DRC), IRAQI POPULATION SURVEY IN LEBANON 70 (2007), *available at* http://urban-refugees.org/wp-content/uploads/2012/09/Iraqi-Population-Survey-in-Lebanon.pdf.
[36] *Id.*
[37] *Famine, Disease, Cause More Refugee Deaths than War*, VOICE OF AMERICA (VOA) (Aug. 5, 2001), *available at* http://www.voanews.com/content/a-13-a-2001-08-05-15-famine-66263632/539239.html (stating that the major causes of deaths among refugees are "a combination of food shortages and infectious diseases").
[38] *See* Areej Abuqudairi, *Iraqi Refugees Remain Vulnerable Despite Aid Efforts*, JORDAN TIMES, Apr. 23, 2013, *available at* http://jordantimes.com/iraqi-refugees-remain-vulnerable-despite-aid-efforts (reporting that Iraqi refugees are not eligible to work in Jordan except for extremely rare cases when a Jordanian employer sponsors an Iraqi refugee); *see also* Babak Deghanpisheh, *Iraqi Refugees in Syria Feel New Strains of War*, WASH POST, Apr. 10, 2013, *available at* http://articles.washingtonpost.com/2013-04-10/world/38415037_1_syria-refugees-damascus (noting that before the Syrian conflict broke out, Iraqi refugees in Syria depended on aid from nongovernmental organizations or cash from "odd jobs" because they were not allowed to officially work).
[39] THE BROOKINGS INSTITUTION—LONDON SCHOOL OF ECONOMICS PROJECT ON INTERNAL DISPLACEMENT & THE INTERNATIONAL RESCUE COMMITTEE, IMPROVING PROSPECTS FOR DURABLE SOLUTIONS FOR IRAQI INTERNALLY DISPLACED PERSONS AND REFUGEES: A ROUNDTABLE DISCUSSION HOSTED BY BROOKINGS—LSE PROJECT ON INTERNAL DISPLACEMENT AND THE INTERNATIONAL RESCUE COMMITTEE 7 (2012), *available at* http://www.brookings.edu/~/media/events/2012/2/24%20iraq%20displacement/event%20report.pdf.
[40] *See* Nicholas A. Heras, *Going Nowhere Fast: Iraqi Refugees*, FAIR OBSERVER, June 19, 2012, at 1, *available at* http://www.fairobserver.com/article/going-nowhere-fast-iraqi-refugees-part-1-2.
[41] *Cf.* ARNE STRAND ET AL., CHR. MICHELSEN INSTITUTE, BETWEEN TWO SOCIETIES: REVIEW OF IRAQI NATIONALS TO IRAQ (IRRINI) PROGRAMME (2011), *available at* http://www.cmi.no/publications/file/4155-between-two-societies-review-of-the-information.pdf. One study on a Norwegian program, the Information, Return, and Reintegration of Iraqi Nationals to Iraq (IRRINI), which was developed to facilitate the voluntary return and reintegration of persons from Iraq, suggests that vocational training and education in the host country can enhance return conditions by better preparing those considering return. *Id.* at 77. In addition to offering start-up cash upon returning to Iraq, the study found that courses in topics such as English, computer literacy, first aid, birth assistance, secretarial skills, car

mechanics, and other educational programs tailored to the individual seeking return may render the refugees more resourceful, therefore increasing the likelihood of a sustainable return. *Id.* This study may suggest that creating better conditions in the host country does not lead to refugees feeling "too comfortable" and wanting to stay.

[42] *See* THE BROOKINGS INSTITUTION—LONDON SCHOOL OF ECONOMICS, *supra* note 39, at 5.

[43] *Id.*

[44] Integrated Reg'l Info. Networks (IRIN), *Still No Clear Policy to Tackle Displacement*, IRIN MIDDLE EAST, Sept. 4, 2012, *available at* http://www.irinnews.org/report/96240/IRAQ-Still-no-clear-policy-to-tackle-displacement. UNHCR and the International Organization for Migration (IOM) concluded that ninety percent of people displaced by the recent conflict wanted to integrate locally in their areas of displacement—either because sectarian tensions prohibited their return or because they have nothing to go home to. *Id.* Those who fled to the autonomous Kurdish region in northern Iraq have settled there, in some cases, seemingly permanently, even changing their identification cards to read "Kurdish" instead of "Arab." *Id.* But nearly half a million others continue to eke out an existence in 382 settlements across Iraq and observers say the government has no real strategy to deal with them. *Id.*

[45] The New York Times reported, for example, that after the start of the recent Syrian uprisings "near-record numbers of displaced families [began] pouring back, but instead of kindling a much-needed reconciliation they are in some cases reviving the resentments and suspicions created by bloody purges that carved Iraq into archipelagos of Sunnis, Shiites and Kurds after the American-led 2003 invasion." Jack Healy & Yasir Ghazi, *As Displaced Return to Iraq, New Tensions for Neighbors*, N.Y. TIMES, Mar. 24, 2012, *available at* http://www.nytimes.com/2012/03/25/world/middleeast/as-the-displaced-return-to-iraq-new-tensions-arise.html?pagewanted=1&ref=global-home.

[46] THE BROOKINGS INSTITUTION—LONDON SCHOOL OF ECONOMICS, *supra* note 39, at 8; *see* UNRWA, *Iraqi Refugees in Syria Reluctant to Return to Home Permanently: Survey*, UNHCR (Oct. 8, 2010), *available at* http://www.unhcr.org/cgi-bin/texis/vtx/search?page=search&docid=4caf376c6&query=2010%20survey#hit2

[47] Peter Van der Auweraert, *Land and Property Issues in Iraq: Present Challenges and Future Solutions*, *in* RESOLVING IRAQI DISPLACEMENT: HUMANITARIAN AND DEVELOPMENT PERSPECTIVES (Elizabeth Ferris ed., 2010).

[48] *See Iraq Property Claims Programme*, INTERNATIONAL ORGANIZATION FOR MIGRATION, *available at* http://www.iom.int/cms/en/sites/iom/home/what-we-do/reparation-programmes/iraq-property-claims-programme.html (last visited May 23, 2013).

[49] THE BROOKINGS INSTITUTION—LONDON SCHOOL OF ECONOMICS, *supra* note 39, at 6.

[50] *Id.*

[51] AMNESTY INT'L, IRAQ: SUFFERING IN SILENCE: IRAQI REFUGEES IN SYRIA 11 (2008), *available at* http://www.amnesty.org/en/library/asset/MDE14/010/2008/en/7f39d610-2042-11dd-a784-8b9c94c1f93f/mde140102008eng.pdf.

[52] Press Release, UNICEF, Little Respite for Iraq's Children in 2007 (Dec. 21, 2007), *available at* http://www.unicef.org/infobycountry/media_42256.html.

[53] Astrid van Genderen Stort, *Iraqi Refugee Families Need Help to Educate Their Children*, UNHCR (July 31, 2007), *available at* http://www.unhcr.org/46aefe094.html.

[54] INT'L ORG. FOR MIGRATION (IOM), *supra* note 19, at 16.

[55] Hannah Tappis et al., *Domestic Violence Among Iraqi Refugees in Syria*, 33 HEALTH CARE FOR WOMEN INT'L 285 (2012); *see also* AMNESTY INT'L, *supra* note 51.

[56] *See* Integrated Reg'l Info. Networks (IRIN), *Syria: Fears Over Gender-based Violence in Iraqi Community* (Apr. 6, 2009), *available at* http://www.unhcr.org/refworld/docid/49db17ab19.html; IRIN, *Jordan: Increased Domestic Violence Among Iraqi Refugees–IOM Report* (Apr. 29, 2008), *available at* http://www.unhcr.org/cgi-bin/texis/vtx/refworld/rwmain?docid=4820057f1e.

[57] ASHLEY JONATHAN CLEMENTS, TRAPPED! THE DISAPPEARING HOPES OF IRAQI REFUGEE CHILDREN 12 (2007), *available at* http://reliefweb.int/sites/reliefweb.int/files/resources/1E3FBD8A6411E5F0C12572FB004C22D2-Full_Report.pdf.

[58] Integrated Reg'l Info. Networks (IRIN), *IRAQ: Domestic Violence Against Children on the Rise* (May 24, 2007), *available at* http://www.irinnews.org/Report.aspx?ReportId=72350.

[59] Clements, *supra* note 57.

[60] Integrated Reg'l Info. Networks (IRIN), *supra* note 58.

[61] Among the Iraqi refugee community, UNHCR reported 200 cases of sex or gender based violence in Syria between January and May of 2008, and 4380 cases in Jordan in 2007. UNHCR, IRAQ SITUATION UPDATE: APRIL-MAY 2008 (2008).

[62] AMNESTY INT'L, *supra* note 51 (reporting about, among other things, the detention of nine girls in a Damascus juvenile center in March 2008 for the crime of prostitution).

[63] Elizabeth G. Ferris, *The Role of Non-Governmental Organizations in the International Refugee Regime*, *in* PROBLEMS OF PROTECTION: THE UNHCR, REFUGEES, AND HUMAN RIGHTS 117, 128 (Niklaus Steiner, Mark Gibney & Gil Loescher eds., 2003); *see also* George Packer, *Betrayed: The Iraqis Who Trusted America the Most*, NEW YORKER, Mar. 26, 2007, at 69 (noting that "few Iraqis could get work permits" in Syria).

[64] Alistair Lyon, *Iraqi Refugees Turn to Sex Trade in Syria*, REUTERS, Dec. 31, 2007, *available at* http://www.reuters.com/article/worldNews/idUSL2966165920071231?sp=true.

[65] *See* THE ECONOMIST INTELLIGENCE UNIT, *Refugee Returns Increase in 2012,* Mar. 6, 2013, *available at*

http://www.eiu.com/index.asp?layout=displayIssueArticle&issue_id=1230243507&opt=full (noting that in 2012 the largest number of Iraqi refugees returned to Iraq since 2004, with a majority coming from Syria). The number of returning Iraqi refugees reached nearly 85,000 in 2012 and is linked to the turmoil in Syria, "with sixty-nine percent of returnees coming from there, compared with just three percent from Jordan, which hosts the second-largest Iraqi refugee population." *Id.*
[66] Integrated Reg'l Info. Networks (IRIN), *IRAQ: Returnees from Syria – A "Humanitarian" Crisis in the Making*, IRIN MIDDLE EAST, July 27, 2012, http://www.irinnews.org/report/95964/IRAQ-Returnees-from-Syria-a-humanitarian-crisis-in-the-making (quoting Yaseen Ahmed Abbas, the president of the Iraq Red Crescent (IRC), "I think we will face a humanitarian crisis regarding this issue . . . You should expect pressure on everything in Iraq by having such a large number of people in a short time. It's not easy.").
[67] *See* Serene Assir, *Iraqis in Syria: The Loss of a Last Refuge*, ALAKHBAR ENGLISH, Mar. 15, 2012, *available at* http://english.al-akhbar.com/node/5224.
[68] Felicity Arbuthnot, *Syrians, Iraqis, Palestinians: No Place to Hide*, PALESTINE CHRONICLE, July 25, 2012, *available at* http://palestinechronicle.com/old/view_article_details.php?id=19434.
[69] Jack Healy, *Syrian Kurds Flee into Iraqi Refugee Limbo*, N.Y. TIMES, Mar. 9, 2012, at A4, *available at* http://www.nytimes.com/2012/03/09/world/middleeast/syrian-kurds-flee-into-iraqi-refugee-limbo.html?pagewanted=all&_r=0.
[70] *See* Jacob Resneck & Krasimir Yankov, *Syrian Kurds Find Refuge in Iraq's Kurdish Region,* WASH. TIMES, Dec. 4, 2012, *available at* http://www.washingtontimes.com/news/2012/dec/4/syrian-kurds-find-refuge-in-iraqs-kurdish-region/?page=all; *see also* Amnesty Int'l, *More than 1.3 Million Refugees from Syria in Dire Need of Increased International Support*, Apr. 24, 2014, *available at* http://www.amnesty.org/en/news/more-13-million-refugees-syria-dire-need-increased-international-support-2013-04-24 (reporting that as of April 2013, "133,840 [Syrian] refugees were registered in Iraq, with the majority being hosted in the Kurdish region.").
[71] *See* Voice of America, *U.S. Officials Say More Than 12,000 Iraqi Refugees Resettled in U.S. This Year*, UNHCR REFUGEES DAILY, Sept. 15, 2008, *available at* http://www.unhcr.org/cgi-bin/texis/vtx/refdaily?pass=463ef21123&id=48cf4f268.
[72] *See* U.S. DEPT. OF STATE, PROPOSED REFUGEE ADMISSIONS FOR FISCAL YEAR 2013 5 (2013), *available at* http://www.state.gov/documents/organization/198157.pdf.
[73] *See* U.S. DEPT. OF STATE, STATUS OF U.S. REFUGEE RESETTLEMENT PROCESSING FOR IRAQI NATIONALS 1-2 (2008), *available at* http://oig.state.gov/documents/organization/109296.pdf
[74] BUREAU OF NEAR EASTERN AFFAIRS, U.S. DEP'T OF STATE, IRAQ STATUS REPORT 7 (2010), *available at* www.state.gov/documents/organization/145285.pdf (showing 47,841 Iraqi refugees admitted beginning with the start of a new program during the 2007 fiscal year to July 21, 2010, and approximately 3,000 other Iraqis

admitted under special visas for interpreters and other employees of the U.S. government).

[75] Stephen H. Legomsky, *Humanitarianism Will Provide Better Refuge*, CHRISTIAN SCIENCE MONITOR, Feb. 16, 1996, *available at* http://www.csmonitor.com/1996/0216/16181.html.

[76] Also, up until 1999, the USSR (and former USSR) received high percentages of allocated numbers, especially compared to the continent of Africa (58,300 to 2,000 for 1990). KAREN MUSALO ET AL., REFUGEE LAW AND POLICY: A COMPARATIVE AND INTERNATIONAL APPROACH 77-79 (2011). At its inception in 1980 and until 1999, most of the U.S. resettlement efforts focused on Asia and the former Soviet Union, with approximately half the refugees coming from those two regions in 1990. *See id.* Then, over the past 7-9 years, the focus expanded: under the current program the population of resettled refugees spans 70 nationalities with processing taking place in 100 countries. *See id.*; U.S. DEPT. OF STATE, PROPOSED REFUGEE ADMISSIONS FOR FISCAL YEAR 2013 5 (2013), *available at* http://www.state.gov/documents/organization/198157.pdf.

[77] *See* National Defense Authorization Act for Fiscal Year 2008, Pub. L. No. 110-181, § 1244 (2008).

[78] *See The End of the Special Immigrant Visa?*, THE LIST PROJECT TO RESETTLE IRAQI ALLIES, *available at* http://thelistproject.org/the-end-of-the-special-immigrant-visa/ (last visited Feb. 12, 2013),

[79] Immigration & Nationality Act (INA) § 212(d)(5)(A).

[80] *Id.*

[81] James Glanz & Thom Shanker, *U.S. Opens a Sheltered Path to Asylum for Some Iraqis*, N.Y. TIMES, May 25, 2007, *available at* http://www.nytimes.com/2007/05/25/washington/25asylum.html?pagewanted=all.

[82] Kevin Whitelaw, *When Helping America is a Death Sentence,* U.S. NEWS & WORLD REP., Oct. 1, 2007, at 33, *available at* http://www.usnews.com/news/iraq/articles/2007/09/22/a-brave-iraqi-prosecutor-who-took-on-the-militias-escapes-to-america.

[83] ANDREW HARPER, *Where to Now? Decreasing Options for Displaced Iraqis,* MIGRATION INFO. SOURCE (Sept. 2007), *available at* http://www.migrationinformation.org/Feature/display.cfm?ID=644.

[84] HUMAN RIGHTS FIRST, IRAQI REFUGEES IN JORDAN AND SYRIA: FACTSHEET 2 (2007), *available at* http://www.humanrightsfirst.org/wp-content/uploads/pdf/irp-jordan-syria.pdf.

[85] Nicholas Kristof, *Books, Not Bombs*, N.Y. TIMES, June 26, 2008, at A23, *available at* http://www.nytimes.com/2008/06/26/opinion/26kristof.html.

[86] MATTHEW J. GIBNEY, THE ETHICS AND POLITICS OF ASYLUM: LIBERAL DEMOCRACY AND THE RESPONSE TO REFUGEES 250 (2004).

[87] *See generally* Michele R. Pistone & John J. Hoeffner, *Unsettling Developments: Terrorism and the New Case for Enhancing Protection and Humanitarian Assistance for Refugees and Internally Displaced Persons, Including Victims of Natural Disasters*, 42 COLUM. HUM. RTS. L. REV. 613 (2011).

[88] COUNCIL ON FOREIGN RELATIONS, INDEPENDENT TASK FORCE REPORT NO. 63: U.S. IMMIGRATION POLICY 31 (2009), *available at* http://www.cfr.org/immigration/us-immigration-policy/p20030.

[89] *See* Massimo Calabresi, *Confronting Iraq's Exodus*, TIME, Mar. 2, 2007, *available at* http://www.time.com/time/magazine/article/0,9171,1595248,00.html (noting that 18 Iraqi refugees were admitted in 2005 and asserting that the Bush Administration was reluctant to acknowledge and address the Iraqi refugee crisis because "doing so would be an admission of failure in Iraq"); *see also* Samantha Power, *Access Denied*, TIME, Sept. 26, 2007, at 33 (stating that the Bush Administration was "in denial about the refugee crisis" and "pretend[ed]" it did "not exist" so as to not "undermine . . . arguments for staying"); Frank Rich, *Operation Freedom from Iraqis*, N.Y. TIMES, May 27, 2007, at WK10 (asserting that President Bush's "silence about Iraq's mass exodus" was "part of a policy . . . to keep the Iraqi plight out of sight"); Packer, *supra* note 63, at 53, 72 (quoting a claim by former Deputy Secretary of State Richard Armitage that no one in the Bush Administration was thinking about resettling Iraqis in the U.S. because "you'd be considered a traitor to the President's policy," and an anonymous official who expressed the fear that resettling Iraqis would signal "'that it's game over' in Iraq").

[90] *See* U.S. DEPT. OF STATE, DEPT. OF STATE BUREAU OF POPULATION, REFUGEES, AND MIGRATION, EXPEDITED PROTECTION AND RESETTLEMENT OF REFUGEES FACT SHEET (2011), *available at* http://www.state.gov/j/prm/releases/factsheets/2011/181021.htm.

[91] *See* REFUGEE COUNCIL USA, POLICY FRAMEWORK: RECOMMENDATIONS AND ACTIONS FOR THE OBAMA ADMINISTRATION AND THE 113TH CONGRESS 10 (2013), *available at* http://www.rcusa.org/uploads/pdfs/RCUSA_2013_FINAL.pdf

[92] *See* HUMAN RIGHTS FIRST, HOW TO REPAIR THE U.S. ASYLUM AND REFUGEE RESETTLEMENT SYSTEMS: BLUEPRINT FOR THE NEXT ADMINISTRATION 17 (2012), *available at* http://www.humanrightsfirst.org/wp-content/uploads/pdf/asylum_blueprint.pdf. Although the Bureau of Population, Refugees, and Migration (PRM) drafted global guidelines in 2011, regional guidelines that pertain to specific areas would better reflect local processing realities. *Id.* Moreover, while a few resettlement countries have faster systems in place than the United States, this should not stop the United States from restricting and strengthening its resettlement program. *See* REFUGEE COUNCIL USA, *supra* note 91. Strengthening is needed because the faster systems in other countries sometimes do not respond to the most at-risk individuals, for example, Iraqi refugees who worked with the U.S. military. *See* HUMAN RIGHTS FIRST, *supra* note 92.

[93] *See* HUMAN RIGHTS FIRST, *supra* note 92.

[94] *Id.*

[95] U.S. COMM'N ON INT'L RELIGIOUS FREEDOM, USCIRF ANNUAL REPORT 2013: IRAQ 12 (2013), *available at* http://www.uscirf.gov/images/Iraq%202013.pdf.

[96] AM. BAR ASS'N, COMM'N ON IMMIGRATION, REFORMING THE IMMIGRATION SYSTEM, EXECUTIVE SUMMARY (2010), *available at*

http://www.americanbar.org/content/dam/aba/migrated/media/nosearch/immigration_reform_executive_summary_012510.authcheckdam.pdf.
[97] Hannah Allam, *U.S. Pledge to Help Iraqis Who Aided Occupation Largely Unfulfilled*, MCCLATHCY NEWSPAPERS, Mar. 14, 2013, *available at* http://www.mcclatchydc.com/2013/03/14/185851/us-pledge-to-help-iraqis-who-aided.html#.UaiuO0CTgb1 (citing an official from the Department of Homeland Security).
[98] *See* HUMAN RIGHTS FIRST, *supra* note 92, at 18. Suspected TB cases take six to eight weeks to confirm, resulting in significant delays for refugees that end up being free of TB. *Id.*
[99] *See* REFUGEE COUNCIL USA, *supra* note 91, at 24.
[100] *Id.*
[101] *See* Allam, *supra* note 97.
[102] *See id.* At the very least, Congress should amend the Refugee Crisis in Iraq Act of 2007, National Defense Authorization Act for Fiscal Year 2008, Pub. L. No. 110-181, § 1241, 122 Stat. 3 (2008), so that special immigrant visas can still be given until the allotment for Iraqis is exhausted. *See* REFUGEE COUNCIL USA, *supra* note 91, at 25.
[103] *See* REFUGEE COUNCIL USA, *supra* note 91, at 14.
[104] *See id.*; UNHCR, *supra* note 15.
[105] *See* Michael Hollifield, M.D. et al., *The Refugee Health Screener -15 (RHS-15): Development and Validation of an Instrument for Anxiety, Depression, and PTSD in Refugees*, 35 GENERAL HOSPITAL PSYCHIATRY 202, 208 (2013). A potentially useful screening test that may be implemented is RHS-15, which allows screening for a range of common mental disorders across refugee populations as opposed to other tests which only screen for a single disorder. *See id.* Furthermore, the test appears both promising and efficient: it can be self-administered or clinician administered by interpreters, it is generally only four to twelve minutes long, and the psychometric properties are reportedly "very good." *Id.*
[106] *See* CTR. FOR VICTIMS OF TORTURE, TORTURE VICTIMS RELIEF ACT, *available at* http://www.cvt.org/what-you-can-do/advocate/torture-victims-relief-act.
[107] *See* REFUGEE COUNCIL USA, *supra* note 91, at 8.
[108] *See id.*
[109] *See id.*
[110] *See* HUMAN RIGHTS FIRST, *supra* note 92, at 15.
[111] *See id.*
[112] *See supra* note 8.
[113] *See* HUMAN RIGHTS FIRST, *supra* note 92, at 21.
[114] *Id.* at 19-21.
[115] *See* COUNCIL ON FOREIGN RELATIONS, *supra* note 88.
[116] When portions of a majority group leave their homes, their culture lives on in those who remain. But the flight of minority groups, which groups may be particularly vulnerable to the pressures that cause displacement, can mean the loss to history of a language, a religion, and unique cultural practices and traditions. Even if some members of a minority group remain, a tipping point can be reached

in which the group's future viability comes into question. There is substantial fear that such a dynamic is now playing out in Iraq, as "grave conditions affect[] . . . Chaldo-Assyrian Christians, Yazidis, Sabean Mandaeans, and other minority religious communities [who] suffer widespread violence." UNITED STATES COMMISSION ON INTERNATIONAL RELIGIOUS FREEDOM, ANNUAL REPORT OF THE UNITED STATES COMMISSION ON RELIGIOUS FREEDOM 32 (2007), *available at* http://www.aina.org/reports/uscirf2007.pdf. The deterioration and possible destruction of such communities represents an incalculable loss both to cultural diversity and to historic understanding. *See id.*

CHAPTER SIX

UNLOCKING PROTRACTED REFUGEE SITUATIONS: LESSONS FROM FOUR ASIAN CASE STUDIES[1]

BILL FRELICK*

Protracted refugee situations do not unlock themselves. To state the obvious, if such situations were easily unlocked they would not be protracted. Ideally, the resolution of refugee situations, whether short term or protracted, happens after fundamental changes occur in the country of origin that allow most refugees to return. The optimal solution is that refugees' rights as citizens are restored and they are enabled to recover their losses and become productive and fulfilled members of their home societies.

The resolution of refugee situations that involves repatriation as a component is highly problematic where a fundamental and durable change in the country of origin has not occurred that allows refugees' rights as citizens to be fully restored. There are nevertheless cases where protracted situations have been resolved where such changes have not occurred in the country of origin. These cases have usually involved significant investment and effort by a variety of actors, including local host states, donor or resettlement countries outside the region, the United Nations High Commissioner for Refugees ("UNHCR") and other intergovernmental agencies, nongovernmental organizations ("NGOs"), and usually at least some engagement by the countries of origin. While internationally coordinated agreements to resolve refugee situations affirm as a matter of course the need to ensure the rights of refugees, in practice, they have more often demonstrated an international consensus to contain refugee flows and to manage migration than solidarity to protect refugees and to ensure human rights.

Refugee protection principles—most fundamentally, the principle of *non-refoulement*—are most likely to be sacrificed or play a secondary role where some combination of the following factors prevails: compassion fatigue, the unwillingness of donors to provide money and other assistance to maintain refugees in protracted situations, and the sense of host countries that the refugees represent a never-ending burden. Other factors include deteriorating conditions in host countries, including host country conflict that engulfs refugees or rising tensions with local communities that erode humanitarian space; the presence or perceived presence of non-refugees among refugee populations, including not only economic migrants but also combatants and others who are or appear to be security threats. Additional factors that can undermine refugee protection are the desire of the international community to use refugee and internally displaced persons ("IDP") returns as a means of achieving peace-building in the country of origin; and the desire of the refugees themselves to move on with their lives and escape stagnant, demoralizing disenfranchisement and destitution even when the situation in the country of origin remains precarious.

This chapter will look at how the international community has worked to unlock protracted refugee situations in Asia. It will first examine two examples of resolved protracted refugee situations in Southeast Asia from the 1970s to the 1990s, the continuing outflow of Vietnamese refugees throughout the region after the Vietnam War and the Cambodian exodus to Thailand and along its border as a result of the Khmer Rouge genocide and following the Vietnamese invasion in December 1978. The chapter will then look at two contemporary examples of protracted refugee situations in Asia that are at different stages of potentially being resolved: that of the Bhutanese refugees in Nepal and of the Burmese refugees in Thailand.

Vietnamese Refugees and the Comprehensive Plan of Action

From the first international conference on Indochinese refugees in 1979 onwards, international cooperation to resolve the situation of refugees arriving in the neighboring states in Southeast Asia after the end of the Vietnam War was based on the *quid pro quo* of temporary asylum by first asylum countries and refugee resettlement by countries outside the region.[2] At the time, there was no prospect for fundamental changes in Vietnam that would allow for safe and voluntary refugee repatriation nor any willingness of other countries in the region (with the exception of the

Philippines) to consider offering permanent asylum to Vietnamese refugees and integrating them into their societies.

The protracted Southeast Asian refugee situation occurred during the Cold War when the United States and other non-communist states were engaged in what the authors of one history of the era called the "calculated kindness" of creating a refugee regime that would not only provide refuge to those who "voted with their feet" by fleeing from communist ruled countries, but would also score points in the grand ideological battle of the time.[3] It was an era symbolized by the Berlin Wall, and characterized both by a prima facie recognition that people who fled communist countries were refugees and by an "exilic bias" that repatriation would not be an option available to them.[4] Whether from the Warsaw Pact countries of Eastern Europe, Cuba in the Western Hemisphere, or China, North Korea, or Vietnam in Asia, the act of leaving without permission itself was grounds for being persecuted. People exercising their right to leave these countries established *sur place* claims for refugee status based on the likelihood of persecution for the act of leaving, notwithstanding other grounds for fearing persecution, such as political dissent.[5]

The prima facie recognition of Vietnamese refugees was also closely linked to the commitment made by the United States and other resettlement countries to resettle the refugees; the unwillingness of first-asylum countries to provide secure and permanent asylum; and their increasing willingness to block asylum entirely by towing boats out to sea or pushing back asylum seekers at land borders. As W. Courtland Robinson observed, "UNHCR and the Western countries realized that—lacking other durable solutions—temporary haven for the boat people would have to be purchased, on a one-to-one ratio if necessary, with resettlement offers."[6]

The 1979 conference that resulted in the first asylum/third country resettlement *quid pro quo* also produced a Vietnamese government agreement "to make every effort to stop illegal departures."[7] Vietnam agreed to the "moratorium" on boat departures under pressure from the French, British, and Americans.[8] That the Western powers pushed Vietnam to stop boat people from leaving represented a remarkable departure from their promotion heretofore of the right to leave, a right enshrined in article 13(2) of the 1948 Universal Declaration of Human Rights ("UDHR") and in article 12(2) of the International Covenant on Civil and Political Rights ("ICCPR"), which had come into force in 1976. It was also noteworthy that the discussion did not focus on ameliorating the root causes of refugee flows—such as violations of human rights in

Vietnam—but rather on having Vietnam contain the irregular flow and manage it through orderly departures.

In part as a result of ongoing repression in Vietnam, but also because of *prima facie* refugee recognition and the prospect of being resettled outside the region, high numbers of asylum seekers continued to leave Vietnam more than a decade after the end of the Vietnam War. As there seemed to be no end in sight to departures, and as the availability of resettlement places could not keep pace with the numbers of refugees continuing to leave, policy-makers in the region and beyond began to question whether the newer arrivals were *bona fide* refugees. The principle of first asylum in the region came under great strain by the late 1980s. A number of first-asylum states, most notably Thailand, Malaysia, and Hong Kong, adopted so-called "humane deterrence" policies intended to make conditions of asylum so restrictive that other asylum seekers would be deterred from coming.[9] But a renewed wave of Vietnamese boat people in 1988 and 1989 flushed away any remaining wishful thinking that the exodus of asylum seekers from Vietnam would be deterred. It also spurred littoral states in the region, particularly Malaysia, to take drastic measures to push boats out to sea with the result that many asylum seekers drowned or fell under the vicious predations of pirates.

Consequently, in July 1989, another international conference convened to resolve the refugee problem, adopting a Comprehensive Plan of Action ("CPA") for Indochinese Refugees.[10] According to the definitive history of the Indochinese exodus and the international response, "the CPA, first and foremost, was an effort to control migration."[11] It rested on three prongs:

- First-asylum states' initiation of refugee screening and their willingness to maintain refugees in temporary asylum pending durable solutions;
- Vietnam's cooperation in preventing clandestine departures, in facilitating refugee repatriation and in receiving screened-out returnees, and in allowing UN monitoring of returnees and tolerating orderly departure programs; and
- the support of countries outside the region for maintaining temporary asylum in the region by providing financial support for camps and by offering significant levels of refugee resettlement by resettling both long-stayers who arrived before a cut-off date and newer arrivals who were determined to be refugees under the new screening procedures.

The CPA marked a paradigm shift away from regarding presumptively as refugees people leaving a communist state and toward looking at the boat people phenomenon as a mixed flow of refugees and economic migrants. Instead of assuming all Vietnamese asylum seekers were refugees, host governments in the region began to institute refugee status determination ("RSD") screening on the understanding that screened-in refugees would be resettled in third countries and screened-out rejected asylum seekers would return to Vietnam, preferably, but not necessarily, voluntarily.

This, of course, could only happen with the cooperation of Vietnam and with some assurances that returnees would not be persecuted. To that end, Vietnam agreed to waive prosecution of returned boat people for their illegal departure (but did not agree to waive prosecution for other crimes or offences).[12] Vietnam also agreed to allow UNHCR to monitor returnees. UNHCR's monitoring of returnees, including rejected asylum seekers, marked a "break in the exilic focus of its traditional protection mandate" and served to instill "a measure of confidence" in regional screening because it "did not uncover any significant incidence of abuse and persecution" of returnees.[13] However, an internal UNHCR evaluation finding that UNHCR's country office "lack[ed] the most rudimentary documentary evidence relating to arrest, trial and sentence, and imprisonment"[14] suggests that the fact that UNHCR monitors uncovered no significant incidence of abuse does not necessarily mean that such abuses were not occurring.

Vietnam also agreed to reinvigorate the Orderly Departure Program ("ODP") as an alternative to irregular boat departures. In the years 1991-1995, orderly departures averaged 66,000 per year. Many of the refugees already in countries of first asylum were induced to opt for voluntary return by a related program that turned refugee principles on their head: the Resettlement Opportunities for Vietnamese Returnees ("ROVR") program promised refugees a place in the ODP interview queue if they agreed to go back to Vietnam, the country where they claimed to have a well-founded fear of being persecuted. Remarkably, 80,000 Vietnamese repatriated during the years of the CPA—1989 to 1997, many taking advantage of ROVR (or its predecessor, called Track II).[15]

This unprecedented innovation in refugee resettlement: the direct, orderly departure of "refugees" directly from their home country fundamentally contradicts the refugee definition that requires alienage. Orderly home-country resettlement processing raises concerns that refugee processing from the country of origin could be a form of expulsion. Refugee programs could morph into immigration programs while at the same time serving as a pretext to block access to asylum for people with immediate needs to flee persecution who are unable to obtain official travel documents and wait in the orderly departure queue.[16]

The refugee status determination screening was controversial and criticized as having swung the pendulum from regarding asylum seekers as *prima facie* refugees to essentially requiring them to overcome a presumption that "most of the boat people were not refugees."[17] The screening procedures were criticized for being "strictly perfunctory, in the sense that it was done as a deterrent exercise to future asylum seekers."[18]

Even more controversial than the quality of the screening procedures was the treatment of the screened-out asylum seekers who were not willing to return voluntarily.[19] The mandatory detention, conditions of detention, and forced returns from Hong Kong, whose RSD procedure had the highest rejection rates in the region, were particularly tense and violent.[20] Ironically, UNHCR's monitoring presence for voluntary returnees in Vietnam allowed the Hong Kong government to argue that rejected returnees "did not need international protection [because] UNHCR was on hand in the SRV [Socialist Republic of Vietnam] to ensure that returnees were not ill-treated."[21]

Whether the CPA ultimately succeeded in securing rights for asylum seekers, refugees, and screened-out migrants, it nevertheless achieved its objective of stopping the irregular migration flow out of Vietnam. In 1989, some 70,000 Vietnamese irregular "boat people" landed or were picked up in the region. By 1992, the number had dropped to 41.[22]

Cambodian Refugees in Thailand

The Cambodian refugee situation that arose from the Khmer Rouge genocide and spiked with the Vietnamese invasion of that country demonstrated the full array of abuses and dysfunction that characterize protracted situations. The misery of Cambodian refugees in Thailand in the decade of the 1980s was exacerbated by the Thai government's political objectives, which trumped humanitarian principles by condoning the militarization of the camps along the Thai-Cambodian border, and by the United Nations High Commissioner for Refugees' ("UNHCR") inability or unwillingness to recognize as refugees about 300,000 Cambodians displaced along the Thai border or to provide basic protection to them. A marginalized UNHCR instead focused its attention on a relatively smaller number of refugees who arrived before a cut-off date or later managed to overcome considerable obstacles to reach UNHCR-established camps in the Thai interior. UNHCR eventually was able to facilitate the resettlement of about 200,000 of these refugees, but "the bulk of Cambodian refugees remained beyond the reach of UNHCR and had little prospect of resettlement."[23]

In this regard, both the Thai and US governments subverted any pretext of humanitarian neutrality and, whether due to incapacity or unwillingness, stood by as the civilian character of border refugee camps was utterly compromised.[24] For whatever humanitarian good was achieved in feeding displaced civilians (they were not called refugees) along the Thai-Cambodian border, the aid effort to the border camps was also being used by the US and Thailand to bolster their efforts to support the armed Cambodian resistance groups in their fight against the Vietnamese occupation forces and the Vietnamese-installed Cambodian government.[25] With UNHCR refusing to operate in the border camps, an *ad hoc* agency without a protection mandate, the United Nations Border Relief Operation ("UNBRO") was established at the urging—and funding—of the US government. UNBRO drew largely from the World Food Program, which, according to William Shawcross, "was still providing the Thai army with thousands of rations a day for use in the northern and southern sectors, and which had rarely displayed… qualms about either the legalities or the moralities of the process…"[26] In reality, the border camps were controlled by various armed resistance factions, including in some camps the Khmer Rouge. Camp residents were subjected to forced recruitment, forced relocations, forced labor, the requirement to pay "taxes" to armed groups, *refoulement*, and other abuses and exploitation at the hands of both the Cambodian armed groups and the Thai security forces that were supposedly there to protect them.[27] In part because the civilian character of the border camps had been compromised, they were also subjected to attacks by Vietnamese forces.[28]

UNHCR, the sole international agency with a comprehensive refugee protection mandate, not only sat out engagement with the Cambodian refugees at the border, but remained largely silent in the face of repeated Thai violations of the principle of *non-refoulement*, various actors' failure to adhere to international standards of humanitarianism, as well as other abuses perpetrated against the Cambodians by Thai authorities and Cambodian armed groups.[29]

Cambodians were excluded from the CPA, and concerted international efforts to resolve the Cambodian refugee situation did not begin until the signing of the Paris Peace Accord in October 1991. The Accord included a provision on refugee repatriation, which set out the conditions for voluntary return in safety, security and dignity, with freedom of movement and choice of domicile upon return.

A United Nations Transitional Authority in Cambodia ("UNTAC") was established to oversee implementation of the Accord, and UNHCR was designated as the lead agency on refugee repatriation. Instead of creating an out-of-country voting mechanism for Cambodian refugees to have a voice in democratization, the UN used the May 1993 elections as a target date for refugee repatriation. This suggests that UNTAC and UNHCR regarded the return of refugees as an instrument for the peace-building exercise rather than regarding a durable peace as the prerequisite for safe, dignified, and sustainable repatriation. Daniel Unger noted that mass refugee repatriations occurred not only before elections had achieved some level of political stability but also prior to demobilization of armed groups:

> The largest repatriation, much of it of an involuntary nature, came with the Cambodian peace settlement. Between March 1992 and May 1993, 362,000 Cambodians returned to Cambodia from Thailand. The Khmer Rouge threatened to repatriate in excess of 70,000 Cambodians under its control independently of the UN scheme. Following these repatriations, the United Nations Transitional Authority in Cambodia (UNTAC) supervised nominal demobilization of various factions in Cambodia and subsequent elections.[30]

Despite the Peace Accord, there were continuing problems of intimidation and control of returnees, particularly by the Khmer Rouge. Slow and inadequate landmine clearance and a lack of arable property to offer returnees (so that most opted for cash that was insufficient to buy land) also obstructed returns and hampered successful reintegration.[31]

Lessons Learned from the Resolution of the Vietnamese and Cambodian Refugee Situations

In both Vietnam and Cambodia, the willingness of the country of origin to engage with the international community by allowing the presence of international humanitarian agencies to facilitate and monitor repatriation was key to "unlocking" the protracted situation, whether or not those same agencies, once granted access, were sufficiently vigilant in defending the rights of returnees. The Vietnam CPA experience effectively ended a reigning presumption of the Cold War era that repatriation to communist countries was not a viable alternative for refugees because fundamental and durable changes to the root causes of their refugee flight had not occurred, as well as the presumption that people fleeing communist regimes should be regarded as refugees.

Although more of a fundamental change from the situation that had caused refugees to flee could be seen in Cambodia than in Vietnam, the changes that had occurred there could hardly be characterized as stable or durable. Neither Vietnam nor Cambodia could be considered a reliable guarantor of the human rights of returning refugees at the time they were repatriating. But both home governments did cooperate in resolving these protracted situations, though respect for human rights and conflict resolution in both cases were far from satisfactory.

Successful resolution of these protracted refugee situations also came thanks in significant measure to international engagement inside the countries of origin: in Cambodia, UNTAC support for the election of a new government and UNHCR's engagement in repatriation; in Vietnam, UNHCR monitoring and the Orderly Departure Program. Donor and resettlement states also made significant contributions, human and financial. Between 1975 and 1997, about 1.3 million Southeast Asian refugees were resettled to third countries from the first asylum states or directly from Vietnam. Resettlement is a far from perfect outcome for most refugees as it effectively means conceding the loss of one's homeland, but it is often the best of the available alternatives for providing permanent legal protection and the promise of a productive life.

Local integration, the other "durable solution" prong, called the "forgotten solution" by one analyst, was virtually absent in the Vietnamese and Cambodian refugee situations.[32] At best, regional neighbors were willing to provide temporary refuge, usually in closed, overcrowded camps. In this context, third-country resettlement from the outset was fundamentally a tool of international protection, the price of keeping doors at least partially open and to prevent expulsions, and only later, and secondarily, a durable solution to resolve the protracted situation.

Bhutanese Refugees in Nepal[33]

More than 16 years after being expelled from Bhutan in a rash of ethnic cleansing in the early 1990s, about 108,000 Nepali-speaking Lhotshampa ("people of the south") refugees remained stagnating in seven refugee camps in the eastern corner of Nepal. The Lhotshampas were not only refugees, but also stateless, as no government was willing to acknowledge them as their nationals.

Glossed over by its image as a peaceable Shangri-La, Bhutan escaped international scrutiny and censure, and with each passing year memories of the ethnic cleansing faded and accountability slipped further and further away. Bhutan continued steadfastly to refuse any responsibility for expelling its people and for creating a huge stateless population. In July 2010, Prime Minister Jigme Y. Thinley referred to the refugees as illegal immigrants.[34]

Sitting in refugee camps for years takes a severe social and psychological toll on people, and the Bhutanese refugees in Nepal were no exception. During a 2006 visit this author met women and children in the camps who had been the victims of domestic and sexual violence, and saw that depression was rife. As the years dragged on with no solutions in sight, services and aid dwindled.

Year after year, negotiations between the governments of Nepal and Bhutan failed to bring the refugee situation a single step closer to resolution. Finally, after years of ineffective negotiations, Bhutan agreed, in principle, to allow *bona fide* Bhutanese citizens who were forcibly evicted to return. However, even after a long-negotiated nationality verification exercise produced what the Bhutanese government agreed were a handful of Bhutanese nationals in the refugee camps, it allowed none to return.[35]

The US government decided to take the first significant step to breaking the impasse, and in 2008 began resettling Bhutanese refugees from Nepal and calling on other resettlement countries to make resettlement commitments as well. As of this writing, about 65,000 refugees have been resettled, including more than 60,000 to the United States; the US has said that it will take all eligible refugees who want to come.

While there is no denying that the resettled refugees have had opportunities they could hardly have imagined during the time they were stuck in the camps, none of the refugees this author interviewed in 2006 gave resettlement as their first choice; in almost every case, their first choice was to go home.

For many still in the camps—for older refugees, in particular, who remember their lives in Bhutan and still mourn their losses—watching their compatriots leave has been a bitter experience. An estimated 12,000 refugees are projected to remain in the camps after the conclusion of the resettlement program in 2015. Some have refused the resettlement offer because they are still holding onto their right to return to their homeland. If none of these refugees is allowed to return to Bhutan, it will send the wrong message: that a government can get away with a mass expulsion of its population on ethnic lines with no consequences at all.

Another segment of the residual camp population is ineligible for resettlement, or prefers to stay in Nepal. Many of these, having married Nepalese spouses, have developed close ties to Nepal and would prefer to stay there as naturalized Nepalese citizens. A 57-year-old refugee farmer shared his thoughts on the durable solutions for his plight:

> If I do not go back to Bhutan, my choice would be to stay in Nepal. I want Nepal to give me land and citizenship. I don't want to sit in the camp. I

> want land and a house. But if Nepal says no, I prefer to stay in this camp. I know nothing of the United States... I am unskilled. I don't speak their language. I can only find work here. My life is here. I want my life to stay the same way. I don't want to go to some unknown place. I am only a farmer. I want my land. My country is Bhutan. That is my first choice. Otherwise, Nepal or India.[36]

Once resettlement has run its course, it should not be a major hurdle for Nepal to agree to integrate these residual refugees. But that is unlikely to happen until a final issue is resolved: the repatriation of those who hold out to return to their homeland.

Real progress has been made, but the protracted Bhutanese refugee situation is still unresolved. Massive resettlement has not only relieved overcrowding and improved conditions for those who have stayed behind but has also provided new opportunities and hope for a better life for those who have left. But it has neither leveraged the local integration option for those refugees who have developed real ties with Nepal nor any concessions from the Bhutanese government for the return of their own persecuted and disenfranchised nationals.

International efforts to resolve the Vietnamese situation came about as part of a "comprehensive" plan of action, which, like efforts to resolve the Cambodian situation, involved a combination of third-country resettlement and repatriation. A "Core Group" of countries, composed of Australia, Canada, Denmark, the Netherlands, New Zealand, and the United States, attempted to leverage comprehensive solutions when putting the offer of significant resettlement from the camps on the table,[37] but so far, the international efforts to resolve the Bhutanese refugee situation have been anything but comprehensive, as they have relied on resettlement alone. The country of origin—Bhutan—remains utterly uncooperative, and the local host country—Nepal—continues to hold fast in refusing to allow refugees to integrate as it waits for Bhutan to make the first move.

Until the country of origin, Bhutan, allows some refugees to return, particularly the elderly refugees who long to spend their remaining days in their homeland, the situation will continue to fester, even if at a lower level. The job of the international community to resolve this situation, as worthy and beneficial as it has been, will not be complete until Nepal lets refugees with close ties to Nepal naturalize, and Bhutan agrees to acknowledge the historical wrong done to the Lhotshampas and to affirm their right of return.

Burmese Refugees in Thailand[38]

After decades of seemingly never-ending conflict and repression, Burmese refugees, as well as Burma's neighbors and the wider world, are watching the changes there with interest and cautious optimism. For the 140,000 Burmese refugees in Thailand, many stuck in camps on the border for decades, there is now some hope that they might be able to go home.

In 2011, Burma's President Thein Sein called for exiles to return as his government and nearly all ethnic armed groups signed preliminary ceasefire agreements. But, as of this writing in mid-2013, enormous obstacles remain, including a lack of firm political settlements for peace with armed ethnic groups, the contamination of areas of potential return by landmines, the lack of unfettered access to return areas for UNHCR and other human rights monitors and humanitarian and development agencies, and the unresolved issue of restitution of property and land for the displaced.

Given Thailand's history, including the Thai government's forcible return to Laos of more than 4,500 Hmong held in a closed, Thai Army-controlled camp at Huay Nam Khao in December 2009, there has been widespread concern among Burmese refugees and their advocates that Thailand might push for premature repatriation of refugees before adequate protection benchmarks for return are met.[39] The particular fear is that after a superficial presence of UNHCR is established in eastern Burma, the Thai authorities would push for return on the pretext that all is safe if UNHCR is there, notwithstanding whether UNHCR is actually able to provide adequate monitoring or assistance. Thankfully, so far, Thailand is not pushing for hasty returns of the Burmese refugees. In a September 2012 letter to this author, the Thai Ministry of Foreign Affairs said, "Prime Minister Yingluck [Shinawatra]…affirmed Thailand's commitment to providing assistance to the displaced persons from Myanmar until they can return home in safety and dignity or other durable solutions can be found for them."[40]

Since 2004, Thai policy has been to disallow Burmese urban refugees and to insist that all Burmese refugees live in the Thai-Burma border camps, from where their movements are restricted and they are prohibited from working. This has proven to be a recipe for social dysfunction in the camps and, if it continues, will all but ensure that many of the refugees will be ill-prepared to reintegrate successfully when they do go home.

Most of the camps are in isolated mountain locations, accessible only by dirt roads. Some are overcrowded, and all of the camps have experienced cuts in basic assistance, such as food and shelter, from donors who are shifting their attention to programs inside Burma. The isolation of the camps contributes to an environment ripe for abuse of power and impunity, including by Thai officials who are mandated to protect the refugees. After so many years with restrictions on movement and dependency on outside aid, many camp residents experience domestic abuse, depression and other social and mental health problems.

Refugee resettlement of Burmese refugees from the Thai border has been a decidedly mixed blessing. On the positive side, 78,000 people have been taken out of the stagnant dead-end of camp life and been given the opportunity to restart their lives. However, resettlement arguably has made life worse for the refugees remaining behind and appears to have done nothing to resolve the underlying protracted situation. Because many of the better-educated refugees, such as teachers and health workers, have been resettled to countries outside the region, the residual camp population has been left with fewer coping skills.

When the Burmese refugee resettlement program began in earnest in 2005 there were about 140,000 refugees in the Thai border camps. Seven years and 78,000 resettled refugees later, the number of refugees in the camps still stands at about 140,000.[41] Almost person for person, new arrivals have replaced the resettled refugees; instead of relieving camp congestion and closing camps, the camps are as overcrowded as ever and vacated homes have quickly been (sold and) occupied by newcomers. The difference now is that the new arrivals have not been screened or registered so their refugee *bona fides* have not been determined, they are ineligible for resettlement, and their status is even more precarious than that of the registered population.

The Thai government has been unwilling to consider local integration for Burmese refugees. The authorities regard refugees who venture out of the camps as illegal aliens, in part because there is no Thai law that gives legal recognition to refugee status. Thailand, like its Southeast Asian neighbors (with the exception of Cambodia), has not acceded to the 1951 Refugee Convention and prefers to employ broad immigration-based legal categories rather than use an internationally recognized refugee-specific definition that carries with it the obligation to protect. Police, soldiers, and paramilitaries who apprehend camp residents outside the camps either return them to the camps after exacting bribes or forced labor, or send them to immigration detention centers for deportation to Burma.

Refugees can only work legally in Thailand if they remain silent about their refugee claims and present themselves as migrant workers to the Thai Ministry of Labor. The Thai government gives a two-year visa and work permit, renewable once, to migrant workers who register with the Department of Employment and present temporary passports issued by their home governments. After the four-year maximum period of work authorization, migrant workers are required to return to their home countries for a period of three years. By definition, refugees cannot return to their home countries, so migrant worker status is not an option for them.

This leaves Burmese refugees with a stark and unfair choice: either remain in one of the remote refugee camps and be relatively protected from arrest and deportation, but without freedom to move or work, or leave the camp to live and work illegally, at constant risk of exploitation, arrest, and deportation. A significant, but undetermined, number have exercised the latter option and in some cases, have married into local communities– effectively abandoning their refugee status for a life of uncertainty as an undocumented person.

With the prospect on the horizon that safe and voluntary repatriation may become a viable option for most of the Burmese refugees in the border camps, Thailand should initiate a transition from a closed-camp model to an open-camp model that empowers refugees to become self-sufficient and prepares them to reintegrate successfully in Burma when they are able to repatriate.[42]

As Thailand foresees a future that may not involve an encamped refugee population at all, it should establish an asylum procedure grounded in law that meets international refugee standards (that should start by signing and ratifying the 1951 Refugee Convention). Asylum should be open to all nationalities according to the same criteria; recognized refugees should be permitted free movement and authorized to work through a multi-year work visa that could be renewed as long as refugee status is maintaincd.

Those asylum seekers who are rejected after a fair and transparent procedure should be allowed to apply for migrant worker status on the same basis as other migrant workers, based on nationality verification and temporary passports, with the same rights and restrictions as other migrant workers. Access to an asylum procedure will be particularly important for the Shan and Rohingya minorities who have been precluded from recognition as refugees and admission to the camps, which have been dominated by the Karen and Karenni groups. While many Shan, whose language is closer to Thai than the other Burmese ethnic groups, have at least been able to obtain migrant worker status, the Rohingya—because they are stateless—have been rendered ineligible because the Burmese authorities are unwilling to verify them as Burmese nationals and provide them with temporary passports.

Donor governments should promote and facilitate the transition from closed to open camps by reorienting their assistance programs from a care-

and-maintenance model appropriate for sustaining a closed, dependent camp population to a livelihoods-training-and-development model that prepares and empowers refugees for productive lives outside the camps. But the *sine qua non* for such a switch in assistance is that the Thai authorities allow the refugees to move about and work. Work authorization for refugees would not only build refugee skills, but would also contribute to Thailand's economy. By granting refugees work authorization Thailand would also acknowledge the reality that refugees already sneak outside the camps to work illegally. Therefore, one of the clearest and most immediate benefits of work authorization would be to reduce opportunities for corruption and exploitation and to strengthen the rule of law.

In addition to working with UNHCR to establish a fair and transparent refugee screening and registration system for unregistered people living in the refugee camps, the government should also immediately ensure that all refugees, including those living in camps, have full access to the Thai justice system. Police and other security officials who abuse their authority by extorting and mistreating refugees and migrants should be appropriately disciplined or prosecuted.

Meanwhile, the international community should maintain pressure on the authorities in Burma to promote democratization and respect for human rights, including granting citizenship to persons of Rohingya ethnicity on the same basis as others with genuine and effective links to Burma, such as birth, residency, and descent. In addition, pressure needs to be brought to bear on Burma to treat persons of Rohingya ethnicity as equal citizens, addressing the long running hostilities with the ethnic minority groups, and promoting reconciliation with those ethnic communities.

Lessons Learned and To Be Learned

While it may be instructive to compare the four case studies examined in this chapter in order to look for lessons in how protracted refugee situations might be resolved, it needs to be noted that the four cases reflect quite different stages of resolution. The Vietnamese and Cambodian protracted situations are long over and a matter of history; the Bhutanese refugee situation is well on its way to resolution, though at least in terms of numbers, is still in need of durable solutions; and the Burmese situation is still protracted but far from stagnant, and plans to resolve it are moving forward as this chapter is being written.

Although analysts have criticized overreliance on the three traditional durable solutions for resolving protracted refugee situations,[43] an analysis of resettlement, repatriation, and local integration still provides the clearest basis for evaluating whether refugees have indeed ceased to be in need of international protection, and whether their situation can be said to have been resolved.

a. Third Country Resettlement—No Panacea

In the four situations examined in this chapter, the humanitarian good that has been achieved for the individuals who directly benefited from being removed from a protracted situation, should be acknowledged and lauded. Refugees who were resettled were provided permanent protection, given the path to a new citizenship, and the opportunity to start their lives anew (with the caveat that many refugees have struggled in post-admission adjustment and integration not only because of unrealistic expectations and culture shock, but also because of inadequate resources devoted to making the transition to sustained integration in a new, far-away social and cultural environment). But beyond the benefits to resettled refugees themselves, has resettlement succeeded as an instrument that resolves protracted refugee situations or that achieves other strategic objectives? Has resettlement had a positive (or at least no negative) impact on residual camp populations, particularly by improving asylum space or by opening up alternative durable solutions for them?

The post-Vietnam War refugee situation turned almost immediately to resettlement. At the outset, the United States and other countries used resettlement, not with the intention of resolving the refugee situation, but rather as a tool for keeping the doors open to first-asylum countries in the region who made clear their unwillingness to provide more than temporary refuge to asylum seekers pouring out of Vietnam, Laos, and Cambodia in the late 1970s. As the years continued, however, and refugee numbers did not ebb, the first asylum countries came to fear that resettlement was creating a magnet effect and that the outmigration from these three countries would not stop; they also came to doubt that resettlement could keep pace with new arrivals.

For their part, the resettlement countries began to question the wisdom of offering blanket resettlement on a *prima facie* basis. They questioned the motivations of the asylum seekers who in some respects looked more like people seeking immigration opportunities than people fleeing war and persecution. Many of the governmental architects of the CPA from both resettlement and first-asylum countries who attended the 1989 CPA conference came to regard resettlement not as the solution but as an essential part of the problem of the protracted Vietnamese refugee situation.[44]

The Vietnamese refugee experience is unique among the four cases examined in this chapter as the only one that involved significant boat outflows (with the exception of Rohingya boat migrants, a unique subgroup among Burmese refugees whose statelessness will make the resolution of their situation even more difficult—and prolonged—than for that of the other Burmese refugee groups).[45] In none of the other three cases was there any discussion or possibility of home-country refugee processing.

For all its faults, the resettlement of people directly from Vietnam through the ODP—in combination with renewed and strengthened deterrent measures—did provide an alternative to dangerous irregular boat departures and was a key element in ending them. Therefore, not only did resettlement play an essential part in maintaining first asylum, in combination with repatriation, it also contributed significantly to resolving both the Vietnamese and Cambodian refugee situations.

Resettlement has played a different role in the Bhutanese and Burmese refugee situations and the differences are instructive. For the 16 years prior to the Bhutanese resettlement program, there were almost no new arrivals. Unlike the other three situations, which were protracted but not static, only in the Bhutanese refugee situation did new asylum seekers not continue to arrive. This probably reflects that the Lhotshampas generally did not flee fighting, but rather were expelled from Bhutan, and that for the vast majority, their first choice was to go back. The Lhotshampas still in Bhutan, though facing severe discrimination and disenfranchisement, have been committed to staying. They have not shown a desire to leave Bhutan either to join friends and relatives in the camps in Nepal, or to pursue resettlement in the United States or another country.[46] Resettlement from Nepal has had no magnet effect to draw out more asylum (or resettlement) seekers from Bhutan, and therefore has indeed reduced camp overcrowding and, as of this writing, reduced the number of camps in Nepal from seven to two.

In this respect, the Burmese refugee situation is more similar to the Vietnamese one. Some argue that the more than 60,000 asylum seekers who arrived after the resettlement program began fled conditions in Burma, and would have come whether or not a resettlement program existed, and that without resettlement the camp population would be well over 200,000.[47] It is also arguable, however, that the lure of resettlement did draw some people out of Burma and into the camps. Whatever motivated the new arrivals, resettlement out of Thailand utterly failed to reduce camp populations, resulted in decreasing the coping skills of the residual population, and did not appear to have improved access to asylum in Thailand or to leverage other durable solutions.

Unlike the Vietnamese and Cambodian experiences, resettlement was not part of a comprehensive solution for either the Burmese or Bhutanese refugees, so no other durable solutions came into play. Resettlement of Bhutanese refugees from Nepal relieved the overcrowding of refugee camps and resulted in improvements in conditions. But for the Burmese refugees in Thailand, resettlement did not reduce the number of refugees, and achieved no other strategic objectives. In fact, it had a negative impact on the residual camp population of "creaming off" the more highly skilled refugees, and leaving a higher proportion of people in the camps with fewer coping skills. It also left a much higher proportion of unregistered refugees in the camps, since being registered was a prerequisite for resettlement, and those who arrived after 2004 were not allowed to register. Consequently, nearly 50 percent of the residual camp population is unregistered.

Finally, although resettlement has been a major component of all four of the cases examined in this chapter, in fact it is not a solution that is available in most protracted situations. Even within the Burmese refugee population, for example, it has never helped more than a relatively few of the 250,000 or more Rohingya refugees in Bangladesh. Resettlement was never available for the Cambodians displaced on the Thai border nor has it played any significant role in resolving Asia's largest and longest refugee crisis—the Afghan refugees in Pakistan and Iran.

Resettlement countries have total discretion to decide who and how many refugees they are willing to take. Choosing which of the world's refugees to resettle, therefore, is a thoroughly political process. The choice is often propelled more by foreign policy considerations or by finding refugees who will be popular with domestic constituencies than by objectively considering which refugees are most vulnerable and in greatest need of rescue.

To the extent that policy makers intend to use resettlement as a tool to leverage strategic objectives, the numbers of refugees resettled need to be significant enough to make an impact. This requires not only great political will but enormous financial and human resources. To put in perspective the potential role of resettlement as a key for unlocking protracted refugee situations one need only look at the Dadaab camps in Kenya, which opened more than 20 years ago and hold more than 450,000 Somali refugees. A UNHCR official commented on the futility of resettlement as a tool for creating more asylum space or for achieving broader goals such as resolving the protracted situation: "We resettle some 8,000 people per year, and Dadaab is receiving some 9,000 new refugees per month."[48]

b. Repatriation—More Than Just Return

All four cases examined in this chapter underscore the point that repatriation needs to be understood as more than simply people returning back from whence they came. In the refugee context, repatriation fundamentally means a restoration of rights: the right to enjoy meaningful citizenship, a home and livelihood, peace and security. Even if Bhutan were suddenly to allow the Bhutanese refugees to return, for example, the promise would be empty if not accompanied by a restoration of rights as well as a viable and sustainable means to reintegrate.

A focus on numbers of returns as the measure for success in resolving refugee situations is understandable but not helpful; it creates pressure to push refugees back prematurely. Repatriation before conditions are right not only risks endangering the returnees, but may also overwhelm the absorptive capacity of local communities in areas of return, exacerbate political and ethnic tensions, and cause additional displacement that destabilizes fragile post-conflict situations.

A far more effective approach to ensure that repatriation is safe and sustainable is to take a gradual approach that engages the refugees themselves and the communities to which they will be returning. This allows refugees to build confidence over time by encouraging cross border movement, first through look-and-see visits, and then by longer stays for home reconstruction, field planting, and infrastructure development. Instead of one-time repatriation, host countries should promote and facilitate back and forth movement that enables families and communities to return in stages as their capacity for sustainable reintegration improves and their confidence in their acceptance back home is restored.

c. Local Integration—Drop the Taboo

The very notion of permanent integration of refugees in neighboring host states has for decades been anathema throughout Africa, the Middle East, and Asia. Efforts to put local integration on the agenda of UNHCR's Executive Committee have run into stone walls of opposition.[49] Faced with this taboo, UNHCR has mostly settled for calling on local host countries to maintain temporary asylum with the understanding that the only durable solutions under consideration for most refugee situations in the developing world will be resettlement or repatriation. That was certainly the case in the Vietnamese and Cambodian situations and, thus far, has been UNHCR's operating assumption for both the Bhutanese refugees in Nepal and the Burmese in Thailand.

Advocates on behalf of Bhutanese and Burmese refugees (including this author) have studiously avoided asking Nepalese and Thai officials to grant refugees in their countries permanent asylum or citizenship, out of fear that this could cause a backlash that would shut down asylum entirely. Instead, advocates call for open camps, freedom of movement, work authorization, and other measures that would promote *de facto* integration of the refugees.

Advocating for *de facto* integration is not just a matter of political expediency. In assessing how Guatemalan refugees in Mexico progressively integrated and finally naturalized, Katy Long observed, "[t]he best foundation for successful *de jure* integration is *de facto* integration," particularly when building on existing cultural affinities supported through community-based development.[50]

An approach that desegregates refugees from encampment and allows them to exercise basic rights in the host country not only means they will integrate, it also fits well with the author's preference for a gradual approach to repatriation. Whether they ultimately decide to stay or go home, refugees who have been allowed to develop livelihood skills and have been empowered to make decisions affecting their lives will more likely be stable and self-sustaining after ceasing to be refugees.

The areas where the refugee camps are located in both Nepal and Thailand are places where the local communities and refugee populations share the same language and culture and where community support and family ties (including intermarriage between refugees and locals) are strong. It is not hard to imagine that today's refugee camps in eastern Nepal and western Thailand could be tomorrow's towns. The host governments should not fear this, but rather welcome the chance to work with the international community to help them transition from being closed and dependent to being open and self-sustaining. Too often, host governments regard refugees on their soil as a threat or a burden; particularly in Nepal and Thailand, the refugees who want to integrate locally, if given the chance, show all the hallmarks of being able and willing to contribute positively to their host societies.

Had such an approach been taken to the endgame of the Vietnamese and Cambodian refugee situations—gradual repatriation and progressive local integration—the return of the refugees and screened-out asylum seekers might have been far less traumatic and less damaging to human rights principles. Refugees who repatriated might have had less bitterness and resentment toward the governments that sent them back and both returnees and local stayers might have contributed to fostering better relations among the countries in the region and engendering goodwill among their diverse ethnic populations. That, of course, is a matter of speculation, but it is a hypothesis that could still be tested in attempts to resolve the Bhutanese and Burmese refugee situations.

Notes

* Director of Human Rights Watch's Refugee Rights Program.

[1] An earlier version of this essay was presented orally at the Expert Meeting on International Cooperation to Share Burden and Responsibilities, June 27, 2011, Amman, Jordan.

[2] A classic study focused on another region examines many of these elements: REPATRIATION UNDER CONFLICT IN CENTRAL AMERICA (Mary Ann Larkin, Frederick C. Cuny, & Barry N. Stein, eds., 1991).

[3] GIL LOESCHER & JOHN A. SCANLAN, CALCULATED KINDNESS: REFUGEES AND AMERICA'S HALF-OPEN DOOR, 1945 TO THE PRESENT (1986).

[4] Gervase Coles, *Approaching the Refugee Problem Today*, *in* REFUGEES AND INTERNATIONAL RELATIONS 373, 387-93, 403-4, (Gil Loescher & Laila Monahan, eds., 1989).

[5] *See generally* ALAN DOWTY, CLOSED BORDERS: THE CONTEMPORARY ASSAULT ON FREEDOM OF MOVEMENT (1987).

[6] W. COURTLAND ROBINSON, TERMS OF REFUGE: THE INDOCHINESE EXODUS & THE INTERNATIONAL RESPONSE 31 (1998).

[7] *Id.* at 57 (quoting UN Secretary General Kurt Waldheim's closing remarks).

[8] WILLIAM SHAWCROSS, THE QUALITY OF MERCY: CAMBODIA, HOLOCAUST AND MODERN CONSCIENCE 94 (1984).

[9] Dennis McNamara, *The Origins and Effects of 'Humane Deterrence' Policies in South-East Asia*, *in* REFUGEES AND INTERNATIONAL RELATIONS 123 (Gil Loescher & Laila Monahan eds., 1989).

[10] Despite calling itself a comprehensive plan of action for Indochinese refugees, the CPA was focused almost exclusively on Vietnamese refugees. As in 1979, Cambodian refugees were ignored completely. Although nominally included in the conference, by 1989, Laotian refugees were also pretty much ignored as well. *See* Robinson, *supra* note 6, at 189, 222-26.

[11] *Id.* at 193.

[12] *Id.* at 266.

[13] Richard Towle, *Processes and Critiques of the Indo-Chinese Comprehensive Plan of Action: An Instrument of International Burden-Sharing?* 18:3-4 INT'L J. REFUGEE L. 537, 557-559, 567 (2006).

[14] UNHCR Internal Memorandum, *Vietnam Mission Report*, (July 20, 1995) (quoted in Robinson, *supra* note 6, at 266).
[15] Robinson, *supra* note 6, at 221, 260.
[16] For a critique of in-country refugee resettlement processing on these grounds in Haiti, *see* Bill Frelick, *In-Country Refugee Processing of Haitians: The Case Against*, 21:4 REFUGEE 66 (2003).
[17] Arthur Helton, *Refugee Determination under the Comprehensive Plan of Action: Overview and Assessment*, 5:4 INT'L J. REFUGEE L. 544, 548 (1993); *see also* James C. Hathaway, *Labelling the 'Boat People': The Failure of the Human Rights Mandate of the Comprehensive Plan of Action for Indochinese Refugees*, 15:4 HUM. RTS Q. 686 (1993); Robinson, *supra* note 6, at 201-09.
[18] SARA ELLEN DAVIES, LEGITIMIZING REJECTION: INTERNATIONAL REFUGEE LAW IN SOUTHEAST ASIA 207 (2008).
[19] *See generally* ASIA WATCH, INDEFINITE DETENTION AND MANDATORY REPATRIATION: THE INCARCERATION OF VIETNAMESE IN HONG KONG (1991); *see also* LAWYERS COMMITTEE FOR HUMAN RIGHTS, INHUMANE DETERRENCE: THE TREATMENT OF VIETNAMESE BOAT PEOPLE IN HONG KONG (1989).
[20] Robinson, *supra* note 6, at 201, 215-21. Initially, in April 1989, Hong Kong approved only three of 1,300 Vietnamese being screened, and none of the three were screened as refugees but rather for family reunification. Hong Kong's screenings were challenged in the courts, and its approval rate rose to an overall 18.8 percent by the end of the CPA, much improved from the beginning but still among the lowest of any of the states in the region (the overall CPA recognition rate for the region was 27.9 percent). *See* Towle, *supra* note 13, at 549-50.
[21] *Id.* at 557.
[22] Robinson, *supra* note 6, at 193.
[23] Daniel Unger, *Ain't Enough Blanket: International Humanitarian Assistance and Cambodian Political Resistance*, *in* REFUGEE MANIPULATION: WAR, POLITICS, AND THE ABUSE OF HUMAN SUFFERING (Stephen John Stedman & Fred Tanner eds., 2003), at 28.
[24] Shawcross, *supra* note 8, at 229, 287, 305.
[25] *Id.* at 340-43, 345.
[26] *Id.* at 353, 340-43; *see also* FIONA TERRY, CONDEMNED TO REPEAT? THE PARADOX OF HUMANITARIAN ACTION 128-30, 138-39 (2002); Unger, *supra* note 23, at 36-40.
[27] *See* Terry, *supra* note 26, at 122-3, 126-128, 132, 137, 139; Unger, *supra* note 23, at 47-50.
[28] *See* Robinson, *supra* note 6, at 85-95.
[29] The most famous *refoulement* incident occurred at Preah Viharn in June 1979 when the Thai authorities forced 40,000 Cambodians at gunpoint down a cliff into a minefield. "UNHCR's remarkable failure to formally or publicly protest the mass expulsions of Cambodians from Thailand during 1979 must be seen as one of the low points of its protection history." Robinson, *supra* note 6, at 49 (quoting UNHCR official Dennis McNamara); *see also* Unger, *supra* note 23, at 30, 53; Terry, *supra* note 26, at 142; Shawcross, *supra* note 8, at 88-92.

[30] Unger, *supra* note 23, at 45.
[31] Marita Eastmond & Joakim Öjendal, *Revisiting a 'Repatriation Success': The Case of Cambodia*, *in* THE END OF THE REFUGEE CYCLE? REFUGEE REPATRIATION & RECONSTRUCTION 38, 42-43, 51-52 (Richard Black & Khalid Koser eds., 1999).
[32] Karen Jacobsen, *The Forgotten Solution: Local Integration for Refugees in Developing Countries*, *in* NEW ISSUES IN REFUGEE RESEARCH (2001).
[33] This section draws on the author's research for the Human Rights Watch report, *Last Hope: The Need for Durable Solutions for Bhutanese Refugees in Nepal and India*, (2007), *available at* http://www.hrw.org/sites/default/files/reports/bhutan0507webwcover.pdf (hereafter *Last Hope*).
[34] Jigme Thinley, *Bhutan's Prime Minister*, AL JAZEERA (July 8, 2010), http://www.aljazeera.com/programmes/101east/2010/07/20107815544364980.html (see video at 23:13).
[35] See *Last Hope*, *supra* note 33, at 40-42.
[36] Interview, in Sanischare camp, Nepal (Nov. 14, 2006) (published in *Last Hope*, *supra* note 33, at 60).
[37] *Communique of the Core Working Group on Bhutanese Refugees in Nepal*, FOREIGN AFF. & INT'L TRADE CANADA (May 16, 2007), http://nepal.usembassy.gov/bhutan_05-16-2007.html.
[38] This section draws on the author's research for the Human Rights Watch report, *Ad Hoc and Inadequate: Thailand's Treatment of Refugees and Asylum Seekers*, (2012).
[39] Robert Horn, *Will Thailand Send 140,000 Refugees Back to Burma?* TIME (April 17, 2011).
[40] Letter No. 1002/1574 from Vijavat Isarabhakdi, Director-General, Dep't. of Int'l Orgs., Thai Ministry of Foreign Aff., to Bill Frelick, Director, Refugee Program, Hum. Rts Watch, (Sept. 12, 2012) (on file with author).
[41] Camp statistics are reported in annual reports from The Border Consortium (TBC), available at http://www.tbbc.org/resources/resources.htm#reports. For detailed analysis of camp population statistics, see *Ad Hoc and Inadequate*, *supra* note 38, at 22-25.
[42] Cf. also the challenges faced by Iraqi refugees described in Pistone's chapter in this volume, challenges which need to be overcome, should repatriation, resettlement, reintegration, or any kind of new start become a viable option.
[43] Katy Long, *Permanent Crises? Unlocking the Protracted Displacement of Refugees and Internally Displaced Persons* (Refugee Stud. Ctr., Univ. of Oxford, Research Paper, Oct. 2011), *available at* http://www.rsc.ox.ac.uk/publications/rsc-reports/Unlocking-protracted-displacement-policy-overview.pdf/view.
[44] See Robinson, *supra* note 6, at 188.
[45] Hum. Rts Watch, *Perilous Plight: Burma's Rohingya Take to the Seas*, (2009).
[46] *Last Hope*, *supra* note 33, at 27-36.
[47] Interview with Sally Thompson, Deputy-Director, Thailand-Burma Border Consortium, Bangkok, Thailand (8 June 2011). The name of the organization has since changed to The Border Consortium (TBC).

[48] Quoted in Anna Lindley & Anita Haslie, *Unlocking Protracted Displacement: Somali Case Study* 38 (Refugee Stud. Ctr., Internal Displacement Monitoring Ctr., Norwegian Inst. of Int'l Aff., Working Paper No. 79, 2011).
[49] UNHCR, *The State of the World's Refugees 2012: In Search of Solidarity*, 70 (2012).
[50] Long, *supra* note 43, at 24.

CHAPTER SEVEN

CLIMATE-RELATED DISPLACEMENT: THE PERILOUS PATH TOWARDS NORMATIVE DEVELOPMENT

AGNÈS HURWITZ*

I. Introduction

While there is much uncertainty on actual figures and estimates, there is little doubt that an increasing number of people and communities are severely affected by climate change-related processes and will have to move as a result.[1]

It is not surprising, therefore, that the humanitarian impact of climate change and environmental degradation has increasingly captured the attention of scholars and policy-makers. Academic studies have laid the ground for important policy initiatives, which have contributed to greater awareness about these questions, specifically as regards displacement.[2]

The United Nations High Commissioner for Refugees ("UNHCR") has played a leading role in these processes. It took an active part in the Inter-Agency Standing Committee's ("IASC") Task Force on Climate Change, and presented, in cooperation with other agencies, several submissions on climate change's impact on displacement to the Ad Hoc Working Group on Long-Term Cooperative Action of the UN Framework Convention on Climate Change ("UNFCCC").[3]

The commemorations of the anniversaries of the 1951 Convention relating to the Status of Refugees and of the 1961 Convention on the Reduction of Statelessness have provided a unique opportunity to examine these questions in greater depth. An expert roundtable on climate change and displacement was held in February 2011 at the Rockefeller Bellagio Center,[4] and served as a steppingstone to the Nansen Conference on Climate Change and Displacement in the 21st Century hosted in June 2011.[5] The Conference Chairperson's Summary, and in particular, the so-called "Nansen Principles" thus reflected the current policy consensus on climate-related displacement.[6] As a result of these processes, there is now greater clarity on the core protection concerns that arise as a result of climate-related displacement and a clearer strategy on how to move these issues on the policy agenda.

The present chapter offers an overview of this recent policy work and examines what has been achieved, as well as ongoing challenges in terms of normative and policy development.

The article begins by examining the thorny question of the linkage between displacement and climate change. Some of the key protection-related recommendations adopted through the aforementioned processes will then be presented and analyzed. The final section of the chapter examines these various policy initiatives from the perspective of norm-making under the international refugee protection regime.

II. Managing Risks and Uncertainty: Understanding the Cause and Effect Relationship between Climate Change and Displacement

One of the most vexing issues when discussing climate change and displacement is the perennial question of the causal relationship between climate change processes and displacement, and the evidence thereof.[7] The difficulty stems in part from a misunderstanding of the way in which scientists measure the impact of human activity on the climate system, and in turn, assess the impact of climate change on human mobility.

Even if there is no absolute demonstrability of the human influence on the climate system, there is, in scientific terms, a high degree of certainty about it. In its 2007 Report, the International Panel on Climate Change ("IPCC") concluded that it was "very likely" or more than 90% probable, that most of the planet's warming was attributable to human activity.[8] Importantly, uncertainty works both ways, and the likely effect could be smaller but also larger than what is currently projected.[9]

While such high level of probability has been found at the global level, it is far more difficult to demonstrate such causality on a smaller scale. It is the risk of individual events happening over time and their frequency, which is predicted, rather than their specific occurrence. In other words, while human activities have been found to play a contributing role, a single climate event or process cannot be directly and exclusively attributed to human-induced climate change. A multitude of factors will come into play, such as "land-use change, air pollution, wildfires, changing biodiversity," among others.[10]

These preliminary points are important to help clear misunderstandings about the links between climate change processes and displacement. Here as well, the assessment is based on probability, risk, and multi-causality rather than absolute certainty and direct correlation.

The 2007 IPCC Report addressed at length the effect of both gradual changes in the climate, as well as extreme weather events on human systems, finding, in particular, large-scale displacement to be a likely consequence of extreme events.[11] It also noted the high vulnerability of certain regions or countries, and projected considerable impacts of climate change in Asia and Africa due to their association with other environmental and human stresses.[12] Impacts of human-induced climate change highlighted in the report and likely to be relevant for human mobility relate to increased water scarcity, reduced crop yields, and health risks.[13]

The Report of the Secretary-General on climate change and its security implications reached similar conclusions, noting that "[t]he scale of migration and displacement, both internal and cross-border, is expected to rise with climate change, as is the proportion of population movements considered 'involuntary.'"[14] However, in the same way as the effects of human-induced climate change on ecosystems do not occur in isolation, climate change processes multiply the risk, along with other drivers, of forced displacement, and act, to quote the Secretary-General's Report, as a "threat multiplier."[15]

Likewise, the Report on Migration and Global Environmental Change by Foresight – a UK government scientific think tank – emphasized that while environmental change will affect migration now and in the future, "the range and complexity of interactions between these drivers means that it will rarely be possible to distinguish individuals for whom the environmental factors are the sole driver."[16] It concludes that the "estimates of the numbers of environmental/climate migrants" that have been published "are methodologically unsound, as migration is a multi-causal phenomenon and it is problematic to assign a proportion of the actual or predicted number of migrants as moving as a direct result of environmental change."[17] As drily put by Climate Central, a US-based think tank, "[c]limate change will force people to move, but whether it is a million people or a hundred million is hard to say."[18]

As chronicled by Warner in a paper commissioned for the Bellagio Expert Roundtable, climate change negotiators have progressively acknowledged the impacts of climate change processes on human systems and human mobility, a recognition that culminated in the adoption of the Cancun Adaptation Framework.[19] Measures related to migration, displacement, and planned relocation are now expressly mentioned under

Paragraph 14(f) of the Cancun Adaptation Framework and are part of a broader range of measures on adaptation.[20] This is particularly important, as it constitutes a formal recognition by States Parties to the UNFCCC of the linkages between climate change and displacement and of the need for States and for the international community to adopt measures in this respect, including measures on protection and assistance. It also opens new opportunities in terms of funding by the Green Climate Fund,[21] which was set up to finance adaptation measures.[22]

From a protection perspective, the above analysis carries important implications:

- climate change-related hazards will disproportionately affect UNHCR's "populations of concern", whose vast majority live in developing countries and are most vulnerable, due to their status, precarious livelihoods and presence in fragile security environments, to the impacts of climate change processes and events;
- climate change is likely to impact human mobility, multiplying the risk and frequency of internal and external displacement; [23]

These preliminary considerations demonstrate that the need for humanitarian agencies to consider how climate change is going to impact their work is, from both a protection and operational perspective, not only timely but also urgent.

III. Climate-Related Displacement: Protection Considerations

The question of the scope and nature of the protection to be provided to populations affected by climate-related processes has received increased consideration in recent years by scholars and policy-makers alike.[24] In policy terms, there has been growing involvement of the United Nations in disaster-risk reduction,[25] in providing humanitarian assistance after disaster resulting from a natural hazard,[26] and in highlighting the human rights implications of environmental processes and policies.[27] The primary body tasked with the codification and progressive development of international law, the International Law Commission, working under the authority of the General Assembly's Sixth Committee, is also examining the question of the protection of persons in the event of disasters, although it primarily focuses on the international law applicable amongst states to the provision of emergency relief and assistance.[28]

In one of its submissions to the UNFCCC, UNHCR and partner agencies identified five different climate-related events and processes which will have a likely impact on human mobility, and examined the protection concerns that would arise as a consequence of these events. The events identified were: 1) hydro-meteorological extreme hazards; 2) planned evacuations of areas at risk of disaster; 3) environmental degradation and/or slow onset extreme hazards; 4) significant permanent losses in state territory as a result of the rise in sea levels; and 5) armed conflict and violence over shrinking natural resources.[29]

Although some academics have disputed this taxonomy,[30] it resulted from in-depth discussions within the IASC Informal Group on Displacement and Climate Change, and has been regarded as a useful analytical framework in policy circles. The aforementioned Bellagio Expert Roundtable and the Nansen Conference relied on this framework to achieve consensus amongst experts and key stakeholders about the applicability of international protection frameworks with regard to climate related displacement, and to identify the major protection concerns that would require increased attention in the coming years. The following section will analyze each of these protection areas.

External Displacement Related to Sudden-Onset Events: Addressing the Normative Gap

There is now broad agreement that, notwithstanding the applicability of the fundamental protections enshrined in international human rights law and international humanitarian law,[31] existing international instruments on external displacement are not properly tailored to provide protection in an indiscriminate manner in situations of climate-related external displacement.[32] These instruments have not been applied to persons who are forced or compelled to cross an international border because of a sudden-onset disaster, and who cannot return to their country of origin as a result of such events, either temporarily or permanently. Nor do they apply to people who cannot return because their land has become uninhabitable as a result of the long-term effects of climate change. They also have been primarily interpreted in an individualistic manner, while climate-related displacement will likely require group consideration.[33]

It is clear, for instance, that the Refugee Convention was not meant to apply in most of these situations. UNHCR's *Handbook and Guidelines on Procedures and Criteria for Determining Refugee Status* explains that

> [t]he expression "owing to well-founded fear of being persecuted"–for the reasons stated–by indicating a specific motive automatically makes all other reasons for escape irrelevant to the definition. *It rules out such persons as victims of famine or natural disaster, unless they also have well-founded fear of persecution*[34] for one of the reasons stated. Such other motives may not, however, be altogether irrelevant to the process of determining refugee status, since all the circumstances need to be taken into account for a proper understanding of the applicant's case.[35]

The Convention could nonetheless apply where "victims of natural disasters flee because their government has consciously withheld or obstructed assistance in order to punish or marginalize them on one of the five [Convention] grounds."[36] Such situations may take place during armed conflicts, situations of generalized violence, public disorder, political instability, or even in peacetime.

Regional refugee instruments, such as the 1969 OAU Convention Governing Specific Aspects of Refugee Problems in Africa and the 1984 Cartagena Declaration on Refugees, extend the definition of a "refugee" to persons fleeing "events seriously disturbing public order." While this language may have been construed by some as possibly including situations where persons flee sudden-onset disasters, it should be noted that this phrase was originally meant to refer to "war-like" situations, *i.e.* public disturbances resulting in violence, and there currently is no practice supporting a more expansive interpretation.[37]

Complementary protection standards may also offer some level of protection in situations of external displacement. Only a few rights are currently recognised as giving rise to an obligation of *non-refoulement*, however.[38] In the present context, the most relevant of these rights are the prohibition on return to a real risk of arbitrary deprivation of life, or to inhuman or degrading treatment, although it bears noting that the way courts have construed this prohibition means that it does not seem to be applicable to situations of general poverty, unemployment, lack of resources or medical care, for instance.[39] It is therefore unlikely that it would apply in natural disaster situations.

Whether flight related to the impacts of climate change could meet the relatively high threshold adopted in human rights jurisprudence is, in other words, far from clear. As noted by McAdam, "it will likely take some decades before the negative impacts of climate change, interacting with underlying socio-economic vulnerabilities, could, in and of themselves, be regarded as constituting a violation of Article 3 giving rise to protection from removal."[40] The Bellagio Summary of Deliberations refers nonetheless to "the practice of a diverse number of countries in granting some form of permission to remain to persons fleeing natural disasters" which "supports an understanding that such persons are in need of international protection, even if only temporarily."[41]

Based on the above, experts concurred that a significant normative gap existed with respect to climate-related external displacement. Both the Bellagio Summary of Deliberations and the Nansen Principles recommended therefore that "States, in conjunction with UNHCR, elaborate a guiding framework or instrument and devise a more coherent and consistent response to the protection needs of people displaced externally due to sudden-onset disasters."[42]

It is important to note that this recommendation does not necessarily entail the negotiation of a new treaty as the preferred solution and end goal. McAdam makes a persuasive case against the conclusion of a treaty, arguing that this would not be the appropriate approach given the specificity of displacement patterns related to climate and environmental change, the danger of "hardening" a concept of "climate refugees" that would likely exclude a large number of people in need of protection, and the very reluctance of those at risk to be labeled "refugees."[43] The Foresight report sees as well the difficulty of pinning down the cause of flight as an insuperable problem,[44] but this is not as relevant given the language of the Nansen Principles and Bellagio Deliberations, which refer exclusively to flight resulting from a sudden-onset disaster, for the very reason, that in such cases the triggering event is easy to identify.

The original idea was in fact to suggest the adoption of Guiding Principles along the lines of the Guiding Principles on Internal Displacement.[45] This was abandoned, however, due to the concern that some states would take issue with the Guiding Principles approach, which is premised on the fact that its provisions merely restate existing international law and therefore consists in the endorsement, without negotiation, of a text previously prepared by experts in close consultation with relevant agencies.[46]

Instead, the notion of a guiding framework, *i.e.* a soft law instrument distinct from guiding principles, was adopted to highlight the issue as being of international concern while recognizing at the same time that the complexity and range of displacement patterns call for a certain level of flexibility and for tailored responses. As noted by Kälin, "soft law is more appropriate where there are factual uncertainties, as it is flexible and allows scope to experiment with new ideas."[47]

Aside from the value of developing a guiding framework, which remains a longer term prospect, the focus at this time should be placed on advocacy by civil society organizations together with UNHCR to encourage states to develop adequate legislation addressing the protection needs of persons externally displaced due to sudden-onset climate-related events.[48] This would contribute to the emergence of relevant state practice and thereby bolster multilateral efforts to develop protection standards on external displacement.

Internal Displacement: Addressing the Implementation Gap

According to most estimates and academic studies, climate-related displacement will primarily be internal, and in some cases lead at a later stage to external displacement.[49] The importance of addressing the protection concerns of internally displaced persons who are fleeing as a result of climate-related processes was therefore recognized early on by policy-makers and UNHCR.

The Guiding Principles on Internal Displacement reflect and consolidate existing international law and expressly apply to situations of natural and human-made disasters.[50] The concept of "disaster" in the Guiding Principles is generally understood as a "serious disruption of the functioning of a community or a society causing widespread human, material, economic or environmental losses which exceed the ability of the affected community or society to cope using its own resources."[51] The Guiding Principles accordingly cover persons displaced internally by sudden-onset disasters related to climate change and/or variability as well as those displaced internally by such slow-onset disasters as drought, desertification and salinization.[52]

The universal standards enshrined in the Guiding Principles have been supplemented and reinforced by the adoption of regional instruments, namely, the 2009 African Union Convention on the Protection and Assistance of Internally Displaced Persons in Africa, which makes express reference to climate change as a driver of internal displacement, and the 2006 Great Lakes Protocol on the Protection and Assistance to Internally Displaced Persons.[53]

Humanitarian agencies have already taken steps to ensure the implementation of relevant protection standards for climate-related internal displacement. The Global Protection Cluster Working Group *Handbook for the Protection of Internally Displaced Persons*[54] and the *IASC Operational Guidelines on the Protection of Persons in Situations of Natural Disasters* offer advice to those involved in efforts to prevent, respond to and support recovery after disasters.[55]

While both the IDP normative framework and the related guidelines are relatively well developed, policy-makers have recognized the need to further strengthen protection at the operational level. There remain, for instance, gaps in protection delivery at the field level, including in relation to: the security and safety of affected communities, particularly women, children, older persons and persons with disabilities; access to emergency treatment and other health services; replacement of identity documentation; access to shelter; and services, programmes and resources for rehabilitation and reconstruction.[56]

At the institutional and structural levels, there is agreement on the fact that the challenge of climate change requires a fundamental rethinking of the way various actors of the international system operate, and that "traditional barriers between the humanitarian and development fields–be they institutional, funding related, or conceptual–should not be allowed to stifle the changes needed to alleviate suffering and strengthen resilience."[57] Ideally, protection considerations should thus be integrated and considered as part of disaster-risk reduction and adaptation plans, which is rarely the case.[58]

One issue which has been relatively neglected by humanitarian actors up until now, but will certainly require further attention, is the use of planned relocation for populations living in disaster-prone areas and in post-disaster situations where the area of origin of displaced populations has become uninhabitable.[59] Another circumstance where planned relocation may be contemplated is where populations have to be relocated to build new infrastructure to better adapt to climate change, or to turn certain areas into bio-fuel production zones.[60]

From a human rights perspective, a state may have certain obligations to take measures to prevent or mitigate the impact of natural hazards and thereby guarantee the protection of individuals' right to life, property and privacy.[61] The Chairman's Summary of the Nansen Conference recognizes that a "State's duty to protect people entails an obligation to help people move from zones where they face a danger," while stressing that "moving communities in anticipation of climate-related hazards may precipitate vulnerability rather than avoiding it, and should only be considered when adequate alternatives that enable people to rebuild their lives are available."[62] There is a clear tension between distinct public policy objectives that find their expression under international human rights law, and which will in many instances be difficult to reconcile.

Nansen Principle X further articulates the fundamental international standards applicable in such situations, namely: non-discrimination, consent, empowerment, participation, and partnerships with those directly affected, with due sensitivity to age, gender, and diversity aspects for those displaced and those who might choose to remain. Specific guidelines have also been elaborated by development actors dealing with situations of 'development forced displacement and resettlement' ("DFDR"), some of which might be transferable to planned relocation, effected to prevent or respond to disaster.[63] There is no doubt, however, that additional guidelines on protection of populations during processes of planned relocation will have to be elaborated for and by humanitarian actors. Recent relocation experiences on account of disaster prevention have provided ample evidence of the major risks that these carry for local communities.[64]

The Risk of Whole-Nation Displacement: Low-Lying Islands and Coastal States

Climate change, possibly entailing "whole-nation displacement," will have a severe impact on many small islands and/or low-lying coastal states. [65] These impacts include: "loss of coastal land and infrastructure due to erosion, inundation, sea-level rise and storm surges; an increase in the frequency and severity of cyclones, creating risks to life, health and homes; loss of coral reefs, with attendant implications for food security and the ecosystems on which many islanders' livelihoods depend; changing rainfall patterns, leading to flooding in some areas, drought in others and threats to fresh water supplies; salt-water intrusion into agricultural land; and extreme temperatures."[66] In human rights terms, these processes have the potential to affect the right to self-determination, the right to life, the right to an adequate standard of living, the right to health and the right of indigenous peoples recognized under international human rights law.[67]

It has even been suggested that the territories of some small island and/or low-lying coastal states may disappear altogether owing to sea-level rise, leaving its inhabitants stateless.[68] UNHCR had until recently relied on such an assumption.[69] The experts gathered at the Bellagio roundtable opined, however, that such a position needed reviewing.

First of all, the main cause of displacement for the populations of low-lying island States will not be the "disappearance" of the territory. As noted by McAdam, "the Atlantis-style predictions that have captivated the imagination of some are unlikely to materialise as the means by which states cease to exist."[70] Rather, "the cumulative effects of sea-level rise and its related ecological impacts–when compounded by pre-existing stresses such as overcrowding, unemployment, poor infrastructure, pollution, environmental fragility, etc.–may render these territories uninhabitable."[71] The main reason why people will not remain in the longer term will be the lack of fresh water supply. A large majority of the population of these states will likely have to leave long before the land is submerged by sea-level rise.[72] Additionally, although cyclones or king tides may trigger more sudden, temporary (and internal) movements, most movement away from small island and/or low-lying coastal states will generally be gradual.[73]

Secondly, the international community will continue to give prevalence to the presumption of continuity and of legal personality of these states.[74] In other words, the loss of habitable territory will not necessarily entail a loss of statehood, and population movements will not therefore constitute an existential threat.[75]

That said, there are important humanitarian and protection concerns with respect to low-lying island and coastal states and UNHCR has encouraged the international community to consider existing policy, legal, operational, humanitarian and resource responses, including adaptation measures, such as planned relocation and/or migration, in accordance with the right of self-determination of these communities.[76] As affirmed in the Nansen Principles, states have a primary responsibility to protect their populations, which may in turn entail the mobilization of relevant regional and international organizations, arrangements and resources.[77]

Slow-Onset Processes: Whither Humanitarian Protection?

Slow-onset processes fundamentally challenge current normative categories and policy frameworks. While they may not seem as dramatic as rapid-onset extreme weather events, slow-onset processes can cause catastrophic disruption to society, the economy and the environment, including in some cases, violent conflict.[78]

Yet, their humanitarian consequences tend to be overlooked and misunderstood as compared with sudden-onset events, where there is an obvious, isolated and unequivocal trigger leading to displacement. Although the humanitarian consequences can certainly be extremely severe over time, they will fit uneasily within current complementary protection approaches, which require the demonstration of an imminent risk.[79]

In many cases, mobility resulting from slow-onset processes will be regarded as voluntary migration,[80] and may therefore not be treated with the same level of attention by humanitarian actors, notwithstanding the fact that the predicted scale, magnitude and impact of displacement and migration caused by slow-onset events is likely to exceed State capacity in many regions.[81]

There are two key implications for international policy-makers. First, humanitarian agencies may have to rethink the scope of their protection work. The Foresight Report, along with a number of academic scholars, suggests that given the multi-causality of mobility and the impossibility of identifying a single cause of flight, a global protection approach should be based on the needs of refugees and displaced persons rather than on what led them to leave.[82] While this is a sensible approach in principle, it overlooks the difficulty of securing protection for the existing categories of displaced persons. In other words, expanding the personal scope of protection will not necessarily enhance the level and quality of protection afforded. In fact, evidence is to the contrary. A recent study on the arrival of Somalis in Kenya as a result of the 2011 drought provides an excellent illustration of this dilemma. It noted the ambivalent response of the Kenyan Government, which allowed entry, but would not register these recent arrivals, possibly because of the perceived reasons of their flight, and suggested that these new influxes could, in the future, put the whole process of *prima facie* recognition of refugee status in jeopardy.[83]

Second, as will be discussed below, international cooperation will be key to finding fresh ways to address the humanitarian consequences of slow-onset processes.[84] One example is the *Security in Mobility* project supported by the United Nations Office for the Coordination of Humanitarian Affairs ("OCHA"), the International Organization for Migration ("IOM") and the United Nations Environment Programme ("UNEP"), which called for the development by governments in Eastern Africa of a policy to facilitate safe movement of pastoralists within their countries and across borders.[85] Regional intergovernmental organizations can play an important role in addressing displacement events that have regional implications, including through the design and implementation of programmes for the assistance and protection of persons whose livelihoods are affected by climate processes.[86]

International Cooperation and Shared State Responsibilities

Climate change raises important questions regarding shared responsibilities and international cooperation. In the realm of displacement, one requirement of international cooperation to address both internal and external displacement resulting from disaster is that it should involve the country of origin.[87] This is an important difference compared to more traditional refugee flows, where the cooperation of the country of origin is rarely expected, given that its authorities will often be responsible for the flight of displaced populations.[88]

The International Law Commission's discussions on the protection of persons in the event of disaster are instructive in this regard.[89] Draft article 5, provisionally adopted by the Commission, affirms that:

> [i]n accordance with the present draft articles, States shall, as appropriate, cooperate among themselves, and with the United Nations and other competent intergovernmental organizations, the International Federation of the Red Cross and Red Crescent Societies and the International Committee of the Red Cross, and with relevant non-governmental organizations.

According to the fourth report of the Special Rapporteur, "[t]he draft article recognizes that the duty to cooperate is incumbent upon not only third States, but also affected States where such cooperation is appropriate." The report also suggests that there is in international law a duty of the affected state to seek assistance from the international community if its national response capacity is overwhelmed.[90]

The independent expert on human rights and international solidarity supported a similar understanding in his report to the Human Rights Council:

> [t]he obligations related to international assistance and cooperation are complementary to the primary responsibility of States to meet their national human rights obligations. International cooperation rests on the premise that developing countries may not possess the necessary resources for the full realization of rights set forth in human rights covenants and conventions. There is a shared responsibility for development met by States' national obligations and the obligations of international cooperation, facilitating global implementation.[91]

These statements are particularly valuable in that they offer important clarifications on the nature of the duty to cooperate in the realm of emergency relief. They also point to the need for both scholars and practitioners to revisit the concept of international cooperation and consider ways to foster international cooperation to address climate-related displacement. Greater consideration should be given to innovative approaches on the best way to engage countries of origin of climate-related externally displaced persons in the provision of protection outside their borders.[92]

IV. Considerations on the Policy and Norm-Making Process

The international protection regime has in recent years experienced serious challenges in terms of securing the support of states to strengthen and further develop protection standards. This fact has been noted by UNHCR for several years, and has become a matter of concern.[93]

In this context, the suggestion that the complex question of climate change should be addressed by UNHCR was certainly controversial. A fierce debate had already arisen with regard to UNHCR's role in natural disaster situations under the Global Protection Cluster. UNHCR had put forward to the Executive Committee the request made by the United Nations Emergency Relief Coordinator for UNHCR to take the lead in natural disaster situations on a pilot basis,[94] but the response of the Executive Committee was unequivocally negative. The High Commissioner had no choice but to indicate that UNHCR's lead would not proceed with the pilot scheme at this time and that the previous arrangement,[95] despite its operational flaws, would remain in place until further proposals were presented by UNHCR.[96] Many internal and external observers also felt that it was perhaps a little futile to look at such an "emerging" issue when there were very "traditional" refugee crises unraveling at the time in Libya, Yemen, Côte d'Ivoire and many other places that needed immediate attention. These were in addition to the many longstanding and protracted situations, which remained unresolved.

There were, on the other hand, a number of good reasons to pursue this agenda. The 60th anniversary commemorations, which focused on protection gaps,[97] provided a unique opportunity to undertake policy research and development on emerging issues, which at other times could easily be relegated as secondary. There was also interest at the highest level, and from some key states, not least Norway, in the issue, and an auspicious convergence with the 150th anniversary of the birth of Fridtjof Nansen, known for his concern for the environment but also for his role as the first High Commissioner for Refugees in the 1920s. Finally, despite the existence of the aforementioned refugee crises, many key players were aware that climate change and its consequences were no longer a prospective concern and were already having an impact on livelihoods, human mobility, and UNHCR's beneficiaries in many parts of the world.

Given the relatively new and potentially contentious nature of the topic, the approach had to be cautious and incremental. UNHCR had issued a policy paper in 2009 highlighting the possible existence of a normative gap, since the Refugee Convention was not drafted to apply in the vast majority of climate-related external displacement cases.[98] The issue was then presented at the 2010 High Commissioner's Dialogue on Protection Challenges, which highlighted a number of drivers of displacement, such as population growth, food insecurity, water scarcity, and climate change.[99]

The February 2011 meeting held at the Rockefeller Foundation Bellagio Center was convened by UNHCR as a closed meeting of experts. The meeting addressed both the internal and external displacement dimensions of climate change, as well as the question of whether statelessness would occur with respect to low-lying island states. The outcomes of this meeting were then used for the preparation of the Nansen Conference on Climate Change and Displacement, an intergovernmental conference hosted by the Norwegian Government to celebrate the 150th anniversary of Fridtjof Nansen's birth.[100] The event brought together humanitarian, environment and development experts to discuss the linkages between climate change and displacement. It led to the adoption of the so-called *Nansen Principles*, which reflected the policy consensus on ways to address and respond to this new challenge and provided a policy framework for addressing climate related displacement. The *Principles* outlined key areas of engagement at the national, regional, and international levels.

The Nansen Conference served as a sounding board to test the possibility of including a reference to climate-related displacement in the final Ministerial Communiqué to be adopted by high-level representatives of 155 states at the Ministerial Meeting—the closing event of the 2011 commemorations of the 60th anniversary of the 1951 Refugee Convention and the 50th anniversary of the 1961 Convention on the Reduction of Statelessness. It was also important in terms of advocating for state pledges addressing climate-related displacement. The pledges and the Communiqué were disappointing, however.[101] Reference to climate-change displacement was removed from the final version of the Communiqué due to the reluctance of many states to formally recognize the existence of a normative and protection gap, and the text only alludes to "evolving patterns of displacement."[102] Only a handful of states, namely Norway, Switzerland, Germany, Mexico and Costa Rica made a common pledge, which called for "a more coherent and consistent approach at the international level to meet the protection needs of people displaced externally owing to sudden-onset disasters, including where climate change plays a role."[103] The pledge endorsed the language of both the Bellagio Summary of Deliberations and the Nansen Principles. Latvia and Argentina made timid references to the consequences of climate change in protection terms, while Burundi and China recognized the importance of, respectively, disaster risk reduction and disaster relief.[104]

It is tempting to underscore the limited impact of these efforts and the continuing resistance of the majority of states to explicitly support the inclusion of the issue on the protection agenda. Yet, given the generalized disinterest in normative development, the unfavorable political context, the conceptual conundrum around the linkages between climate change and displacement, and the relatively low expectations that had been set from the start, one should consider these various processes and policy steps as qualified successes, to the extent that they generated policy consensus around some key protection concerns.

As a follow up to the Nansen Conference, the Nansen Initiative was launched in October 2012 by Norway and Switzerland to pursue this agenda, including normative and institutional measures to protect persons forced to leave their countries as a consequence of natural disasters.[105] Interestingly, the focus is now on *natural disasters* broadly understood, including geophysical disasters, probably the result of a conscious decision to sidestep the climate/displacement nexus issue. It is worth recalling that notwithstanding the language of Nansen Principle IX, the Chairperson's Summary also stated that "[f]rom a protection perspective, there is no compelling reason to distinguish between displacement due to climate-related and other disasters."[106]

The Initiative aims to formulate a protection agenda that will lead to concrete activities in the fields of prevention, protection and assistance during cross-border displacement, and return and other permanent solutions for the period following a natural disaster. This will include:

- the formulation of a common understanding among participating governments of the issue, its dimensions and the challenges faced by relevant stakeholders;
- the identification of good practices and tools for the protection of persons displaced across borders in the context of natural disasters;
- an agreement on key principles that should guide states and other relevant stakeholders in the three areas of inter-state/international cooperation, standards of protection of displaced people, and operational responses;
- the preparation of recommendations on the respective role and responsibilities of relevant actors and stakeholders; and
- the presentation of an action plan for follow-up, identifying further normative, institutional and operational developments needed at national, regional and international levels.[107]

The Nansen Initiative also entails consultations with governments and civil society representatives in regions particularly affected by natural disasters, and will convene a global dialogue to formulate a protection agenda. The Initiative is headed by a steering group of six to eight representatives from the global North and South, chaired by Norway and Switzerland, and assisted by a consultative committee made up of civil society and international organization representatives.

V. Conclusion

Climate-related displacement is a paradoxical subject of study. It raises a number of unprecedented issues and protection concerns and has generated an abundance of scholarly work and policy initiatives in a short amount of time.

Yet, it has forced researchers and policy-makers to revisit some of the key questions that stand at the heart of forced migration and refugee law scholarship. It has reopened the fundamental debate on who ought to be protected and on the boundaries between forced and voluntary migration. It has generated new policy approaches and innovative norm-making processes, which raise important questions on the nature and evolution of international refugee law, and for that matter, public international law. Finally, it has reinforced the crucial importance of international cooperation as a constitutive element of the international protection regime. Regardless of what one might think of the current infatuation with the topic, there is little doubt that it has revived necessary scholarly debates and spawned innovative policy work.

Notes

[*] DPhil (Oxon) LL.M (Cantab) LL.B (Brussels). This article is based in part on work conducted by the author as climate change focal point and Senior Research Officer within UNHCR's Division of International Protection from 2009 until 2011. The author is grateful to José Riera and Jane McAdam for their comments on earlier versions. All errors and inaccuracies are the author's sole responsibility.

[1] THE GOV'T OFFICE FOR SCIENCE, LONDON, FORESIGHT, MIGRATION AND GLOBAL ENVIRONMENTAL CHANGE: FUTURE CHALLENGES AND OPPORTUNITIES, FINAL PROJECT REP. 9 (2011), *available at* http://www.bis.gov.uk/assets/foresight/docs/migration/11-1116-migration-and-global-environmental-change.pdf (hereafter FORESIGHT).

[2] *See, e.g.*, U.N. Secretary-General, *Climate Change and its Possible Security Implications*, U.N. Doc. A/64/350 (Sept. 11, 2009) (hereafter Secretary-General Report on Climate Change); Eur. Consult. Ass., *Environmentally Induced*

Migration and Displacement: A 21st-Century Challenge, Doc. No. 11785 (Dec. 23, 2008); Int'l Org. for Migration, *Migration, Environment and Climate Change: Assessing the Evidence* (F. Laczko & C. Aghazarm eds., 2009); U.N. UNIV. SERIES, CLIMATE CHANGE AND MIGRATION: RETHINKING POLICIES FOR ADAPTATION AND DISASTER RISK REDUCTION, U.N. No. 15/2011 (2011).

[3] *See* IASC Informal Group on Migration/Displacement and Climate Change, *Climate Change, Migration and Displacement: Who Will Be Affected?*, (Oct. 31, 2008); U.N. Framework Convention on Climate Change [UNFCCC], 5th sess. of the Ad Hoc Working Group on Long-Term Cooperative Action under the Convention (AWG-LCA 5), Bonn, Ger., Mar. 29 – Apr. 8, 2009, *Submission by the International Organization for Migration (IOM), the United Nations High Commissioner for Refugees, and the United Nations University (UNU) in cooperation with the Norwegian Refugee Council (NRC) and the Representative of the Secretary-General on the Human Rights of Internally Displaced Persons (RSG on the HR of IDPs): Climate Change, Migration and Displacement: Impacts, Vulnerability, and Adaptation Options*, (Feb. 6, 2009); UNFCCC, June 1-12, 2009, Bonn, Ger., *Submission of UNHCR, supported by IOM and NRC: Climate Change and Statelessness: An Overview to the 6th Session of the Ad Hoc Working Group on Long-Term Cooperative Action (AWG-LCA 6) under the UN Framework Convention on Climate Change*, (May 15, 2009); UNFCCC, 6th sess. of the Ad Hoc Working Group on Long-Term Cooperative Action under the Convention (WAG-LCA 6), June 1-12, 2009, Bonn, Ger., *Submission by UNHCR, in cooperation with the Norwegian Refugee Council, the Representative of the Secretary-General on the Human Rights of Internally Displaced Persons, and the U.N. Univ.: Forced Displacement in the Context of Climate Change: Challenges for States under International Law*, (May 20, 2009); UNFCCC, 6th sess. of the Ad Hoc Working Group on Long-Term Cooperative Action under the Convention (WAG-LCA 6), June 1-12, 2009, Bonn, Ger., *Non Paper of UNHCR, IOM, Norwegian Refugee Council, UNU, with the support of the Representative of the Secretary-General on the Human Rights of Internally Displaced Persons: Comments and Proposed Revisions to the Negotiating Text Prepared by the Chair of the UNFCCC Ad Hoc Working Group on Long-Term Cooperative Action*, (June 5, 2009).

[4] *See* UNHCR, *Expert Roundtable Climate Change and Displacement: Identifying Gaps and Responses*, Feb. 22-25, 2011, Rockefeller Foundation Bellagio Center, *available at* http://www.unhcr.org/4dd1186c9.html.

[5] *See* Nansen Conference on Climate Change and Displacement in the 21st Century, June 5-7, 2011, *Report on the Nansen Conference on Climate Change and Displacement in the 21st Century*, *available at* http://d2530919.hosted213.servetheworld.no/expose/global/download.asp?id=2280&fk=1633&thumb= (hereafter Nansen Conference).

[6] *Id.* at 5, 18.

[7] *See* J. MCADAM, CLIMATE CHANGE, FORCED MIGRATION, AND INTERNATIONAL LAW 16 (Oxford Univ. Press 2012).

---

[8] W. Collins, R. Colman, J. Haywood, M. R. Manning, & P. Mote, *The Physical Science Behind Climate Change: Why are Climatologists So Highly Confident that Human Activities are Dangerously Warming Earth?*, SCIENTIFIC AMERICAN, Oct. 6, 2008, *available at* http://www.scientificamerican.com/article.cfm?id=science-behind-climate-change.

[9] Royal Society, *Climate Change: A Summary of the Science*, Sept. 2010, *available at* http://royalsociety.org/uploadedFiles/Royal_Society_Content/policy/publications/2010/4294972962.pdf.

[10] Intergovernmental Panel on Climate Change [IPCC], § 14.4.9, *Interacting Impacts*, (2007), *available at* http://www.ipcc.ch/publications_and_data/ar4/wg2/en/ch14s14-4-9.html (references in quotation omitted); *see also* Collins, Colman, Haywood, Manning, & Mote, *supra* note 8.

[11] IPCC, § 7.4.1, *General Effects*, (2007), *available at* http://www.ipcc.ch/publications_and_data/ar4/wg2/en/ch7s7-4-1.html.

[12] *See* UNFCCC, *Climate Change: Impacts, Vulnerabilities and Adaptation in Developing Countries*, (2007), *available at* http://unfccc.int/resource/docs/publications/impacts.pdf; for Africa, see IPCC, *Executive Summary*, (2007), *available at* http://www.ipcc.ch/publications_and_data/ar4/wg2/en/ch9s9-es.html; for Asia, see IPCC, *Executive Summary*, (2007), *available at* http://www.ipcc.ch/publications_and_data/ar4/wg2/en/ch10s10-es.html; *see also* Secretary-General Report on Climate Change, *supra* note 2, ¶ 54.

[13] *See* IPCC, Climate Change 2007: Synthesis Report, at 53, Table 3.2., *available at* http://www.ipcc.ch/pdf/assessment-report/ar4/syr/ar4_syr.pdf .

[14] Secretary-General Report on Climate Change, *supra* note 2, ¶ 54.

[15] *Id.* ¶ 13.

[16] FORESIGHT, *supra* note 1, at 9 (quotation marks in quote omitted).

[17] *Id.* at 11; N. Myers, *Environmental Refugees in a Globally Warmed World*, 43 BIOSCIENCES 252, 257 (1993) estimates that 150 million people will be displaced by 2050. Christian Aid estimates that "unless strong preventative action is taken, between now and 2050, climate change will push the number of displaced people globally to at least 1 billion." Christian Aid, *The Human Tide: The Real Migration Crisis*, 22 (May 2007). For a critique of these figures, see McAdam, *supra* note 7, at 26.

[18] *See* CLIMATE CENTRAL, GLOBAL WEIRDNESS: SEVERE STORMS, DEADLY HEAT WAVES, RELENTLESS DROUGHT, RISING SEAS AND THE WEATHER OF THE FUTURE 142 (Pantheon Books 2012); *see also* Nansen Conference, *supra* note 5, ¶ 5.

[19] K. Warner, *Climate-Induced Displacement and the UNFCCC*, UNHCR LEGAL AND PROTECTION POLICY RESEARCH SERIES 12 (May 2011), *available at* http://www.unhcr.org/4df9cc309.pdf.

[20] Adaptation is defined by the UNFCCC as "adjustment in natural or human systems in response to actual or expected climatic stimuli or their effects, which moderates harm or exploits beneficial opportunities." *See* UNFCCC, *Glossary of Climate Change Acronyms*, http://unfccc.int/essential_background/glossary/items/3666.php.

[21] The Green Climate Fund was established during the Cancun Conference of Parties to contribute to the achievement of the United Nations Framework Convention on Climate Change (UNFCCC). In the context of sustainable development, the Fund will provide support to developing countries to limit or reduce their greenhouse gas emissions and to adapt to the impacts of climate change, taking into account the needs of those developing countries particularly vulnerable to the adverse effects of climate change, *see* http://gcfund.net/home.html.

[22] W. Kälin, *From the Nansen Principles to the Nansen Initiative*, 41 FORCED MIGRATION REV. 48 (2012).

[23] *See* Jean-François Durieux, Bonn Climate Talks, Bonn, Ger., Apr. 6, 2009, *Climate Change and Forced Migration Hot Spots*, *available at* http://www.unhcr.org/4a1e4e342.html.

[24] *See, e.g.*, McAdam, *supra* note 7; R. ZETTER, UNIV. OF OXFORD REFUGEE STUDIES CENTRE, PROTECTING ENVIRONMENTALLY DISPLACED PEOPLE: DEVELOPING THE CAPACITY OF LEGAL AND NORMATIVE FRAMEWORKS (2011), *available at* http://www.rsc.ox.ac.uk/pdfs/workshop-conference-research-reports/Zetter-%20EnvDispRep%2015022011.pdf; F. Dun & F. Gemenne, *Defining Environmental Migration: Why It Matters So Much, Why It Is Controversial and Some Practical Processes Which May Help Move Forward*, 6 REVUE EN LIGNE ASYLON(S) (2008), *available at* http://terra.rezo.net/article847.html; F. Gemenne, *Coping with Desertification: Migration as a Forced Choice and a Livelihood Strategy*, *in* DESERTIFICATION: MIGRATION, HEALTH, REMEDIATION AND LOCAL GOVERNANCE 41-54 (A. Ozer & D. Swinne eds., 2008); F. Gemenne, P. Brücker & D. Ionesco, Int'l Org. for Migration, *The State of Environmental Migration 2011*, (2012), *available at* http://www.iddri.org/Publications/Collections/Analyses/SEM%202011_web.pdf.

[25] *See* U.N. Office for Disaster Risk Reduction [UNISDR], *Hyogo Framework for Action 2005-2015: Building the Resilience of Nations and Communities to Disasters*, A/CONF.206/6 (2005).

[26] *See* I.A.S.C., *Operational Guidelines on Human Rights and Natural Disasters: Protected Persons Affected by Natural Disasters*, (June 2006), *available at* http://www.humanitarianinfo.org/iasc/pageloader.aspx?page=content-products-products&productcatid=1.

[27] UNOHCHR, *Study on the Relationship between Climate Change and Human Rights*, U.N. Doc. A/HRC/10/61, at 15 (Jan. 2009).

[28] U.N. Int'l Law Comm'n, *Fourth Report of the Special Rapporteur on the Protection of Persons in the Event of Disaster*, U.N. Doc. A/CN.4/590 (Dec. 11, 2007).

[29] *See Climate Change, Migration and Displacement: Who Will Be Affected?*, *supra* note 3.

[30] For examples, see McAdam, *supra* note 7, at 18.

[31] *See* J. McAdam & B. Saul, *An Insecure Climate for Human Security? Climate-Induced Displacement and International Law* 1 (Univ. of Sydney, Working Paper No. 4), *available at*

---

http://sydney.edu.au/law/scil/documents/2009/SCILWP4_Final.pdf.
[32] *See* McAdam, *supra* note 7, at 42.
[33] *Id.* at 87.
[34] Emphasis added.
[35] UNHCR, *Handbook on Procedures and Criteria for Determining Refugee Status under the 1951 Convention and the 1967 Protocol relating to the Status of Refugees*, HCR/1P/4/Eng/Rev.2 (Jan. 1992).
[36] UNHCR, 6th Sess. of the Ad Hoc Working Group on Long-Term Cooperative Action under the Convention, *Forced Displacement in the Context of Climate Change: Challenges for States under International Law*, at 9-10 (May 20, 2009).
[37] *See* McAdam & Saul, *supra* note 31, at 373; McAdam, *supra* note 7, at 46-49.
[38] J. McAdam *Climate Change Displacement and International Law: Complementary Protection Standards*, UNHCR LEGAL AND PROTECTION POLICY RESEARCH SERIES, *available at* http://www.unhcr.org/4dff16e99.pdf; *see also* McAdam, *supra* note 7, at 80-81.
[39] McAdam, *supra* note 7, at 54.
[40] *Id.* at 76.
[41] UNHCR, Expert Roundtable on Climate Change and Displacement, Bellagio, Italy, 22-25 Feb. 2011, *Summary of Deliberations on Climate Change and Displacement*, ¶ 10, (April 2011), *available at* http://www.unhcr.org/4da2b5e19.pdf (hereafter Bellagio Summary of Deliberations). Additionally, the Bellagio Principles note that "a large number of countries provide various forms of 'humanitarian' or other statuses to persons who, at the time of a natural disaster, were already within their jurisdiction but cannot be returned to their countries of origin owing to the destruction caused by the natural disaster. This shows a trend at the national level to accept such persons on an individual basis." *See id.* ¶ 11.
[42] *See* Nansen Conference on Climate Change and Displacement in the 21st Century, June 5-7, 2011, *Chairperson's Summary*: *Nansen Principles*, ¶ IX, *available at* http://www.internal-displacement.org/8025708F004BE3B1/(httpInfo Files)/07114855541F4A32C12578D3005D174F/$file/nansen-conference-climate-change-and-displacement-summary-and-principles-june2011.pdf (hereafter Nansen Conference Summary); Bellagio Summary of Deliberations, *supra* note 41, ¶ 12. See below on the pledges that endorsed this recommendation.
[43] McAdam, *supra* note 7, at 193-200.
[44] FORESIGHT, *supra* note 1, at 151.
[45] See, however, the cautiously worded suggestion on the value of considering the *content* of the Guiding Principles for the purpose of setting out applicable protection standards on external displacement. Bellagio Summary of Deliberations, *supra* note 41, ¶ 13.
[46] *See* W. Kälin, *The Guiding Principles on Internal Displacement as International Minimum Standard and Protection Tool*, 24 REFUGEE SURV. Q. 27, 29 (2005).
[47] W. Kälin and N. Schrepfer, *Protecting People Crossing Borders in the Context of Climate Change: Normative Gaps and Possible Approaches*, UNHCR LEGAL AND PROTECTION POLICY RESEARCH SERIES 71 (Feb. 2012), *available at*

http://www.unhcr.org/4f33f1729.pdf.
[48] For an overview of the limited state practice and legislation addressing disaster-related displacement, see McAdam, *supra* note 7, at 99.
[49] Nansen Conference Summary, *supra* note 42, ¶ 5.
[50] UNHCR, *Guiding Principles on Internal Displacement: Introduction-Scope and Purpose*, ¶ 2, U.N. Doc. E/CN.4/1998/53/Add.2 (June 2001) (reprinted Oct. 2004).
[51] Brookings-Bern Project on Internal Displacement, *IASC Operational Guidelines on the Protection of Persons in Situations of Natural Disasters*, at 55, 58, (Jan. 2011). For an analysis of natural disasters, see B. FERRIS, BROOKINGS INST., THE POLITICS OF PROTECTION, THE LIMITS OF HUMANITARIAN ACTION 201 (2011).
[52] *See* Nansen Conference Summary, *supra* note 42, ¶ 19.
[53] A.U., African Union Convention for the Protection and Assistance of Internally Displaced Persons in Africa ("Kampala Convention"), Kampala, Uganda, Oct. 22, 2009, art. 5.4, *available at* http://www.unhcr.org/refworld/docid/4ae572d82.html; Int'l Conference on the Great Lakes Region, *Protocol on the Protection and Assistance to Internally Displaced Persons*, Nov. 30, 2006, *available at* http://www.internal-displacement.org/8025708F004BE3B1/(httpInfoFiles)/29D2872A54561F66C12572FB002BC89A/$file/Final%20protocol%20Protection%20IDPs%20-%20En.pdf.
[54] *See* Global Protection Cluster Working Group, *Handbook for the Protection of Internally Displaced Persons*, (June 2010), *available at* http://www.refworld.org/cgi-bin/texis/vtx/rwmain?docid=4790cbc02.
[55] *See Operational Guidelines on Human Rights and Natural Disasters*, *supra* note 51.
[56] Nansen Conference Summary, *supra* note 42, ¶ 16.
[57] *Id.* ¶ 17.
[58] In this respect, see Zetter, *supra* note 24.
[59] *See* E. Ferris, *Protection and Planned Relocations in the Context of Climate Change*, UNHCR LEGAL AND PROTECTION POLICY RESEARCH SERIES NO. 27 (Aug. 2012), *available at* http://www.unhcr.org/5024d5169.html. Note that relocation across international borders has also been contemplated for the inhabitants of small island states. *See* McAdam & Saul, *supra* note 31, at 15-17.
[60] *See Study on the Relationship between Climate Change and Human Rights*, *supra* note 27, ¶¶ 65-67.
[61] *See, e.g.*, Budayeva & others v. Russia, App. Nos. 15339/02, 21166/02, 11673/02 & 15343/02, Eur. Ct. H.R. (2008), *available at* *http://hudoc.echr.coe.int/sites/eng/pages/search.aspx?i=001-85436#{%22itemid%22:[%22001-85436%22]}*
[62] Nansen Conference Summary, *supra* note 42, ¶ 12.
[63] *See* The World Bank, World Bank Operational Policy on Involuntary Resettlement 4.12, (updated Feb. 2011), http://web.worldbank.org/WBSITE/EXTERNAL/PROJECTS/EXTPOLICIES/EXTOPMANUAL/0,,contentMDK:20064610~menuPK:64701637~pagePK:64709096~piPK:64709108~theSitePK:502184,00.html.
[64] *See* Zetter, *supra* note 24.

[65] McAdam & Saul, *supra* note 31, at 369.
[66] Bellagio Summary of Deliberations, *supra* note 41, ¶ 27; *see Climate Change: Impacts, Vulnerabilities and Adaptation in Developing Countries*, *supra* note 12, at 25.
[67] McAdam & Saul, *supra* note 31, at 374-375.
[68] For a discussion of these claims, see S. Parks, *Climate Change and the Risk of Statelessness: The Situation of Low-Lying Island States*, UNHCR LEGAL AND PROTECTION POLICY RESEARCH SERIES (May 2011), http://www.unhcr.org/4df9cb0c9.html.
[69] *Submission of UNHCR, supported by IOM and NRC: Climate Change and Statelessness*, *supra* note 3.
[70] *See* J. McAdam, *"Disappearing States," Statelessness and the Boundaries of International Law* 4 (Univ. NSW Law Working Paper No. 2, 2010). McAdam recognizes that this imagery was also aggressively exploited by the governments of small island states to draw attention to their plight. *Id.*¶ 3-4.
[71] Bellagio Summary of Deliberations, *supra* note 41, ¶ 28; McAdam, *"Disappearing States," supra* note 70; *see also* Park, *supra* note 68, at 9.
[72] Bellagio Summary of Deliberations, *supra* note 41, ¶ 28.
[73] *Id.* ¶ 29.
[74] McAdam, *"Disappearing States," supra* note 70, at 6, 9-10, 12, 21; *see also* Park, *supra* note 68.
[75] Bellagio Summary of Deliberations, *supra* note 41, ¶ 30.
[76] *Id.* ¶ 31; McAdam, *supra* note 7, at 143; *See* McAdam & Saul, *supra* note 31, at 374.
[77] Nansen Conference Summary, *supra* note 42, ¶ II.
[78] Bellagio Summary of Deliberations, *supra* note 41, ¶ 33.
[79] McAdam, *supra* note 7, at 84-85.
[80] Kälin & Schrepfer, *supra* note 47, at 40.
[81] Bellagio Summary of Deliberations, *supra* note 41, ¶ 34.
[82] FORESIGHT, *supra* note 1, at 152.
[83] V. Kolmannskog, *Gaps in Geneva, Gaps on the Ground: Case Studies of Somalis Displaced to Kenya and Egypt during the 2011 Drought* 7 (UNHCR New Issues in Refugee Research, Working Paper No. 248, Dec. 2012), *available at* http://www.unhcr.org/50c88dbc9.html. The Kenyans cited "security concerns" but the UNHCR officials interviewed believe this decision may have been based on flight motives.
[84] Bellagio Summary of Deliberations, *supra* note 41, ¶¶ 34-38.
[85] United Nations Environment Programme (UNEP), Urgent Action Needed for Pastoralists to Cope with Climate Change (June 29, 2010), http://www.unep.org/climatechange/News/PressRelease/tabid/416/language/en-US/Default.aspx?DocumentId=628&ArticleId=6634.
[86] Bellagio Summary of Deliberations, *supra* note 41, ¶¶ 34, 36.
[87] Kälin, *The Guiding Principles on Internal Displacement as International Minimum Standard and Protection Tool*, *supra* note 46, at 79.

[88] Note, however, that "comprehensive plans of action" may involve the country of origin as well. *See* A. HURWITZ, THE COLLECTIVE RESPONSIBILITY OF STATES TO PROTECT REFUGEES 156 (Oxford Univ. Press 2009).
[89] U.N. Int'l Law Comm'n, *Fourth Report of the Special Rapporteur on the Protection of Persons in the Event of Disaster*, ¶ 38, U.N. Doc. A/CN.4/643 (May 11, 2011) (Eduardo Valencia-Ospina, author).
[90] *Id.* ¶ 39.
[91] OHCHR, *Promotion and Protection of All Human Rights, Civil, Political, Economic, Social and Cultural Rights, Including the Right to Development*, ¶ 21, U.N. Doc. A/HRC/9/10 (Aug. 15, 2008).
[92] See in this regard UNHCR, *International Cooperation to Share Burdens and Responsibilities*, Discussion Paper, June 2011, http://www.refworld.org/cgi-bin/texis/vtx/rwmain?docid=4e9fed232
[93] Agnès Hurwitz, *Norm-Making in International Refugee Law: Challenges and Complexity, Proceedings of the 106th Annual Meeting*, 106 AMERICAN SOC'Y OF INT'L L. PROCEEDINGS 430, 430-433 (2013).
[94] UNHCR Exec. Comm., *Draft Report of the 51st Meeting of the Standing Committee (June 21-23, 2011)*, ¶¶ 30-36, U.N. Doc. EC/62/SC/CRP.25 (Sept. 16, 2011). *See generally* UNHCR Exec. Comm., *UNHCR's Role in Support of an Enhanced Humanitarian Response for the Protection of Persons Affected by Natural Disasters*, ¶ 4, U.N. Doc. EC/62/SC/CRP.19 (June 6, 2011) (and sources cited therein, namely, UNHCR Exec. Comm., *Questions and Answers on UNHCR's Protection Cluster Coordination Role in Natural Disasters*, U.N. Doc. EC/62/SC/INF./1 (Feb. 23, 2011).
[95] At country level, the humanitarian protection leadership role in natural disaster situations is currently decided on a case-by-case basis by UNHCR, OHCHR, and UNICEF, the three protection mandated agencies, under the leadership of the Humanitarian Coordinator/Resident Coordinator. The decision on leadership is dependent on the in-country capacity of each agency to fulfill the role and responsibilities of protection cluster lead agency for the specific emergency. *See Protection in Natural Disasters*, GLOBAL PROTECTION CLUSTER, *available at* http://www.globalprotectioncluster.org/en/areas-of-responsibility/protection-in-natural-disasters.html.
[96] UNHCR Exec. Comm., *Draft Report of the 51st Meeting of the Standing Committee (June 21-23, 2011)*, ¶ 32, U.N. Doc. EC/62/SC/CRP.25 (Sept. 16, 2011).
[97] UNHCR, High Commissioner's Dialogue on Protection Challenges: Protection Gaps and Responses (Dec. 2010), *available at* http://www.unhcr.org/pages/4ca099226.html.
[98] UNHCR, *Climate Change, Natural Disasters and Human Displacement: A UNHCR Perspective*, (Aug. 14, 2009), *available at* http://www.unhcr.org/4901e81a4.html.
[99] UNHCR, *High Commissioner's Dialogue on Protection Challenges: Background Paper: Protection Gaps and Responses*, (Nov. 30, 2010), *available at* http://www.unhcr.org/4cebeeee9.html.

[100] Nansen Conference on Climate Change and Displacement in the 21st Century, June 5-7, 2011, *available at* http://www.nansenconference.no/.

[101] UNHCR, Ministerial Intergovernmental Event on Refugees and Stateless Persons, Dec. 7-8, 2011, *Ministerial Communiqué*, HCR/MINCOMMS/2001/6 (Dec. 8, 2011).

[102] *See id.* ¶ 10.

[103] For a compilation and analysis of pledges, see UNHCR, Ministerial Intergovernmental Event on Refugees and Stateless Persons, Dec. 7-8, 2011, *Pledges 2011*, (May 2012), *available at* http://www.unhcr.org/4ff55a319.html.

[104] *Id.*

[105] Confédération Suisse, Better Protection for Persons Displaced by Natural Disasters (Feb. 10, 2012), *available at* http://www.admin.ch/aktuell/00089/index.html?lang= en&msg-id=46195.

[106] Nansen Conference Summary, *supra* note 42, ¶ 5.

[107] Kälin, *From the Nansen Principles to the Nansen Initiative*, *supra* note 22, at 49.

CHAPTER EIGHT

THE US "MATERIAL SUPPORT" BAR TO REFUGEE PROTECTION: AN EXPANSIVE APPROACH THROUGH A NARROW LENS

KRISTINE A. HUSKEY[*]

I. Introduction

Immediately following the tragedy of September 11, 2001, the United States was, quite understandably, intensely concerned with security across the board. Even now, more than a decade later, national security considerations seem to permeate most matters in the US—from domestic policy to foreign policy and everyday affairs.[1] Travel[2], in particular, has changed dramatically due to security concerns, whether flying[3] or using mass transit; national security is implicated in protests of Wall Street[4] and natural disasters.[5] Concomitantly, various laws have been enacted to increase national security, but which have negatively affected civil liberties and rights. The Posner approach of sacrificing rights for more security may seem compelling because it suggests that security can be obtained in exchange for civil liberties and rights; the more liberties and rights are sacrificed, the more security is acquired.[6] This premise, however, applies an all-encompassing approach through a very narrow lens. It is all-encompassing because it implies that security can be had in all circumstances, and it is too narrow because it concerns itself with the protection of national security, leaving other objectives for secondary consideration.

Furthermore, as part of this post-9/11 approach, international law and institutions have been viewed with great suspicion.[7] This extreme caution towards all things foreign, combined with the desire to tip the scales toward national security, has had the most severe impact on non-US citizens and legal residents—both inside and outside the United States.

The all-encompassing national security approach resulted in the broad sweeps to pick up and detain without trial non-US citizens at Guantanamo, and those part of the PENTTBOM investigation.[8] In both scenarios, the fear of inadvertently releasing a "terrorist" weighed more heavily than the fear of locking up innocent people. With respect to refugees and asylum seekers, the same fear has resulted in a similar narrow approach to people seeking humanitarian protection. In this case, the fear of inadvertently letting a terrorist *into* the country has far outweighed the goal of protecting those in desperate need of refuge. Since 9/11, the US does not so much as have a state response to the global refugee crises. Rather, it has a (somewhat ethno-nationalistic/xenophobic) national security response to aliens.

This type of national security approach to a humanitarian objective—that is, protecting persons who cannot return to their home countries due to fear of persecution—has resulted in exceptionally expansive laws that exclude otherwise deserving refugees from entry or other protections in the United States. One key component of the national security laws affecting refugee admission is the much-criticized "material support for terrorism" bar in the Immigration and Nationality Act. The bar is broad in scope and has been interpreted to apply without exception, essentially excluding aliens who represent no threat to US security. This is, of course, problematic on its own accord for the human impact, but it is also troubling with respect to US obligations under international law and in light of international norms.

This chapter provides a brief history of the evolution of the terrorism bar in US law, focusing on "material support," and then addresses the current version of the material support bar, including the non-designated terrorist organization provision, and the various concerns that have arisen over the application of such provisions. Lastly, the chapter addresses the US material support bar in light of US obligations under international law and with respect to international norms, concluding that the failure to require a nexus between the support/activity and US national security puts the US out of step on both accounts.

II. US Law

A. Evolution of the Terrorism Bar—A Brief History

Exclusion of aliens from the United States for national security reasons began in earnest with the Immigration and Nationality Act ("INA") of 1952.[9] The relevant provisions aimed at keeping out aliens who sought to enter the United States to engage in activities that would be prejudicial to the "welfare, safety, or security of the United States," or that were prohibited by US law *and* relating to espionage, sabotage, or other activity subversive to its national security.[10] Among other grounds, an alien was also excludable if he advocated or belonged to an organization that advocated the use of force to overthrow the government of the United States.[11] The national security exclusionary grounds in the original INA were directly related to the safety and security of the United States.[12]

The Immigration Act of 1990, amending the INA, contained the first reference to "terrorist activity," and laid the foundation upon which the terrorism-related bars now rest. While the previous grounds for exclusion had a causal relationship to the protection of the United States, the 1990 Act appeared to shift to a general "condemnation of terrorism" [13] by rendering aliens who *had* engaged in "terrorist activities" excludable.[14] "Terrorist activity" was defined as "any activity which is unlawful under the laws of the place where it is committed" and which involved acts typically associated with terrorism, such as hijacking, sabotage, assassination, or using a nuclear device, explosive or firearm (other than for mere personal gain), with an intent to harm people or cause substantial damage to property.[15] The 1990 Act also contained the first reference to "material support," rendering an alien excludable for providing material support to any entity "conducting" a terrorist activity, or providing such support to an individual, believing that individual had committed or planned to commit terrorist activity.[16]

The Anti-Terrorism and Effective Death Penalty Act ("AEDPA") of 1996 extended the definition of "terrorist activity" to include membership or acting as a representative of a terrorist organization.[17] Thus, past commission of a terrorist activity or the likelihood of committing such an activity was no longer the lynchpin for exclusion.[18]

Less than forty-five days after the events of 11 September 2001, the US Congress passed the Uniting and Strengthening America by Providing Appropriate Tools Required to Intercept and Obstruct Terrorism Act of 2001 (the "Patriot Act").[19] Generally speaking, the Patriot Act enhanced and expanded the government's authority to engage in surveillance, investigate, designate, prosecute, exclude, and circumscribe protections to any individuals or groups perceived (even speculatively) to be connected (even remotely) with terrorism. Regarding aliens and immigration matters, prophylactic security efforts increased tenfold.

The Patriot Act amended the INA by adding three more grounds to the existing five for terrorism-related inadmissibility. It redefined "terrorist activity" and introduced the current three-tier system of terrorist organizations.[20] Under the current INA, a "Tier I" terrorist organization is any group designated under section 219 as a foreign terrorist organization ("FTO"); a "Tier II" organization is a group so designated through public notice by the Secretary of State, in consultation with the Attorney General or Secretary of Homeland Security; and a "Tier III" group is known as an "undesignated terrorist organization." [21] This third tier is particularly controversial for its broad scope, as it defines a terrorist organization as "a group of two or more individuals, whether organized or not, which engages in, or has a subgroup which engages in [terrorist] activities" as described in three previous sub-clauses in the statute.[22]

Four years later, in the continuing attempt to limit potential terrorist access to the United States, Congress passed the REAL ID Act of 2005 directed at several aspects of US counter-terrorism efforts. The Act included a section addressing inadmissibility due to terrorist-related activities.[23] The REAL ID Act enlarged the terrorism bar even further by including three additional types of terrorist activity in which two or more individuals could engage, that would render them an "undesignated terrorist organization."[24] Thus, prior to 2005, an alien could engage in terrorist activity by affording material support to an undesignated terrorist group that directly committed, planned or gathered information for terrorist activities.[25] After REAL ID, an alien was excludable for providing material support to an organization that engaged in the aforementioned activities, as well as for providing support to an undesignated terrorist organization that may have indirectly supported terrorist activity by providing material support itself to an undesignated terrorist organization or subgroup.[26]

The REAL ID Act also substantially relaxed the *mens rea* requirement. Previously, the material support bar applied in the case of an undesignated terrorist organization unless the alien could prove that he did not know and should not reasonably have known that the support would *further* the organization's terrorist activity.[27] REAL ID amended this provision to apply the bar unless the alien could demonstrate by "clear and convincing" evidence that he did not know and should not reasonably have known that the undesignated terrorist organization was a terrorist organization as defined by the statute.[28]

Though the REAL ID Act, and later the Consolidated Appropriations Act, provided for the possibility of a waiver from some of the terrorism bars, the effect of the Patriot Act and the REAL ID Act combined was a vast expansion of the terrorism-related bars which adversely impacted thousands of individuals seeking humanitarian protections.

B. Waiver/Exemption Authorities

The scope of authority for waiving application of the material support for terrorism bar to both individuals and groups has similarly undergone piecemeal modification in response to concern over the unintended consequences of the exclusion provisions.

Included in the Patriot Act was a provision giving authority to the Secretary of State and/or the Attorney General in consultation with one another to determine when and whether the material support clause should not apply.[29] The REAL ID Act added a provision addressing Tier III organizations and allowing waivers in cases of subgroups that engaged in terrorist activity.[30] This provision did not provide similar authority with respect to groups that had directly engaged in violent activity, even if for a legitimate cause, thus barring groups such as Cuban anti-Castro freedom fighters and the Vietnamese Montagnards who fought alongside US forces.[31] The Secretary of the Department of Homeland Security ("DHS") eventually waived application of the material support bar to aliens who had provided assistance to specific groups, including, among others, the Chin National League for Democracy, the Tibetan Mustangs and the Cuban Alzados.[32]

However, asylum seekers who themselves were victims of terror were continually denied refugee protection for providing material support to terrorist organizations, even when that support was coerced or given under duress. Due to the lack of interpretative flexibility in the language of the provision, and an attitudinal shift towards over-broad interpretation, decision-makers and government attorneys simply ignored the context in which the support occurred, and failed to take into account whether such support was coerced.[33] Egregious examples of the expansive reach of the provision involve individuals who were forced to pay ransoms or bribes to save their and/or a family member's life;[34] individuals who were kidnapped and forced to provide medical services;[35] and individuals who were abducted, gang-raped, and forced to cook and clean.[36] These victims either had their applications for permanent status placed on hold or were denied asylum due to the "material support" bar, which does not recognize extenuating circumstances.

In 2007, two much-needed DHS directives gave immigration officers the ability to grant waivers to aliens who had provided material support under duress to undesignated or designated terrorist groups.[37] Under both directives, in addition to proving duress, the "totality of the circumstances" must be such as to warrant a waiver.[38] Given that the authority is discretionary, the directives do not create any substantive or procedural right legally enforceable against the US or its officers. In other words, an alien has neither a legal right to a duress exemption before an asylum officer or an immigration judge or board, nor any recourse in court.

The Consolidated Appropriations Act of 2008 ("CAA") expanded the waiver authority to reach nearly all cases involving terrorism-related bars.[39] Relevant here, immigration officers can waive application of the "terrorist organization" definition to any Tier III organization with some exceptions.[40] Tier I and II groups, however, were not included in the CAA and thus, individuals who have provided assistance to designated groups are still barred by the material support provision unless granted a specific waiver such as that provided by the duress exemption.[41] Notably, the CAA discretionary authority does not apply in cases pending removal.

In 2011, DHS Secretary Napolitano determined that the bar would not apply with respect to the provision of medical care except when an alien knowingly provides medical care on behalf of a Tier I or II group.[42] She exercised her authority more recently, bringing potential relief to refugees and asylees who had already been granted protection but whose applications for permanent residence or reunification with family members had been on hold for many years due to terrorism-related grounds. These grounds remain applicable throughout an alien's life, as they can be reasserted by the government at the time an alien applies for status adjustment or reunification.[43] Specifically, an exemption is now available for persons already granted asylum or refugee status if they engaged in, providing material support to most, but not all, Tier III groups.[44]

Concerns with Waivers/ Exemptions

While the law now provides broad authority to grant exemptions from most of the terrorism-related inadmissibility grounds, the authority must be exercised by a government agency. According to human rights advocacy groups, the waiver process has been cumbersome and DHS has acted too slowly and in piecemeal fashion, thereby putting hundreds of asylum seekers in limbo while their cases are on hold—placing them in detention or at risk of deportation, or separating families while the executive branch decides how to proceed.[45]

Additionally, the already prolonged and paralyzed waiver process is exacerbated while agency officials seek to determine whether the groups to which individuals have provided support fall within the ever-expanding category of Tier III organizations, due to the logistical hurdles in researching groups that may be defunct or don't actually exist. Further delaying the process are foreign policy debates about whether the organization itself should be granted a group-based waiver, which in turn affects the individual who provided support.

The dissenting judge in *Khan v. Holder* aptly described the waiver process when he concluded:

> I, however, am less sanguine than [the majority] are about the efficacy of this waiver provision. First, the waiver is entirely discretionary and unreviewable. [citations omitted]. Second, the waiver requires the assent of three separate agencies, posing a daunting bureaucratic obstacle to implementation. Third, even without this high administrative hurdle, a waiver seems to me a haphazard and inefficient means of avoiding outcomes–such as classifying the US military as a terrorist organization–that Congress clearly never intended.[46]

In light of the often catastrophic consequences for individuals for whom protections are delayed or denied, a legislative solution allowing judicial flexibility would be more appropriate than allowing the backlog of cases to increase, or simply enlarging the scope of waiver authority. Without a solution, courts will continue to apply the material support bar expansively because, as discussed below, the courts view the statute as not allowing for consideration of all of the circumstances surrounding the provision of material support, as well as for the nature of an undesignated terrorist organization.

C. The "Material Support" Bar in Practice

"[T]he statute may go too far, but that is not the business of the courts."[47]

It is difficult to ascertain the quantifiable impact of the material support bar as the numbers of individuals denied refugee protections (through refugee admission, asylum grant, permanent residence, etc.) on the basis of "material support" grounds are not specifically tracked. However, the precipitous decline in the number of refugee admissions after the Patriot Act (2001) and the REAL ID Act (2005), as well as the continuing decline of asylum approvals since 2001, are indicative of an intensely security-weighted approach to a humanitarian endeavor. Moreover, DHS has consistently made clear that the drop in numbers is largely due to enhanced security measures and legislation such as the Patriot Act and REAL ID.[48]

For example, in 2002, refugee admissions decreased 72 percent from the previous year, dropping from 66,000 in 2001 to 18,652 in 2002. [49] In 2006, admissions decreased 23 percent, dropping from 53,738 in 2005 to 41,150 in 2006. [50] Refugee admissions have not increased to their pre-2001 levels. In 2011, approximately 56,000 persons were admitted as refugees.[51] With respect to asylum, the number of persons granted asylum was: 39,161 in 2001; 28,734 in 2003; 26, 252 in 2006; and 24,988 in 2011.[52] Asylum grants reached a low in 2010 of 21,056.[53]

The application of the material support bar in individual cases, including interpretation of the Tier III provision, underscores the concern that the terrorism bar in particular is having wide-ranging and unintended consequences on persons deserving of protection, reflected in the declining numbers above. The statutory language of both provisions is overly expansive, and has been interpreted by decision-makers as such, with few or no exceptions, thus rendering inadmissible aliens who were forced to provide material support to terrorists. In fact, in most cases it is this support which formed the very basis of these victims' asylum claims. Individuals have also been barred for providing *de minimis* support to groups, some of which have no intention to harm US national security. Moreover, there is no requirement of an individualized intent to further terrorist activity. These concerns are addressed below.

Minimal Mens Rea Requirement

Perhaps the most troubling aspect of the material support provision is the extremely weak *mens rea* requirement. In this regard, the Patriot Act and Real ID together changed the entire approach to the "material support for terrorism" bar in two important ways. First, prior to 2001, an alien was excludable if material support was provided *for use in conducting terrorist activity*, or if there was knowledge that the recipient (an individual) had committed or planned to commit a terrorist activity. The Patriot Act amended the language so that the material support paragraph ((a)(3)(B)(iv)(VI)) only requires the alien to know that his action is "affording" material support to the recipient of the support, not that the recipient is a terrorist organization.[54]

Second, before REAL ID, the material support bar applied in the case of an undesignated terrorist organization unless the alien could prove he or she did not know and should not reasonably have known that the support would *further* the *terrorist activities* of the organization.[55] Now, an alien has to prove by clear and convincing evidence that he did not know (or should not reasonably have known) that the undesignated organization was a terrorist organization. The intent of the support is wholly irrelevant.

Deserving refugees have been denied asylum on this basis. For example, in *Singh-Kaur v. Ashcroft*, the Third Circuit held that "if you give money (or raise money to be given) for the teaching of arithmetic to children in an elementary school run by Hamas, you are providing material support to a terrorist organization even though you are not providing direct support to any terrorist acts."[56] The Ninth Circuit concluded similarly, finding that the petitioner was ineligible for asylum or withholding of removal because the alien's intention in soliciting funds for nonviolent activity was irrelevant to the "terrorist activity" definition. Under the INA, even when an organization has separate political and militant wings, money donated to an organization's political wing is considered to support the militant wing as well.[57] The court reasoned that money is fungible, so giving support intended to aid an organization's peaceful activities frees up resources that can be used for terrorist acts.[58]

This line of reasoning was the issue during the many years of litigation in *Humanitarian Law Project* (*HLP*), culminating in a Supreme Court decision in 2010 which addressed criminal liability for material support to organizations that conduct both terrorist and non-terrorist activities.[59] In *HLP*, the Court determined that with respect to the criminal-law material support statute (2339B), the only *mens rea* requirement for criminal liability is proof that the actor intended to provide support to a designated foreign terrorist organization, even if the material support was intended to support the organization's legitimate or non-terrorist activities.[60] The Court relied heavily on the "fungibility" of money theory, described above, and the Congressional statement in enacting 2339B that "foreign organizations that engage in terrorist activity are so tainted by their criminal conduct that any contribution to such an organization facilitates that conduct."[61] A DHS official conveyed this same sentiment in his testimony before Congress—also quoting the criminal statute—regarding the material support bar in the INA, which, while not assigning criminality, has the effect of denying otherwise deserving aliens refugee status.[62]

Two important points should be noted. First, the statute at issue in *HLP*—2339B—makes it a crime to provide material support to a *designated* foreign terrorist organization (FTO). Thus, the *HLP* "strict liability" standard should be wholly inapposite in the case of an alien seeking refugee protection who has provided material support to an undesignated terrorist organization.[63] In this latter category, the *mens rea* requirement comes into play in the sub-clause of the Tier III provision, which allows the alien to prove he did not know the organization was a terrorist organization.

Second, congressional sentiment about the "tainted-ness" of terrorist organizations was made in the context of a statute that contains a complex process for designating foreign terrorist organizations, which includes the requirement that the terrorist activity threaten the national security of the United States.[64] Ascribing this same rationale in the instance of support provided to undesignated terrorist organizations effectively denies humanitarian protection to refugees who have no nefarious designs against the United States or any connection to activity that might threaten the United States. Indeed, DHS has said as much: "[b]ecause the material support bar casts a broad net, its scope may include those who do not present a risk to US national security and to whom the United States is sympathetic and willing to provide refuge."[65] As addressed below, the failure to require a link between a threat to national security and the denial of entry is greatly at odds with international law, not to mention the human cost, barring individuals who have been victims of terror themselves.

No Explicit Duress or Coercion Exception

Prior to the DHS directives making available a duress waiver in most cases, the lack of a duress exception in the material support statutory bar had been a source of deep concern to many, not to mention the several thousand individuals who were denied refugee protection owing to such failure.[66] Several stark examples have already been mentioned above but one example illustrates the reverberating impact of the bar: Colombians fleeing persecution by the Revolutionary Armed Forces of Colombia ("FARC"), who together with another armed group have controlled almost 75 percent of Colombian territory.[67]

In 2005, the United Nations High Commissioner for Refugees ("UNHCR") reported there were approximately 46,000 Colombian asylum seekers in the region.[68] For those attempting to come to the United States, the material support bar was a severe obstacle.[69] Many civilians were (and still are) forced to pay a *vacuna* or "war tax" to or feed and shelter FARC soldiers simply to stay alive.[70] A fact-finding investigation by the Georgetown University Law Center Human Rights Institute documented that in the case of Colombian refugees, in 73 percent of instances in which material support was provided, it was provided under duress—either by force or threat of force.[71] Such individuals were (and still are) considered inadmissible under the material support bar.[72] For several years, UNHCR limited its referral of Colombians to the US Refugee Admissions Program due to the material support inadmissibility provision although, since the availability of the duress waivers, UNHCR has begun increasing referrals to the US program.[73] While the availability of waivers ameliorates some of the problems, their piecemeal application still constitutes an obstacle for the thousands of Colombians who need protection. In 2010, US government agencies estimated there were some 400,000 asylum seekers and persons in refugee-like situations in surrounding countries, with UNHCR recognizing at least 55,000 Colombians as refugees in Panama, Ecuador, Venezuela, and Costa Rica.[74]

Despite the sliver of hope the US Supreme Court may have held out in the *Negusie v. Holder* case with respect to reading a duress exception into the persecutor bar provision,[75] courts have continued to take a strict approach to the material support statute, barring aliens who qualify as refugees but who provided support under duress to terrorist organizations. In two recent cases, both aliens were found to have had credible claims of persecution as well as credible testimony demonstrating that they provided support only under duress or coercion, but the Fourth and Ninth Circuits both emphasized the lack of an express exception in the statute, barring the aliens from protection under the material support provision.[76] Both courts pointed to the availability of the duress waiver and thus, congressional intent to leave it to the executive branch to determine who might be granted a waiver.[77] Illustrating the tension between the original intent of the INA and the overriding attention paid to national security, the Fourth Circuit concluded: "we should defer to Congress' chosen method to try to strike a correct balance between the United States' humanitarian obligations and national security."[78]

No De Minimis Requirement

The bar has also been heavily criticized for the expansive way in which agency officials, the Board of Immigration Appeals ("BIA") and federal courts have interpreted "material support." Indeed, one might say that "material support" has been interpreted in such a way as to read "material" right out of the statutory language.[79] US officials and courts mostly have been interpreting "material support" to include *any* act of support, no matter how small, how infrequent, or unrelated to the terrorist activities of the group. While the statute provides examples of material support, such as a "safe house, transportation, communications, and funds," among other items, it does not define "material" in any way.[80] Consequently, there is no *de minimis* of support requirement in the statute, and it has not been interpreted by decision makers to include one.

In *In re S-K*, the applicant argued that the type and amount of support she provided was not material, specifically, that trivial or unsubstantial amounts of assistance were not within the statutory bar.[81] In response, DHS asserted that the exemplary list of "material support" in the statute was meant to have an expanded reach and "cover virtually all forms of assistance, even small monetary contributions."[82] With some exceptions, immigration judges, the BIA, and courts have generally agreed with DHS lawyers and have declined to interpret "material" to have a *de minimis* requirement, thus barring aliens for providing *immaterial* or inconsequential types of support.[83] In 2012, the Fourth Circuit in *Barahona v. Holder* deferred to the determinations of the Immigration Judge ("IJ") and the BIA that "there is no exception in the Material Support Bar for de minimis activities on behalf of a terrorist organization."[84]

The failure to recognize some *de minimis* threshold distorts the meaning of "material" and ultimately, the intent of the statutory provision. As the dissent in *Singh-Kaur* recognized, "'material support' by its plain language, should mean that the act affording support must be of a kind and degree that has relevance and importance to terrorist activity, terrorists, or terrorist organizations."[85]

Additional Concerns with "Material Support"

The strict language of the statute and lack of exceptions present obstacles in addition to those highlighted above. For example, there is no statutory exception for support provided before the age of consent. This may bar individuals who provided material support at a young age but who may not be able to prove the required level of "duress" or coercion (other than the mere fact of their young age) for obtaining a waiver.[86] Also problematic are attempts by DHS and US Department of Justice ("DOJ") officials to interpret political speech and activity as "material support."[87] And, until recently, medical care was also construed as "material support."[88] Prior to October 2011, aliens who provided medical care to terrorists would have been providing material support and would be statutorily barred unless they could obtain a waiver by proving duress. This rule is contrary to the principle of medical neutrality and a violation of medical ethics.[89] As discussed above, Secretary Napolitano issued a directive providing for a waiver in the case of medical care, except that provided to a Tier I or II organization. [90] The effect of the medical care waiver remains to be seen.

D. Material Support to Tier III Terrorist Organizations

The material support bar alone has presented many obstacles to deserving refugees. Combined with the exceptionally expansive Tier III category—undesignated terrorist organizations—the material support bar significantly undermines the humanitarian goals of refugee protection.

An alien is inadmissible to the United States if he has provided material support to a group of two or more individuals, whether organized or not, which engages in, or has a subgroup which engages in, "terrorist activity," defined to include the use of any weapon or dangerous device with the intent to endanger the safety of anybody or cause substantial damage to property.[91] This intricate layer of definitions can be interpreted to encompass any number of people who use, at any given moment in time, any implement to cause harm to persons or substantial harm to property.[92] Indeed, under the Tier III definition, "[a]ny group that has used a weapon for any purpose other than for personal monetary gain can, under this statute, be labeled a terrorist organization."[93]

Further, any organization or group of individuals is considered an undesignated terrorist organization if it has a "subgroup" that engages in "terrorist activity."[94] The statute does not define "subgroup" or require that the activities of the subgroup be integral to the larger group, or even require that the subgroup be more than loosely associated with the larger group. DHS has in fact taken the position that the terrorist activities of one member group of a broad coalition make every member group in that coalition a terrorist organization.[95]

Significantly, the statute does not take into account the purpose, motivation, or goal of the group engaged in the "violent" activity. This has proven to be embarrassing to the US and devastating to people who have supported pro-democracy groups. It has included in some cases groups which the US itself has supported or considered an ally. One clear example of this policy consequence is the well-known case of *S-K*. In this case, the asylum seeker was a Burmese Christian and a Chin, an ethnic minority in Burma. She had donated money to the Chin National Front ("CNF"), an organization that had engaged in armed conflict with the Burmese government for the purpose of securing freedom for ethnic Chin people. *S-K* pointed out that Burma was a military dictatorship which regularly abused human rights, as the US has recognized. She further demonstrated that CNF was allied with the National League of Democracy, which the US recognizes as the legitimate representative of the Burmese people, and which was also recognized by the United

Nations. Acknowledging that those facts were not necessarily in dispute, the BIA, nonetheless, concluded:

> Congress intentionally drafted the terrorist bars to relief very broadly, to include even those people described as 'freedom fighters,' and it did not intend to give us discretion to create exceptions for members of organizations to which our Government might be sympathetic . . . there is no exception in the Act to the bar to relief in cases involving the use of justifiable force to repel attacks by forces of an illegitimate regime.[96]

The concurrence recognized that such a strict interpretation of the statute would include organizations that the United States government has not viewed as terrorist organizations because their activities coincided with US foreign policy objectives. [97] As DHS conceded in *S-K*, an individual who assisted the Northern Alliance against the Taliban in Afghanistan in the 1990s would have been providing "material support" and barred from asylum under the current statute.[98]

Indeed, the strict statutory language has led to absurd results, denying protection to people who have assisted the US in previous conflicts. For example, DHS has found inadmissible Iraqi citizens who served as interpreters to the US military during the overthrow of Saddam Hussein, on account of their past association with a Kurdish group which was allied with the United States.[99] In fact, all Iraqi groups that took part in the uprising against Saddam Hussein after the first Gulf War would fall within the Tier III category.[100]

In *S-K*, on remand, though the applicant was granted asylum,[101] the BIA held that its earlier decision still stands with respect to determinations involving the applicability and interpretation of the material support provisions in the INA.[102] Therefore, even today, pro-democracy groups that fight against oppressive regimes may still be considered terrorist organizations under the statute, barring anyone who has provided material support to such groups from asylum or other refugee protections.[103]

Moreover, the process for determining what organizations and "sub-groups" are Tier III terrorist organizations is decentralized and initially an *ad hoc* administrative decision made by consular authorities or asylum officers. There is no uniform process for assessing the dangerousness of the alleged terrorist organization or subgroup that is endangered by the "terrorist activity" of the group, and/or whether the "terrorist activity" is the dominant characteristic of the group. These are all considerations that enter into the formal designation process for Tier I and II groups.[104] If and when the decision is reviewed by a court, the judge must give deference to the agency determination.[105]

Ultimately, if an alien is found to have provided material support to a Tier III undesignated terrorist organization, the burden is on the individual to prove by clear and convincing evidence that he did not know or should not reasonably have known that the organization was a terrorist organization.[106]

In sum, the ever-expanding Tier III definition has enveloped groups that pose no threat to the United States or who have not committed conduct in violation of international law. The provision has allowed the government to deny protections to aliens who have associated with such groups, including the provision of even the smallest amount of "support."

III. Reconciling the US "Material Support" Bar with International Law and Norms

As described above, the statutory language barring aliens who have provided material support to terrorist organizations is expansive and vague; such provisions typically are asserted by government officials and interpreted by decision-makers to apply with little exception. The sheer over-breadth of the material support bar in language and application, particularly in combination with the Tier III organizations category and definitions thereof, is inconsistent with international treaty law insofar as denials of refugee protections are meant to be restrictive in nature.[107] Further, such over- breadth appears to be inconsonant with international law norms.

The pertinent international obligations of the United States derive from the Protocol Relating to the Status of Refugees (the "Protocol"), which adopts in substance the 1951 Convention Relating to the Status of Refugees (the "Refugee Convention").[108] In signing and ratifying the Protocol, the US undertook a commitment to grant protections to persons who meet the international legal definition of a refugee, with limited exceptions as set forth in the Refugee Convention. The Convention requires contracting states to grant refugee status to individuals with a "well-founded fear of being persecuted for reasons of race, religion, nationality, membership of a particular social group or political opinion" and who are unable or unwilling to return to their own country for protection on account of such fear.[109] Persons not entitled to such status are those who have committed a crime against peace, a war crime, crimes against humanity, a serious non-political crime outside the country of refuge, or acts contrary to the principles of the United Nations.[110]

The US also took on the obligation of *non-refoulement*, which forbids a state from returning a refugee to any territory where his life or freedom would be threatened on account of the same enumerated grounds, excepting a refugee for whom there are:

> [R]easonable grounds for regarding as a danger to the security of the country in which he is, or who, having been convicted by a final judgment of particularly serious crime, constitutes a danger to the community of that country.[111]

Importantly, the Refugee Convention (and Protocol) withholds protections in two distinct categories: exclusion from refugee status if an individual has committed certain crimes; and non-application of the *non-refoulement* obligation to a person with refugee status who is a danger to the security of the country.[112] In US domestic law, the INA terrorism bar, however, makes a refugee inadmissible on numerous grounds that are cumulatively broader than the relevant grounds in the Refugee Convention. The INA terrorism bar conflates exclusion from refugee status and exceptions to *non-refoulement*.[113] The language in the latter clause of the Convention plainly seeks to except refugees from this protection only where there is a connection between the danger posed by the refugee and the security of the country in which he is seeking protection. Yet, the US material support bar—despite the assertion that it derives from the Convention's article 33.2 exception—requires no such connection. [114] As regards material support to organizations, there is no requirement that the alien intends to further the terrorist activity of the organization, or that the support actually further the activity or the terrorist intent of the organization. In the case of a non-designated terrorist organization, there is no requirement that the organization implicate a threat to the security of the United States.[115]

US courts have been largely dismissive of aliens' international law claims regarding the material support bar, including the Tier III provision.[116] The case of *Khan v. Holder* illustrates well the US approach to balancing national security concerns and humanitarian obligations. Khan, who solicited funds for the nonmilitant wing of a non-designated organization fighting against an illegitimate government, argued that the INA incorporates international law, thereby compelling a more narrow reading of "terrorist activity."[117] Specifically, Khan asserted that legitimate armed resistance is not a violation of international law and therefore not "terrorist activity." Further, he claimed that his actions, designated as "terrorist activity" under the INA, were not covered by any of the exclusion grounds articulated in Articles 33.2 or 1F of the Refugee Convention, which are the only bases for exceptions to *non-refoulement* (removal). The court was unreceptive to international law in general, finding that the Protocol is not self-executing and therefore does "not have the force of law in American courts."[118] In light of the *Charming Betsy* doctrine,[119] the court went on to consider the petitioner's argument, but declined to find the INA's definition inconsistent with the Protocol because it found that the US has determined that any alien who has engaged in terrorist activity as defined by the INA (section 212(a)(3)(B)) is a danger to the security of the United States.[120]

Following the *Khan* court's reasoning, the Ninth Circuit recently rejected an asylum seeker's argument that involuntary material support as a basis for exclusion conflicts with the Protocol. [121] The court concluded that because the determination of refugee status is incumbent upon the contracting state in whose territory the refugee finds himself, Congress was free to find that an alien who provides material support to a terrorist organization, even if under duress, is a danger to the United States.[122]

The rationale underlying these two decisions demonstrates how the US position on its obligations under the Protocol is highly problematic. As a preliminary matter, while it may be up to the contracting state to determine refugee status, interpretative authority suggests that any exclusions or exceptions are to be interpreted restrictively.[123] Moreover, exceptions to *non-refoulement* under the Refugee Convention do not denigrate refugee status. Rather, they exclude a person from a subsidiary protection and are limited to individuals who pose a danger to the security of the state in which the refugee seeks protection.[124] Under the INA, exclusion from refugee status may occur with no such relationship between the "terrorist activity"—*e.g.,* material support—and the security of the United States. This is particularly so with respect to Tier III organizations.

Won Kidane's survey of the anti-terrorism and immigration laws of four common law jurisdictions (Australia, Canada, United Kingdom, and the US), found that the United States is the only state that does not require a nexus between the terrorist conduct, which disqualifies the alien seeking refuge, and the state's security.[125] Kidane concluded that the US definition of terrorism used to exclude aliens is:

> [S]ignificantly broader than all of the other jurisdictions because of the addition of the tier III terrorist group category, the material support bar linked to this particular category, the lack of a national security nexus requirement, and the addition of an independent children and spouses of terrorists category. The US net is cast so wide that it is often likely to catch Burmese monks, not real terrorists.[126]

The decision by the European Court of Justice ("ECJ") in *Federal Republic of Germany v. B&D* also serves to illustrate the deviation by the

US from international legal norms. Relying on Council Directive 2004/83/EC, in *B&D*, the ECJ, asked to determine whether affiliation with a listed terrorist organization would be a sufficient condition to deny asylum and revoke refugee status, concluded that "the mere fact that the person concerned was a member of such an organization cannot automatically mean that the person must be excluded from refugee status."[127] The Court held that an exclusion decision may not be based solely on membership in a terrorist organization but requires an individual assessment of specific facts to determine whether the person falls within an exception and individual responsibility is established.[128] Notably, the Court also made clear that such an individual assessment would include "the true role" of the person accused of association and "any pressure" or other factors that might have influenced his conduct.[129] *B&D* thus stands for the proposition that in denying a person international protection, an individualized analysis that takes into account the totality of the circumstances is appropriately required even where counter-terrorism mechanisms are at issue.[130]

IV. Conclusion

Under US law, the "material support bar," coupled with the Tier III provision, is indeed a high and heavy bar to refugee protection. Though criticism has been directed at several aspects of the material support bar and the terrorism bar in general, the most problematic has been the steel-like inflexibility created by the lack of a duress exception and a *de minimis* requirement. Thus, an individual could be excluded from protection even if he gave minuscule support, under threat, to a terrorist. The overbreadth of the Tier III—undesignated terrorist organization—category, which would include a disorganized band of rock throwers protesting a tyrannical government, merely exacerbates the problem. Decision makers, such as consulate officials, asylum officers and judges, have not had the authority to grant exceptions, while DHS attorneys appear to be consistently advocating a strict interpretation of the exclusionary language. As illustrated above, the bar has affected thousands and thousands of deserving individuals, many of whom were seeking protection as victims of terrorism.

Over the years, there has been a slow trickling of legislative modifications and agency directives that have generated the authority to grant waivers. This waiver process, however, has been besieged with bureaucracy, delay, and a lack of uniformity, and continues to result in the denial of protection to many refugees who merit it. Moreover, if a case gets to court, there is still no legislative leeway allowing or suggesting that exceptions could be granted from the bench. Even recently, courts continue to interpret the language of the material support bar rigidly, that is, without consideration to the type of support given and the recipient of such support and, ultimately, whether any of it directly affects US national security.

An approach that fails to require a nexus between the dangerousness of the individual and the security of the nation is considerably out of step with international law and norms. Given that these protections are, in fact, international obligations to which the US is legally bound, this approach is of great concern—first, for the individuals whom it impacts and second, for the additional strain on the rule of law, which the US has already stretched in much of its post 9/11 counter-terrorism response.

At the end of the day, the material support bar is a general approach to terrorism, as there appears to be minimal requirement that a *bona fide* refugee's activities correlate to national security. This is not to say that the bar is wholly ineffective. Certainly, keeping out all refugees would decrease the possibility of letting in a terrorist. But this line of reasoning gives very little thought to humanitarian protection as an objective and substantially more thought to national security, as discussed in the Introduction of this chapter. Given what is at stake—whether it be life and liberty of individuals, legal obligations, or the rule of law— the US greatly undermines its commitment to human rights, as well as its own security, by sacrificing humanitarian protection for the appearance of national security.

Notes

---

[*] Kristine A. Huskey is a visiting associate clinical professor at the James E. Rogers College of Law, The University of Arizona. She is the founder of the National Security Clinic at the University of Texas School of Law and author of JUSTICE AT GUANTANAMO: ONE WOMAN'S ODYSSEY AND HER CRUSADE FOR HUMAN RIGHTS (2009). The author wishes to thank Matteo Quattrocchi for his very valuable contributions to the conception of and research for this work and without whom this chapter would not have been possible. The author also thanks Katelyn Kimber, a law student at Georgetown University Law Center, for her research assistance, and Tom Syring for his editorial input. This chapter was originally presented on the panel "State Responses to Refugee Flows," as part of the symposium from which this book originates.

[1] Shortly after 9/11, retail stores appeared to be requesting more and more personal information from in-store customers, such as phone numbers, email addresses, and

zip codes, some personnel even asserting "national security reasons" for obtaining such information.

[2] The nationwide "If You See Something, Say Something" public awareness campaign in the US is heralded as a "simple and effective program to raise public awareness of indicators of terrorism and terrorism-related crime, and to emphasize the importance of reporting suspicious activity to the proper local law enforcement authorities." DEP'T OF HOMELAND SEC., http://www.dhs.gov/if-you-see-something-say-something-campaign (last visited April 3, 2013).

[3] The Transportation Security Administration (TSA), an agency within the United States Department of Homeland Security, screens all passengers before airline travel. Such screenings, at a minimum, require assorted outerwear and accessories, including shoes, to be removed and passage through a detector that has been criticized by privacy advocates.

[4] Naomi Wolf, *Revealed: How the FBI Coordinated the Crackdown on Occupy*, THE GUARDIAN, Dec. 29, 2012, *available at* http://www.guardian.co.uk/commentisfree/2012/dec/29/fbi-coordinated-crackdown-occupy.

[5] *See, e.g.*, DEP'T OF HOMELAND SEC., *The Strategic National Risk Assessment in Support of PPD, A Comprehensive Risk-Based Approach Toward a Secure and Resilient Nation* (Dec. 2011), *available at* http://www.dhs.gov/xlibrary/assets/rma-strategic-national-risk-assessment-ppd8.pdf.

[6] Richard A. Posner, *The Law: Security v. Civil Liberties*, THE ATLANTIC MONTHLY, Dec. 2001, *available at* http://www.theatlantic.com/past/docs/issues/2001/12/posner.htm; *see generally* RICHARD A. POSNER, NOT A SUICIDE PACT: THE CONSTITUTION IN A TIME OF NATIONAL EMERGENCY (2006).

[7] *See, e.g.*, Rep. Sandy Adams, *Ban Foreign Law from Courts*, THE WASH. TIMES, Mar. 9, 2011, *available at* http://www.washingtontimes.com/news/2011/mar/9/in-recent-years-supreme-court-justices-have-interj/ (noting more than a dozen states that introduced legislation aimed at outlawing the use of international law in American courts).

[8] PENTTBOM was the codename for the Federal Bureau of Investigation's (FBI) investigation into the September 11, 2001 terrorist attacks that occurred in the US. The acronym stands for Pentagon/Twin Towers Bombing Investigation.

[9] Immigration and Nationality Act (INA) of 1952, Pub. L. No. 82-414, 66 Stat. 163 (codified as amended in 8 U.S.C. §§ 1101-1503 (1952)).

[10] *Id.* § 212(a)(27), (29).

[11] *Id.* § 212(a)(28)(F).

[12] *See id.* § 212(a)(27)-(29).

[13] Scott Aldworth, *Terror Firma: The Unyielding Terrorism Bar in the Immigration and Nationality Act*, 14 LEWIS & CLARK L. REV., 1159, 1166 (2010).

[14] Immigration Act of 1990, § 601, Pub. L. No. 101-649, § 601(a), 104 Stat. 4978, 5069 (amending section § 212 of the INA [8 U.S.C. 1182]).

[15] *Id.* § 601(a) (setting forth revised (a)(3)(B)(ii)).

[16] *See id.* The 1990 Act defined "engage in terrorist activity" to include "to commit, in an individual capacity or as a member of an organization, an act of terrorist activity or an act which the actor knows, or reasonably should know, affords material support to any individual, organization, or government in conducting a terrorist activity at any time, including any of the following acts:

(I) The preparation or planning of a terrorist activity.
(II) The gathering of information on potential targets for terrorist activity.
(III) The providing of any type of material support, including a safe house, transportation, communications, funds, false identification, weapons, explosives, or training, to any individual the actor knows or has reason to believe has committed or plans to commit an act of terrorist activity.
(IV) The soliciting of funds or other things of value for terrorist activity or for any terrorist organization.
(V) The solicitation of any individual for membership in a terrorist organization, terrorist government, or to engage in a terrorist activity."

[17] Antiterrorism and Effective Death Penalty Act (AEDPA) of 1996, Pub. L. No. 104-132, § 411, 110 Stat. 1214.
[18] The Attorney General was also given the authority to waive the exclusion if he or she determined the alien was not a danger to the security of the United States. *Id.* § 421. This discretionary power was later narrowed. Illegal Immigration Reform and Immigrant Responsibility Act (IIRIRA) of 1996, Div. C, Pub. L. No. 104-208, § 604, 110 Stat. 3009.
[19] The Uniting and Strengthening America by Providing Appropriate Tools Required to Intercept and Obstruct Terrorism Act of 2001 (Patriot Act), Pub. L. No. 107-56, 115 Stat. 272.
[20] *Id.* § 411 (amending INA § 212 [8 U.S.C. 1182]).
[21] INA § 212(a)(3)(B)(vi)(I), (II), (III).
[22] *Id.* § 212(a)(3)(B)(vi)(III).
[23] Emergency Supplemental Appropriations Act for Defense, the Global War on Terror, and Tsunami Relief, 2005, Div. B--REAL ID Act of 2005, Pub. L. No. 109-13, 119 Stat. 231, 302.
[24] The REAL ID Act also contained other provisions directed at refugee status, such as heightening a corroboration requirement, but these issues are beyond the scope of this chapter.
[25] Patriot Act, § 411(a).
[26] REAL ID Act, § 103(a).
[27] *See* Patriot Act, § 411(a).
[28] *Id.* One would think that *if* a "terrorist organization" is not designated by a US agency, it is reasonable to assume that one may not "reasonably have known" whether an organization is engaged in terrorist activities.
[29] The Patriot Act, § 411(a)(1)(F).

[30] The REAL ID Act, § 104. Section 104 of the REAL ID Act also includes the same waiver authority regarding material support as the Patriot Act, but adds the Secretary of Homeland Security, which was not an existing position at the time of the passage of the Patriot Act. *Id.*

[31] *Hearing on Oversight of U.S. Refugee Admission and Policy Before the Subcomm. on Immigration, Border Security and Citizenship of the S. Comm. on the Judiciary*, 109th Cong. 2 (Sept. 27, 2006) (testimony of Ellen Sauerbrey, Asst. Sec. for the Bureau of Population, Refugees and Migration) (expressing concern that the waiver authority did not provide flexibility in all refugee cases).

[32] Interoffice Memorandum from U.S. Citizenship and Immigration Services, *Processing the Discretionary Exemption to the Inadmissibility Ground for Providing Material Support to Certain Terrorist Organizations* 3 (May 24, 2007).

[33] *See* Human Rights First, *Denial and Delay, The Impact of the Immigration Law's "Terrorism Bars" on Asylum Seekers and Refugees in the United States*, 24 (2009), *available at* http://www.humanrightsfirst.org/wp-content/uploads/pdf/RPP-DenialandDelay-FULL-111009-web.pdf [hereinafter *Denial and Delay*].

[34] R.K. was kidnapped by members of the Liberation Tigers of Tamil Eelam (LTTE) and forced to pay a ransom of 50,000 rupees for his release. R.K. then sought asylum in the United States, chosen because it was a country known for speaking out against Tamil brutality. Although the immigration judge determined that R.K. paid the LTTE under duress, he ultimately agreed with DHS attorneys who argued "there is no duress exception to the material support definition" and "had Congress intended to include such a duress exception to the material support definition, it could have done so." As a result, R.K. was denied asylum. *See* Human Rights First, *Abandoning the Persecuted: Victims of Terrorism and Oppression Barred from Asylum*, 7 (Sept. 2006), *available at* http://www.humanrightsfirst.org/wp-content/uploads/pdf/06925-asy-abandon-persecuted.pdf; Jeremiah Marquez, *Some Refugees in Legal Paradox*, ASSOCIATED PRESS, Sept. 26, 2006, *available at* http://www.rcusa.org/uploads/pdfs/ms-mediaart-ap9-26-06.pdf.

[35] B.T., a Nepalese government employee and healthcare worker, was kidnapped by Maoist Rebels and forced at gunpoint to provide medical treatment to injured militia. He was then tortured by the Royal Nepalese Army for providing assistance to the rebels. Although he was granted asylum by a US immigration judge, DHS appealed the decision, placing B.T.'s case on indefinite hold. Prosecutors had argued that the material support bar did not include an exception for providing medical care under duress. *See* Brief of the Physicians Committee for Human Rights as Amicus Curiae Supporting Respondent, Matter of B.T.; Melanie Nezer, *The 'Material Support' Problem: An Uncertain Future for Thousands of Refugees and Asylum Seekers*, 12 BENDER'S IMM. BULL. 2 (2005).

[36] After Sierra Leonean rebels killed one family member with machetes, they raped Helene and her daughter and held the family captive for four days in their own home. Although Helene was designated a refugee by the United Nations High Commissioner for Refugees and DHS initially agreed with the designation, DHS put her case on hold because the "shelter" constituted material support to a terrorist

group. *See* Jennie Pasquarella, *Victims of Terror Stopped at the Gate to Safety: The Impact of the "Material Support to Terrorism" Bar on Refugees*, 13(3) HUM. RTS. BRIEF 28 (Spring 2006) (citing US Dep't of State, Bureau of Population, Refugees and Migration, *Case Summaries*; Editorial, *Terrorist or Victims?*, N.Y. TIMES, Apr. 3, 2006).

[37] *See* 72 Fed. Reg. 9958 (Mar. 6, 2007) (Tier III groups) and 72 Fed. Reg. 26138 (May 8, 2007) (Tier I and II groups).

[38] *Id.* When considering the totality of the circumstances, factors to be considered may include: amount, type, and frequency of material support, the nature of the activities committed by the terrorist organization, the alien's awareness of those activities, the length of time since the support was provided, and any other relevant factors. *Id.*

[39] Consolidated Appropriations Act of 2008 (CAA), Pub. L. 110-161, Div. J, § 691(a), 121 Stat. 1844 (2007).

[40] *Id.* § 691(a). Waivers do not extend to any group that has engaged in terrorist activity against the United States or another democratic country, or that has purposefully engaged in a pattern or practice of terrorist activity that is directed at civilians. *Id.*

[41] *Id.* The CAA also specifies that certain groups are not considered terrorist organizations for INA purposes.

[42] 76 Fed. Reg. 70463 (Nov. 14, 2011); *see also* Policy Memorandum from U.S. Citizenship and Immigration Services, *Implementation of the New Exemption Under INA Section 212(d)(3)(B)(i) for the Provision of Material Support in the Form of Medical Care*, 3-4 (Nov. 21, 2011) (explaining that "on behalf of" of a designated terrorist organization means the alien is providing medical care as the organization's physician, or his services are furthering the group's terrorist aims).

[43] 77 Fed. Reg. 49821 (Aug. 17, 2012). Tier III groups that have targeted US interests or persons, engaged in torture, or used child soldiers are not included in this exemption.

[44] *Id.* At the time the exemption was granted, it was estimated that there were roughly 3500-4000 refugees who had been granted protection but whose permanent residence or reunification applications were on hold due to non-violent associations with "terrorist organizations" under the INA, solely by virtue of the fact that the organizations engaged in the use of armed force as non-state actors.

[45] *See, e.g.*, *Denial and Delay*, *supra* note 33, at 41-49; Refugee Council USA, *The Problem of Terrorism-Related Inadmissibility Grounds (TRIG) and the Implementation of the Exemption Authority for Refugees, Asylum Seekers, and Adjustment of Status Applicants* (*Terrorism-Related Inadmissibility Grounds Backgrounder*) (2009), *available at* http://www.rcusa.org/index.php?page=material-support-issue.

[46] Khan v. Holder, 584 F.3d 773, 787 (9th Cir. 2009) (Nelson, J., dissenting).

[47] Hussain v. Mukasey, 518 F.3d 534, 538 (7th Cir. 2008).

[48] *See* OFFICE OF IMMIGRATION STATISTICS, DEP'T OF HOMELAND SEC., REFUGEES AND ASYLEES 2011, ANNUAL FLOW REPORT 3 (May 2012) [hereinafter REFUGEES AND ASYLEES 2011]; OFFICE OF IMMIGRATION STATISTICS, DEP'T OF HOMELAND

SEC., REFUGEES AND ASYLEES 2006, ANNUAL FLOW REPORT 3 (May 2007) [hereinafter REFUGEES AND ASYLEES 2006]; OFFICE OF IMMIGRATION STATISTICS, DEP'T OF HOMELAND SEC., 2002 Y.B. OF IMMIGRATION STATISTICS 52, 54 (2003) [hereinafter 2002 Y.B.].

[49] 2002 Y.B., *supra* note 48, at 59.

[50] REFUGEES AND ASYLEES 2006, *supra* note 48, at 3.

[51] REFUGEES AND ASYLEES 2011, *supra* note 48, at 1.

[52] OFFICE OF IMMIGRATION STATISTICS, DEP'T OF HOMELAND SEC., 2011 Y.B. OF IMMIGRATION STATISTICS 43 (Table 16) (2012) [hereinafter 2011 Y.B.]. Unlike many jurisdictions, the United States distinguishes people seeking refugee status and who are outside the US from those seeking the same and already in the US or at a US port of entry. Individuals outside the US apply for "refugee status" while those in the US apply for "asylum status." To be eligible for either status, one must meet the definition of a "refugee" under section 101(a)(42) of the INA, which is "a person unwilling or unable to return to his or her country of nationality because of persecution or a well-founded fear of persecution based on race, religion, nationality, membership in a particular social group, or political opinion." REFUGEES AND ASYLEES 2011, *supra* note 48, at 1.

[53] *Id.*

[54] INA § 212(a)(3)(B)(VI). *See, e.g.*, American Academy of Religion v. Napolitano, 573 F.3d 115, 131 (2d Cir. 2009) (concluding that material support bar does not require knowledge that recipient of alien's material support was a terrorist organization but only provides alien with defense contained in § 212(a)(3)(B)(iv)(VI)(dd) that an alien can prove he did not know the organization was a terrorist one).

[55] *See generally* text, *supra*, at Part I.A.

[56] 385 F.3d 293, 299–300 (3d Cir. 2004).

[57] Khan v. Holder, 584 F.3d 773, 777, 785 (9th Cir. 2009).

[58] *Id.* at 777 (citing Humanitarian Law Project v. Reno, 205 F.3d 1130, 1136 (9th Cir. 2000)); *see also* Hussain v. Mukasey, 518 F.3d 534, 538 (7th Cir. 2008) (finding that providing material support to a terrorist organization is engaging in terrorist activity even if support is confined to non-terrorist activities of the organization).

[59] *See* Holder v. Humanitarian Law Project, 130 S.Ct. 2705 (2010) and prior history.

[60] *Id.* at 2727.

[61] *Id.* at 2710 (citing § 301(a), 110 Stat. 1247 (note following § 2339B)).

[62] *The "Material Support" Bar: Denying Refuge to the Persecuted?, Hearing Before the Subcomm. on Human Rights and the Law of the S. Comm. on the Judiciary*, 110th Cong. 1 (Sept. 19, 2007) (statement of Paul Rosenzweig, Deputy Assistant Sec'y. for Policy, Dep't of Homeland Sec.) [hereinafter "Rosenzweig Statement"] ("the Courts and Congress have recognized that 'foreign organizations that engage in terrorist activity are so tainted by their criminal conduct that any contribution to such an organization facilitates that conduct'" (citing Humanitarian Law Project v. Reno, 205 F.3d 1130, 1136 (9th Cir. 2000) and AEDPA, § 301(a)(7))).

[63] *But see* Khan, 584 F.3d 773 (undesignated terrorist organization) and Hussain, 518 F.3d 534 (undesignated terrorist organization); *see generally* Tom Syring, *Protecting the Protectors or Victimizing the Victims Anew? "Material Support of Terrorism" and Exclusion from Refugee Status in U.S. and European Courts*, 18 ILSA J. INT'L & COMP. L. 597, 602-603 (2012).
[64] *See* AEDPA, § 302 (revising INA § 219).
[65] *See* Rosenzweig Statement.
[66] *See, e.g.*, Mark Fleming, et al. eds., *Unintended Consequences: Refugee Victims of the War on Terror*, 37 GEO. J. INT'L L. 759, 794-801 (2006) [hereinafter *Unintended Consequences*]; Human Rights First, *Abandoning the Persecuted*, 6-7 (2006); *see generally* Gregory F. Laufer, *Admission Denied: In Support of a Duress Exception to the Immigration and Nationality Act's "Material Support for Terrorism" Provision*, 20 GEO. IMMIGR. L.J. 437 (2006).
[67] Pasquarella, *supra* note 36, at 30.
[68] U.S. DEP'T OF STATE, U.S. DEP'T OF HOMELAND SEC., AND U.S. DEP'T OF HEALTH AND HUMAN SERVICES, PROPOSED REFUGEE ADMISSIONS FOR FISCAL YEAR 2006, 33 (2005) [hereinafter PROPOSED REFUGEE ADMISSIONS FOR 2006], *available at* http://jfs.ohio.gov/refugee/docs/FY-2006-Report-to-the-Congress.pdf.
[69] *See id.* at 4 (noting "material" support ground has slowed Colombian refugee processing considerably). *See, e.g.*, Arias v. Gonzales, 143 F. Appx. 464, 466 (3d Cir. 2005) (affirming the immigration judge's (IJ) and Board of Immigration Appeals' (BIA) decision finding Arias barred under material support statute regardless of whether his support was voluntary or involuntary).
[70] *Unintended Consequences*, *supra* note 66, at 788-790; PROPOSED REFUGEE ADMISSIONS FOR 2006, *supra* note 68, at 34; UNHCR, *International Protection Considerations Regarding Colombian Asylum-Seekers and Refugees*, ¶¶ 55, 57, 89 (Mar. 2005), *available at* http://www.unhcr.org/refworld/docid/3d92d4204.html.
[71] *Unintended Consequences*, *supra* note 66, at 795-96.
[72] PROPOSED REFUGEE ADMISSIONS FOR 2006, *supra* note 68, at 4 (an individual who provides money, food, shelter or other assistance to an organization which engages in terrorist activity is inadmissible even when the individual was compelled or coerced to provide such support).
[73] U.S. DEP'T OF STATE, U.S. DEP'T OF HOMELAND SEC., AND U.S. DEP'T OF HEALTH AND HUMAN SERVICES, PROPOSED REFUGEE ADMISSIONS FOR FISCAL YEAR 2010, 37 (2009), *available at* http://www.state.gov/documents/organization/181382.pdf.
[74] U.S. DEP'T OF STATE, U.S. DEP'T OF HOMELAND SEC., AND U.S. DEP'T OF HEALTH AND HUMAN SERVICES, PROPOSED REFUGEE ADMISSIONS FOR FISCAL YEAR 2012, 35 (2011).
[75] *See* Aldworth, *supra* note 13, at 1184 (addressing Negusie v. Holder, 129 S.Ct. 1159 (2009), in which the Supreme Court appeared to open up the possibility that the "persecutor's bar" might be inapplicable if such persecution was under duress).
[76] *See* Barahona v. Holder, 691 F.3d 349, 354 (4th Cir. 2012); Annachamy v. Holder, 686 F.3d 729, 734 (9th Cir. 2012).
[77] *See* Barahona, 691 F.3d at 355; Annachamy, 686 F.3d at 736.

[78] Annachamy, 686 F.3d at 737.
[79] Singh-Kaur v. Ashcroft, 385 F.3d 293, 303 (3d Cir. 2004) (Fisher, J., dissenting) ("I conclude that Congress did not intend 'material support' to embrace acts that are not of importance or relevance to terrorism. To hold otherwise reads 'material' out of 'material support' and treats half of the statutory term as surplusage.").
[80] INA § 212(a)(3)(B)(iv)(VI).
[81] In re S-K-, 23 I. & N. Dec. 936, 942-944 (BIA 2006).
[82] *Id.* at 945 (the BIA went on to state that "material support" was a "term of art" and that all the listed types of assistance are covered regardless of whether they are independently "material.").
[83] *See, e.g.*, Singh-Kaur, 385 F.3d 292; *see also Denial and Delay*, *supra* note 33, at 33-34; *but see* Matter of L-H, 2009 Immig. Rptr. LEXIS 963 (BIA July 10, 2009) (unpublished opinion) (reversing immigration judge's decision that "one packed lunch and the equivalent of $4 US dollars" was material support). *See also Unintended Consequences*, *supra* note 66, at 801-803 (noting in a 2004 briefing to UNHCR on the application of the material support bar, staff from US Embassy stated that if a person gave "even a glass of water" to a member of an armed group, that act would qualify as material support and result in the individual being barred from the US resettlement program).
[84] Barahona v. Holder, 691 F.3d 349, 353 (4th Cir. 2012).
[85] Singh-Kaur, 385 F.3d at 304-305. The majority pointed to the criminal counterpart for material support (18 U.S.C. 2339A) and found it would be incongruous to conclude that a person who provides food and sets up tents for terrorists could be jailed for life but the same conduct could not prohibit admission to the United States. *Id.* at 298-299. This ignores the fact that while the list in 2339B contains many examples of types of material support, the statute also requires that the support be provided knowing or intending that it will be used to carry out, or in preparation for, a terrorist act. *See* 18 U.S.C. 2339A(a).
[86] *See Denial and Delay*, *supra* note 33, at 32; *Unintended Consequences*, *supra* note 66, at 804-805 (case study of "Laura" who was required to cook for FARC members who took over her family's home).
[87] *Denial and Delay*, *supra* note 33, at 34-37 (*e.g.*, denying permanent residence to Iranian who had provided material support by publishing and passing out pro-Shah propaganda; deeming speech, posters, and authorship of certain articles in support of pro-democratic movements "material support").
[88] *Id.* at 37.
[89] *See* World Medical Ass'n, *International Code of Medical Ethics* (1949) (adopted at the 3rd Assemb. in London) (as amended), *available at* http://www.wma.net/en/30publications/10policies/c8/index.html. *See also The "Material Support" Bar: Denying Refuge to the Persecuted?, Hearing Before the Subcomm. on Human Rights and the Law of the S. Comm. on the Judiciary*, 110th Cong. 1 at 138 (Sept. 19, 2007) (statement of Physicians for Human Rights) ("If the provision of medical care were to be considered 'material support' under the INA, the result would be that healthcare workers would be required to deny medical care to certain wounded persons. Under such a reading of the INA

healthcare workers would be in the untenable position of deciding whether a life is worth saving, whether a person has committed a crime or terrorist act, and whether a group should be denied medical treatment—a form of political decision-making incompatible with medical ethics and international law.").

[90] 76 Fed. Reg. 70463 (Nov. 14, 2011).

[91] 8 U.S.C. § 1182(a)(3)(B)(iv)(VI), (vi)(I), (II), (III), and (iii)(V)(bb).

[92] This definition has been colloquially summarized as "two guys and a gun" on account of the low threshold required to turn any act of violence by more than one person into a terrorist act. *See, e.g.*, Press Release, Human Rights First, Eight Years After Enactment of Patriot Act Provisions, Human Rights First Report Outlines Needed Reforms (Nov. 11, 2009), *available at* http://www.humanrightsfirst.org/2009/11/11/overly-broad-immigration-provisions-redefine-thousands-of-legitimate-refugees-asylum-seekers-as-terrorists/.

[93] In re S-K-, 23 I. & N. Dec. 936, 948 (BIA 2006) (Osuna, BIA member, concurring). S*ee also* Hussain v. Mukasey, 518 F.3d 534, 537 (7th Cir. 2008) ("the statutory definition of 'terrorist organization' is broad enough to encompass a pair of kidnappers") (citations omitted); Singh v. Wiles, 747 F. Supp. 2d 1223, 1227 (W.D. Wa. 2010) (noting terrorist activities described in statute "are exceedingly broad in scope").

[94] 8 U.S.C. § 1182(a)(3)(B)(vi)(III).

[95] *Denial and Delay*, *supra* note 33, at 29-30.

[96] In re S-K-, 23 I. & N. Dec. at 941.

[97] *Id.* at 948. The concurring opinion went so far as to state that arguably by supporting CNF, SK was acting consistently with US foreign policy. *Id.* at 950.

[98] *Id.* at 948.

[99] *Denial and Delay*, *supra* note 33, at 4.

[100] *Id.* at 26. *See also* Khan, 584 F.3d at 787 (Nelson, J., concurring) (pointing out that any individual or group who assisted the US in invading Afghanistan or Iraq would be ineligible for asylum or withholding of removal because the US military, whose activities were "indisputably unlawful" in those countries, would qualify as a Tier III organization).

[101] Matter of S-K-, 24 I. & N. Dec. 475 (BIA 2008).

[102] *Id.* at 477.

[103] *See* Annachamy, 686 F.3d at 733-34 (no exception for groups that engage in "legitimate political violence"); Khan, 584 F.3d at 787 (acknowledging that armed resistance by Jews against the government of Nazi Germany might be a terrorist organization under the statute); *see also* Cheema v. Ashcroft, 383 F.3d 848, 858 (9th Cir. 2004) ("[o]ne country's terrorist can often be another country's freedom-fighter."). Groups suffering the same fate might include, among others: the Afghan mujahidin groups that fought against the Soviet Union in the 1980's with US support; The Sudan People's Liberation Movement/Army (SPLM/SPLA), the South Sudanese armed opposition movement that after years of civil war in pursuit of self-determination is now the ruling party of an autonomous Government in South Sudan; any group that has used armed force against the regime in Iran since the 1979 revolution; and The Movement for Democratic Change (MDC), the main

political opposition to President Robert Mugabe of Zimbabwe. *See Denial and Delay*, *supra* note 33, at 26.
[104] *See* Won Kidane, *The Terrorism Bar to Asylum in Australia, Canada, the United Kingdom, and the United States: Transporting Best Practices*, 33 FORDHAM INT'L L.J. 300, 354 (2010); *Denial and Delay*, *supra* note 33, at 21.
[105] *See, e.g.*, Barahona, 691 F.3d at 354 (citing Chevron U.S.A., Inc. v. NRDC, Inc., 467 U.S. 837, 844 (1984), in which the US Supreme Court set forth the principle requiring deference to agencies in interpreting a statute that is within its subject matter jurisdiction and is ambiguous or unclear).
[106] 8 U.S.C. § 1182(a)(3)(B)(iv)(VI)(dd).
[107] *See* UNHCR, HANDBOOK ON PROCEDURES AND CRITERIA FOR DETERMINING REFUGEE STATUS, ¶ 149, U.N. Doc. HCR/IP/4/Eng/REV.1 (1979) (reedited, Geneva, Jan. 1992) [hereinafter UNHCR HANDBOOK].
[108] U.N. Convention Relating to the Status of Refugees, July 28, 1951, 19 U.S.T. 6259, 189 U.S.T.S. 137 (entered into force July 28, 1951) [hereinafter Refugee Convention]; Protocol Relating to the Status of Refugees, Jan. 31, 1967, 19 U.S.T. 6223, 606 U.N.T.S. 267 (entered into force Oct. 4, 1967).
[109] Refugee Convention, art. 1.A.2.
[110] *Id.* art. 1.F.
[111] Refugee Convention, arts. 33.1, 33.2.
[112] *Id.*, arts. 1.F, 33.2.
[113] Alice Farmer, *Non-Refoulement and Jus Cogens: Limiting Anti-Terror Measures that Threaten Refugee Protection*, 23 GEO. IMMIGR. L.J. 1, 15-17 & accompanying notes (2008). This results in potentially limiting future protections for a person who meets the definition of refugee and who falls within the exceptions in Article 33.2 but may not pose a similar risk in another state. *See id.*, at n.92.
[114] *See, e.g.*, Annachamy, 686 F.3d at 740; Khan, 584 F.3d at 783-84.
[115] *See infra*, text, Part I.C; *see also, e.g.*, Hussain, 518 F.3d at 538 ("It is likewise irrelevant that MQM-H does not appear to harbor any hostile designs against the United States; the statute does not require that the terrorist organization be a threat to us.").
[116] *See, e.g.*, Barahona, 691 F.3d at 353 ("it is well-established that Congress may enact statutes that conflict with international law"); Annachamy, 686 F.3d at 739; Khan, 584 F.3d at 782-784; McAllister v. Att'y Gen., 444 F.3d 178, 187 (3d Cir. 2006).
[117] Khan, 584 F.3d at 781, 783.
[118] *Id.* at 783.
[119] Under US law, the Charming Betsy doctrine essentially provides that domestic legislation should be interpreted to avoid conflict with international law. *See* Murray v. The Charming Betsy, 2 Cranch 64, 6 U.S. 64 (1804) ("It has also been observed that an act of Congress ought never to be construed to violate the law of nations if any other possible construction remains..."). *See also* Hamdi v. Rumsfeld, 124 S.Ct. 2633 (2004); INS v. St. Cyr, 533 U.S. 289 (2001); Sale v.

Haitian Centers Council, Inc., 509 U.S. 155 (1993). The Supreme Court has explicitly relied upon the Charming Betsy doctrine in at least a dozen cases.

[120] *Id.* at 784 (citing Murray v. The Charming Betsy, 2 Cranch 64, 6 U.S. 64 (1804) and 8 U.S.C. ¶ 1182(a)(3)(B)). The court also noted that the discretionary waiver allowed for an exemption from the broad statutory definition of "terrorist activity." *Id* at 782.

[121] Annachamy, 686 F.3d at 739.

[122] *Id.* at 740.

[123] UNHCR HANDBOOK, *supra* note 107, Foreword, ¶ II, ¶ 149; Farmer, *supra* note 113, at 11 & accompanying notes; Elihu Lauterpacht & Daniel Bethlehem, *The Scope and Content of the Principle of Non-Refoulement: Opinion, in* REFUGEE PROTECTION IN INTERNATIONAL LAW: UNHCR GLOBAL CONSULTATIONS ON INTERNATIONAL PROTECTION 133-34 (Erika Feller et al. eds., 2003).

[124] *See* Refugee Convention, art. 33.2.: "…or, having been convicted by a final judgment of a particularly serious crime, constitutes a danger to the community of that country."

[125] Kidane, *supra* note 104, at 350.

[126] *Id.* at 357.

[127] Joined Cases C-57/09 & C-1-1/09, Fed. Rep. of Ger. v. B & D, 2010 E.C.R. I-000 ¶ 88 (2010) (referring to Council Directive 2004/83/EC, Minimum Standards for the Qualification and Status of Third Country Nationals or Stateless Persons as Refugees or as Persons Who Otherwise Need International Protection and the Content of the Protection, 2004 O.J. (L 304) (EC), which assists in implementing EU member states' obligations under the Refugee Convention).

[128] *See id.* ¶¶ 90-97; *see also* Syring, *supra* note 63, at 610-613.

[129] *See* B & D, ¶ 97.

[130] *See* Syring, *supra* note 63, at 612-613.

CHAPTER NINE

THE SIRENS AND THE EMPEROR: THE EUROPEAN UNION BETWEEN ATTRACTION AND INTERVENTION

TOM SYRING*

"What potions have I drunk of Siren tears,
Distill'd from limbecks foul as hell within,
Applying fears to hopes, and hopes to fears,
Still losing when I saw myself to win!"[1]

I. Introduction

Few regions have seen such a persistent–albeit not uninterrupted or unchallenged–move among well-established, independent states towards greater integration into an intergovernmental, and to some degree even supranational, entity[2] in the past couple of decades as the area now constituting the European Union ("EU").[3] At a time when the quest for independence and secession of states still loomed large in a post-Soviet era,[4] and despite war and dissolution in its immediate neighborhood (the former Yugoslavia)–now to a certain extent already forming an integral part of it–the European project proceeded towards greater unity in a number of key legal and policy areas at the expense of the individual Member States' sovereign right to decide upon the shape and content of those core competencies. This process culminated on 1 November 1993 in the entry into force of the Maastricht Treaty establishing the European Union.[5] In response to the EU's growing attraction as an asylum destination, outside pressures from overseas wars and refugee situations, and internal pressures from uneven capabilities and 'burden-distribution' within Europe, one of the most prominent regulatory areas of particular concern has been the creation of a 'common asylum policy,' a goal pursued by the European Union since the Tampere European Council in 1999.[6]

Through the efforts to create internal policy conformity and an increasingly active European Common Foreign and Security Policy ("CFSP"), disemboguing over the years in more than 30 civilian and military EU missions and interventions abroad,[7] the states forming the European Union have had a significant influence on protracted refugee situations. This impact has been felt both overseas (based on EU action–and inaction–abroad) and within the Union, where asylum policies have left refugees in legal limbo due to lack of coordination, willingness or ability among EU Member States to assume responsibility for asylum applications.[8]

This chapter examines the European Union's dual role as both a passive recipient and an active party with regard to refugee situations. On the one hand, the EU may be perceived as a safe and rather wealthy[9], 'luscious' destination of refuge, attracting, like Sirens once seafarers, now refugees, asylum seekers, and migrants alike.[10] On the other hand, the EU may be said to represent a powerful and at times seemingly harsh and ruthless actor–'Emperor'[11]–'fending off' and pushing back immigrants and others trying to reach its shores, and intervening in new and old crises abroad.

These two-fold characteristics evoke ambivalent impressions of the EU's role in, or contributions to, protracted refugee situations, applying, from a refugee's point of view, 'fears to hopes, and hopes to fears'[12]. This article assesses the evolution and status of the Common European Asylum System ("CEAS") and the EU's growing role and impact as a foreign policy actor involved in various international peace, stabilization, and security missions, evaluating the EU's track record in the area of asylum law and policy and foreign and security policy with respect to dealing with refugees within the EU and abroad.

The chapter starts with an introduction to the problems with the European asylum system, tracing the development of an EU-wide asylum policy that led to the creation of CEAS, examining its impact on refugees trying to gain access to protection within the European Union,[13] and assessing consequences and remaining challenges ahead (Section II). The ensuing section scrutinizes the EU's role as a foreign policy actor, focusing on EU interventions, missions, and other operations within the framework of CFSP, and what effect these actions–or omissions[14]–may have had on creating or sustaining unresolved refugee situations (Section III). After thus having examined two types of potential *explanans* for the creation or lack of resolution of various refugee situations, this chapter concludes by contemplating future challenges to the EU's CEAS and CFSP, taking into account the tension between the persistent forces of attraction and intervention (Section IV).

II. European Asylum Law and Policy

Commenting on European countries' attitude towards refugee flows in the wake of the Arab Spring, the United Nations High Commissioner for Refugees ("UNHCR") António Guterres called the European Union's asylum system "extremely dysfunctional."[15] In his opinion, faced with the 2011 events in North Africa, the dominant message from Europe had "not been of solidarity and enthusiasm, but of concern about a possible invasion of people."[16] That attitude, he indicated, needed to change.

As an illustration of the malfunctioning of the system, the head of UNHCR cited the wide variations in acceptance rates among EU Member States for refugees from the same country. For example, the chances for an Afghan refugee to prevail in his asylum claim last year ranged from 8% to 91%, depending on which EU Member State the application for protection was lodged in. Lack of generosity, a shrinking "humanitarian space", and unpredictability had become "the name of the game."[17] With a view to these shortcomings, Guterres pleaded "for the EU to review its attitudes on migration and to asylum, and try to build a new platform of cooperation with countries of origin, countries of transit and countries of destination on the issue of 'people on the move.'"[18]

To be sure, many of these points of critique have a global dimension, may be true of other regions as well, and are a reflection of the weakness of the international protection regime, which is built around individual (state) responsibility based on the requirements of the 1951 Refugee Convention,[19] yet depends on international cooperation, solidarity, and 'burden-sharing.' Terminologically, it would be more appropriate and more respectful towards refugees who seek protection, but also represent a human resource for the host states to which they flee, to rather use the expression 'responsibility-sharing.' After all, quite apart from moral obligations, taking in refugees is a legal responsibility flowing from the Refugee Convention.[20] I employ the term 'burden-sharing' deliberately, however, in order to emphasize this side of the problem. Bluntly speaking, if all states assumed their part of this shared legal 'responsibility,' there would be no 'burden' left to share.

Of course, few states or regions take in significantly more of a share of refugees than those who cross into their territory and apply for protection.

One path for states to increase their share consists in accepting a certain amount of quota refugees and providing 'third-country resettlement'[21] opportunities. Admission rates vary within other regions besides Europe, as do the types of protection or residence permits other regions grant, their duration and even the definitions they apply to 'people on the move.' Whether vulnerable people are defined as refugees, forced or voluntary migrants, internally displaced persons ("IDPs") or various other categories has an immediate impact on whether a receiving state will accept them on their territory. But irrespective of definitional or systemic actualities, as a matter of fact, countries closest to a conflict area usually receive and bear the lion's share of refugees, and as a political reality most of today's mass refugee crises, including those discussed in this volume, take place outside Europe.

Finally, taking these circumstances at face value, and stating the obvious, that generosity is "not proportionate to wealth,"[22] even where a country or region were to adopt a positive, yet realist, position towards assuming greater responsibility for refugees as a lode star for its asylum policy, it might still end up adopting a 'crisis situational approach': From a purely utilitarian point of view, having as a guiding principle to 'invest' resources as close as possible to the place of origin of a conflict or refugee situation might make sense.

For obvious reasons the first priority should be to prevent violent conflict and other 'refugee generating crises' *ab initio* (including those caused by natural disasters, climate change, and resource scarcity of any kind [23]).The second priority should consist of allocating help and resources in the country or region of crisis. Looking e.g. at the particularly war-prone North and South Kivu and Katanga provinces in the eastern part of the Democratic Republic of the Congo, such an approach would entail lending support to IDPs on the Congolese side, and refugee camps on the Tanzanian, Rwandan, or Zambian side. Help on the ground to Somali refugees in neighboring countries would mean allocating resources to Kenya,[24] while investing in the plight of Iraqi refugees would, until recently, have entailed sending money and foreign aid to neighboring Jordan and Syria. Of course, with the prolonged civil war in Syria, the direction of the flow of refugees is not so straightforward any more, and partly reversed, with many Syrians also fleeing to Iraq for protection.[25] A last priority, and currently the only *de lege lata* obligation flowing from the Refugee Convention, would be to assume responsibility for refugees coming to one's borders or crossing into one's country.

To be sure, the costs of 'processing' asylum applications and hosting refugees are notoriously hard to calculate, differ from country to country (including within the EU) and, as stated above, states should regard receiving and accepting refugees as an act of humanity, an asset, and a resource.

But if we, for the sake of argument, cynically and shortsightedly, were to look at the costs of having the current asylum system in place and then were to calculate the costs per refugee within a given country's asylum system, including application procedures and translations, potential appeals, lawyers, interpreters, time spent, housing, and many other facts and needs (not to mention the refugees' own expenses–material and immaterial ones), those resources could arguably be spent differently and yield more benefits for a greater number of refugees. In *that* sense, adopting a purely utilitarian line of reasoning towards resource allocation vis-à-vis refugees might be justified.

Norway may serve as a useful example. Although outside the EU, it is still bound by the EU laws and directives governing CEAS. Due to its salary level and costs of living, Norway will be on the upper end of the scale of costs, but even so, a cost-benefit calculation illustrates the utilitarian comparison quite well. Norway receives about 10,000 asylum applications each year. Based on 2013 numbers, the Norwegian Immigration Appeals Board alone (excluding about 50% of applicants who received asylum at the first instance through the Norwegian Directorate of Immigration[26]) spends about $51 million a year.[27] Of this figure, more than two thirds is spent on asylum appeals, the remainder on other matters of immigration, including appeals regarding applications for family unification, work permits, and the like. Far greater sums however are spent by the lower body, the Directorate of Immigration, whose budget covers everything from initial processing, asylum interviews, to interpreters and reception centers, thus amounting to about $705 million.[28]

Assuming that at least two thirds of this sum is spent on asylum applications,[29] even a conservative estimate amounts to $470 million. If one includes the Appeals Board budget spent on such cases, the figure rises to more than $500 million–and this is still restricted to the immediate costs associated with processing and adjudicating asylum applications, excluding resources spent on voluntary ('VARP')[30] and involuntary returns. VARP costs include seed money, reintegration support, airfare, and assistance from organizations such as IOM (International Organization for Migration). The costs of involuntary returns include police escorts and associated expenditures. Dividing the total costs by the number of total annual asylum claims lodged in Norway yields an estimated $50,000 per application–adjusted for successful applications, this number might even be twice as high.[31]

In order to avoid misunderstandings, this is not an argument to justify reducing domestic refugee reception capacities, or raising the bar to access to asylum. Rather, by employing a utilitarian approach, one can imagine just how much conditions could be improved for the lives of individuals in regions of crisis for the amount of just one flight made 'unnecessary'—that is, where sufficient resources had been invested to improve conditions before people were forced to flee. The potential benefit is even greater if one takes into account that in many of these countries the per capita GDP may be as low as a few hundred dollars[32].

Of course, having a focus on what could be done abroad, to the detriment of accepting refugees in the respective (Western) countries of asylum, any such argument would be at a loss for good answers to accusations of 'paying off' refugee flows and would attract suspicion–and often rightfully so–of having alternative motives. A prime example in that regard is the latest contribution to the discussion of refugee burden-sharing by Australian Prime Minister Kevin Rudd who announced a bilateral agreement with Nauru, according to which refugees arriving in Australia "will be sent offshore for processing and will be free to 'settle and reside in Nauru.'"[33] The announcement set off a firestorm of criticism for Australia's dubious motivations underlying the new policy.

There is no doubt that access to asylum and the right to seek protection should not be just a matter of money and numbers. Keeping borders open to refugees represents an intrinsic value, and a fundamental premise on which the international protection regime is built. But setting that aside for a moment, it is reasonable to conclude that states should and indeed *do* have every incentive to invest much more in the countries and regions of crises than they do today, to spend significantly more foreign aid in order to preempt the need of people fleeing over great distances, and to engage far more resources in overseas countries of refuge and asylum. Yet, caught in some combination of 'chicken game' and free-rider problem,[34] from a Refugee Convention's point of view, states are only directly responsible for refugees crossing their respective country's borders and thus, apparently only then, feel the need to react and spend significant resources on them.

The remainder of this section focuses on 'burden-' and 'responsibility-sharing' in the context of the EU asylum system from its first inception till now, and the challenges associated with the creation of CEAS.

II. 1. From Dublin to Stockholm and Beyond–Towards a Common European Asylum System (CEAS)

From the 1980s onwards, there has been increasing cooperation on matters of asylum and migration among European states. To begin with, this process took shape outside the framework of the then European Community. Subsequently, the Treaty of Maastricht[35] granted the EU competences, albeit initially still rather modest ones, in that field of law and policy overlap.

The origin of European cooperation on asylum may be traced to the work of the Ad Hoc Group on Migration,[36] established in 1986, which eventually led to the adoption of the *Convention determining the state responsible for examining an application for asylum lodged in one of the Member States of the European Community* in 1990, also known as the first *Dublin Convention.*[37]

As asylum applications in Western states were experiencing a peak,[38] the Treaty of Maastricht formally transferred intergovernmental cooperation on asylum and migration into the institutional framework of the EU, identifying asylum in article K of the Treaty as one of the so-called nine "matters of common interest" in Justice and Home Affairs ("JHA"), and emphasizing that these matters were to be dealt with in compliance with the 1950 European Convention on Human Rights[39] and the 1951 Refugee Convention.

In practice, the specific institutional arrangements established by the Treaty of Maastricht[40] meant that EU Member States remained the dominant actors in the early stages of the EU asylum policy. The European Council was only required to "fully associate" the Commission to its work on asylum, and to keep the European Parliament informed about its asylum initiatives. The European Court of Justice had no jurisdiction in matters of asylum.[41]

II.1.a The First Phase of CEAS–Tampere

These parameters were soon to change. Following the adoption of the Treaty of Amsterdam in 1997 and its entry into force on 1 May 1999,[42] the EU launched the first phase of CEAS, the so-called Tampere Programme, charged with implementing the Treaty provisions. According to Article 73(k)[43] of the Treaty of Amsterdam, the Council was to adopt a series of measures, viz. criteria and mechanisms for determining the Member State responsible for considering an asylum application; minimum standards concerning the reception of refugees; a definition of 'refugee'; and procedures governing the asylum process. Article 73(k) also called for the adoption of minimum standards regarding the granting of temporary protection to displaced persons and persons otherwise in need of international protection, and for furthering a balance of efforts ('burden-sharing') among Member States.

Furthermore, article 73(p)[44] of the Treaty of Amsterdam strengthened the role of the European Court of Justice in asylum matters, albeit restricting its jurisdiction to specific instances. For example, according to article 68.3 (ex article 73(p), "[t]he Council, the Commission or a Member State may request the Court of Justice to give a ruling on a question of interpretation of this Title ['Title IV–Visas, Asylum, Immigration and other Policies Related to Free Movement of Persons'], but the ruling given by the Court in response to such a request "shall not apply to judgments of courts or tribunals of the Member States which have become res judicata." Moreover, under article 68.2, the Court was not to have "jurisdiction to rule on any measure or decision taken pursuant to Article 62(1) relating to the maintenance of law and order and the safeguarding of internal security."

While giving the European Court of Justice at least some formal role, the Treaty of Amsterdam ensured that the Court would not be in a position to challenge (or be able to overturn) final decisions of Member States' domestic courts, or Member States' domestic or inter-EU border control measures.

The Tampere Summit aimed at following up on these new (Amsterdam) Treaty provisions, and stated in its conclusions for the first time the EU's intentions to develop a 'Common European Asylum System', which was meant to encompass not only common legal standards, but also a more coordinated European asylum policy, and in that sense went significantly beyond Amsterdam. While the Treaty of Amsterdam had only provided for the adoption of 'minimum standards,' at Tampere the EU heads of state and government foresaw the adoption of *common* minimum standards, eventually leading to "a common asylum procedure and a uniform status for those who are granted asylum valid throughout the Union."[45]

In fulfilling the requirements of the Amsterdam Treaty, the first phase of CEAS saw the adoption of a number of legislative instruments pertaining to the subjects qualifying for protection, the procedures employed for determining protection status, and the reception conditions in the various EU Member States. The Temporary Protection Directive[46] established provisions on temporary protection for displaced persons in the context of a mass influx of persons in need of protection. The existence of a 'mass influx' situation was to be collectively determined by the Council with a qualified majority vote. However, every Member State was to assess its own reception capacity in a spirit of 'Community solidarity.'[47]

Hence, while representing a first attempt at 'burden-sharing,' absent any financial burden (re)distribution or legal enforcement mechanisms, 'sharing' was still mainly restricted to a moral sense of responsibility and solidarity.

The Reception Conditions Directive[48] laid down minimum standards regarding the reception of asylum seekers, which every Member State was required to provide, including information distributed upon arrival, freedom of movement, residence, material reception conditions, and health care. While the Reception Directive may be regarded as being motivated, in part, by the goal of reducing the perceived need or incentives for asylum seekers to move from one Member State to another in search of somehow decent enough reception conditions, the so-called Dublin II Regulation[49] establishing the criteria and mechanisms for determining the Member State responsible for examining an asylum application lodged in one Member State by a third-country national, was spurred in at least equal measure by the needs and interests of the receiving states. Based on criteria of state responsibility, the regulation aimed at coping with problems associated with so-called "'asylum-shopping' (i.e. multiple applications for asylum across the EU by the same person) and 'refugees in orbit' (i.e. asylum-seekers unable to find a State accepting to examine their application in the EU)."[50]

One of the core principles underlying the Dublin system stipulates that the state responsible for the presence of an asylum seeker in the territory of the EU—that is, the state representing the applicant's 'port of entry' into the EU—is the state responsible for processing his or her application, with mandatory transfers and returns to that state of first entry within the EU, if and where such initial entry may be established.

The Asylum Qualification Directive[51] then turned from those mainly procedural aspects to the more substantive legal rules. It established "minimum standards for the qualification and status of third-country nationals or stateless persons as refugee or as persons who otherwise need international protection and the content of the protection granted," outlining the criteria for qualifying for refugee status, or subsidiary protection, respectively. Compared to what had been the norm in most EU Member States prior to the adoption of this legal instrument, the Qualification Directive represented a positive *novum* in several ways. For the purpose of refugee status determination, the Directive now also recognized non-state actors as potential actors of persecution or serious harm; it codified previous *ad hoc* practices of complementary protection, thus establishing a 'subsidiary protection' regime;[52] and it broadened the scope of the concept of 'acts of persecution.'

In sum, the Qualification Directive led to several fundamental changes in a number of Member States' asylum legislation and practice,[53] which, in turn, reinforced the new EU asylum regime.

The Asylum Procedures Directive[54] provided minimum standards with respect to asylum procedures within a Member State pertaining to access to asylum, the right to personal interviews, legal assistance and representation, appeals, and detention, among other issues. This was in distinct contrast to the Dublin II Regulations, which pertained mostly to the organization of such procedures across the EU between Member States. The Directive also defined the concepts of 'safe country of origin' and 'safe third country,' which granted Member States a right to dispense with examining an application for asylum lodged by a person originating from, or having transited through, a country considered as 'safe'. These provisions were to gain importance in ensuing discussions of Member States' return options regarding refused applicants for asylum.

This first phase of CEAS was generally successful in establishing a common ground regarding qualification for refugee status, temporary protection, asylum procedures, and reception conditions, albeit–in line with its point of departure–only on the level of 'minimum standards.'

To be sure, for some states even such leveling meant a significant increase in asylum and protection standards offered,[55] and Member States with preexisting or intended higher protection standards were free to retain or adopt them. However, in a collective protection regime with inherent free-rider problems, incentives for an individual state to introduce (from a refugee's vantage point) more favorable conditions than the bare minimum required are, unsurprisingly, largely absent.

II.1.b The Second Phase of CEAS–The Hague

Starting in 2004 with the adoption of the Hague Programme,[56] CEAS entered its second phase, which aimed at moving beyond minimum standards to develop a European protection regime based on common asylum procedures, and a subsidiary protection or refugee status valid throughout the EU. The Hague Programme for the first time contemplated the possibility of jointly processing asylum applications, both inside and outside the EU. It also introduced the idea of a 'European support office' to enhance practical cooperation among Member States,[57] which eventually was to disembogue into the European Asylum Support Office ("EASO"). Other proposals, which aimed at overcoming flaws in the first phase of CEAS, included 'recasts'[58] of the various directives and regulations pertaining to reception conditions, asylum procedures, asylum qualification, and responsibility allocation for asylum applications across the EU. Putting these suggestions into a binding agreement proved more difficult though.

The Treaty of Lisbon, entering into force on 1 December 2009, remedied some of those shortcomings.[59] It enabled the EU to

> adopt measures for a common European asylum system comprising: (a) a uniform status of asylum for nationals of third countries, valid throughout the Union; (b) a uniform status of subsidiary protection for nationals of third countries who, without obtaining European asylum, are in need of international protection; (c) a common system of temporary protection for displaced persons in the event of a massive inflow; (d) common procedures for the granting and withdrawing of uniform asylum or subsidiary protection status; (e) criteria and mechanisms for determining which Member State is responsible for considering an application for asylum or subsidiary protection; (f) standards concerning the conditions for the reception of applicants for asylum or subsidiary protection; (g) partnership and cooperation with third countries for the purpose of managing inflows of people applying for asylum or subsidiary or temporary protection.[60]

The Lisbon Treaty also stated that any common policy on asylum, subsidiary, and temporary protection must be in accordance with the 1951 Refugee Convention, and other relevant treaties.[61] It accepted the Charter of Fundamental Rights of the European Union[62] (which now included in its Article 18, as amended by the Treaty, a "right to asylum") as binding on all Member States[63], and provided for the EU to accede, as an entity, to the European Convention for the Protection of Human Rights and Fundamental Freedoms.[64]

Furthermore, "[i]n the event of one or more Member States being confronted by an emergency situation characterised by a sudden inflow of nationals of third countries" the Treaty envisaged that "the Council, on a proposal from the Commission, may adopt provisional measures for the benefit of the Member State(s) concerned. . . after consulting the European Parliament."[65]

Finally, the Treaty of Lisbon expanded the European Court of Justice's competence to all matters pertaining to the Area of Freedom, Security and Justice ("AFSJ"), including EU asylum policy,[66] and strengthened the role of the European Parliament in asylum matters by including this area of competence in its ordinary legislative procedure[67] (thereby reducing the influence of the Council).

While the Treaty of Lisbon thus included a number of potential improvements, going beyond mere minimum standards and towards higher common standards in asylum matters, it suffered from a lack of any deadlines and hence of teeth and incentives. This contrasted sharply with the Amsterdam Treaty, which had stated that the various measures had to be adopted within five years of the Treaty's entry into force. For example, Article 63b of the Lisbon Treaty stipulates that implementation of the various measures under Chapter 2 ('Policies on Border Checks, Asylum and Immigration') "shall be governed by the principle of solidarity and fair sharing of responsibility." However, specific acts of solidarity and responsibility sharing, such as those for the benefit of a Member State experiencing a sudden inflow of nationals from third countries, still depended on 'provisional measures' that may or may not be adopted by the Council following proposal from the Commission, and after consultation with the European Parliament.

Considering the diverging interests at stake and the rather cumbersome procedures even in emergency situations, it does perhaps not come as a surprise that, to date, few of the various suggested changes to the EU asylum regime have actually been adopted or 'recast,' as provided for in the Dublin Treaty.

II.1.c The Third Phase of CEAS–Stockholm and Beyond

Finally, at the Stockholm meeting, Member States negotiated follow-up measures to the Treaty of Dublin. The so-called Stockholm Programme,[68] the EU's latest five-year 'action plan' thus far, envisioned the establishment of a "common area of protection and solidarity based on a common asylum procedure and a uniform status for those granted international protection," and contemplated the possibility of joint processing of asylum applications, coordinated by a European Asylum Support Office (EASO).[69] While this Programme further acknowledged the need to promote "[e]ffective solidarity with the Member States facing particular pressure,"[70] the proposed means still appeared to be inadequate. No compulsory 'burden-sharing' was suggested. Instead, the EU continued to rely on "voluntary and coordinated sharing of responsibility"[71]–with all the downfalls such a generally noble idea entails in the face of free-rider problems. Some of those challenges and shortcomings are discussed below.

The first legally binding aftermath of the Stockholm negotiations was the adoption of the recast[72] Qualification Directive (Directive 2011/95/EU)[73] pertaining to the standards for the qualification of third-country nationals or stateless persons as beneficiaries of international protection. Not surprisingly (considering it being of more than just a political nature), while recognizing the Stockholm Programme's objective of establishing a common area of protection and solidarity, the recast Qualification Directive included rather scaled-down ambitions.

To be sure, it proclaimed that, in line with the 1989 United Nations Convention on the Rights of the Child, "[t]he 'best interests of the child' should be a primary consideration of Member States when implementing this Directive,"[74] and emphasized that, absent necessary and objectively justified exceptions, "beneficiaries of subsidiary protection status should be granted the same rights and benefits as those enjoyed by refugees."[75] The Directive claimed that its overriding objective was to create a uniform status of protection throughout the EU which "cannot be sufficiently achieved by the Member States," but, due to its scale and effects, would "be better achieved at Union level." However, apart from those few, positive developments the document stopped right there, leaving to the future measures that the Union "may adopt" to that end.[76]

Thus, aside from confirming the principles underlying the original Directive 2004/83/EC, the recast only "to achieve a *higher level of approximation* of the rules on the recognition and content of international protection on the basis of higher standards."[77] To that end, resources of the European Refugee Fund and of the European Asylum Support Office are to be mobilized to support Member States in their efforts to implement the standards set forth in the second phase of CEAS, "in particular . . . those Member States which are faced with specific and disproportionate pressure on their asylum systems, due in particular to their geographical or demographic situation."[78]

The most recent follow up to the Stockholm Programme occurred on 26 June 2013 when the EU passed three further legislative acts in the area of asylum law and policy, two recast directives, and one recast regulation.[79] Regulation No 604/2013[80] establishing the criteria and mechanisms for determining the Member State responsible for examining an application for international protection represented a recast of Council Regulation (EC) No 343/2003, now also including stateless persons within its purview in addition to third-country nationals. Under the heading of 'solidarity measures,' the recast Regulation advocates establishing an Asylum Intervention Pool, within the framework of EASO, consisting of asylum support teams. These teams are tasked with assisting Member States facing particular pressure, and where applicants for international protection are unable to benefit from adequate standards.[81]

Acknowledging that "a well-functioning Dublin system is essential for the CEAS," the Regulation foresees a "comprehensive 'fitness check,'" consisting of "an evidence-based review covering the legal, economic and social effects of the Dublin system, including its effects on fundamental rights."[82] It also aspires to establish a process of early warning, aiming at detecting and ultimately preventing the deterioration, or collapse of asylum systems.[83] Where the European Commission establishes that a Member State's asylum system is not functioning properly, "it shall, in cooperation with EASO, make recommendations to that Member State, inviting it to draw up a preventive action plan"[84] and, that failing to produce results, it can request a "crisis management action plan" be drawn up "at the latest within three months of the request."[85]

The Regulation strengthens the rights of families by expanding the definition of dependency relations that are to be protected. It establishes that family ties which trigger a binding responsibility criterion regarding the Member State responsible for examining an application for international protection may also consist of "a relation of dependency between an applicant and his or her child, sibling or parent on account of the applicant's pregnancy, maternity, state of health, or old age."[86]

Furthermore, it enhances the rights of applicants in underlining that "Member States shall provide for a *reasonable* period of time within which the person concerned may exercise his or her right to an effective remedy"[87] in the form of an appeal or review, in fact and in law, against the decision to be transferred to another Member State for examination of an application for protection. But aside from those few improvements regarding an applicant's legal position, the threat of a non-functioning or substandard asylum system, whether brought about by outside pressure or internal policies, or a combination thereof, is ultimately still only to be remedied by recommendations to the Member State concerned—and by a future, hoped-for early warning system, and an aspiration of "genuine and practical solidarity" among Member States.[88]

The recast Asylum Procedures Directive (Directive 2013/32/EU[89]) on common procedures for granting and withdrawing international protection also lays claim to the principles of solidarity and fair sharing of responsibility.[90] With the help of EASO and the European Refugee Fund, it aims at further approximation and development of procedural rules throughout the Union, including providing adequate training to officials likely to first come into contact with potential applicants, *i.e.* those officials conducting land and maritime border surveillance, in order to enhance their ability to recognize and deal with applications for international protection.[91]

To avoid secondary movements of applicants, the Directive calls for common criteria for designating a third country as a safe country of origin, *i.e.* a country to which, absent specific or exceptional arguments to the contrary, an applicant generally may be returned.[92] In the case of States Parties to the European Convention for the Protection of Human Rights and Fundamental Freedoms, the concept of a 'safe country' may entail "that no, or no full, examination of the application for international protection" has to take place.

However, applicants shall be allowed to challenge the application of the concept of a "European safe country on the grounds that the third country concerned is not safe *in his or her particular circumstances*."[93] Extradition of an applicant to other third countries may in any case only take place where there is no risk of direct or indirect *refoulement*.[94] In other words, the competent authorities must be satisfied that an applicant would neither be returned to persecution or torture, inhuman or degrading treatment or punishment in his home country, nor be extradited from there to another country where he or she may risk such serious harm.

While Member States shall ensure that examination procedures in the first instance are concluded within six months of the lodging of the application, in complex cases, situation of mass influx of applicants or lack of collaboration on the part of the applicant, this time limit may be extended to fifteen months.[95] Where the situation in the country of origin is uncertain and makes it difficult for the responsible authorities to decide, another six months may be added. In any event, procedures shall be concluded "within a maximum time limit of 21 months from the lodging of the application."[96]

Similar to the recast Regulation, the recast Procedures Directive raises some minimum standards with regard to the maximum length of time for an application to be decided at first instance, and with respect to an applicant's right to appeal the application of the concept of a 'European safe county' to his individual case. Whether such appeals are given proper consideration by the various national authorities and how the other enhancements actually play out remains to be seen.

Finally, among the substantive changes introduced by the recast Reception Directive (Directive 2012/33/EU[97]) on standards for the reception of applicants for international protection are prohibiting the imposition of "*unnecessary or disproportionate* documentation or other administrative requirements on applicants before granting them the rights to which they are entitled,"[98]and restricting detention to specific needs associated with identity verification, forced return of an applicant, national security or public order. A person may not be detained for the sole reason that he or she is an applicant for international protection, and the grounds for detention must be established in national law.[99] Also, Member States are not only to "put in place relevant mechanisms in order to ensure that appropriate guidance, monitoring and control of the level of reception conditions are established," but are henceforth required to "submit relevant information" in that regard to the European Commission.[100]

The recast Reception Directive thus puts certain restrictions on the way Member States may limit applicants' rights, and obliges them to report on the measures taken in order to ensure reception conditions are of a certain standard. But how 'unnecessary or disproportionate documentation requirements' or 'national security or public order' needs will be interpreted, and what effect a duty to report on national reception conditions to the European Commission will have on the reception standards across the European Union, only the future will show.

The recast Qualification Directive, the first of the 'revamped' legislative acts following the adoption of the Stockholm Programme, defined as its main objective "to ensure that Member States apply common criteria for the identification of persons genuinely in need of international protection […] and to ensure that a minimum level of benefits is available for those persons in all Member States."[101] One of its key aims was to "help to limit the secondary movement of applicants for international protection between Member States, where such movement is purely caused by differences in legal frameworks."[102] The ensuing Regulations and Directives introduced EASO and the European Refugee Fund as resources to be used in detecting and ultimately preventing the breakdown of asylum systems within the EU, raising minimum standards regarding procedures and reception conditions, and promoting 'genuine and practical solidarity' within the EU. However, for the time being, aspirations for establishing a truly uniform area of asylum, with joint asylum application processing across Member States and refugee status valid throughout the EU seem to have been put on hold.

But such 'modesty' also—and perhaps unwittingly—points to challenges on a much deeper level, engrained in the spinal cord of national jurisprudence that forms the backbone of every 'living'[103] legal system. In fact, as Guy Goodwin-Gill has stated, "[m]any currently perceived divergences in national practice under the Refugee Convention may be more about the facts and appreciations of facts, than about law or 'interpretation', strictly so called."[104]

Hence, even if the 'level of approximation' were to reach its highest plane, with identical legal norms in all participating countries, the outcome of *e.g.* a refugee status determination process might still vary across the

EU, and "the idea of a fully uniform system [may] be an impossible target, even within the European Union and a Common European Asylum System."[105] While adopting a common legal basis is of vital importance in any attempt at sowing the seeds of a unified legal system, its success may depend on externalities that can only be outlined, not guaranteed by the legal texts themselves.

In the *de facto* absence[106] of an international court tasked with enforcing the rules laid down in the Refugee Convention (as initially envisioned in the Convention's Article 38,[107] stipulating that disputes, but then also only between States Parties, be settled by the International Court of Justice), achieving a genuinely uniform legal framework, application, and area of protection, may depend on jurisprudential cooperation across borders.

In that sense, it may be argued that as long as the EU consists of sovereign states with diverging legal systems and traditions, "the role of transnational jurisprudence (and therefore of national courts and tribunals as decision-makers) is […] essential to the establishment of a truly 'common' European asylum system."[108]

The various recasts contributed to raising the standards of protection in certain Member States by promoting, for example, 'the best interest of the child' as a primary consideration, and establishing subsidiary protection on an equal footing with refugee status. The Stockholm Programme is correct in aiming for a uniform refugee status throughout the Union and in realizing that absent such unity "[e]ffective solidarity with the Member States facing particular pressure"[109] needs to be promoted. Alas, progress with respect to enforcing much needed responsibility-sharing is still slow. Meanwhile, problems related to differences in standards, geography and resources continue.

II.2 From Sirenum Scopulos to Lampedusa–Persisting Challenges to CEAS

While the refugee regime was initially designed to cope with the aftermath of the Second World War and hence focused on European refugees fleeing the horrors and consequences of war, today the majority of migrants and refugees entering Western, and especially European states, travel from afar. Though forming part of the same area constituting the European Union, for geopolitical reasons, since the Southern regions often represent the closest port of entry into Europe, countries in the South and Southeast of Europe such as Italy and Greece are more likely to receive large numbers of refugees, mainly from Asian and African countries, than their Central and Northern European counterparts. They are, unfortunately, bearing the brunt of the EU asylum policies designed to avert so-called 'asylum-shopping,' the activity of applying multiple times in different countries for asylum.

The Dublin II regime was established precisely to prevent asylum shopping; it is based on the premise that the territory where a person enters the EU to seek asylum determines where his or her application has to be processed and decided. Whenever it was detected that a person had made a second application in another EU Member State or other state participating in the Dublin regime, that applicant would be sent back to the country through which he initially entered. That, however, further contributed to an unbalanced 'burden-sharing' status quo with countries closest to the ports of entry receiving the highest number of asylum seekers. While the already deteriorating system of refugee status determination and reception capacities in some particularly exposed EU countries degenerated further due to lack of economic resources and perhaps also incentives,[110] countries at the periphery, such as those in the north of Europe, received an unduly low share of the total number of applicants entering the EU.

The conflicting interests were highlighted in the *M.S.S. v. Belgium & Greece*[111] case before the Grand Chamber of the European Court of Human Rights, which underscores some of the inherent challenges to CEAS. The applicant, M.S.S., had entered the EU through Greece, where he had been fingerprinted, detained, and then issued with an order to leave the country. He left Greece, traveled through France, and entered Belgium, where he applied for asylum, basing his claim for protection on the risk of being murdered by the Taliban in reprisal for his work as an interpreter for the international air force troops stationed in Kabul. During the registration process, Belgian authorities discovered that M.S.S. had already been registered in Greece and, based on Article 10 § 1 of the Dublin Regulation, submitted a request to the Greek authorities to take charge of his asylum application as the first country of entry into the 'Dublin area'–irrespective of the fact that, at the time, it was known that Greece, overwhelmed by the number of asylum seekers arriving at its borders, had no functioning asylum system. When Greek authorities failed to respond within the two-month period provided for in Article 18 § 1 of the Regulation, Belgium, considering this to be a tacit acceptance of its request, transferred the applicant to Greece, where he was first detained and eventually released pending the outcome of his asylum request–with poor prospects of receiving any real examination of the merits of his asylum application, or any effective remedy to challenge his detention and living conditions.

As to Greece, the Grand Chamber acknowledged that states which form the external borders of the European Union, were experiencing considerable difficulties in coping with the increasing influx of migrants and refugees, and that the situation was exacerbated by the transfers of asylum seekers by other Member States in application of the Dublin Regulation, especially in the present context of the economic crisis. However, the Court emphasized that "having regard to the absolute character of Article 3 (of the European Convention on Human Rights, prohibiting torture, and inhuman or degrading treatment or punishment), that cannot absolve a State of its obligations under that provision."[112]

As to Belgium, the Court held *inter alia* that it would be incompatible with the purpose and object of the Refugee Convention for States Parties to the Dublin Regulation to be absolved of all responsibility *vis-à-vis* the Convention within the "Dublin area." Accession to the Dublin Regulation and other international treaties was not in itself sufficient to ensure adequate protection against ill-treatment, especially where, as in the present case, reliable sources reported asylum practices that clearly violated principles of the Convention. In such circumstances, Belgium as the transferring state should not merely have assumed that the applicant would be treated in conformity with the Convention standards, but should also have verified how the receiving country, Greece, actually applied its asylum legislation and procedures.[113]

The Court's opinion criticized both countries: Greece for the current conditions of detention and subsistence awaiting asylum seekers, and Belgium for "intentional blindness" for failing to properly scrutinize the adequacy of protection against *refoulement* in Greece, despite the fact that circumstances had called for application of the sovereignty clause. However, the Grand Chamber's judgment also exposed serious flaws in the current European asylum regime, based as it is on a presumption of equality and cooperation among safe countries, but still failing to adequately account for systemic inequalities and states' self-interest. The judgment acknowledged those challenges, yet underlined that neither uneven burden-distribution (Greece), nor a state's minimalist reading of the Dublin Regulation (Belgium), could absolve Member States of their responsibilities *vis-à-vis* the Convention or other applicable international treaties, including the 1951 Refugee Convention.

In order to control the growing number of refugees and migrants attempting to enter Europe, Frontex, the EU's joint border patrol force, has increased its activities in recent years by dispatching patrol boats to the Aegean Sea to block arrival of mostly African irregular immigrants and refugees, and by heightening control around the EU's outer (land) frontiers such as those near the Greek town of Nea Vissa, bordering Turkey, which has become a main corridor for illegal entry into Europe by Middle Eastern and North African people seeking protection, or a better future[114].

This 'surge' in Frontex activity has been criticized for attaching paramount importance to preventing entry of migrants and asylum seekers, rather than protecting human beings who have the right to, and are in need of, protection. To put policies into perspective, in 2012 the Frontex budget amounted to almost 90 million euros, while the office tasked with enhancing protection standards throughout the EU (EASO) was left with little more than 10 million euros. At the same time, in October 2013, the European border surveillance system ("EUROSUR"), the EU's new electronic wall, was to be launched, with an estimated cost of about 338 million euros for the period 2011-2020, further reducing many people's chances of even applying for asylum.[115]

The danger of sacrificing fundamental rights in the face of countervailing forces has also been expressed in a recent report of the Committee on Migration, Refugees, and Displaced Persons to the Parliamentary Assembly, Council of Europe, on the human rights responsibilities of the border agency:

> Frontex has to face the difficulty of having two masters: the European Union and its member States. In Brussels, the latter might be very keen on respecting human rights. However, back in their capitals and at the borders, they may see the priority more in terms of migration management.[116]

Upset by the uneven distribution of burden within the EU asylum system, countries on top of the port of entry statistics increasingly also aimed at entering into bilateral agreements with countries serving as hubs on the way to Europe. As a case in point, prior to the ousting and death of Muammar Gaddafi, Italy and Libya reportedly executed an agreement that compensated Libya in return for cracking down on illegal migration routes stemming from, or in any case leading through, Libya. That agreement included an opening for Italian authorities to swiftly return intercepted boat migrants to Libya–a country which is not a State Party to the Refugee Convention–before they could even reach Italian shores. The agreement was criticized for not sufficiently differentiating between illegal migrants and genuine refugees, and in many cases not even having the necessary procedures in place for making a well-informed decision in regard to refugee status determinations of the people intercepted at sea before they were returned.[117]

In the 2012 case of *Hirsi Jamaa and others v. Italy,*[118] the European Court of Human Rights, again sitting as a Grand Chamber, reiterated the gist of the judgment in *M.S.S. v. Belgium & Greece*, and observed that

> Libya's failure to comply with its international obligations was one of the facts denounced in the international reports of that country. In any event, [...] the existence of domestic laws and the ratification of international treaties guaranteeing respect for fundamental rights [as in said bilateral agreement between Italy and Libya] are not in themselves sufficient to ensure adequate protection against the risk of ill-treatment where, as in the present case, reliable sources have reported practices resorted to or tolerated by the authorities which are manifestly contrary to the principles of the Convention [...] Italy cannot evade its own responsibility by relying on its obligations arising out of bilateral agreements with Libya.[119]

Thus, the Court unanimously held that there had been a violation of Article 3 of the European Convention on Human Rights on the part of Italy by exposing the applicants to the risk of being subjected to ill-treatment in Libya and to being repatriated to Somalia and Eritrea, the applicants' home countries from which they had fled.

Concerns have also been raised that readmission agreements, even where their conclusion would not be contrary *per se* to any provisions of international law, contribute to potential violations of refugee rights, including the denial of access to protection due to the accelerated procedures of expulsion which generally form part of such accords.[120] Paying-off and redirecting refugee flows in that fashion to countries less concerned with, or feeling less bound by, the Refugee Convention–and the granting of rights pronounced therein–jeopardizes the fairness of the asylum system and thus the very idea underlying the concept of granting protection to those in need. With the fall of Gaddafi and the rise of new regimes in various countries in the region in the aftermath of the Arab Spring, that particular agreement had been discontinued, and now even larger groups of people are fleeing at the present time. None of this has helped individuals already prevented from applying for protection.

Even in the absence of restrictive, bilateral agreements, people attempting to cross into Europe face numerous hazards and obstacles. With tightened border controls, people trying to enter the EU are taking ever-greater risks in order to literally find an opening and sometimes their 'port of entry' is merely a rock, such as the small Italian island of Lampedusa, 127 miles off Sicily and 70 miles off Tunis. Lampedusa, due to its remote location *en route* from North Africa to Europe, has become the first, and often last, destination of many migrants and refugees taking to the sea, risking the journey to safety in overcrowded and unsuitable craft, only to come–if they make it at all–to an equally overcrowded island, with few chances of proceeding any further.

The latest tragedy of Lampedusa, and one of the worst disasters in recent years, occurred in early October 2013, when a vessel carrying about 500 African migrants and refugees sank less than half a mile off the shore of this tiny island, killing at least 250 people.[121] The disaster raised anew questions regarding the EU border regime and the strict Italian immigration laws.[122]

Like the Sirens in Greek mythology calling upon (soon to be forlorn) seafarers, luring them with their enchanting music and voices to shipwreck, the lure of Europe combined with the many obstacles of safely reaching its shores has become many a refugee's undoing. And while ancient writers did not entirely agree on where to place what Virgil[123] and Ovid[124] had called Sirenum scopulos (Siren Island), in many ways Lampedusa has become its modern day counterpart.

II.3 Improving the System?

As discussed above, from its inception until today, the idea of establishing a European approach to asylum has undergone many changes and revisions, and while it has raised the level of protection in some areas, in others the leveling across the EU has had a detrimental effect on people's access to asylum. And despite continuous, albeit slow progress, many challenges remain to be addressed.

But what should an active, positive European asylum law and policy be? What could contribute to resolving the sort of protracted refugee situations discussed throughout this volume?

Although it is feasible to have much better international conflict monitoring systems in place, it will never be entirely possible to prevent crisis situations, whether caused by armed conflict, environmental disasters, or other forces. There will always be refugees and people in need of protection. Europe's contribution may consist of various forms of aid offered abroad, in the country or region mostly affected by such crises; however, its greatest contribution at present is its approach towards receiving and dealing with refugees as a Union—for better or for worse.

Some desirable enhancements to the current EU asylum *acquis* have already been pronounced in the various EU work plans (most recently the Stockholm Programme), although in the face of Member States' resistance not all have found their way into a recast or new directive yet. Notably, at Stockholm the possibility of joint processing of asylum applications, coordinated by EASO, was suggested, to reduce the need or incentives for applicants to engage in secondary movements within the European Union in search of a better chance of applying for and receiving international protection. Transforming such 'EU asylum *desiderata*' into binding law would be a starting point. But more is needed.

One proposal is the establishment of unified, centralized asylum processing conducted by mixed asylum teams of officers of various nationalities. These might be structured along the lines of the Asylum Intervention Pool, and tasked with deploying asylum support teams, but on a permanent basis and not just for countries and regions temporarily experiencing a high influx of migrants and asylum seekers. At minimum, a higher level of regular, institutionalized exchange of personnel should be pondered. The more unified the asylum procedures and assessments, the more even-handed they might be expected to be conducted across the EU. And perhaps it might be worth considering the establishment of a central institution to process all asylum applications within the EU that would decide on refugee status valid throughout the Union, and then distribute successful applicants across the EU according to a quota system. This might work in similar fashion to the current system operated by UNHCR of states accepting a certain quota of refugees for resettlement in their country.

To be sure, as *e.g.* James Hathaway has underlined,[125] one may claim that the right to seek asylum also includes a right to decide where to apply for asylum, rendering a rule that restricts a refugee's choice in that regard contrary to international law. Such a concern would certainly be valid in the context of a first country of entry/asylum discussion, where an asylum seeker's fingerprints–even if taken against his will, while he was trying to transit through one, in order to apply in another state–could determine where his application for asylum would be decided, and a right to stay granted or denied. However, if a unified and centralized asylum procedure could be established, with refugee status valid throughout the EU, such argument would become obsolete. If the same asylum system were to apply to the entire Union, with an ensuing right to move and eventually settle anywhere within its borders, the need or right to apply at a specific port of entry would evaporate.

Furthermore, the EU should significantly increase the number of UNHCR refugees accepted for resettlement. Generally speaking, the vast majority of those the most in need of help and protection never even make it to the shores and borders of Europe. After all, while the exact flight routes are often unknown, being on the run and traveling great distances is demanding and expensive. On average, only those who are relatively resourceful stand a chance of being able to pay for, undertake and survive such a trip. All the others tend to be more easily forgotten. It is with respect to these, the most vulnerable left behind, that the EU has the greatest potential to change its course, increase its efforts and 'make a difference.'

In addition, there needs to be a re-orientation from the single-minded focus on security to greater humanitarian need. While border control is a necessary and legitimate concern, a greater focus on refugee protection, as opposed to the too- defensive approach taken by Frontex, seems to be called for, understanding refugees foremost as people in need, not as a potential threat to Europe. Of course, as has been pointed out, where an application lodged at a specific port of entry remains the respective country's obligation, any plan for a more 'human' and refugee focused approach to Frontex' border control remains a lofty promise. The national implementers (which Frontex consists of and depends on) lack incentives to put their best efforts into such an approach, knowing that they ultimately create more obligations for their own states.

However, as long as the EU and CEAS are composed of individual Member States as opposed to a 'United States of Europe,' individual states will be responsible for independently assessing each asylum claim, providing appropriate procedures, reception, and living conditions. Considering the reluctance of Member States to adopt significant changes to the current state of affairs, even in the face and aftermath of the recent Lampedusa disasters, true burden sharing may still have to travel a long way before becoming a reality. In the meantime, closer scrutiny, reporting requirements, and an active use of EASO and the European Refugee Fund, with a view to balancing uneven burden distribution, may be the best to hope for.

III. The EU's Role as a Foreign Policy Actor

Under the umbrella of the CFSP and the Common Security and Defence Policy ("CSDP"), along with the European External Action Service ("EEAS") headed by the High Representative of the Union for Foreign Affairs and Security Policy, established in 2010,[126] the EU has become increasingly active on the international level. It has launched some 30 international security, stabilization, and peace missions abroad, of a civilian as well as military character.[127] From the Congo to Kosovo, from Somalia to South Sudan, through action and inaction abroad, the states forming the European Union have had a at times significant impact on the lives and living conditions of people in the respective countries and regions affected, including on various protracted refugee situations originating there. In the same way, EU foreign policy decisions to invite, support, fight, or blacklist certain groups of people but not others, thereby engaging in political trade-offs, have directly or indirectly contributed to inflict pain and suffering on those in need and deserving of help.

In the ensuing section, various EU actions and omissions will be presented and evaluated, highlighting the fact that all political decisions to engage or disengage in conflicts and crisis situations have the potential to seriously affect the lives of a great number of people, and that an omission to act, or (re)act, in an appropriate way, may entail just as much responsibility as an active intervention abroad.

To be sure, EU Member States, individually or as a group, are often engaged overseas in collaboration with other states and organizations, including the UN and its various agencies, with NATO, or with more loosely defined 'coalitions of the willing.' States also employ soft power in the form of development aid which, contrary to pronounced goals, may have unintended repercussions. As has been pointed out in the Congo context, though it is just as valid elsewhere:

> [D]onors . . . usually insist that this money is politically neutral, that it does not directly benefit the political elite. This is true, as most of the money is for schools, roads, health care, and water projects. But *all development is deeply political.* By taking over the financing of most public services, donors take pressure off . . . the government to respond to the needs of its citizens.[128]

Having these alternative and at times competing avenues to achieving foreign policy goals in mind is important when attempting to gauge the EU's role as a foreign policy actor. As the above lines have indicated, discarding actions taken and contributions made by Member States, individually or as partners in separate operations, the EU's impact *as a Union* remains rather limited. Even in situations where Member States engage in joint action as a European Union, their room to maneuver varies significantly, depending on a mission's mandate; whether a mission has been invited by the respective country; the situation 'on the ground;' whether the government is in control throughout the country or several domestic, regional, or international actors are competing for influence; whether a violent conflict is still unfolding; or whether the crisis situation mainly pertains to the result of 'force majeure.'

But while the scope of intervention may depend on such variables, there is always a certain 'margin of appreciation' when faced with a given situation, and that margin may be applied towards acting–and attempting to improve in some way the conditions of live, if not to say the chances of survival, for those affected–or failing to act. In the following, a number of such decisions and their consequences, *i.e.* resulting missions or omission, will be depicted, paying particular attention to some of the most neglected refugee situations.

III.1 EU Missions and Interventions Abroad

About one third of all EU missions launched abroad have been in part, or in their entirety of a military character. However, as this does not seem to have been their distinctive feature with respect to their success, or failure, in the following no distinction will be made in that regard when presenting various cases. Rather, the depiction will follow a chronological order in this non-exclusive list.

III.1.a Democratic Republic of the Congo (DRC)

While war had been raging in this country since 1998, it was not until 2003 that the European Union became directly engaged. Following a peace agreement between the DRC and the Ugandan government and removal of Ugandan troops from the Eastern Congolese region of Ituri, fighting erupted again between various militia factions, leading to a major humanitarian crisis with about 500,000 to 600,000 IDPs. With the 700 United Nations Organization Mission in the Democratic Republic of the Congo ("MONUC") troops stationed there unable to address the situation appropriately, the EU Member States decided, encouraged by the UN Secretary General, to launch Operation Artemis ("RD Congo") within the framework of its European security and defense policy.[129] EU Artemis would create an historical example, as it was the "first European military operation deployed without NATO support."[130]

The mission's mandate was to stabilize the security conditions and improve the humanitarian situation in Bunia, the main town in the Ituri region of the Orientale province, and one of the many recurring points of conflict in the war-torn eastern part of the DRC. The mission was also tasked with protecting the airport and the IDPs in the camps in Bunia, and with generally contributing to the safety of the civilian population. The operation consisted of about 2,000 troops, concentrated around the town of Bunia, and lasted for only three months. The troops quickly secured the airport, the five entry points to Bunia, and forced the militia fighters to withdraw before eventually handing over power to a newly deployed UN contingent. Due to its quite limited scope, it is hard to gauge the mission's success.[131] In the short run, Operation Artemis fulfilled the mandate's objective of securing the airport, town, and population. However, shortly after the mission's withdrawal, fighting erupted anew and has continued in short intervals. When fighting peaked again in the Kivu region in late 2008, the EU decided not to intervene.[132] Even today, strife and armed conflict is a fact of life for a great many people in the eastern part of the DRC, in particular in the eastern-most provinces of Katanga, North- and South Kivu, and Orientale.

The EU's next active mission in the DRC was EUPOL Kinshasa,[133] the first civilian European defense and security operation to be deployed in Africa, whose main purpose was to support the Congolese National Police's Integrated Police Unit in keeping order during the electoral period in 2006. The EU's police mission deployed from April 2005 to June 2007, following a request by the Congolese authorities. Taking the fragile internal security situation in the aftermath of the national elections into account, EUPOL Kinshasa was not discontinued, but rather transformed into EUPOL RD Congo in 2007.[134] EUPOL RD Congo's mandate continues today, and has evolved over time to include providing assistance, mentoring, support and advice to the Congolese authorities on all matters of security sector reform ("SSR"), policing and its interaction with the justice system. EUPOL RD Congo eventually expanded its deployments to encompass police reform in Goma (North Kivu) and Bukavu (South Kivu), though the impact of this extension has been limited due to persistent fighting in this part of the country. Addressing active warfare is outside the mission's civilian mandate.

Both missions seem to have suffered from the ambivalent consequences of their success, and the above stated fact that all development aid is deeply politicized.

As to the latter, by improving the transitional government's capacity to deal with mass demonstrations and political rallies during the crucial periods of the electoral campaign, the EU missions may have unduly and perhaps unwittingly chosen sides in a supposedly open and democratic electoral competition. By taking some of the 'heat' off the incumbents, the missions' contribution may have made it easier for the government to concentrate its resources on winning the elections without adequately paying heed towards the population's needs.

As to the former, the government of Joseph Kabila, which prevailed in both the 2006 and in the 2011 elections, aided in part by these EU missions, felt legitimized, and seemed "less keen to pursue a genuine police reform, thereby reducing opportunities for international cooperation and incentives for coordination among donors."[135] This ultimately reduced the international community's leverage for positive change, whether within SSR in general, or in regard to the plight of the most vulnerable people.

Following an official request by the Congolese government, the EU decided to establish an advisory and assistance mission for security reform in the DRC ("EUSEC RD Congo"[136]). The mission's mandate included supporting the integration of the Congolese army, good governance in the field of security, army reform–in particular separating the chain of payment from the chain of command–and conducting a census of the Congolese army. EUSEC was groundbreaking for EU foreign and security policy in that it was "the first of its kind; a 'civilian' mission designed to provide 'military' advice."[137] Along with EUPOL RD Congo, the EUSEC mission is still ongoing though its mandate has evolved over time and now explicitly includes a gender focus, and the protection of children affected by armed conflict.

EUSEC may be credited with a number of achievements, notably conducting a census to establish the actual number of soldiers in the armed forces with the help of biometric records and military identity cards. The effort to separate the chain of payment from the chain of command[138] also contributed to better oversight, enhancing the pay and standing of the individual soldier, and, by extension, reducing soldiers' incentives to extort the population.

While some of these achievements may have also contributed to improving the situation of the most vulnerable people, serious obstacles reduce the likelihood of a lasting, positive impact. Once commanding officers could no longer unabatedly siphon off soldiers' pay, they soon found other ways of diverting funds.[139] Furthermore, the mission's SSR efforts had to be conducted in a context of protracted armed conflict, which added to an environment of unpredictability. Finally, despite EUSEC's efforts to introduce a statute outlining the conditions under which prospective soldiers (including former rebels) may join (or be integrated into) the new army, and to address the equally urgent subject of soldiers' sexual abuse of the population,[140] "[t]o date, no vetting has ever taken place. As a result numerous unsavory characters joined the new integrated army, sometimes in senior positions,"[141] with all the negative repercussions this may have for the orderly conduct of soldiers in the army, and for the refugee, IDP, or otherwise most vulnerable population at large.

Finally, following adoption of UN SC Resolution 1671 (2006) on 25 April 2006, authorizing the temporary deployment of an EU force to support MONUC, the EU launched a military operation (EUFOR RD

Congo[142]) assisting MONUC during the election process (along with EUPOL Kinshasa, the EU's civilian mission which had already been deployed at that time). EUFOR RD Congo was conducted in full agreement with the DRC authorities and in close cooperation with them and MONUC. In addition to exerting a stabilizing role during the election process, its mandate included deterrence of violence, protection of civilians, airport protection in Kinshasa and, if need be, evacuation of individuals in danger. EUFOR consisted of about 4,000 troops and was deployed for four months, starting on 30 July 2006, and concentrated its activities on the capital Kinshasa.

Akin to the problems faced by EUPOL Kinshasa, and perhaps not surprisingly, considering its cooperation with the sitting regime, EUFOR was initially suspected of partiality and to support incumbent president Kabila by the local population.[143] While some of these prejudices diminished in the course of the mission, given its scant geographical and temporal scope, EUFOR's success remained limited. Even though its mere presence may have had a preventive effect, it did not face any serious military challenges during its time of deployment and critics argued that the European "Union welcomed the operation mainly for internal purposes in that it afforded an opportunity to show the EU flag and to demonstrate the Union's military capabilities and autonomy."[144] Certainly, its rather limited presence and duration may be questioned. In any case, once EUFOR had left the DRC, conflict between president Kabila and the opposition erupted again, as the country as a whole was neither safer, nor the individual less vulnerable than before, and especially in the eastern parts, violent conflict continues still today.[145]

III.1.b Chad/Central African Republic

Chad has been at war since 1964, with continued instability on the Chad-Sudan-Central African Republic borders linked to the presence of groups across all three borders that are directly or indirectly involved in various kinds of violence. In 2003-2004 the first massive inflow of refugees from Darfur entered Chad, exacerbating an existing Chadian internal political crisis and local tensions between ethnic groups. By 2006 the situation had turned into a humanitarian disaster.[146] Attacks from Sudanese (at times via the Central African Republic) and Chadian armed groups and Janjaweed militias targeting specific ethnic communities, the use of recruitment camps and child soldiers, and a general environment of impunity led the international community to call for international intervention to restore security and protect the population in the area.

The EU, unable to intervene directly in Sudan, eventually decided to "act on the margin of Darfur, i.e. in the neighbouring region of Chad where around 400,000 refugees and displaced people had fled."[147] With French-led efforts to mobilize its European partners, a joint action under UNSC Resolution 1778 of 25 September 2007 was eventually adopted, leading to the launch of a military mission (EUFOR Tchad/RCA[148]) on March 2008. The mission's mandate, complementary to the UN Mission to Central African Republic and Chad ("MINURCAT"), lasted a year, and consisted of 3,700 troops. The mandate included protecting civilians in danger, in particular refugees and internally displaced persons, facilitating the delivery of humanitarian aid, and generally helping to improve security in the area. It was the logistically most complex operation deployed within the framework of CFSP thus far.[149]

Challenges in terms of cooperation were twofold. On the one hand, as the mission was meant to work along with, and eventually hand over the reins to, MINURCAT, cooperation with the United Nations was crucial. Some in the UN Department of Peacekeeping Operations ("UN DPKO") however, had voiced opposition to the very idea of having a peacekeeping operation in Eastern Chad, based on concerns that the conditions identified by the Brahimi Report[150]—that there needs to be a peace to keep, firm commitments of troops, and a clear mandate and instructions—had not been satisfied. On the other hand, Chadian authorities were also hard to convince, as they feared an international presence would limit their room for maneuver.[151]

While there seems to have been consensus that EUFOR Tchad/RCA contributed to a safer environment and increased security, at least in the area where the soldiers patrolled, there also were concerns about a security vacuum created by the departure of the mission. Furthermore, in an effort to prove the success of the mission, pressure was apparently brought to bear to prematurely induce substantial IDP returns.[152] EUFOR Tchad/RCA has been the largest, most multinational EU operation in Africa thus far, with 23 cooperating EU Member States. When the mission ended, the European Council hailed its success, and stated the European Union would remain "active at a political and diplomatic level in Chad, in the Central African Republic and especially in Sudan."[153]

Considering that the security and humanitarian situation in the region today remains highly volatile, the mission's success in terms of its mandate of protecting civilians in danger, in particular refugees and IDPs, is at least questionable. It also points to the more general problem of measuring success where an acute refugee flow and crisis turns into a protracted refugee situation, which persists far beyond an operation's time frame and mandate, and may raise questions about the sensibility of (relatively) short missions in the face of potentially long-lasting crises, which ethnically-fueled conflicts, as in the present case, have a tendency to turn into.

III.1.c Somalia

Following decades of fighting in Somalia, the *de facto* absence of a central government, and a continuing increase in piracy activity off the coast of Somalia, the UNSC adopted a number of resolutions, calling on states and regional organizations to "undertake all necessary measures that are appropriate in Somalia, for the purpose of suppressing acts of piracy,"[154] and asking all states "to criminalize piracy under their domestic law and favourably consider the prosecution of suspected, and imprisonment of convicted, pirates apprehended off the coast of Somalia."[155]

Paying heed to those resolutions, states intensified their presence in the Gulf of Aden, which included the first-ever European Union-led naval force ("EU NAVFOR") executing operation "Atalanta."[156] While there was general recognition that the root causes of piracy are to be found in Somalia's protracted internal crisis and that a maritime operation alone would not adequately address the problem of a weak or 'failed state' *per se*, it was also recognized that some aspects of piracy constituted a direct threat to the lives of the Somali population.[157] Having a piracy problem in one's 'maritime backyard' or being associated with a piracy infested region in turn further undermines the legitimacy of an already weak government and "increases pressure towards falling into the latter category of the weak state/failed state continuum,"[158] and contributes to the need for countermeasures.

The launching of *Atlanta* came in the context of an already grave humanitarian situation in Somalia, which, *inter alia*, has led to a refugee population of close to half a million Somalis in the Dadaab refugee camp in Kenya alone. *Atalanta*'s mandate, extended most recently until December 2014 and now also covering Somali coastal territory and internal waters in its Area of Operation,[159] includes a broad range of protection activities. It is entrusted with safeguarding World Food Programme ("WFP") vessels delivering aid to displaced persons in Somalia; protecting other vulnerable shipping off the Somali coast; and deterring, preventing and repressing suspected pirates. The last part of the mission allows the EU navies to resort to force to deter acts of piracy and armed robbery at sea, and, where necessary, to arrest, detain, transfer and prosecute suspected pirates.

Based on the sheer size of the area to be covered, even the limited focus of a mission confined to the oceans faced major challenges.

> With presence, however, comes the problem of effective patrolling, which again is closely tied to the concept of jurisdiction and law enforcement . . . in practice, states patrolling the Gulf of Aden have shied away from prosecuting, sometimes even from arresting, suspected pirates due to anticipated legal difficulties and expenses. Yet, without serious and visible efforts at prosecution and punishment, the preventive and deterring effect of increased patrols is at best reduced.[160]

EU NAVFOR in cooperation with NATO and other international operations, and on-board security measures adopted by the shipping industry, eventually contributed to some decline in successful pirate attacks off Somalia. The specific effect of the various efforts is, however, not easily established, as the increased international military presence also has led to a diversification and spread of pirates' area of operation, moving towards less patrolled and policed territory. Improvement of the security and humanitarian situation within Somalia beyond the protection of WFP shipments would require more than a maritime operation.

Realizing that the challenges around the Horn of Africa would depend on a comprehensive approach, including efforts to promote political progress, governance, rule of law, and responses to development and humanitarian needs, the European Union established EUTM Somalia[161] in support of UNSC Resolution 1872 (2009). EUTM Somalia, launched in April 2010, is an EU military training mission tasked with strengthening the Somali Federal Government and Somali government institutions. In accordance with its mandate, the mission aims at "improving the living conditions of the population, including in the field of security and delivery of basic services . . . [and] supports . . . the search for an inclusive process in Somalia."[162] Its mandate currently runs until March 2015. Despite some modest progress and the establishment of a federal government after many years of a transitional government, the government and the federal state will continue to be weak, and the security and humanitarian situation for the population continue to be challenging for years to come.

III.1.d Mali

After Islamist fighters captured two-thirds of the country in 2012, and amid growing fears in Europe that Mali could turn into a platform for future terrorist attacks,[163] the European Union eventually launched a training mission for Mali armed forces, EUTM Mali,[164] on 18 February

2013. The mission, established at the request of the Malian authorities and in accordance with UNSC Resolution 2085 (2012), aims at restoring constitutional and democratic order. It assists the Malian authorities to exercise full sovereignty over the entire country; to neutralize organized crime and terrorist attacks by providing expertise and advice, in particular regarding logistics, command and control; and to train combat units. The mission's mandate does not include combat operations, however. EUTM is based in part on the EU's comprehensive Strategy for Security and Development in the Sahel, recognizing that the Sahel is one of the poorest regions in the world which simultaneously

> faces . . . the challenges of extreme poverty, the effects of climate change, frequent food crises, rapid population growth, fragile governance, corruption, unresolved internal tensions, the risk of violent extremism and radicalisation, illicit trafficking and terrorist-linked security threats.[165]

At the core of the Strategy lies the insight that the "problems facing the Sahel not only affect the local populations but increasingly impact directly on the interests of European citizens" as the "fragility of governments impacts on the stability of the region and the ability to combat both poverty and security threats." Realizing that "[p]overty creates inherent instability that can impact on uncontrolled migratory flows" and that the "security threat from terrorist activity by Al-Qaida in the Maghreb (AQIM), which has found a sanctuary in Northern Mali, is focused on Western targets," the Sahel Strategy in general, and EUTM Mali in particular, may be described just as much as a European preventive and defensive operation as a mission in support a government under attack, or a population suffering the mutually reinforcing consequences of poverty, food shortage, and armed conflict. EUTM Mali's initial mandate is for 15 months. Evaluating the mission's success may have to wait until long after the end of that time frame.

III.2 EU Omissions and Trade-Offs

While there may be many ways of circumscribing a neglected refugee situation, a good point of departure may be to contemplate the so-called CNN-effect at play; scrutinize how much attention a given situation has received in the media relative to the actual scope of the problem. The 2004 Tsunami represents a prime example, where governments around the world pledged more money in one week than was made available to the United Nations' emergency assistance for all of Africa.[166]

Neglect is a political act of intentional overlooking. It may entail just as much responsibility as its counterpart, engagement, the decision to actively face a crisis situation. In its 2013 report,[167] the Norwegian Refugee Council ("NRC") identified the following (here in alphabetical order) as ten of the most neglected refugee situations in the world: Burma (Myanmar), Central African Republic, Democratic Republic of the Congo, India, Indonesia (West Papua), Iraq, North Korea, Nigeria, Sudan (Darfur), and Western Sahara.

Some of these country's refugee situations continue in their protracted state despite and sometimes because of being the subject of missions and operations. Many are far from being solved or even near a solution, while others reflect EU decisions to neglect them by not sending any (civilian or military) mission, or not contributing in any way whatsoever. Of course, apart from various missions, there are many ways of helping to alleviate a crisis situation, including providing development aid. Also, sometimes, in spite of willingness to act, actively intervening, or being present in a country is not an option, for geopolitical, military, or other reasons. At times, the EU cannot agree on a common policy or has chosen not to act, in (misguided) deference to a Member State with particular interests in the respective country of crisis. Furthermore, the EU is just one of many international actors. But where the end result is one of broad neglect, as in the refugee situations stated above, at least co-responsibility, if not complicity, may be assumed. Some of these situations have been described in other chapters in this volume.

Burma (Myanmar) is still among the countries with a major refugee and IDP problem, despite recent progress in other areas including the first signs of a less repressive regime. More than 200,000 people are regarded by the authorities as illegal immigrants, 125,000 IDPs were living in the state of Rakhine alone, most of them in overcrowded camps without basic services.[168]

More than ten years after the US-led invasion of Iraq and the ousting of the Baath regime, the security situation in that country is still highly volatile; an estimated 1.1 million people are internally displaced, and almost 800,000 refugees live in neighboring countries. At the same time, Syrians are increasingly fleeing across the border these days, with more than 140,000 people already living as refugees in Iraq.[169]

The Central African Republic ("CAR"), despite having been a crisis in the making for quite some years, and in spite of the EU having had a mission (EUFOR Tchad/RCA) in the country, today represents one of the most crucial humanitarian crises, with 206,000 IDPs, 88% of whom live in constant fear, and 200,000 refugees from CAR having fled to neighboring countries.

The Democratic Republic of the Congo ("DRC") has been a focal point of EU operations and missions abroad for more than a decade, but despite progress on some levels, overall the missions have been marred by various degrees of administrative infighting, coordination problems, underfunding, restrictive mandates, lack of commitment of participating states, and a general inability of the international community as a whole to engage long enough at a time in order to understand and deal comprehensively with the country's complex problems. Last year's attack on Goma in the eastern part of DRC by the militia group M23 alone caused the displacement of an additional 140,000 people.

And while the EU arguably has sufficient leverage to help find a solution to the Western Sahara protracted refugee situation, with more than 165,000 Saharawi refugees living in Algeria ever since the Moroccan occupation in 1975, some EU Member States have defended a *status quo* that is neither in line with moral obligations, nor with international law.[170] Despite UN recognition of POLISARIO as the representative of the people of Western Sahara, active, positive EU engagement with the group is limited.

Finally, similar acts of omission, presumably equally based on attempted or expected trade-offs, explain the treatment accorded the People's Mojahedin Organization of Iran ("PMOI"), which was put, and then kept for many years, on a terrorist black list for no justifiable reason, as has eventually been admitted and proven in various courts.[171]

As a matter of fact, European diplomats had previously acknowledged that the PMOI figured prominently as a bargaining chip, with Tehran insisting that the PMOI be listed as terrorists in exchange for benevolent behavior of various kinds, and also to the U.S. such furtive overtures were not foreign.[172] The unwarranted terrorist designation not only seriously hampered the organization's participation in international political fora to present their case and advocate their cause; it also effectively prevented its members from receiving refugee status and the opportunity to resettle in a safe country. In the meantime, their members were under lethal attack in their current host country (Iraq), and faced persecution in their home country (Iran), in spite of previously having formally received status from the United States as protected persons under the Fourth Geneva Convention.[173]

In an effort to redeem themselves from false accusations of being involved in terrorism, and placed on a terror list, the PMOI eventually turned to the European Court of Justice.[174] Already in a 2006 judgment, the Court of First Instance[175] ruled that a Council decision placing the PMOI on the terror list was unlawful,[176] which in turn led the Proscribed Organisations Appeal Commission ("POAC") to characterize the ensuing decision of the United Kingdom Home Secretary (who had initiated placing the group on an EU terror list) to keep the PMOI on the terror list as "perverse."[177] Subsequent efforts on the part of France to appeal the judgment removing the PMOI from the EU list of terrorist organizations were finally dismissed by the Grand Chamber of the Court of Justice on 21 December 2011,[178] reconfirming the former court's judgment and evaluation of the terrorist organization designation procedure as severely flawed.

Interestingly, in a related decision in the United States, following a petition for a writ of mandamus filed by the PMOI in response to the U.S. Secretary of State's failure to make a final, judicially reviewable decision on the organization's terrorist designation, a U.S. Court of Appeals first criticized the Secretary's progress in responding to the initial petition for removal from the terror list as "ha[ving] been–to say the least–slow going,"[179] before ordering her to either deny or grant the PMOI's petition not later than four months from the date of the issuance of its opinion. If the Secretary failed to act within that period of time, the Court indicated that it would grant the petition for a writ of mandamus setting aside the terrorist designation. On September 21, 2012, ten days before the court-imposed deadline, the Secretary of State announced she would delist the PMOI. The terrorist designation has now been effectively revoked.[180]

IV. Conclusion

No state, nor union of states, acts in a vacuum, and every action or omission may have serious consequences. And while a union may act in unison, it is accountable vis-à-vis each of its members, and responsible to the outside world for all acts of its member states. The European Union possesses such a dual role, in general in its internal and external relations, and in particular as both a passive recipient or bystander, and an active party in regard to refugee situations, both at home and abroad.

In light of increasing refugee flows, one of the EU's main challenges is to strike a balance between establishing a common legal basis, and not exacerbating geographical or economic differences across the Member States that lead to a dysfunctional asylum system. The actions taken since Stockholm, with various recast Directives and Regulations being adopted, were a step towards the idea of a truly uniform EU refugee regime, but progress with respect to enforcing much needed responsibility-sharing is still slow. Considering resources wasted on insufficiently organized domestic asylum procedures, there is plenty of room for improvement. If all EU Member States were to assume a fair part of their shared responsibility, there should not be any burden left to share.

Perhaps most striking, though not surprising, is the view of the big picture. Looking at the burden shared by countries neighboring some of the most fatal, violent, and war-torn regions and areas of protracted conflict, the contribution of European countries looks quite bleak, and serves as a befitting reminder that much more could and should be done by better-off regions, such as the EU, to both take in more of the most vulnerable refugees and spend more resources on enhancing the situation of refugees abroad. At times the EU has been actively engaged in civilian and military missions and operations abroad, intervening or omitting to act in crisis areas with varying success, and for a variety of motives, often under the concealing umbrella of a common foreign and security policy.

As the chapters in this volume have demonstrated, successfully countering protracted refugee situations depends on strong, concerted, and long-term commitment by national, regional, and international actors. But the major lesson may be that protection for all those who are still waiting for tomorrow may only materialize when the law prevails over the politics underlying unresolved refugee crises.

Notes

[*] The author is Co-Chair of the International Refugee Law Interest Group of the American Society of International Law and currently serves at the Norwegian Immigration Appeals Board. He has previously taught at the University of Oslo and at Boston University as a Lecturer in International Law and Visiting Fulbright Scholar. The views expressed in this chapter are those of the author alone and do not necessarily reflect the views of the Norwegian Immigration Appeals Board.

[1] WILLIAM SHAKESPEARE, *Sonnet CXIX, in* THE ILLUSTRATED STRATFORD SHAKESPEARE, 1020 (Bounty Books, 1993).

[2] The EU "is more than a regime, but less than a fully-fledged federation." Christian Kaunert & Sarah Léonard, *The European Union Asylum Policy after the Treaty of Lisbon and the Stockholm Programme: Towards Supranational Governance in a Common Area of Protection?,* 31 REFUGEE SURV. Q. 1, 5 (2012). Due to the complexity of the European Union governing system supranationalism exists only in the two European Communities inside the EU, *i.e.* the Economic Community, and the European Atomic Energy Community (EURATOM). Asylum matters are not yet governed supranationally.

[3] There are other organizations, such as the African Union (AU), the Association of Southeast Asian Nations (ASEAN), the Caribbean Community (CARICOM), Cooperation Council for the Arab States of the Gulf (CCASG), the Union of South

American Nations (UNASUR), or the League of Arab States which have adopted some policies that may eventually lead to greater integration of the kind ascribed to the EU, but none is currently even close to intending as much. Thus, with regard to normative theoretical discussion of supranational entities, the EU still remains "the only available model." Rainer Bauböck, *Why European Citizenship? Normative Approaches to a Supranational Union*, 8 THEORETICAL INQUIRIES IN L. 453, 455 (2007).

[4] Lithuania formally declared restoration of independence from the Soviet Union, Estonia and Latvia followed suit on Aug. 20, 1991 and Aug. 21, 1991, respectively, and the Czech Republic and present-day Slovakia became independent states on Jan. 1, 1993, after the peaceful dissolution of Czechoslovakia.

[5] Formally, the Treaty on European Union (TEU), signed on Feb. 7, 1992.

[6] Presidency Conclusions, Tampere European Council (Oct. 15-16, 1999).

[7] Under the umbrella of the Common Foreign and Security Policy (CFSP) and the Common Security and Defence Policy (CSDP), the EU has launched some 30 international security, stabilization, and peace missions abroad. For an overview, *see* European Union External Action Service (EEAS), Security and Defence–CSDP, *available at* http://www.eeas.europa.eu/csdp/index_en.htm.

[8] For an illustrative report with a particular focus on the lack of appropriate reception conditions in Greece and Turkey, and the failure of the EU's asylum system to adequately cope with those flaws, *see e.g.* Hum. Rts. Watch, *Stuck in a Revolving Door: Iraqis and Other Asylum Seekers and Migrants at the Greece/Turkey Entrance to the European Union*, 1-56432-411-7 (Nov. 26, 2008).

[9] According to Eurostat (the statistical office of the European Union), the economy of the European Union generated a GDP (Gross Domestic Product) of more than €12,894 trillion (close to $17,000) in 2012, making it the largest economy in the world (data *available at* http://epp.eurostat.ec.europa.eu/tgm/table.do?tab=table&init=1&language=en&pcode=tec00001&plugin=1). And while GDPs and standards of living vary greatly within the EU, even the EU-wide average GDP of €25,600 (about $34,000) per capita (in comparison, the United States is listed at €39,300 or about $52,100), is still exponentially more than the GDP per capita for the ten countries where the most people fled from in 2012. Syria, Mali, Sudan, Somalia, Democratic Republic of the Congo, Eritrea, South-Sudan, Côte d'Ivoire, Iraq, Afghanistan, average at less than $1,314 (calculated based on data taken from NORWEGIAN REFUGEE COUNCIL, FLYKTNINGREGNSKAPET 2013 ['REFUGEE BALANCE 2013'] 143 (2013), and UNITED NATIONS, NATIONAL ACCOUNTS MAIN AGGREGATES DATABASE (DEC. 2012), UNITED NATIONS STATISTICS DIVISION (using 2011 numbers as the most recent data set), *available at* http://unstats.un.org/unsd/snaama/selbasicFast.asp.) The poorest three among those countries in GDP per capita (Somalia: $112; Democratic Republic of the Congo: $237; Eritrea: $482) lag even further behind.

[10] 'Refugees' here refers to persons fulfilling the requirements of the 1951 Refugee Convention; 'asylum seekers' denotes persons applying for protection also on other than Convention grounds. 'Forced migrants' is a generic term for all persons compelled to leaving their former home (country), but is employed here to refer to

persons not necessarily seeking protection from harm suffered at the hands of others, but rather alleviation of a nature- or socio-economically inflicted situation, such as famine, poverty, natural disasters etc.

[11] This term is employed here to emphasize the powerful impact EU asylum law and foreign policy may have on those affected by its actions. Apart from that, of course, no comparisons with monarchical titles or powers are intended.

[12] Shakespeare, *supra* note 1, at 1020.

[13] Through association agreements and the so-called Schengen Treaty, EU asylum laws and policy, such as the various EU Directives, are also applied outside the confines of the EU Member States. This is also true for Norway, which is not a state within the EU, yet, as a member of the 'Schengen-area,' is bound by those Directives.

[14] As Jason K. Stearns put it, with particular regard to the long-lasting conflict in the Congo: "Overall, however, the greatest sins of Western governments have been ones of omission and ignorance, not of direct exploitation," JASON STEARNS, DANCING IN THE GLORY OF MONSTERS: THE COLLAPSE OF THE CONGO AND THE GREAT WAR OF AFRICA, XXII (Public Affairs, 2012).

[15] *UN Official Calls EU's Asylum System 'Extremely Dysfunctional'*, EURACTIVE. COM (Mar. 21, 2012), *available at* http://www.euractiv.com/justice/un-official-calls-eus-asylum-sys-news-511622.

[16] *Id.*

[17] *Id.*

[18] *Id.*

[19] United Nations Convention Relating to the Status of Refugees, July 28, 1951, 189 U.N.T.S. 150 (entered into force on Apr. 22, 1954) [hereinafter 'Refugee Convention'].

[20] *Cf. id.*, at art. 3 ("The Contracting States shall apply the provisions of this Convention to refugees without discrimination as to race, religion or country of origin").

[21] *See also* Bill Frelick's chapter on 'Unlocking Protracted Refugee Situations: Lessons from Four Asian Case Studies' in this volume.

[22] *See supra* note 15.

[23] *See also* Agnès Hurwitz' chapter on 'Climate-related Displacement: The Perilous Path towards Normative Development' in this volume.

[24] Dadaab in Kenya remains the largest refugee camp in the world today, housing more than 450,000 Somali refugees.

[25] *See* Michele Pistone's chapter on 'The Iraqi Refugee Crisis and the U.S. Response' in this volume.

[26] In Norway, everyone has a right to appeal, and receives free legal aid up to the appeals level. Thus, understandably, practically everyone not receiving a positive decision at the lower instance does in fact exercise his right to appeal.

[27]*See* Justis-og Beredskapsdepartementet ['Ministry of Justice and Public Security'], Tildelingsbrev 2013 Utlendingsnemnda ['Budget 2013 Norwegian Immigration Appeals Board'] 12 (Jan. 29, 2013), *available at*

http://www.regjeringen.no/upload/JD/Vedlegg/tildelingsbrev/Tildelingsbrev_UNE_2013.pdf.
[28] *See* Justis- og Beredskapsdepartementet, Tildelingsbrev 2013 Utlendingsdirektoratet ['Budget 2013 Norwegian Directorate of Immigration'] 20-21 (Jan. 29, 2013), *available at* http://www.regjeringen.no/upload/JD/Vedlegg/tildelingsbrev/Tildelingsbrev_UDI_2013.pdf.
[29] And likely much more, as the largest post in the budget (about $250 million) is reserved for costs associated with (refugee) reception centers–which, by definition, are only concerned with people applying for protection, not with other aspects pertaining to immigration.
[30] To be sure, the term 'Voluntary Assisted Return Program' ('VARP') for rejected asylum seekers has been criticized for its euphemism, as it disregards the absence, or in any case strong reduction, of the element of voluntarism in the face of an often imminent threat of an expulsion order.
[31] According to data provided by IMDI ['Directorate of Integration and Diversity'], in 2012 about 9,800 persons applied for asylum, half of whom received a positive decision at the lower instance, and about one thousand were accepted upon appeal. In addition, another thousand refugees were accepted for resettlement (mostly in cooperation with UNHCR), thus introducing a further element of uncertainty with respect to the above numbers for 'application expenditures'. *See* IMDI, FAKTA OM ASYLSØKERE OG FLYKTNINGER ['FACTS ON ASYLUM SEEKERS AND REFUGEES'], *available at* http://www.imdi.no/no/Fakta-og-statistikk/Fakta-om-asylsokere-og-flyktninger/ .
[32] For the Democratic Republic of the Congo per capita GDP in 2011 was a mere $237, for Somalia $112, and even the per capita GDP of the ten countries where most people fled from in 2012 averaged only $1,314. *See also supra* note 9.
[33] Cf. *Kevin Rudd Announces New Asylum Seeker Processing and Refugee Settlement Deal with Nauru*, ABC NEWS, Aug. 5, 2013, *available at* http://www.abc.net.au/news/2013-08-03/rudd-announces-asylum-policy/4863226. To be fair, some of the rhetoric may be attributed to the election campaign in Australia at the time. However, the mere fact that parties even consider such a stance beneficial to their election prospects is quite telling.
[34] *I.e.*, the delusive perception that, on the one hand, whichever country opens its gates first or widest (lowers its legal bars to granting applications for refugee status), will be 'stuck' with the largest share of all refugees, and, on the other hand, the more one country contributes in terms of taking in refugees, the less others have to deal with.
[35] Treaty on European Union, Jul. 20. 1992, 1992 O.J. (C 191)(entry into force on Nov. 11, 1993) [hereinafter Treaty of Maastricht].
[36] E. Guild, *The Impetus to Harmonise: Asylum Policy in the European Union in* REFUGEE RIGHTS AND REALITIES: EVOLVING INTERNATIONAL CONCEPTS AND REGIMES 313 (F. Nichols & P. Twomey eds.,Cambridge University Press 1999).
[37] Official Journal, 1997 O.J. (C 254/1).

[38] El-Enany, Nadine & Thielemann, Eiko R. *The impact of EU asylum policy on national asylum regimes in* THE AREA OF FREEDOM, SECURITY AND JUSTICE: MYTH OR REALITY? TAKING STOCK OF THE LISBON TREATY AND THE STOCKHOLM PROGRAMME 98 (Wolff, Sarah, Goudappel, Flora & de Zwaan, Jaap W. eds., Asser Press 2011).

[39] Convention for the Protection of Human Rights and Fundamental Freedoms, as amended by Protocols Nos. 11 and 14, Nov. 4, 1950, ETS 5 (entry into force on Sep. 3, 1953).

[40] *See in particular* articles K.4 and K.6 of the Treaty of Maastricht.

[41] Christian Kaunert & Sarah Léonard, *supra* note 2 at 8.

[42] Treaty of Amsterdam Amending the Treaty on European Union, the Treaties Establishing the European Communities and Related Acts, Oct. 2, 1997, 1997 O.J. (C 340).

[43] In the Consolidated Version of the Treaty Establishing the European Community (TEC), Dec. 29, 2006, 2006 O.J. (C 321/E/1), this article was to be renamed Article 63.

[44] To become Article 68 in the consolidated version of the Treaty.

[45] Presidency Conclusions, *supra* note 6.

[46] Council Directive 2001/55/EC, 2001 O.J. (L 212/12), of 20 July 2001 on minimum standards for giving temporary protection in the event of a mass influx of displaced persons and on measures promoting a balance of efforts between Member States in receiving such persons and bearing the consequences thereof.

[47] K. Hailbronner, *Asylum Law in the Context of a European Migration Policy in* EUROPE'S AREA OF FREEDOM, SECURITY AND JUSTICE 41 (N. Walker ed., Oxford University Press 2004).

[48] Council Directive 2003/9/EC, 2003 O.J. (L31/18) of 27 January 2003 laying down minimum standards for the reception of asylum seekers.

[49] Council Regulation 343/2003, 2003 O.J. (L 50/1) (EC), of 18 February 2003 establishing the criteria and mechanisms for determining the Member State responsible for examining an asylum application lodged in one of the Member States by a third-country national.

[50] Christian Kaunert & Sarah Léonard, *supra* note 2, at 11.

[51] Council Directive 2004/83/EC, 2004 O.J. (L 304/12), of 29 April 2004 on minimum standards for the qualification and status of third-country nationals or stateless persons as refugees or as persons who otherwise need international protection and the content of the protection granted.

[52] *See e.g.* Jane McAdam, *The European Union Qualification Directive: The Creation of a Subsidiary Protection Regime*, 17 INT'L J. OF REFUGEE L. 461 (2008) (generally praising the codification process, but criticizing the disproportionate differentiation made between refugees and those receiving subsidiary protection).

[53] H. Storey, *EU Refugee Qualification Directive: A Brave New World?*, 20 INT'L J. OF REFUGEE L., 1 (2008).

[54] Council Directive 2005/85/EC, 2005 O.J. (L 326/13) of 1 December 2005 on minimum standards on procedures in Member States for granting and withdrawing refugee status.

---

[55] Notably, e.g. Portugal and Spain had to lift restrictions on admissibility of asylum claims, see M. Fullerton, *"Inadmissible in Iberia: The Fate of Asylum Seekers in Spain and Portugal" in* 17 INT'L J. OF REFUGEE L., 659 (2005).
[56] Presidency Conclusions, Brussels European Council (Nov. 4-5, 2004), and The Hague Programme: Strengthening Freedom, Security and Justice in the European Union, 2005 O.J. (L 53/1)(EC).
[57] *See supra* note 56, at annex I, 18.
[58]A 'recast' denotes a particular EU amendment procedure that "simultaneously makes the desired amendment, codifies that amendment with the unchanged provisions of the earlier act, and repeals that act." 'Interinstitutional Agreement of 28 November 2001 on a more structured use of the recasting technique for legal acts (EC), No. 2002/C 77/01 of 28 November 2001, recital 5, 2001 O.J. (C 77/1).
[59] Treaty of Lisbon Amending the Treaty on European Union and the Treaty Establishing the European Community, Dec. 13, 2007, 2007 O.J. (C 306) 1 [hereinafter Treaty of Lisbon].
[60] *Id.*, at art. 63.2.
[61] *Id.*, at art. 63.1.
[62] Charter of Fundamental Rights of the European Union, Dec. 18, 2000, 2000 O.J. (C 364/01) (entered into force on Dec. 1, 2009).
[63] *See* Treaty of Lisbon, *supra* note 59 at art. 6.1.
[64] *Id.*, at art. 6.2.
[65] *Id.*, at art. 63.3.
[66] Since the entry into force of the Treaty of Lisbon, the European Court of Justice has been renamed 'Court of Justice of the European Union' (CJEU), consisting of the General Court (previously 'Court of First Instance'), and the higher Court of Justice.
[67] *See supra* note 59, at art. 63.2.
[68] The Stockholm Programme – An Open and Secure Europe Serving and Protecting Citizens, 2010 O.J. 6.2.2 (L 115/01).
[69] *Id.*, at 6.2.
[70] *Id.*, at 6.2.2.
[71] *Id.*
[72] As to a definition of 'recast' for the purpose of EU law terminology, *cf. supra* note 58.
[73] Council Directive 2011/95/EU, 2011 O.J. (L 337/9) (of the European Parliament and of the Council of 13 December 2011 on standards for the qualification of third-country nationals or stateless persons as beneficiaries of international protection, for a uniform status for refugees or for persons eligible for subsidiary protection, and for the content of the protection granted (recast)).
[74] *Id.*, at ¶ 18.
[75] *Id.*, at ¶ 39.
[76] *Id.*, at ¶ 49.
[77] *Id.*, at ¶10. (Emphasis added).
[78] *Id.*, at ¶11.

---

[79] The difference lies in the immediacy of enforceability. While both are legislative acts, an EU regulation becomes immediately enforceable as law in all Member States simultaneously, whereas directives generally first need to be transposed into the respective Member States' national law.
[80] Regulation (EU) of the European Parliament and of the Council of 26 June 2013 establishing the criteria and mechanisms for determining the Member State responsible for examining an application for international protection lodged in one of the Member States by a third-country national or a stateless person (recast), Council Directive 604/2013, 2013 O.J. (L 180/31). While entering into force on the twentieth day following that of its publication in the Official Journal of the European Union, according to article 49 the Regulation will not be applicable until early 2014 ("shall only apply to applications for international protection lodged as from the first day of the sixth month following its entry into force").
[81] *Id.*, at ¶ 8.
[82] *Id.*, at ¶ 9.
[83] *Id.*, at ¶ 22.
[84] *Id.*, at art. 33.1.
[85] *Id.*, at art. 33.3.
[86] *Id.*, at ¶. 16.
[87] *Id.*, at art. 27.2. (Emphasis added). Sometimes access to an effective remedy had de facto been precluded by far too brief time frames for appeals.
[88] *Id.*, at ¶ 22.
[89] Council Directive 2013/33/EU, 2013 O.J. (L 180/96) (of the European Parliament and the Council laying down standards for the reception of applicants for international protection (recast). It shall repeal Council Directive 2003/9/EC, 2003 O.J. (L 31/18), with effect from 21 July 2015).
[90] *Id.*, at ¶ 2.
[91] *Id.*, at ¶ 26.
[92] *Id.*, at ¶¶ 40-44.
[93] *Id.*, at art. 39.1-3. (Emphasis added).
[94] *Id.*, at art. 9.3.
[95] *Id.*, at art. 31.3.
[96] *Id.*, at art. 31.5.
[97] *Supra* note 89.
[98] *Id.*, at art. 6.6. (Emphasis added).
[99] *Id.*, at art. 8.
[100] *Id.*, at art. 28.
[101] Council Directive 2011/95/EU, ¶ 12, 2011 O.J. (L 337/9).
[102] *Id.*, at ¶ 13.
[103] In Sepet v. Secretary of State for the Home Department (2003) 1 W.L.R. 856 (Eng.), at §6, Lord Bingham argued (in discussing the Vienna Convention on the Law of Treaties) "that the Convention must be seen as a living instrument in the sense that while its meaning does not change over time, its application will." No less would be true of a set of norms constituting a national legal system.

[104] Guy S. Goodwin-Gill, *The search for the one, true meaning, in* THE LIMITS OF TRANSNATIONAL LAW 205 (Goodwin-Gill & Hélène Lambert eds., Cambridge University Press 2010).
[105] *Id.*
[106] Despite the fact that the International Court of Justice, in principle, is charged with settling disputes between States Parties, "no references have ever been made and none are anticipated". Cf. Goodwin-Gill, *supra* note 104. Increasingly, however, the Court of Justice of the European Union may rise to the occasion in that regard.
[107] Article 38 of the 1951 Refugee Convention (and a similar provision maybe found in Article IV of its 1967 Protocol) stipulates that "[a]ny dispute between parties to this Convention relating to its interpretation or application, which cannot be settled by other means, shall be referred to the International Court of Justice at the request of any of the parties to the dispute."
[108] Hélène Lambert, *Transnational law, judges and refugees in the European Union, in* THE LIMITS OF TRANSNATIONAL LAW 9 (Goodwin-Gill & Hélène Lambert eds., Cambridge University Press 2010).
[109] The Stockholm Programme, *supra* note 68.
[110] In a variation of the aforementioned 'chicken game', in the absence of any significant financial support from other European countries, those most exposed may not have seen many benefits in enhancing conditions on the ground and making it thus perhaps more attractive to 'choose' their country as an entry port– quite the opposite. Despite the fact that the majority of flight routes are not predetermined in detail by refugees fleeing their home country, who often do not even know beforehand through which country they eventually will enter the EU, some of these misconceptions live on.
[111] M.S.S. v. Belgium & Greece (No. 30696), 2011 Eur. Ct. H.R. 09, *available at* http://hudoc.echr.coe.int/sites/eng/pages/search.aspx?i=001-103050.
[112] *Id.*, at ¶ 223.
[113] *Id.* at ¶ 389.
[114] *Cf.* Edward Cody, *Greek Town Becomes Flash Point in War against Muslim Immigrants*, WASHINGTON POST, Nov. 11, 2010, *available at* http://www.washingtonpost.com/wpdyn/content/article/2010/11/11/AR201011110 7562.html.
[115] *See* NORWEGIAN REFUGEE COUNCIL, FLYKTNINGREGNSKAPET 2013 ['REFUGEE BALANCE 2013'] 111 (2013).
[116] Eur. Consult. Ass. *Frontex: Human Rights Responsibilities*, Doc. No. 1361 (Apr. 8, 2013), and Remarks of Mr. Cederbratt ¶ 89, Committee on Migration, Refugees and Displaced Persons, *see also* 25 INT'L J. OF REFUGEE L., 433, 407-434 (2012).
[117] *See Pushed Back, Pushed Around: Italy's Forced Return of Boat Migrants and Asylum Seekers, Libya's Mistreatment of Migrants and Asylum Seekers*, HUM. RTS. WATCH, Sept. 21, 2009, *available at* http://www.hrw.org/reports/2009/09/21/pushed-back-pushed-around-0; *see also Italy to Pay Libya 5 Billion*, N.Y. TIMES, Aug. 31, 2008, *available at*

http://www.nytimes.com/2008/08/31/world/europe/31ihtitaly.4.15774385.html.
[118] Hirsi Jamaa & Others v. Italy (No. 27765), 2012 Eur. Ct. H.R. 09, *available at* http://hudoc.echr.coe.int/sites/eng/pages/search.aspx?i=001-109231.
[119] *Id.* ¶¶ 128-129.
[120] *See e.g.* Mariagiulia Giuffré, *Readmission Agreements and Refugee Rights: From a Critique to a Proposal*, 32 REFUGEE SURV. Q. 79, 79-111(2013), arguing that, in particular in situations of informal border controls and massive and sudden arrivals of migrants and refugees–as in regard to interceptions at sea–where monitoring procedures are generally lacking or insufficient, "the implementation of a readmission agreement may contribute to hinder access of asylum seekers to protection" (*id.*, at 110).
[121] *See Italy Sinking: Bad Weather Hampers Search for Migrants*, BBC NEWS, Oct. 4, 2013, *available at* www.bbc.co.uk/news/world-europe-24392732; *Lampedusa Wreck: EU Proposes Migrant Rescue Mission*, BBC NEWS, Oct. 8, 2013, *available at* http://www.bbc.co.uk/news/world-europe-24440908.
[122] *See Italy Immigration Law Prompts Lampedusa Rescue Row*, EURONEWS, Oct. 5, 2013, *available at* http://www.euronews.com/2013/10/05/italy-immigration-law-prompts-lampedusa-rescue-row.
[123] *See* VIRGIL, AENEID, Book V:864.
[124] *See* OVID, METAMORPHOSES, Book 14:88.
[125] For example at an Expert Seminar on 'Shared Responsibility in International Refugee Law, held at the Amsterdam Center of International Law, University of Amsterdam, May 30, 2011. While neither including any attribution of points of discussion to participants (the seminar was held under Chatham House rules), nor the specific remark stated above, a summary of the presentations and discussion may be found at the SHARES Expert Seminar Report 'Shared Responsibility in International Refugee Law' (May 30, 2011, Amsterdam), *available at* http://www.sharesproject.nl/wp-content/uploads/2012/03/Report-Expert-Seminar-Refugee-Law-2.pdf.
[126] Catherine Ashton is the first and still current incumbent.
[127] Countries of completed missions include Bosnia-Herzegovina (EUPM), Chad and Central African Republic (EUFOR), Democratic Republic of the Congo (ARTEMIS, EUFOR, EUPOL Kinshasa), Former Yugoslav Republic of Macedonia (Concordia, EUPOL PROXIMA, EUPAT), Georgia (EUJUST THEMIS), Guinea-Bissau (EU SSR), Indonesia (Aceh Monitoring Mission), Libya (EUFOR), Sudan (EU Support to AMIS). Missions are currently ongoing in Afghanistan (EUPOL), Bosnia-Herzegovina (EUFOR ALTHEA), Democratic Republic of the Congo (EUSEC, EUPOL RD Congo), Georgia (EUMM), Iraq (EUJUST LEX), Kosovo (EULEX), Libya (EUBAM), Mali (EUTM), Niger (EUCAP SAHEL), Palestinian Territories (EUPOL COPPS, EUBAM RAFAH), Somalia (EUTM, EU NAVFOR Atalanta), South Sudan (EUAVSEC), in addition to support missions strengthening regional capacities of groups of countries, *e.g.* EUCAP Nestor comprising five countries at the Horn of Africa (Djibouti, Kenya, Somalia, Seychelles and Tanzania), and EUBAM (Moldova and Ukraine).
[128] Stearns, *see supra* note 14, at 332. (Emphasis added).

[129] Based on Council Joint Action 2003/423/CFSP, 2003 O.J. (L 143/50), and S.C. Res. 1484, U.N. Doc. S/RES/1484 (May 30, 2003). Missions in French speaking countries usually use French names, and acronyms.
[130] Damien Helly, *The EU Military Operation in DR Congo (Artemis), in* EUROPEAN SECURITY AND DEFENCE POLICY: THE FIRST 10 YEARS (1999-2009) 181, 182 (Giovanni Grevi, Damien Helly, and Daniel Keohane, eds., 2009).
[131] Anand Menon, *Empowering Paradise? The ESDP at Ten*, 85 INT'L AFF. 227, 230 (2009).
[132] Helly, *supra* note 130, at 185.
[133] Based on Council Joint Action 2004/847/CFSP, 2004 O.J. (L 367/30).
[134] Based on Council Joint Action 2007/405/CFSP, 2007 O.J. (L 151).
[135] Thierry Vircoulon, *The EU Police Mission in Kinshasa – DRC (EUPOL Kinshasa) and the EU Police Mission in RD Congo (EUPOL RD Congo), in* EUROPEAN SECURITY AND DEFENCE POLICY: THE FIRST 10 YEARS (1999-2009) 221, 229 (Giovanni Grevi, Damien Helly, and Daniel Keohane, eds., 2009).
[136] Based on Council Joint Action 2005/355/CFSP, 2005 O.J. (L 112).
[137] Caty Clément, *The EU Mission to Provide Advice and Assistance to Security Sector Reform in the Democratic Republic of the Congo (EUSEC RD Congo), in* EUROPEAN SECURITY AND DEFENCE POLICY: THE FIRST 10 YEARS (1999-2009) 243, 244 (Giovanni Grevi, Damien Helly, and Daniel Keohane, eds., 2009).
[138] *Id.*, at 248.
[139] *Id.*, at 247.
[140] Although civilians contribute to the exorbitant number of abuses, most perpetrators are part of armed groups, both militias and the regular army, which led a senior UN official to declare the DRC the 'rape capital of the world'. *See e.g. UN Official Calls DRC 'Rape Capital of the World'*, BBC NEWS, Apr. 28, 2010, *available at* http://news.bbc.co.uk/2/hi/8650112.stm (last visited Nov. 20, 2013).
[141] Clément, *supra* note 137, at 251.
[142] Based on Council Joint Action 2006/319/CFSP, 2006 O.J. (L 116/98).
[143] Claudia Major, *The Military Operation EUFOR RD Congo 2006, in* EUROPEAN SECURITY AND DEFENCE POLICY: THE FIRST 10 YEARS (1999-2009) 311, 317 (Giovanni Grevi, Damien Helly, and Daniel Keohane, eds., 2009).
[144] *Id.*, at 320.
[145] *See e.g. DRC Insurgency Not Over*, DEUTSCHE WELLE, Nov. 12, 2013, *available at* http://www.dw.de/drc-insurgency-not-over/a-17220556 (last visited Nov. 20, 2013).
[146] *See* Int'l Crisis Group [ICG], '*Chad: A New Conflict Resolution Framework*', at 25, 28, Afr. Rep. No. 144 (Sep. 24, 2008).
[147] Damien Helly, *The EU Military Operation in the Republic of Chad and in the Central African Republic (Operation EUFOR Tchad/RCA), in* EUROPEAN SECURITY AND DEFENCE POLICY: THE FIRST 10 YEARS (1999-2009) 339, 340 (Giovanni Grevi, Damien Helly, and Daniel Keohane, eds., 2009).
[148] Based on Council Joint Action 2007/677/CFSP, 2007 O.J. (L 323/57).
[149] *See* Helly, *supra* note 147, at 342.

[150] Rep. of the Panel on United Nations Peace Operations, U.N. Doc. A/55/305–S/2000/809 (Aug. 21, 2000) *available at* http://www.un.org/en/ga/search/view_doc.asp?symbol=A/55/305 (last visited Nov. 20, 2013).
[151] Winrich Kuehne, *How the EU Organizes and Conducts Peace Operations in Africa: EUFOR/MINURCAT*, at 19, ZIF Report 03/09 (Mar. 2009).
[152] Helly, *supra* note 147, at 346.
[153] European Union External Action Service (EEAS)–Mission Description: EUFOR Tchad/RCA, *available at* http://www.eeas.europa.eu/csdp/missions-and-operations/eufor-tchad-rca/mission-description/index_en.htm (last visited Nov. 20, 2013).
[154] S.C. Res. 1851, ¶ 6, U.N. Doc. S/RES/1851 (Dec. 16, 2008).
[155] S.C. Res. 1950, ¶ 13, U.N. Doc. S/RES/1950 (Nov. 23, 2010).
[156] Established according to EU Council Joint Action 2008/851/CFSP, 2008 O.J. (L 301/33).
[157] Damien Helly, *EU NAVFOR Somalia: The EU Military Operation* Atalanta, *in* EUROPEAN SECURITY AND DEFENCE POLICY: THE FIRST 10 YEARS (1999-2009) 339, 340 (Giovanni Grevi, Damien Helly, and Daniel Keohane, eds., 2009).
[158] Tom Syring, *'Candide' or Pessimism: Fighting Piracy and Transnational Crime in Uncharted Waters*, 2:1 INTERDISCIPLINARY POL. STUD. 48, 51 (2012).
[159] Council Decision 2012/174/CFSP, 2012 O.J. (L 89/69).
[160] Tom Syring, *A Pirate and a Refugee: Reservations and Responses in the Fight against Piracy*, 17 ILSA J. OF INT'L & COMP. L. 437, 442 (2011). (Footnote omitted).
[161] Based on Council Decision 2010/197/CFSP, 2010 O.J. (L 87/33).
[162] European Union External Action Service (EEAS)–Common Security and Defence Policy: EUTM Somalia, *available at* http://www.eeas.europa.eu/csdp/missions-and-operations/eutm-somalia/pdf/fact sheet_eutm_somalia_en.pdf (Dec. 2, 2013).
[163] Sebastian Moffett, *EU Considers Sending 200 Troops to Train Mali Army*, REUTERS, Oct. 30, 2012, *available at* http://www.reuters.com/article/2012/10/30/us-mali-crisis-eu-idUSBRE89T1DB20 121030 (last visited Nov. 10, 2013).
[164] Based on Council Decision 2013/87/CFSP, 2013 O.J. (L 46/27).
[165] European Union External Action Service (EEAS)–Strategy for Security and Development in the Sahel, *available at* http://www.eeas.europa.eu/africa/docs/sahel_strategy_en.pdf
[166] *See* NORWEGIAN REFUGEE COUNCIL, FLYKTNINGREGNSKAPET 2013 ['REFUGEE BALANCE 2013'] 15 (2013). Of course, not all the money pledged while the cameras were on, was eventually actually paid. But the 2004 Tsunami was still an example of an extraordinary commitment by the international society, which, irrespective of how cruel that disaster was, may appear out of proportion relative to other, similar or worse crises.
[167] *Id.*, at 16-19.

[168] Numbers and descriptions of refugee situations in the following are based, in part, on the account in NRC's 'Refugee Balance 2013', *see supra* note 166. As to Burma, *see also* Frelick's chapter, *supra* note 21.
[169] *See also* Pistone's chapter, *supra* note 25.
[170] *See also* Jeffrey Smith's chapter on 'State of Exile: The Saharawi Republic and Its Refugees' in this volume.
[171] For a detailed account, *see also* Tom Syring, *Protecting the Protectors or Victimizing the Victims Anew? "Material Support of Terrorism" and Exclusion from Refugee Status in US and European Courts*, 18 ILSA J. OF INT'L & COMP. L. 597-614 (2012).
[172] *See e.g.* KENNETH KATZMAN, Cong. Research Serv., RL32048, IRAN: U.S. CONCERNS AND POLICY RESPONSES at 33 (Nov. 29, 2004), indicating that Iran had refused to extradite certain Al Qaeda leaders because Iran viewed them as a bargaining chip to persuade the United States to extradite to Iran member of the Iranian opposition group PMOI based in Iraq.
[173] Fourth Geneva Convention Relative to the Protection of Civilian Persons in Time of War, Aug. 12, 1949, 75 U.N.T.S. 287 (entered into force Oct. 21, 1950).
[174] The ECJ is now generally referred to as the Court of Justice of the European Union (CJEU).
[175] This Court is now commonly referred to as the 'General Court'.
[176] *See* Case T-228/2, Organisation des Modjahedines du peuple d'Iran [People's Mojahedin Org. of Iran] v. Council of the Eur. Union, 2002 O.J. (C 247) 20 (Ct. of First Instance Dec. 12, 2006), *available at* http://eurlex.europa.eu/LexUriServ/LexUriServ.do?uri=CELEX:62002A0228:EN:HTML.
[177] Proscribed Organizations Appeal Commission, Appeal No. PC/02/2006, ¶ 19 (Nov. 30, 2007), *available at* http://www.statewatch.org/terrorlists/PC022006%20PMOI%20FINAL%20JUDGMENT.pdf.
[178] *See* Case C-27/09 P, France v. People's Mojahedin Org. of Iran, (Grand Chamber Dec. 21, 2011), *available at* http://curia.europa.eu/juris/document/document.jsf?text=&docid=117189&pageIndex=0&doclang=en&mode=doc&dir=&occ=first&part=1&cid=479256 (last visited Oct.12, 2013).
[179] Petition For A Writ of Mandamus To Enforce This Court's Mandate, *In Re* People's Mojahedin Org. of Iran, No. 12-1118 (D.C. Cir. 2012), at 10.
[180] For details on 'material support' bars in U.S. law and the procedures for designation as a foreign terrorist organization (FTO), see also Kristine Huskey's chapter on 'The US "Material Support" Bar to Refugee Protection: An Expansive Approach through a Narrow Lens' in this volume. For a brief analysis of the U.S. Court of Appeals judgment, *see also* Tom Syring, *U.S. Court Issues Writ of Mandamus, Effectively Removing Organization from Terror List:* In Re *People's Mojahedin Organization of Iran,* ASIL INSIGHTS (Nov. 16, 2012).

CONTRIBUTORS

Karen AbuZayd served as Under Secretary General and Commissioner-General of the United Nations Relief and Works Agency (UNRWA) for Palestine refugees in the Near East from June 2005 until January 2010. In August 2000 she had been appointed Assistant Secretary-General and Deputy Commissioner General of UNRWA. She carried out her duties from UNRWA Headquarters in Gaza, overseeing the education, health, social services and microfinance programs for 4.7 million Palestine Refugees in the occupied Palestinian territory (West Bank and Gaza), Jordan, Syrian and Lebanon. Since September 2000, an additional focus was to ensure necessary emergency relief (food, shelter and employment) in the occupied Palestinian territories and Lebanon.

Before joining UNRWA, Karen worked for the Office of the United Nations High Commissioner for Refugees (UNHCR) for 19 years. She began her humanitarian career in Sudan in 1981, dealing with Ugandan, Chadian and Ethiopian/Eritrean refugees, seconded for five of those years to the Office of the Sudanese Commissioner for Refugees. She moved to Namibia in 1989 as Senior Program Coordinator for the return of apartheid-era refugees, and transferred to Sierra Leone in 1990 to head the UNHCR Freetown office, settling 100,000 Liberians in 600 villages along the Sierra Leone border.

After directing the South African repatriation and the Kenya-Somalia operations at UNHCR's Geneva Headquarters from 1991–93, she moved to Sarajevo as Chief of Mission until 1995, supervising protection, airlift and convoy activities, working closely with UNPROFOR. Following a year as Deputy Director of Operational Support in UNHCR Headquarters, she spent two years as Chef de Cabinet to High Commissioner Ogata and another two years as Regional Representative for the U.S. and the Caribbean in Washington, D.C.

Before joining the UN, she lectured in Political Science at Makerere University in Uganda and Juba University in southern Sudan. She has a B.Sc. from Depauw University in Indiana and an M.A. in Islamic Studies from McGill University in Canada. Her late husband, Professor Abdel Rahman AbuZayd, was from Sudan. She has two sons and two grandsons.

Since retiring in 2010, Karen has joined a number of Middle East and refugee-related Boards (MEPC, AFU, ICCO, NAI), and undertaken numerous public speaking engagements in the U.S., Europe, the Middle East and Africa. She was Distinguished Visiting Professor at American University in Cairo in October 2010 and Distinguished Lecturer at Biblioteca Alexandria in April 2011. She was a member of the 2010 OCHA Advisory Group for the study, 'To Stay and Deliver' and a 2011 external reviewer for UNHCR's Office of the Inspector General.

She received the Spanish UN Association/Catalonia Peace Prize in 2010 and the Austria Golden Medal with Star for Service to The Austrian Republic in 2011.

Susan M. Akram is Clinical Professor at Boston University School of Law, teaching immigration law, comparative refugee law, and international human rights law, and supervising students handling refugee and asylum cases in BU's Asylum and Human Rights program. She is a native of Pakistan, a graduate of the University of Michigan-Ann Arbor (BA), Georgetown University Law Center, Washington DC (JD), and the *Institut International des Droits de l'Homme*, Strasbourg (*Diplôme* in international human rights).

Before joining the faculty at BUSL in 1993, Susan Akram has held the positions of executive director of Boston's Political Asylum/Immigration Representation (PAIR) Project; directing attorney of the immigration project at the public interest law firm, Public Counsel, in Los Angeles; and director of the program for resettling Iraqi refugees from the camps in Saudi Arabia after the First Gulf War. She is a past Fulbright Senior Scholar in Palestine, teaching at Al-Quds University/Palestine School of Law in East Jerusalem; she has taught at the American University in Cairo's Forced Migration Program; and she co-teaches the Palestine Refugee short course at Oxford University's Refugee Studies Centre. She has litigated and advocated for refugees and forced migrants in domestic courts and international venues for the last thirty years.

Among her recent publications are a co-edited volume on *International Law and the Israeli-Palestinian Conflict: A Rights Based Approach to Middle East Peace* (Routledge Press); a co-authored entry on "The Middle East Conflict" in the *Max Planck Encyclopedia of International Law* (Oxford University Press); and a chapter on "The Rights of Palestinian Refugees and Territorial Solutions in Historic Palestine" in the edited volume, *A One-State Solution for Palestine-Israel* (I.B.Taurus Publishers). She writes on the intersection of race, civil rights and immigration; comparative refugee issues, particularly relating to the Middle East; and Palestinian and other refugees in the Arab world. She serves on the Board of Directors of the American Civil Liberties Union of Massachusetts, the

Advisory Committee of the Boston Center for Refugee Health and Human Rights, and is Boston University Law School's representative to the House of Delegates of the Association of American Law Schools.

Bill Frelick, director of Human Rights Watch's refugee program, monitors, investigates, and documents human rights abuses against refugees, asylum seekers, and internally displaced persons, and advocates for the rights and humanitarian needs of all categories of forcibly displaced persons around the world.

Before joining Human Rights Watch, Frelick directed Amnesty International USA's refugee program and the US Committee for Refugees (USCR), which he served for 18 years. He was the editor of USCR's annual World Refugee Survey and monthly Refugee Reports. Frelick has traveled to refugee sites throughout the world and is widely published. He taught in the Middle East from 1979–1983 and was co-coordinator of the Asian Center of Clergy and Laity Concerned from 1976–1979. Frelick has a B.A. from Oberlin College and an M.A. from Columbia University.

Guy S. Goodwin Gill is a Senior Research Fellow of All Souls College, Oxford University, and Professor of International Refugee Law. He is also a Barrister and a member of Blackstone Chambers, London, where he practices in public international law generally, and in human rights, refugee and asylum law. He has worked extensively with the United Nations, including twelve years with UNHCR, has been a member of the Council of the Overseas Development Institute (ODI) since 2007, a Patron of AsylumAid since 2008, and from 1997–2010 he was President of Refugee and Migrant Justice (formerly the Refugee Legal Centre). From 2000–2003, he was President of the Media Appeals Board of Kosovo.

He is the Founding Editor of the *International Journal of Refugee Law* (Oxford University Press) and was Editor-in-Chief from 1989–2001. Recent publications include, 'The Right to Seek Asylum: Interception at Sea and the Principle of *Non-refoulement*', 23 *International Journal of Refugee Law* 443-57 (2011); 'The Search for the One, True Meaning...', in Guy S. Goodwin-Gill & Hélène Lambert, eds., *The Limits of Transnational Law*, Cambridge: Cambridge University Press, 2010, 204-41; 'The Challenge of the Child Soldier', in Hew Strachan & Sibylle Scheipers, *The Changing Character of War*, Oxford: Oxford University Press, 2011, 410-28; 'The Extra-Territorial Reach of Human Rights Obligations: A Brief Perspective on the Link to Jurisdiction', in Laurence Boisson de Chazournes & Marcelo G. Kohen, eds., *International Law and the Quest for its Implementation/Le droit international et la quête de sa mise en oeuvre*: Liber Amicorum *Vera Gowlland-Debbas*, Leiden: Brill, 2010, 293-308; *Brownlie's Documents on Human Rights*, 6th edition with the late Sir Ian Brownlie, Oxford: Oxford University Press, 2010; and *The Refugee in International Law*, 3rd edition with Jane McAdam, Oxford: Oxford University Press, 2007.

Agnès Hurwitz currently works for the UN Development Programme as Global Rule of Law Coordinator, focusing in particular on transitional justice and environmental justice. Prior to joining UNDP, she was the Senior Research Officer at the Division of International Protection of UNHCR in Geneva. She was the main editor of the Legal and Protection Policy Research Series and was also actively involved in policy developments related to the commemorations of the 60th anniversary of the Refugee Convention, in particular as regards climate-related displacement and complementarities between international refugee law and international criminal law.

From 2006 until 2009, she worked at the International Criminal Tribunal for the former Yugoslavia where she held various posts, including Deputy Chef de Cabinet in the Office of the President and trial team coordinator. Between 2004 and 2006, she headed a research project on the rule of law and peacebuilding at the International Peace Institute (formerly International Peace Academy) in New York. She was the Ford Foundation Research Fellow in International Human Rights and Refugee Law at Oxford University's Refugee Studies Centre from 2001 to 2003, where she taught international human rights law, international refugee law, and public international law.

She has published peer-reviewed articles, policy papers and reports on refugee law and rule of law programs. She is the author of a monograph entitled *The Collective Responsibility of States to Protect Refugees* (OUP, 2009) and the editor of Civil War and the Rule of Law: Security, Development, Human Rights (Lynn Rienner Pub., 2008). She completed her DPhil at Oxford University, and holds an LLM in international law from Cambridge University and a BA in Law from the Free University of Brussels.

Kristine Huskey is a visiting associate clinical professor at the James E. Rogers College of Law, The University of Arizona. She is the founder of the National Security Clinic at the University of Texas School of Law. Previously, she held the position of Director of the Anti-Torture Program at Physicians for Human Rights (PHR), where she led PHR's advocacy for strengthening anti-torture policy and practice in the United States, particularly in the national security context. Ms. Huskey also regularly taught a national security seminar at Georgetown University Law Center and was an Associate at the Robert Strauss Center for International Security and Law.

Ms. Huskey has represented several individuals and entities in national security cases, including the Holy Land Foundation and Guantanamo detainees, and was part of the legal team in *Rasul v. Bush* (2004), winning the right of the detainees to challenge their detentions in federal court. She has been to Guantanamo numerous times and has frequently appeared in the media to discuss human rights and war on terrorism issues. Ms. Huskey is the author of *Justice at Guantánamo: One Woman's Odyssey and Her Crusade for Human Rights* and a contributing author to *One of the Guys: Women as Aggressors and Torturers*. She was featured as a "Woman to Watch" in *Marie Claire* (Dec. 2006). She co-authored a chapter on US law and policy governing private military and security contractors in a book on *Multilevel Regulation of Military and Security Contractors: The Interplay between International, European and Domestic Norms* (Hart 2012).

Ms. Huskey was an attorney in the International Litigation practice group at Shearman & Sterling LLP and has taught international law, and international human rights and humanitarian law at Washington College of Law, George Washington University Law School, Howard University School of Law, and Victoria University Law School in New Zealand.

Michele R. Pistone is a Professor of Law at Villanova University School of Law. She is the Founding Director of the Clinic for Asylum, Refugee, and Emigrant Services (CARES), in which she and her students provide free legal representation to asylum seekers fleeing persecution in their home countries.

Professor Pistone was awarded a Fulbright scholarship to lecture at the University of Malta on refugee law and to help to create a refugee law clinic during the spring 2006 semester. She also served as a Visiting Professor at American University's Washington College of Law during the 2008–09 academic year.

Professor Pistone's scholarly interests include asylum and refugee law, legal and clinical education, migration, and Catholic social thought. Among other scholarly publications, Professor Pistone is co-author of a book, entitled *Stepping Out of the Brain Drain: Applying Catholic Social Teaching in a New Era of Migration* (Lexington Books 2007), which looks at migration of skilled and educated workers from the perspective of Catholic social thought. Her articles have appeared in the Columbia

Human Rights Law Review, Harvard Human Rights Journal, Georgetown Immigration Law Journal, Georgetown Journal of Law and Public Policy, the Journal of Catholic Social Thought, and the Fordham Urban Law Journal, among others.

Robert Sloane is an associate professor of law at Boston University School of Law. He has published widely in the fields of public international law, international human rights, international criminal law, asylum law, the law of war, international legal theory and international investment arbitration. Two of his articles have been awarded the Francis Lieber Prize for outstanding scholarship in the field of the law of armed conflict by an author 35 years or younger.

After receiving his J.D. from Yale Law School in 2000, Sloane worked for the International Committee of Lawyers for Tibet (now known as Tibet Justice Center) under the auspices of Yale Law School's Robert L. Bernstein Fellowship in International Human Rights, and since then, has continued to serve as a board member and, from 2006 to date, as Chairman of the Board. In that capacity, among other pro bono work, he provides expert testimony and affidavits for Tibetan asylum seekers and writes reports on the status of and circumstances for Tibetan refugees worldwide. After completing the Bernstein Fellowship, Professor Sloane served two judicial clerkships and practiced international law at Debevoise & Plimpton in New York.

Before joining BU Law, Sloane served as a lecturer and Schell Fellow at Yale and as an associate-in-law at Columbia. He has been a visiting professor at the University of Michigan Law School and Harvard Law School, where he served as the John Harvey Gregory Lecturer in World Organization.

Jeffrey Smith is a Canadian lawyer and law professor who has served as counsel to the Frente POLISARIO for the past three years. He was previously counsel to the United Nations and the government of East Timor (Timor–Leste) in that country for its maritime jurisdiction and oilfield development. His work for the Frente POLISARIO includes all aspects of international humanitarian law, the creation of the Saharawi state, natural resources development, and legal aspects of self-determination. Jeffrey Smith works in Tindouf, Brussels, and Ottawa. His most recent scholarly work is "Fishing for Self-Determination: European fisheries and Western Sahara–The case of ocean resources in Africa's last colony" published in *Ocean Yearbook* in 2013.

Tom Syring currently serves on the Norwegian Immigration Appeals Board. He studied law and political science at the University of Oslo, Norway, and Johannes Gutenberg University Mainz, School of Law, Germany, where he also conducted his doctoral studies, focusing on International Humanitarian Law and International Criminal Law, particularly national and international jurisdictional approaches with respect to punishing the most serious crimes. He has been a Lecturer in International Law, Political Philosophy, and International Politics at the University of Oslo and a Visiting Fulbright Scholar and Lecturer in International Law at Boston University.

Syring's recent publications include book chapters and articles on state-building and constitution drafting, accountability mechanisms and their conduciveness to lasting peace, the nexus between piracy and refugee crises, and between occupation and state responsibility for refugees, as well as discussions of the Court of Justice of the European Union and European Court of Human Rights decisions in *ASIL Insights* and *International Legal Materials*. Current scholarly projects include research on the application of the UN Convention against Transnational Organized Crime to the challenges posed by piracy and armed robbery at sea, a comparative analysis of material support bars in the United States and Europe, and a forthcoming, co-edited volume (with Richard Falk) on *War, Occupation, and Refugees* (Routledge).

Tom Syring is a National Coordinator of the Refugee Case Law Site, a member of the Norwegian Resource Bank for Democracy and Human Rights (NORDEM), and he co-chairs and co-founded the American Society of International Law's Interest Group on International Refugee Law together with Richard Falk.

INDEX